Praise for Michael Hartl's Books and Videos on Ruby on Rails™

"My former company (CD Baby) was one of the first to loudly switch to Ruby on Rails, and then even more loudly switch back to PHP (Google me to read about the drama). This book by Michael Hartl came so highly recommended that I had to try it, and the *Ruby on Rails™ Tutorial* is what I used to switch back to Rails again."

—From the Foreword by Derek Sivers (sivers.org)
　　Formerly: Founder, CD Baby
　　Currently: Founder, Thoughts Ltd.

"Michael Hartl's Rails Tutorial book is the #1 (and only, in my opinion) place to start when it comes to books about learning Rails. . . . It's an amazing piece of work and, unusually, walks you through building a Rails app from start to finish with testing. If you want to read just one book and feel like a Rails master by the end of it, pick the *Ruby on Rails™ Tutorial*."

—Peter Cooper
　　Editor, Ruby Inside

RUBY ON RAILS™ TUTORIAL

Second Edition

Addison-Wesley
Professional Ruby Series

Obie Fernandez, Series Editor

REFACTORING
RUBY EDITION

JAY FIELDS ● SHANE HARVIE
MARTIN FOWLER with KENT BECK

RAILS
ANTIPATTERNS
BEST PRACTICE RUBY ON
RAILS REFACTORING

CHAD PYTEL ● TAMMER SALEH

DISTRIBUTED
PROGRAMMING
WITH RUBY

MARK BATES

THE RAILS 3 WAY

David H. Hansson

OBIE FERNANDEZ

★ Addison-Wesley

Visit **informit.com/ruby** for a complete list of available products.

The **Addison-Wesley Professional Ruby Series** provides readers with practical, people-oriented, and in-depth information about applying the Ruby platform to create dynamic technology solutions. The series is based on the premise that the need for expert reference books, written by experienced practitioners, will never be satisfied solely by blogs and the Internet.

RUBY ON RAILS™ TUTORIAL

Learn Web Development with Rails

Second Edition

Michael Hartl

↟ Addison-Wesley

Upper Saddle River, NJ • Boston • Indianapolis • San Francisco
New York • Toronto • Montreal • London • Munich • Paris • Madrid
Capetown • Sydney • Tokyo • Singapore • Mexico City

The publisher offers excellent discounts on this book when ordered in quantity for bulk purchases or special sales, which may include electronic versions and/or custom covers and content particular to your business, training goals, marketing focus, and branding interests. For more information, please contact:

> U.S. Corporate and Government Sales
> (800) 382-3419
> corpsales@pearsontechgroup.com

For sales outside the United States please contact:
> International Sales
> international@pearson.com

Visit us on the Web: informit.com/aw

Cataloging-in-Publication Data is on file with the Library of Congress.

ISBN 13: 978-0-321-83205-4
ISBN 10:   0-321-83205-1
Text printed in the United States on recycled paper at Edwards Brothers Malloy in Ann Arbor, Michigan.
Fourth printing, November 2013

Editor-in-Chief
Mark Taub

Executive Editor
Debra Williams Cauley

Managing Editor
John Fuller

Full-Service Production Manager
Julie B. Nahil

Project Manager
Laserwords

Copy Editor
Laserwords

Indexer
Laserwords

Proofreader
Laserwords

Reviewer
Jennifer Lindner

Publishing Coordinator
Kim Boedigheimer

Cover Designer
Chuti Prasertsith

Compositor
Laserwords

Contents

Foreword to the First Edition by Derek Sivers   xv

Foreword to the First Edition by Obie Fernandez   xvii

Acknowledgments   xix

About the Author   xxi

Chapter 1   From Zero to Deploy   1

1.1   Introduction   3

    1.1.1   Comments for Various Readers   4

    1.1.2   "Scaling" Rails   7

    1.1.3   Conventions in This Book   7

1.2   Up and Running   9

    1.2.1   Development Environments   10

    1.2.2   Ruby, RubyGems, Rails, and Git   12

    1.2.3   The First Application   17

    1.2.4   Bundler   19

    1.2.5   `rails server`   23

    1.2.6   Model-view-controller (MVC)   25

1.3   Version Control with Git   27

    1.3.1   Installation and Setup   27

    1.3.2   Adding and Committing   30

    1.3.3   What Good Does Git Do You?   31

1.3.4   GitHub   32

1.3.5   Branch, Edit, Commit, Merge   34

1.4   Deploying   39

1.4.1   Heroku Setup   39

1.4.2   Heroku Deployment, Step One   40

1.4.3   Heroku Deployment, Step Two   40

1.4.4   Heroku Commands   41

1.5   Conclusion   43

Chapter 2   A Demo App   45

2.1   Planning the Application   45

2.1.1   Modeling Demo Users   47

2.1.2   Modeling Demo Microposts   48

2.2   The Users Resource   49

2.2.1   A User Tour   51

2.2.2   MVC in Action   56

2.2.3   Weaknesses of this Users Resource   62

2.3   The Microposts Resource   63

2.3.1   A Micropost Microtour   63

2.3.2   Putting the *micro* in Microposts   66

2.3.3   A User has_many Microposts   68

2.3.4   Inheritance Hierarchies   70

2.3.5   Deploying the Demo App   73

2.4   Conclusion   74

Chapter 3   Mostly Static Pages   77

3.1   Static Pages   82

3.1.1   Truly Static Pages   82

3.1.2   Static Pages with Rails   85

3.2   Our First Tests   93

3.2.1   Test-driven Development   93

3.2.2   Adding a Page   99

3.3   Slightly Dynamic Pages   103

3.3.1   Testing a Title Change   103

3.3.2   Passing Title Tests   106

3.3.3   Embedded Ruby   108

3.3.4   Eliminating Duplication with Layouts   111

3.4   Conclusion   114

3.5   Exercises   114
3.6   Advanced Setup   117
        3.6.1   Eliminating `bundle exec`   118
        3.6.2   Automated Tests with Guard   120
        3.6.3   Speeding up Tests with Spork   123
        3.6.4   Tests inside Sublime Text   127

Chapter 4   Rails-Flavored Ruby   129

4.1   Motivation   129
4.2   Strings and Methods   134
        4.2.1   Comments   134
        4.2.2   Strings   135
        4.2.3   Objects and Message Passing   138
        4.2.4   Method Definitions   141
        4.2.5   Back to the Title Helper   142
4.3   Other Data Structures   142
        4.3.1   Arrays and Ranges   142
        4.3.2   Blocks   146
        4.3.3   Hashes and Symbols   148
        4.3.4   CSS revisited   152
4.4   Ruby Classes   153
        4.4.1   Constructors   153
        4.4.2   Class Inheritance   155
        4.4.3   Modifying Built-in Classes   158
        4.4.4   A Controller Class   159
        4.4.5   A User Class   161
4.5   Conclusion   164
4.6   Exercises   164

Chapter 5   Filling in the Layout   167

5.1   Adding Some Structure   167
        5.1.1   Site Navigation   169
        5.1.2   Bootstrap and Custom CSS   175
        5.1.3   Partials   181
5.2   Sass and the Asset Pipeline   187
        5.2.1   The Asset Pipeline   187
        5.2.2   Syntactically Awesome Stylesheets   190

5.3   Layout Links   197
       5.3.1   Route Tests   200
       5.3.2   Rails Routes   202
       5.3.3   Named Routes   205
       5.3.4   Pretty RSpec   207
5.4   User Signup: A First Step   211
       5.4.1   Users Controller   212
       5.4.2   Signup URI   213
5.5   Conclusion   215
5.6   Exercises   217

Chapter 6   Modeling Users   221

6.1   User Model   222
       6.1.1   Database Migrations   223
       6.1.2   The Model File   228
       6.1.3   Creating User Objects   230
       6.1.4   Finding User Objects   233
       6.1.5   Updating User Objects   235
6.2   User Validations   236
       6.2.1   Initial User Tests   236
       6.2.2   Validating Presence   239
       6.2.3   Length Validation   243
       6.2.4   Format Validation   245
       6.2.5   Uniqueness Validation   249
6.3   Adding a Secure Password   254
       6.3.1   An Encrypted Password   255
       6.3.2   Password and Confirmation   257
       6.3.3   User Authentication   260
       6.3.4   User Has Secure Password   263
       6.3.5   Creating a User   265
6.4   Conclusion   267
6.5   Exercises   268

Chapter 7   Sign Up   271

7.1   Showing Users   271
       7.1.1   Debug and Rails Environments   272
       7.1.2   A Users Resource   278

7.1.3   Testing the User Show Page (with Factories)   282

7.1.4   A Gravatar Image and a Sidebar   286

7.2   Signup Form   292

7.2.1   Tests for User Signup   293

7.2.2   Using form_for   297

7.2.3   The Form HTML   301

7.3   Signup Failure   303

7.3.1   A Working Form   303

7.3.2   Signup Error Messages   308

7.4   Signup Success   312

7.4.1   The Finished Signup Form   313

7.4.2   The Flash   315

7.4.3   The First Signup   317

7.4.4   Deploying to Production with SSL   317

7.5   Conclusion   321

7.6   Exercises   321

Chapter 8   Sign In, Sign Out   325

8.1   Sessions and Signin Failure   325

8.1.1   Sessions Controller   326

8.1.2   Signin Tests   330

8.1.3   Signin Form   333

8.1.4   Reviewing Form Submission   336

8.1.5   Rendering with a Flash Message   339

8.2   Signin Success   343

8.2.1   Remember Me   343

8.2.2   A Working sign_in Method   349

8.2.3   Current User   351

8.2.4   Changing the Layout Links   355

8.2.5   Signin upon Signup   359

8.2.6   Signing Out   361

8.3   Introduction to Cucumber (Optional)   363

8.3.1   Installation and Setup   364

8.3.2   Features and Steps   365

8.3.3   Counterpoint: RSpec Custom Matchers   368

8.4   Conclusion   371

8.5   Exercises   372

Chapter 9   Updating, Showing, and Deleting Users   373

9.1   Updating Users   373
        9.1.1   Edit Form   374
        9.1.2   Unsuccessful Edits   380
        9.1.3   Successful Edits   382
9.2   Authorization   385
        9.2.1   Requiring Signed-in Users   386
        9.2.2   Requiring the Right User   390
        9.2.3   Friendly Forwarding   392
9.3   Showing All Users   396
        9.3.1   User Index   396
        9.3.2   Sample Users   403
        9.3.3   Pagination   404
        9.3.4   Partial Refactoring   410
9.4   Deleting Users   413
        9.4.1   Administrative Users   413
        9.4.2   The destroy Action   417
9.5   Conclusion   422
9.6   Exercises   424

Chapter 10   User Microposts   429

10.1   A Micropost Model   429
         10.1.1   The Basic Model   430
         10.1.2   Accessible Attributes and the First Validation   432
         10.1.3   User/Micropost Associations   433
         10.1.4   Micropost Refinements   439
         10.1.5   Content Validations   443
10.2   Showing Microposts   445
         10.2.1   Augmenting the User Show Page   446
         10.2.2   Sample Microposts   450
10.3   Manipulating Microposts   454
         10.3.1   Access Control   456
         10.3.2   Creating Microposts   459
         10.3.3   A Proto-feed   467
         10.3.4   Destroying Microposts   475
10.4   Conclusion   479
10.5   Exercises   480

Chapter 11   Following Users   483

11.1 The Relationship Model   484
      11.1.1 A Problem with the Data Model (and a Solution)   485
      11.1.2 User/Relationship Associations   491
      11.1.3 Validations   495
      11.1.4 Followed users   495
      11.1.5 Followers   500
11.2 A Web Interface for Following Users   503
      11.2.1 Sample Following Data   503
      11.2.2 Stats and a Follow Form   505
      11.2.3 Following and Followers Pages   515
      11.2.4 A Working Follow Button the Standard Way   519
      11.2.5 A Working Follow Button with Ajax   524
11.3 The Status Feed   529
      11.3.1 Motivation and Strategy   530
      11.3.2 A First Feed Implementation   532
      11.3.3 Subselects   535
      11.3.4 The New Status Feed   538
11.4 Conclusion   539
      11.4.1 Extensions to the Sample Application   540
      11.4.2 Guide to Further Resources   542
11.5 Exercises   543

Index   545

Foreword to the First Edition

My former company (CD Baby) was one of the first to loudly switch to Ruby on Rails, and then even more loudly switch back to PHP (Google me to read about the drama). This book by Michael Hartl came so highly recommended that I had to try it, and *Ruby on Rails™ 3 Tutorial* is what I used to switch back to Rails again.

Though I've worked my way through many Rails books, this is the one that finally made me get it. Everything is done very much "the Rails way"—a way that felt very unnatural to me before, but now after doing this book finally feels natural. This is also the only Rails book that does test-driven development the entire time, an approach highly recommended by the experts but which has never been so clearly demonstrated before. Finally, by including Git, GitHub, and Heroku in the demo examples, the author really gives you a feel for what it's like to do a real-world project. The tutorial's code examples are not in isolation.

The linear narrative is such a great format. Personally, I powered through the *Rails Tutorial* in three long days, doing all the examples and challenges at the end of each chapter. Do it from start to finish, without jumping around, and you'll get the ultimate benefit.

Enjoy!

—Derek Sivers (sivers.org)
Formerly: Founder, CD Baby
Currently: Founder, Thoughts Ltd.

Foreword to the First Edition

"If you want to learn web development with Ruby on Rails, how should I start?" For years Michael Hartl has provided the answer as author of the *RailsSpace* tutorial in our series and now the new *Ruby on Rails™ 3 Tutorial* that you hold in your hands (or PDF reader, I guess).

I'm so proud of having Michael on the series roster. He is living, breathing proof that us Rails folks are some of the luckiest in the wide world of technology. Before getting into Ruby, Michael taught theoretical and computational physics at Caltech for six years, where he received the Lifetime Achievement Award for Excellence in Teaching in 2000. He is a Harvard graduate, has a Ph.D. in Physics from Caltech, and is an alumnus of Paul Graham's esteemed Y Combinator program for entrepreneurs. And what does Michael apply his impressive experience and teaching prowess to? Teaching new software developers all around the world how to use Ruby on Rails effectively! Lucky we are indeed!

The availability of this tutorial actually comes at a critical time for Rails adoption. We're five years into the history of Rails and today's version of the platform has unprecedented power and flexibility. Experienced Rails folks can leverage that power effectively, but we're hearing growing cries of frustration from newcomers. The amount of information out there about Rails is fantastic if you know what you're doing already. However, if you're new, the scope and mass of information about Rails can be mind-boggling.

Luckily, Michael takes the same approach as his first book in the series, building a sample application from scratch, and writes in a style that's meant to be read from start to finish. Along the way, he explains all the little details that are likely to trip up beginners. Impressively, he goes beyond just a straightforward explanation of what Rails does and ventures into prescriptive advice about good software development practices, such as test-driven development. Neither does Michael constrain himself to a box delineated by the extents of the Rails framework—he goes ahead and teaches the reader to use tools essential to existence in the Rails community, such as Git and GitHub. In a friendly style, he even provides copious contextual footnotes of benefit to new programmers, such as the pronunciation of SQL and pointers to the origins of *lorem ipsum*. Tying all the content together in a way that remains concise and usable is truly a tour de force of dedication!

I tell you with all my heart that this book is one of the most significant titles in my Professional Ruby Series, because it facilitates the continued growth of the Rails ecosystem. By helping newcomers become productive members of the community quickly, he ensures that Ruby on Rails continues its powerful and disruptive charge into the mainstream. The *Rails Tutorial* is potent fuel for the fire that is powering growth and riches for so many of us, and for that we are forever grateful.

—Obie Fernandez, Series Editor

Acknowledgments

The *Ruby on Rails*™ *Tutorial* owes a lot to my previous Rails book, *RailsSpace*, and hence to my coauthor Aurelius Prochazka. I'd like to thank Aure both for the work he did on that book and for his support of this one. I'd also like to thank Debra Williams Cauley, my editor on both *RailsSpace* and the *Ruby on Rails*™ *Tutorial*; as long as she keeps taking me to baseball games, I'll keep writing books for her.

I'd like to acknowledge a long list of Rubyists who have taught and inspired me over the years: David Heinemeier Hansson, Yehuda Katz, Carl Lerche, Jeremy Kemper, Xavier Noria, Ryan Bates, Geoffrey Grosenbach, Peter Cooper, Matt Aimonetti, Gregg Pollack, Wayne E. Seguin, Amy Hoy, Dave Chelimsky, Pat Maddox, Tom Preston-Werner, Chris Wanstrath, Chad Fowler, Josh Susser, Obie Fernandez, Ian McFarland, Steven Bristol, Pratik Naik, Sarah Mei, Sarah Allen, Wolfram Arnold, Alex Chaffee, Giles Bowkett, Evan Dorn, Long Nguyen, James Lindenbaum, Adam Wiggins, Tikhon Bernstam, Ron Evans, Wyatt Greene, Miles Forrest, the good people at Pivotal Labs, the Heroku gang, the thoughtbot guys, and the GitHub crew. Thanks to Jen Lindner, Patty Donovan (Laserwords), and Julie Nahil and Michael Thurston from Pearson for their help with the book. Finally, many, many readers—far too many to list—have contributed a huge number of bug reports and suggestions during the writing of this book, and I gratefully acknowledge their help in making it as good as it can be.

About the Author

Michael Hartl is the author of the *Ruby on Rails*™ *Tutorial*, the leading introduction to web development with Ruby on Rails. His prior experience includes writing and developing *RailsSpace*, an extremely obsolete Rails tutorial book, and developing Insoshi, a once-popular and now-obsolete social networking platform in Ruby on Rails. In 2011, Michael received a Ruby Hero Award for his contributions to the Ruby community. He is a graduate of Harvard College, has a Ph.D. in physics from Caltech, and is an alumnus of the Y Combinator entrepreneur program.

CHAPTER 1

From Zero to Deploy

Welcome to *Ruby on Rails*™ *Tutorial*. The goal of this book is to be the best answer to the question, "If I want to learn web development with Ruby on Rails, where should I start?" By the time you finish the *Rails Tutorial*, you will have all the skills you need to develop and deploy your own custom web applications with Rails. You will also be ready to benefit from the many more advanced books, blogs, and screencasts that are part of the thriving Rails educational ecosystem. Finally, since the *Rails Tutorial* uses Rails 3, the knowledge you gain here represents the state of the art in web development. (The most up-to-date version of the *Rails Tutorial* can be found on the book's website at http://railstutorial.org; if you are reading this book offline, be sure to check the online version of the Rails Tutorial book at http://railstutorial.org/book for the latest updates.)

Note that the goal of this book is *not* merely to teach Rails, but rather to teach *web development with Rails*, which means acquiring (or expanding) the skills needed to develop software for the World Wide Web. In addition to Ruby on Rails, this skillset includes HTML and CSS, databases, version control, testing, and deployment. To accomplish this goal, *Rails Tutorial* takes an integrated approach: You will learn Rails by example by building a substantial sample application from scratch. As Derek Sivers notes in the foreword, this book is structured as a linear narrative, designed to be read from start to finish. If you are used to skipping around in technical books, taking this linear approach might require some adjustment, but I suggest giving it a try. You can think of the *Rails Tutorial* as a video game where you are the main character and where you level up as a Rails developer in each chapter. (The exercises are the minibosses.)

In this first chapter, we'll get started with Ruby on Rails by installing all the necessary software and by setting up our development environment (Section 1.2). We'll then create our first Rails application, called (appropriately enough) **first_app**. The *Rails Tutorial* emphasizes good software development practices, so immediately after creating our fresh new Rails project we'll put it under version control with Git (Section 1.3). And, believe it or not, in this chapter we'll even put our first app on the wider web by *deploying* it to production (Section 1.4).

In Chapter 2, we'll make a second project, whose purpose is to demonstrate the basic workings of a Rails application. To get up and running quickly, we'll build this *demo app* (called **demo_app**) using scaffolding (Box 1.1) to generate code; since this code is both ugly and complex, Chapter 2 will focus on interacting with the demo app through its *URIs* (sometimes called *URLs*)[1] using a web browser.

The rest of the tutorial focuses on developing a single large *sample application* (called **sample_app**), writing all the code from scratch. We'll develop the sample app using *test-driven development* (TDD), getting started in Chapter 3 by creating static pages and then adding a little dynamic content. We'll take a quick detour in Chapter 4 to learn a little about the Ruby language underlying Rails. Then, in Chapter 5 through Chapter 9, we'll complete the foundation for the sample application by making a site layout, a user data model, and a full registration and authentication system. Finally, in Chapter 10 and Chapter 11 we'll add microblogging and social features to make a working example site.

The final sample application will bear more than a passing resemblance to a certain popular social microblogging site—a site that, coincidentally, was also originally written in Rails. Although of necessity our efforts will focus on this specific sample application, the emphasis throughout the *Rails Tutorial* will be on general principles, so that you will have a solid foundation no matter what kinds of web applications you want to build.

Box 1.1 Scaffolding: Quicker, Easier, More Seductive

From the beginning, Rails has benefited from a palpable sense of excitement, starting with the famous 15-minute weblog video by Rails creator David Heinemeier Hansson. That video and its successors are a great way to get a taste of Rails' power,

---

1. *URI* stands for Uniform Resource Identifier, while the slightly less general *URL* stands for Uniform Resource Locator. In practice, the URI is usually equivalent to "the thing you see in the address bar of your browser."

and I recommend watching them. But be warned: They accomplish their amazing 15-minute feat using a feature called *scaffolding*, which relies heavily on *generated code*, magically created by the Rails `generate` command.

When writing a Ruby on Rails tutorial, it is tempting to rely on the scaffolding approach—it's quicker, easier, more seductive. But the complexity and sheer amount of code in the scaffolding can be utterly overwhelming to a beginning Rails developer; you may be able to use it, but you probably won't understand it. Following the scaffolding approach risks turning you into a virtuoso script generator with little (and brittle) actual knowledge of Rails.

In the *Rails Tutorial*, we'll take the (nearly) polar opposite approach: Although Chapter 2 will develop a small demo app using scaffolding, the core of the *Rails Tutorial* is the sample app, which we'll start writing in Chapter 3. At each stage of developing the sample application, we will write *small, bite-sized* pieces of code—simple enough to understand, yet novel enough to be challenging. The cumulative effect will be a deeper, more flexible knowledge of Rails, giving you a good background for writing nearly any type of web application.

1.1 Introduction

Since its debut in 2004, Ruby on Rails has rapidly become one of the most powerful and popular frameworks for building dynamic web applications. Everyone from scrappy startups to huge companies have used Rails: 37signals, GitHub, Shopify, Scribd, Twitter, LivingSocial, Groupon, Hulu, the Yellow Pages—the list of sites using Rails goes on and on. There are also many web development shops that specialize in Rails, such as ENTP, thoughtbot, Pivotal Labs, and Hashrocket, plus innumerable independent consultants, trainers, and contractors.

What makes Rails so great? First of all, Ruby on Rails is 100 percent open-source, available under the permissive MIT License, and as a result it also costs nothing to download or use. Rails also owes much of its success to its elegant and compact design; by exploiting the malleability of the underlying Ruby language, Rails effectively creates a domain-specific language for writing web applications. As a result, many common web programming tasks—such as generating HTML, making data models, and routing URIs—are easy with Rails, and the resulting application code is concise and readable.

Rails also adapts rapidly to new developments in web technology and framework design. For example, Rails was one of the first frameworks to fully digest and implement the REST architectural style for structuring web applications (which we'll be learning about throughout this tutorial). And when other frameworks develop successful new techniques, Rails creator David Heinemeier Hansson and the Rails core team don't hesitate to incorporate their ideas. Perhaps the most dramatic example is the merger of Rails and Merb, a rival Ruby web framework, so that Rails now benefits from Merb's modular design, stable API, and improved performance.

Finally, Rails benefits from an unusually enthusiastic and diverse community. The results include hundreds of open-source contributors, well-attended conferences, a huge number of plugins and gems (self-contained solutions to specific problems such as pagination and image upload), a rich variety of informative blogs, and a cornucopia of discussion forums and IRC channels. The large number of Rails programmers also makes it easier to handle the inevitable application errors: The "Google the error message" algorithm nearly always produces a relevant blog post or discussion-forum thread.

1.1.1 Comments for Various Readers

The *Rails Tutorial* contains integrated tutorials not only for Rails, but also for the underlying Ruby language, the RSpec testing framework, HTML, CSS, a small amount of JavaScript, and even a little SQL. This means that, no matter where you currently are in your knowledge of web development, by the time you finish this tutorial you will be ready for more advanced Rails resources, as well as for the more systematic treatments of the other subjects mentioned. It also means that there's a *lot* of material to cover; if you don't already have experience programming computers, you might find it overwhelming. The comments below contain some suggestions for approaching the *Rails Tutorial* depending on your background.

All readers: One common question when learning Rails is whether to learn Ruby first. The answer depends on your personal learning style and how much programming experience you already have. If you prefer to learn everything systematically from the ground up, or if you have never programmed before, then learning Ruby first might work well for you, and in this case I recommend *Beginning Ruby* by Peter Cooper. On the other hand, many beginning Rails developers are excited about making *web* applications, and would rather not slog through a 500-page book on pure Ruby before ever writing a single web page. In this case, I recommend following the short interactive tutorial at TryRuby,[2] and then optimally do the free tutorial at Rails for Zombies[3] to get a taste of what Rails can do.

Another common question is whether to use tests from the start. As noted in the introduction, the *Rails Tutorial* uses test-driven development (also called test-first development), which in my view is the best way to develop Rails applications, but it does introduce a substantial amount of overhead and complexity. If you find yourself getting bogged down by the tests, I suggest either skipping them on a first reading or (even better) using them as a tool to verify your code's correctness without worrying about how they work. This latter strategy involves creating the necessary test files (called *specs*) and filling them with the test code *exactly* as it appears in the book. You can then run the test suite (as described in Chapter 5) to watch it fail, then write the application code as described in the tutorial, and finally re-run the test suite to watch it pass.

Inexperienced programmers: The *Rails Tutorial* is not aimed principally at beginning programmers, and web applications, even relatively simple ones, are by their nature fairly complex. If you are completely new to web programming and find the *Rails Tutorial* too difficult, I suggest learning the basics of HTML and CSS and then giving the *Rails Tutorial* another go. (Unfortunately, I don't have a personal recommendation here, but *Head First HTML* looks promising, and one reader recommends *CSS: The Missing Manual* by David Sawyer McFarland.) You might also consider reading the first few chapters of *Beginning Ruby* by Peter Cooper, which starts with sample applications much smaller than a full-blown web app. That said, a surprising number of beginners have used this tutorial to learn web development, so I suggest giving it a try, and I especially recommend the *Rails Tutorial* screencast series[4] to give you an "over-the-shoulder" look at Rails software development.

Experienced programmers new to web development: Your previous experience means you probably already understand ideas like classes, methods, data structures, and others, which is a big advantage. Be warned that if your background is in C/C++ or Java, you

---

2. http://tryruby.org

3. http://railsforzombies.org

4. http://railstutorial.org/screencasts

may find Ruby a bit of an odd duck, and it might take time to get used to it; just stick with it and eventually you'll be fine. (Ruby even lets you put semicolons at the ends of lines if you miss them too much.) The *Rails Tutorial* covers all the web-specific ideas you'll need, so don't worry if you don't currently know a PUT from a POST.

Experienced web developers new to Rails: You have a great head start, especially if you have used a dynamic language such as PHP or (even better) Python. The basics of what we cover will likely be familiar, but test-driven development may be new to you, as may be the structured REST style favored by Rails. Ruby has its own idiosyncrasies, so those will likely be new, too.

Experienced Ruby programmers: The set of Ruby programmers who don't know Rails is a small one nowadays, but if you are a member of this elite group you can fly through this book and then move on to *The Rails 3 Way* by Obie Fernandez.

Inexperienced Rails programmers: You've perhaps read some other tutorials and made a few small Rails apps yourself. Based on reader feedback, I'm confident that you can still get a lot out of this book. Among other things, the techniques here may be more up-to-date than the ones you picked up when you originally learned Rails.

Experienced Rails programmers: This book is unnecessary for you, but many experienced Rails developers have expressed surprise at how much they learned from this book, and you might enjoy seeing Rails from a different perspective.

After finishing the *Ruby on Rails Tutorial*, I recommend that experienced programmers read *The Well-Grounded Rubyist* by David A. Black, which is an excellent in-depth discussion of Ruby from the ground up, or *The Ruby Way* by Hal Fulton, which is also fairly advanced but takes a more topical approach. Then move on to *The Rails 3 Way* to deepen your Rails expertise.

At the end of this process, no matter where you started, you should be ready for the many more intermediate-to-advanced Rails resources out there. Here are some I particularly recommend:

- RailsCasts by Ryan Bates: Excellent (mostly) free Rails screencasts
- PeepCode: Excellent commercial screencasts

- Code School: Interactive programming courses
- Rails Guides: Good topical and up-to-date Rails references
- RailsCasts by Ryan Bates: Did I already mention RailsCasts? Seriously: *RailsCasts*.

1.1.2 "Scaling" Rails

Before moving on with the rest of the introduction, I'd like to take a moment to address the one issue that dogged the Rails framework the most in its early days: the supposed inability of Rails to "scale"—i.e., to handle large amounts of traffic. Part of this issue relied on a misconception; you scale a *site*, not a framework, and Rails, as awesome as it is, is only a framework. So the real question should have been, "Can a site built with Rails scale?" In any case, the question has now been definitively answered in the affirmative: Some of the most heavily trafficked sites in the world use Rails. Actually *doing* the scaling is beyond the scope of just Rails, but rest assured that if *your* application ever needs to handle the load of Hulu or the Yellow Pages, Rails won't stop you from taking over the world.

1.1.3 Conventions in This Book

The conventions in this book are mostly self-explanatory. In this section, I'll mention some that may not be.

Both the HTML and PDF editions of this book are full of links, both to internal sections (such as Section 1.2) and to external sites (such as the main Ruby on Rails download page).[5]

Many examples in this book use command-line commands. For simplicity, all command line examples use a Unix-style command line prompt (a dollar sign), as follows:

```
$ echo "hello, world"
hello, world
```

---

5. When reading the *Rails Tutorial*, you may find it convenient to follow an internal section link to look at the reference and then immediately go back to where you were before. This is easy when reading the book as a web page, since you can just use the Back button of your browser, but both Adobe Reader and OS X's Preview allow you to do this with the PDF as well. In Reader, you can right-click on the document and select "Previous View" to go back. In Preview, use the Go menu: `Go > Back`.

Windows users should understand that their systems will use the analogous angle prompt >:

```
C:\Sites> echo "hello, world"
hello, world
```

On Unix systems, some commands should be executed with **sudo**, which stands for "substitute user do." By default, a command executed with **sudo** is run as an administrative user, which has access to files and directories that normal users can't touch, such as in this example from Section 1.2.2:

```
$ sudo ruby setup.rb
```

Most Unix/Linux/OS X systems require **sudo** by default, unless you are using Ruby Version Manager as suggested in Section 1.2.2; in this case, you would type this instead:

```
$ ruby setup.rb
```

Rails comes with lots of commands that can be run at the command line. For example, in Section 1.2.5 we'll run a local development web server as follows:

```
$ rails server
```

As with the command-line prompt, the *Rails Tutorial* uses the Unix convention for directory separators (i.e., a forward slash /). My *Rails Tutorial* sample application, for instance, lives in

```
/Users/mhartl/rails_projects/sample_app
```

On Windows, the analogous directory would be

```
C:\Sites\sample_app
```

The root directory for any given app is known as the *Rails root*, but this terminology is confusing and many people mistakenly believe that the "Rails root" is the root directory for Rails itself. For clarity, the *Rails Tutorial* will refer to the Rails root as the *application root*, and henceforth all directories will be relative to this directory. For example, the **config** directory of my sample application is

```
/Users/mhartl/rails_projects/sample_app/config
```

The application root directory here is everything before **config**, that is,

```
/Users/mhartl/rails_projects/sample_app
```

For brevity, when referring to the file

```
/Users/mhartl/rails_projects/sample_app/config/routes.rb
```

I'll omit the application root and simply write **config/routes.rb**.

The *Rails Tutorial* often shows output from various programs (shell commands, version control status, Ruby programs, etc.). Because of the innumerable small differences between different computer systems, the output you see may not always agree exactly with what is shown in the text, but this is not cause for concern.

Some commands may produce errors depending on your system; rather than attempt the Sisyphean task of documenting all such errors in this tutorial, I will delegate to the "Google the error message" algorithm, which among other things is good practice for real-life software development. If you run into any problems while following the tutorial, I suggest consulting the resources listed on the Rails Tutorial help page.[6]

1.2 Up and Running

> I think of Chapter 1 as the "weeding out phase" in law school—if you can get your
> dev environment set up, the rest is easy to get through.
> —Bob Cavezza, *Rails Tutorial* reader

It's time now to get going with a Ruby on Rails development environment and our first application. There is quite a bit of overhead here, especially if you don't have

---

6. http://railstutorial.org/help

Tutorial will generally be of a Firefox browser. If you use Firefox, I suggest using the Firebug add-on, which lets you perform all sorts of magic, such as dynamically inspecting (and even editing) the HTML structure and CSS rules on any page. For those not using Firefox, both Safari and Chrome have a built-in "Inspect element" feature available by right-clicking on any part of the page.

A Note about Tools

In the process of getting your development environment up and running, you may find that you spend a *lot* of time getting everything just right. The learning process for editors and IDEs is particularly long; you can spend weeks on Sublime Text or Vim tutorials alone. If you're new to this game, I want to assure you that *spending time learning tools is normal*. Everyone goes through it. Sometimes it is frustrating, and it's easy to get impatient when you have an awesome web app in your head and you *just want to learn Rails already*, but have to spend a week learning some weird ancient Unix editor just to get started. But a craftsman has to know his tools, and in the end the reward is worth the effort.

1.2.2 Ruby, RubyGems, Rails, and Git

> Practically all the software in the world is either broken or very difficult to use. So users dread software. They've been trained that whenever they try to install something, or even fill out a form online, it's not going to work. *I* dread installing stuff, and I have a Ph.D. in computer science.
> —Paul Graham, *Founders at Work*

Now it's time to install Ruby and Rails. I've done my best to cover as many bases as possible, but systems vary, and many things can go wrong during these steps. Be sure to Google the error message or consult the Rails Tutorial help page if you run into trouble.

Unless otherwise noted, you should use the exact versions of all software used in the tutorial, including Rails itself, if you want the same results. Sometimes minor version differences will yield identical results, but you shouldn't count on this, especially with respect to Rails versions. The main exception is Ruby itself: 1.9.2 and 1.9.3 are virtually identical for the purposes of this tutorial, so feel free to use either one.

Rails Installer (Windows)

Installing Rails on Windows used to be a real pain, but thanks to the efforts of the good people at Engine Yard—especially Dr. Nic Williams and Wayne E. Seguin—installing Rails and related software on Windows is now easy. If you are using Windows, go to Rails Installer and download the Rails Installer executable and view the excellent installation video. Double-click the executable and follow the instructions to install Git (so you can skip Section 1.2.2), Ruby (skip Section 1.2.2), RubyGems (skip Section 1.2.2), and Rails itself (skip Section 1.2.2). Once the installation has finished, you can skip right to the creation of the first application in Section 1.2.3.

Bear in mind that the Rails Installer might use a slightly different version of Rails from the one installed in Section 1.2.2, which might cause incompatibilities. To fix this, I am currently working with Nic and Wayne to create a list of Rails Installers ordered by Rails version number.

Install Git

Much of the Rails ecosystem depends in one way or another on a version control system called Git (covered in more detail in Section 1.3). Because its use is ubiquitous, you should install Git even at this early stage; I suggest following the installation instructions for your platform at the Installing Git section of *Pro Git*.

Install Ruby

The next step is to install Ruby. It's possible that your system already has it; try running

```
$ ruby -v
ruby 1.9.3
```

to see the version number. Rails 3 requires Ruby 1.8.7 or later and works best with Ruby 1.9.x. This tutorial assumes that most readers are using Ruby 1.9.2 or 1.9.3, but Ruby 1.8.7 should work as well (although there is one syntax difference, covered in Chapter 4, and assorted minor differences in output).

As part of installing Ruby, if you are using OS X or Linux, I strongly recommend using Ruby Version Manager (RVM), which allows you to install and manage multiple versions of Ruby on the same machine. (The Pik project accomplishes a similar feat on Windows.) This is particularly important if you want to run different versions of Ruby or Rails on the same machine. If you run into any problems with RVM, you can often find its creator, Wayne E. Seguin, on the RVM IRC channel (#rvm on freenode.net).[10] If you are running Linux, I particularly recommend the installation tutorial for Linux Ubuntu and Linux Mint by Mircea Goia.

After installing RVM, you can install Ruby as follows:[11]

```
$ rvm get head && rvm reload
$ rvm install 1.9.3
<wait a while>
```

Here the first command updates and reloads RVM itself, which is a good practice since RVM gets updated frequently. The second installs the 1.9.3 version of Ruby; depending on your system, it might take a while to download and compile, so don't worry if it seems to be taking forever.

Some Linux users report having to include the path to a library called OpenSSL:

```
$ rvm install 1.9.3 --with-openssl-dir=$HOME/.rvm.usr
```

On some older OS X systems, you might have to include the path to the readline library:

```
$ rvm install 1.9.3 --with-readline-dir=/opt/local
```

(Like I said, lots of things can go wrong. The only solution is web searches and determination.)

After installing Ruby, you should configure your system for the other software needed to run Rails applications. This typically involves installing *gems*, which are self-contained packages of Ruby code. Since gems with different version numbers sometimes conflict, it is often convenient to create separate *gemsets*, which are self-contained bundles of gems. For the purposes of this tutorial, I suggest creating a gemset called **rails3tutorial2ndEd**:

```
$ rvm use 1.9.3@rails3tutorial2ndEd --create --default
Using /Users/mhartl/.rvm/gems/ruby-1.9.3 with gemset rails3tutorial2ndEd
```

---

10. If you haven't used IRC before, I suggest you start by searching the web for "irc client <your platform>." Two good native clients for OS X are Colloquy and LimeChat. And of course there's always the web interface at http://webchat.freenode.net/?channels=rvm.

11. You might have to install the Subversion version control system to get this to work.

This command creates (`--create`) the gemset **rails3tutorial2ndEd** associated with
Ruby 1.9.3 while arranging to start using it immediately (`use`) and setting it as the
default (`--default`) gemset, so that any time we open a new terminal window the
1.9.3@rails3tutorial2ndEd Ruby/gemset combination is automatically selected.
RVM supports a large variety of commands for manipulating gemsets; see the documentation at http://rvm.beginrescueend.com/gemsets. If you ever get stuck with RVM,
running commands like these should help you get your bearings:

```
$ rvm --help
$ rvm gemset --help
```

Install RubyGems

RubyGems is a package manager for Ruby projects, and there are many useful libraries
(including Rails) available as Ruby packages, or *gems*. Installing RubyGems should
be easy once you install Ruby. In fact, if you have installed RVM, you already have
RubyGems, since RVM includes it automatically:

```
$ which gem
/Users/mhartl/.rvm/rubies/ruby-1.9.3-p0/bin/gem
```

If you don't already have it, you should download RubyGems, extract it, and then go
to the **rubygems** directory and run the setup program:

```
$ ruby setup.rb
```

(If you get a permissions error here, recall from Section 1.1.3 that you may have to use
sudo.)

   If you already have RubyGems installed, you should make sure your system uses
the version used in this tutorial:

```
$ gem update --system 1.8.24
```

Freezing your system to this particular version will help prevent conflicts as RubyGems
changes in the future.

   When installing gems, by default RubyGems generates two different kinds of
documentation (called ri and rdoc), but many Ruby and Rails developers find that
the time to build them isn't worth the benefit. (Many programmers rely on online
documentation instead of the native ri and rdoc documents.) To prevent the automatic

generation of the documentation, I recommend making a gem configuration file called **.gemrc** in your home directory as in Listing 1.1 with the line in Listing 1.2. (The tilde "~" means "home directory," while the dot **.** in **.gemrc** makes the file hidden, which is a common convention for configuration files.)

Listing 1.1 Creating a gem configuration file.

```
$ subl ~/.gemrc
```

Here **subl** is the command-line command to launch Sublime Text on OS X, which you can set up using the Sublime Text 2 documentation for the OS X command line. If you're on a different platform, or if you're using a different editor, you should replace this command as necessary (i.e., by double-clicking the application icon or by using an alternate command such as **mate**, **vim**, **gvim**, or **mvim**). For brevity, throughout the rest of this tutorial I'll use **subl** as a shorthand for "open with your favorite text editor."

Listing 1.2 Suppressing the ri and rdoc documentation in **.gemrc**.

```
install: --no-rdoc --no-ri
update: --no-rdoc --no-ri
```

Install Rails

Once you've installed RubyGems, installing Rails should be easy. This tutorial standardizes on Rails 3.2, which we can install as follows:

```
$ gem install rails -v 3.2.13
```

To check your Rails installation, run the following command to print out the version number:

```
$ rails -v
Rails 3.2.13
```

Note: If you installed Rails using the Rails Installer in Section 1.2.2, there might be slight version differences. As of this writing, those differences are not relevant, but in the future, as the current Rails version diverges from the one used in this tutorial, these differences may become significant. I am currently working with Engine Yard to create links to specific versions of the Rails Installer.

If you're running Linux, you might have to install a couple of other packages at this point:

```
$ sudo apt-get install libxslt-dev libxml2-dev libsqlite3-dev # Linux only
```

1.2.3 The First Application

Virtually all Rails applications start the same way, with the **rails** command. This handy program creates a skeleton Rails application in a directory of your choice. To get started, make a directory for your Rails projects and then run the **rails** command to make the first application (Listing 1.3):

Listing 1.3 Running **rails** to generate a new application.

```
$ mkdir rails_projects
$ cd rails_projects
$ rails new first_app
      create
      create  README.rdoc
      create  Rakefile
      create  config.ru
      create  .gitignore
      create  Gemfile
      create  app
      create  app/assets/images/rails.png
      create  app/assets/javascripts/application.js
      create  app/assets/stylesheets/application.css
      create  app/controllers/application_controller.rb
      create  app/helpers/application_helper.rb
      create  app/mailers
      create  app/models
      create  app/views/layouts/application.html.erb
      create  app/mailers/.gitkeep
      create  app/models/.gitkeep
      create  config
      create  config/routes.rb
      create  config/application.rb
      create  config/environment.rb
      .
      .
      .
      create  vendor/plugins
      create  vendor/plugins/.gitkeep
         run  bundle install
```

```
Fetching source index for https://rubygems.org/
.
.
.
Your bundle is complete! Use 'bundle show [gemname]' to see where a bundled
gem is installed.
```

As seen at the end of Listing 1.3, running **rails** automatically runs the **bundle install** command after the file creation is done. If that step doesn't work right now, don't worry; follow the steps in Section 1.2.4 and you should be able to get it to work.

Notice how many files and directories the **rails** command creates. This standard directory and file structure (Figure 1.2) is one of the many advantages of Rails; it immediately gets you from zero to a functional (if minimal) application. Moreover, since the structure is common to all Rails apps, you can immediately get your bearings when looking at someone else's code. A summary of the default Rails files appears in Table 1.1; we'll learn about most of these files and directories throughout the rest of this book. In particular, starting in Section 5.2.1 we'll discuss the **app/assets** directory,

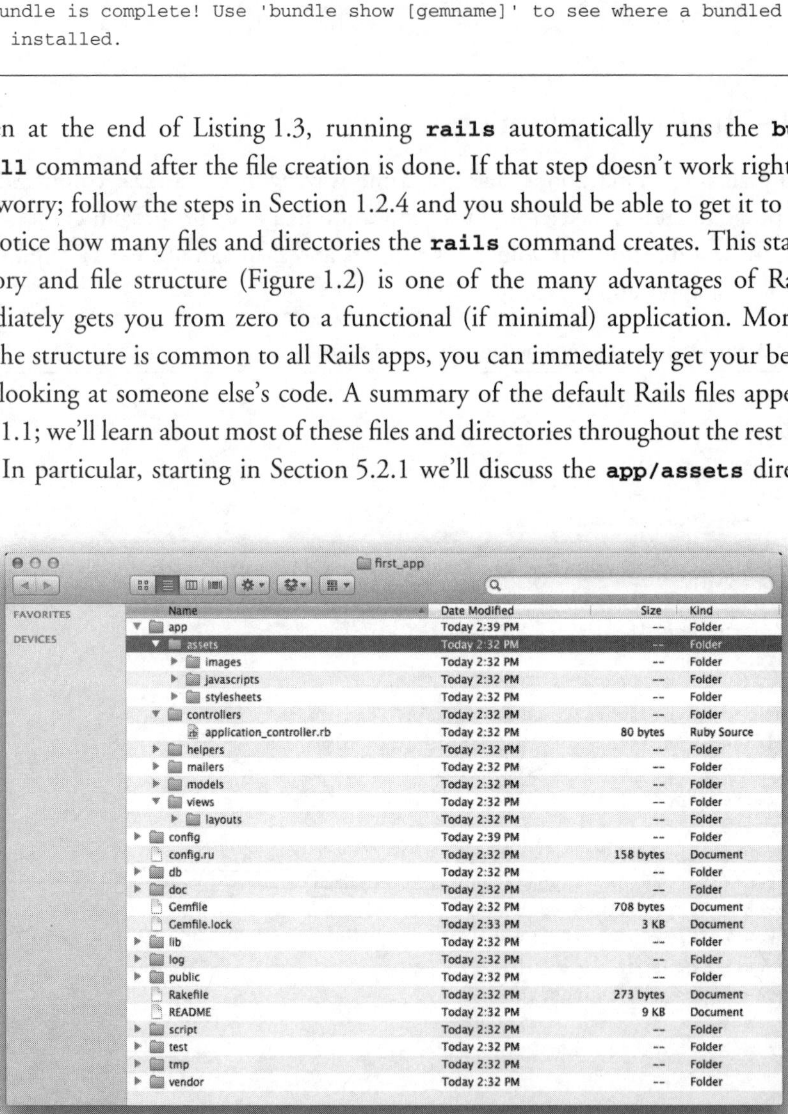

Figure 1.2 The directory structure for a newly hatched Rails app.

Table 1.1 A summary of the default Rails directory structure.

File/Directory	Purpose
`app/`	Core application (app) code, including models, views, controllers, and helpers
`app/assets`	Applications assets such as cascading style sheets (CSS), JavaScript files, and images
`config/`	Application configuration
`db/`	Database files
`doc/`	Documentation for the application
`lib/`	Library modules
`lib/assets`	Library assets such as cascading style sheets (CSS), JavaScript files, and images
`log/`	Application log files
`public/`	Data accessible to the public (e.g., web browsers), such as error pages
`script/rails`	A script for generating code, opening console sessions, or starting a local server
`test/`	Application tests (made obsolete by the `spec/` directory in Section 3.1.2)
`tmp/`	Temporary files
`vendor/`	Third-party code such as plugins and gems
`vendor/assets`	Third-party assets such as cascading style sheets (CSS), JavaScript files, and images
`README.rdoc`	A brief description of the application
`Rakefile`	Utility tasks available via the `rake` command
`Gemfile`	Gem requirements for this app
`Gemfile.lock`	A list of gems used to ensure that all copies of the app use the same gem versions
`config.ru`	A configuration file for Rack middleware
`.gitignore`	Patterns for files that should be ignored by Git

part of the *asset pipeline* (new as of Rails 3.1) that makes it easier than ever to organize and deploy assets such as cascading style sheets and JavaScript files.

1.2.4 Bundler

After creating a new Rails application, the next step is to use *Bundler* to install and include the gems needed by the app. As noted briefly in Section 1.2.3, Bundler is run automatically (via `bundle install`) by the `rails` command, but in this section we'll make some changes to the default application gems and run Bundler again. This involves opening the **Gemfile** with your favorite text editor:

```
$ cd first_app/
$ subl Gemfile
```

The result should look something like Listing 1.4. The code in this file is Ruby, but don't worry at this point about the syntax; Chapter 4 will cover Ruby in more depth.

Listing 1.4 The default **Gemfile** in the **first_app** directory.

```ruby
source 'https://rubygems.org'

gem 'rails', '3.2.13'

# Bundle edge Rails instead:
# gem 'rails', :git => 'git://github.com/rails/rails.git'

gem 'sqlite3'


# Gems used only for assets and not required
# in production environments by default.
group :assets do
  gem 'sass-rails',   '~> 3.2.3'
  gem 'coffee-rails', '~> 3.2.2'

  gem 'uglifier', '>= 1.2.3'
end

gem 'jquery-rails'

# To use ActiveModel has_secure_password
# gem 'bcrypt-ruby', '~> 3.0.0'

# To use Jbuilder templates for JSON
# gem 'jbuilder'

# Use unicorn as the web server
# gem 'unicorn'

# Deploy with Capistrano
# gem 'capistrano'

# To use debugger
# gem 'ruby-debug19', :require => 'ruby-debug'
```

Many of these lines are commented out with the hash symbol #; they are there to show you some commonly needed gems and to give examples of the Bundler syntax. For now, we won't need any gems other than the defaults: Rails itself, some gems related to the asset pipeline (Section 5.2.1), the gem for the jQuery JavaScript library, and the gem for the Ruby interface to the SQLite database.

Unless you specify a version number to the **gem** command, Bundler will automatically install the latest version of the gem. Unfortunately, gem updates often cause minor but potentially confusing breakage, so in this tutorial we'll include explicit version numbers known to work, as seen in Listing 1.5 (which also omits the commented-out lines from Listing 1.4).

Listing 1.5 A **Gemfile** with an explicit version of each Ruby gem.

```
source 'https://rubygems.org'

gem 'rails', '3.2.13'

group :development do
  gem 'sqlite3', '1.3.5'
end


# Gems used only for assets and not required
# in production environments by default.
group :assets do
  gem 'sass-rails',   '3.2.4'
  gem 'coffee-rails', '3.2.2'

  gem 'uglifier', '1.2.3'
end

gem 'jquery-rails', '2.0.0'
```

Listing 1.5 changes the line for jQuery, the default JavaScript library used by Rails, from

```
gem 'jquery-rails'
```

to

```
gem 'jquery-rails', '2.0.0'
```

We've also changed

```
gem 'sqlite3'
```

to

```
group :development do
  gem 'sqlite3', '1.3.5'
end
```

which forces Bundler to install version **1.3.5** of the **sqlite3** gem. Note that we've also taken this opportunity to arrange for SQLite to be included only in a development environment (Section 7.1.1), which prevents potential conflicts with the database used by Heroku (Section 1.4).

Listing 1.5 also changes a few other lines, converting

```
group :assets do
  gem 'sass-rails',   '~> 3.2.3'
  gem 'coffee-rails', '~> 3.2.2'
  gem 'uglifier', '>= 1.2.3'
end
```

to

```
group :assets do
  gem 'sass-rails',   '3.2.4'
  gem 'coffee-rails', '3.2.2'
  gem 'uglifier', '1.2.3'
end
```

The syntax

```
gem 'uglifier', '>= 1.2.3'
```

installs the latest version of the **uglifier** gem (which handles file compression for the asset pipeline) as long as it's greater than version **1.2.3**—even if it's, say, version **7.2**. Meanwhile, the code

```
gem 'coffee-rails', '~> 3.2.2'
```

installs the gem **coffee-rails** (also needed by the asset pipeline) as long as it's lower than version **3.3**. In other words, the **>=** notation always performs upgrades, whereas the ˜> `3.2.2` notation only performs upgrades to minor point releases (e.g., from `3.1.1` to `3.1.2`), but not to major point releases (e.g., from `3.1` to `3.2`). Unfortunately, experience shows that even minor point releases often break things, so for the *Rails Tutorial* we'll err on the side of caution by including exact version numbers for virtually all gems. (The only exception is gems that are in release candidate or beta stage as of this writing; for those gems, we'll use ˜> so that the final versions will be loaded once they're done.)

Once you've assembled the proper `Gemfile`, install the gems using `bundle install`:

```
$ bundle install
Fetching source index for https://rubygems.org/
    .
    .
    .
```

(If you're running OS X and you get an error about missing Ruby header files (e.g., `ruby.h`) at this point, you may need to install Xcode. These are developer tools that came with your OS X installation disk, but to avoid the full installation I recommend the much smaller Command Line Tools for Xcode.[12]) The `bundle install` command might take a few moments, but when it's done our application will be ready to run. *Note:* This setup is fine for the first app, but it isn't ideal. Chapter 3 covers a more powerful (and slightly more advanced) method for installing Ruby gems with Bundler.

1.2.5 `rails server`

Thanks to running `rails new` in Section 1.2.3 and `bundle install` in Section 1.2.4, we already have an application we can run—but how? Happily, Rails comes with a command-line program, or *script*, that runs a *local* web server, visible only from your development machine:[13]

```
$ rails server
=> Booting WEBrick
=> Rails application starting on http://0.0.0.0:3000
=> Call with -d to detach
=> Ctrl-C to shutdown server
```

---

12. https://developer.apple.com/downloads

13. Recall from Section 1.1.3 that Windows users might have to type `ruby rails server` instead.

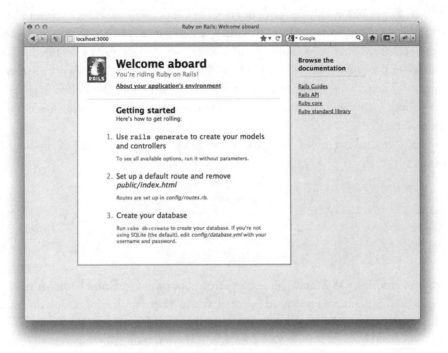

Figure 1.3 The default Rails page.

(If your system complains about the lack of a JavaScript runtime, visit the execjs page at GitHub for a list of possibilities. I particularly recommend installing Node.js.) This tells us that the application is running on port number 3000[14] at the address **0.0.0.0**. This address tells the computer to listen on every available IP address configured on that specific machine; in particular, we can view the application using the special address **127.0.0.1**, which is also known as **localhost**. We can see the result of visiting http://localhost:3000/ in Figure 1.3.

To see information about our first application, click on the link "About your application's environment." The result is shown in Figure 1.4. (Figure 1.4 represents the environment on my machine when I made the screenshot; your results may differ.)

---

14. Normally, websites run on port 80, but this usually requires special privileges, so Rails picks a less restricted higher-numbered port for the development server.

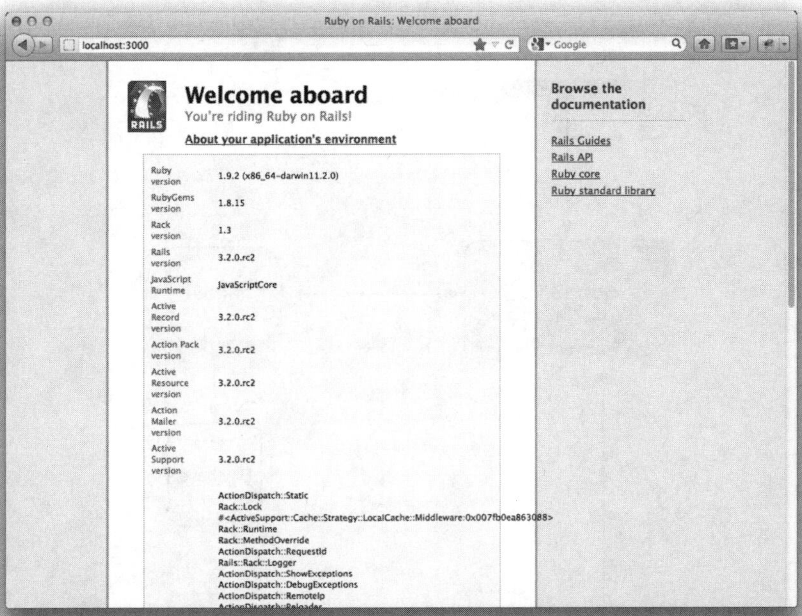

Figure 1.4   The default page with the app environment.

Of course, we don't need the default Rails page in the long run, but it's nice to see it working for now. We'll remove the default page (and replace it with a custom home page) in Section 5.3.2.

1.2.6   Model-view-controller (MVC)

Even at this early stage, it's helpful to get a high-level overview of how Rails applications work (Figure 1.5). You might have noticed that the standard Rails application structure (Figure 1.2) has an application directory called **app/** with three subdirectories: **models**, **views**, and **controllers**. This is a hint that Rails follows the model-view-controller (MVC) architectural pattern, which enforces a separation between "domain logic" (also called "business logic") from the input and presentation logic associated with a graphical user interface (GUI). In the case of web applications, the "domain logic"

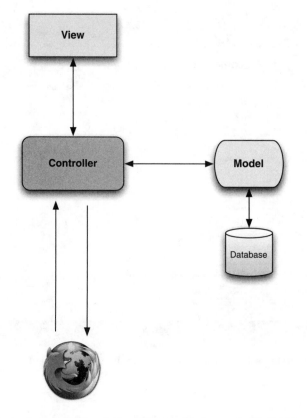

Figure 1.5   A schematic representation of the model-view-controller (MVC) architecture.

typically consists of data models for things like users, articles, and products, and the GUI is just a web page in a web browser.

When interacting with a Rails application, a browser sends a *request*, which is received by a web server and passed on to a Rails *controller*, which is in charge of what to do next. In some cases, the controller will immediately render a *view*, which is a template that gets converted to HTML and sent back to the browser. More commonly for dynamic sites, the controller interacts with a *model*, which is a Ruby object that represents an element of the site (such as a user) and is in charge of communicating with the database. After invoking the model, the controller then renders the view and returns the complete web page to the browser as HTML.

If this discussion seems a bit abstract right now, worry not; we'll refer back to this section frequently. In addition, Section 2.2.2 has a more detailed discussion of MVC in the context of the demo app. Finally, the sample app will use all aspects of MVC; we'll cover controllers and views starting in Section 3.1.2, models starting in Section 6.1, and we'll see all three working together in Section 7.1.2.

1.3   Version Control with Git

Now that we have a fresh and working Rails application, we'll take a moment for a step that, while technically optional, would be viewed by many Rails developers as practically essential, namely, placing our application source code under *version control*. Version control systems allow us to track changes to our project's code, collaborate more easily, and roll back any inadvertent errors (such as accidentally deleting files). Knowing how to use a version control system is a required skill for every software developer.

There are many options for version control, but the Rails community has largely standardized on Git, a distributed version control system originally developed by Linus Torvalds to host the Linux kernel. Git is a large subject, and we'll only be scratching the surface in this book, but there are many good free resources online; I especially recommend *Pro Git* by Scott Chacon (Apress, 2009). Putting your source code under version control with Git is *strongly* recommended, not only because it's nearly a universal practice in the Rails world, but also because it will allow you to share your code more easily (Section 1.3.4) and deploy your application right here in the first chapter (Section 1.4).

1.3.1   Installation and Setup

The first step is to install Git if you haven't yet followed the steps in Section 1.2.2. (As noted in that section, this involves following the instructions in the Installing Git section of *Pro Git*.)

First-time System Setup

After installing Git, you should perform a set of one-time setup steps. These are *system* setups, meaning you only have to do them once per computer:

```
$ git config --global user.name "Your Name"
$ git config --global user.email your.email@example.com
```

I also like to use **co** in place of the more verbose **checkout** command, which we can arrange as follows:

```
$ git config --global alias.co checkout
```

This tutorial will usually use the full **checkout** command, which works for systems that don't have **co** configured, but in real life I nearly always use **git co**.

As a final setup step, you can optionally set the editor Git will use for commit messages. If you use a graphical editor such as Sublime Text, TextMate, gVim, or MacVim, you need to use a flag to make sure that the editor stays attached to the shell instead of detaching immediately:[15]

```
$ git config --global core.editor "subl -w"
```

Replace **"subl -w"** with **"mate -w"** for TextMate, **"gvim -f"** for gVim, or **"mvim -f"** for MacVim.

First-time Repository Setup

Now we come to some steps that are necessary each time you create a new *repository*. First, navigate to the root directory of the first app and initialize a new repository:

```
$ git init
Initialized empty Git repository in /Users/mhartl/rails_projects/first_app/.git/
```

The next step is to add the project files to the repository. There's a minor complication, though: By default Git tracks the changes of *all* the files, but there are some files we don't want to track. For example, Rails creates log files to record the behavior of the application; these files change frequently, and we don't want our version control system to have to update them constantly. Git has a simple mechanism to ignore such files: Simply include a file called **.gitignore** in the application root directory with some rules telling Git which files to ignore.[16]

---

15. Normally this is a feature, since it lets you continue to use the command line after launching your editor, but Git interprets the detachment as closing the file with an empty commit message, which prevents the commit from going through. I only mention this point because it can be seriously confusing if you try to set your editor to **subl** or **gvim** without the flag. If you find this note confusing, feel free to ignore it.

16. If you can't see the **.gitignore** file in your directory, you may need to configure your directory viewer to show hidden files.

Looking again at Table 1.1, we see that the **rails** command creates a default **.gitignore** file in the application root directory, as shown in Listing 1.6.

Listing 1.6 The default **.gitignore** created by the **rails** command.

```
# See http://help.github.com/ignore-files/ for more about ignoring files.
#
# If you find yourself ignoring temporary files generated by your text editor
# or operating system, you probably want to add a global ignore instead:
#   git config --global core.excludesfile ~/.gitignore_global

# Ignore bundler config
/.bundle

# Ignore the default SQLite database.
/db/*.sqlite3

# Ignore all logfiles and tempfiles.
/log/*.log
/tmp
```

Listing 1.6 causes Git to ignore files such as log files, Rails temporary (**tmp**) files, and SQLite databases. (For example, to ignore log files, which live in the **log/** directory, we use **log/*.log** to ignore all files that end in **.log**.) Most of these ignored files change frequently and automatically, so including them under version control is inconvenient; moreover, when collaborating with others they can cause frustrating and irrelevant conflicts.

The **.gitignore** file in Listing 1.6 is probably sufficient for this tutorial, but depending on your system you may find Listing 1.7 more convenient. This augmented **.gitignore** arranges to ignore Rails documentation files, Vim and Emacs swap files, and (for OS X users) the weird **.DS_Store** directories created by the Mac Finder application. If you want to use this broader set of ignored files, open up **.gitignore** in your favorite text editor and fill it with the contents of Listing 1.7.

Listing 1.7 An augmented **.gitignore** file.

```
# Ignore bundler config
/.bundle

# Ignore the default SQLite database.
/db/*.sqlite3
```

```
# Ignore all logfiles and tempfiles.
/log/*.log
/tmp

# Ignore other unneeded files.
doc/
*.swp
*~
.project
.DS_Store
```

1.3.2 Adding and Committing

Finally, we'll add the files in your new Rails project to Git and then commit the results. You can add all the files (apart from those that match the ignore patterns in **.gitignore**) as follows:

```
$ git add .
```

Here the dot "**.**" represents the current directory, and Git is smart enough to add the files *recursively*, so it automatically includes all the subdirectories. This command adds the project files to a *staging area*, which contains pending changes to your project; you can see which files are in the staging area using the **status** command:[17]

```
$ git status
# On branch master
#
# Initial commit
#
# Changes to be committed:
#   (use "git rm --cached <file>..." to unstage)
#
#       new file:   README.rdoc
#       new file:   Rakefile
.
.
.
```

(The results are long, so I've used vertical dots to indicate omitted output.)

---

17. If in the future any unwanted files start showing up when you type **git status**, just add them to your **.gitignore** file from Listing 1.7.

To tell Git you want to keep the changes, use the **commit** command:

```
$ git commit -m "Initial commit"
[master (root-commit) df0a62f] Initial commit
42 files changed, 8461 insertions(+), 0 deletions(-)
create mode 100644 README.rdoc
create mode 100644 Rakefile
.
.
.
```

The **-m** flag lets you add a message for the commit; if you omit **-m**, Git will open the editor you set in Section 1.3.1 and have you enter the message there.

It is important to note that Git commits are *local*, recorded only on the machine on which the commits occur. This is in contrast to the popular open-source version control system called Subversion, in which a commit necessarily makes changes on a remote repository. Git divides a Subversion-style commit into its two logical pieces: A local recording of the changes (**git commit**) and a push of the changes up to a remote repository (**git push**). We'll see an example of the push step in Section 1.3.5.

By the way, you can see a list of your commit messages using the **log** command:

```
$ git log
commit df0a62f3f091e53ffa799309b3e32c27b0b38eb4
Author: Michael Hartl <michael@michaelhartl.com>
Date:   Thu Oct 15 11:36:21 2009 -0700

  Initial commit
```

To exit **git log**, you may have to type **q** to quit.

1.3.3 What Good Does Git Do You?

It's probably not entirely clear at this point why putting your source under version control does you any good, so let me give just one example. (We'll see many others in the chapters ahead.) Suppose you've made some accidental changes, such as (D'oh!) deleting the critical **app/controllers/** directory:

```
$ ls app/controllers/
application_controller.rb
$ rm -rf app/controllers/
$ ls app/controllers/
ls: app/controllers/: No such file or directory
```

Here we're using the Unix **ls** command to list the contents of the **app/controllers/** directory and the **rm** command to remove it. The **-rf** flag means "recursive force", which recursively removes all files, directories, subdirectories, and so on, without asking for explicit confirmation of each deletion.

Let's check the status to see what's up:

```
$ git status
# On branch master
# Changed but not updated:
#   (use "git add/rm <file>..." to update what will be committed)
#   (use "git checkout -- <file>..." to discard changes in working directory)
#
#       deleted:    app/controllers/application_controller.rb
#
no changes added to commit (use "git add" and/or "git commit -a")
```

We see here that a file has been deleted, but the changes are only on the "working tree"; they haven't been committed yet. This means we can still undo the changes easily by having Git check out the previous commit with the **checkout** command (and a **-f** flag to force overwriting the current changes):

```
$ git checkout -f
$ git status
# On branch master
nothing to commit (working directory clean)
$ ls app/controllers/
application_controller.rb
```

The missing directory and file are back. That's a relief!

1.3.4 GitHub

Now that you've put your project under version control with Git, it's time to push your code up to GitHub, a social code site optimized for hosting and sharing Git repositories. Putting a copy of your Git repository at GitHub serves two purposes: It's a full backup of your code (including the full history of commits), and it makes any future collaboration much easier. This step is optional, but being a GitHub member will open the door to participating in a wide variety of open-source projects.

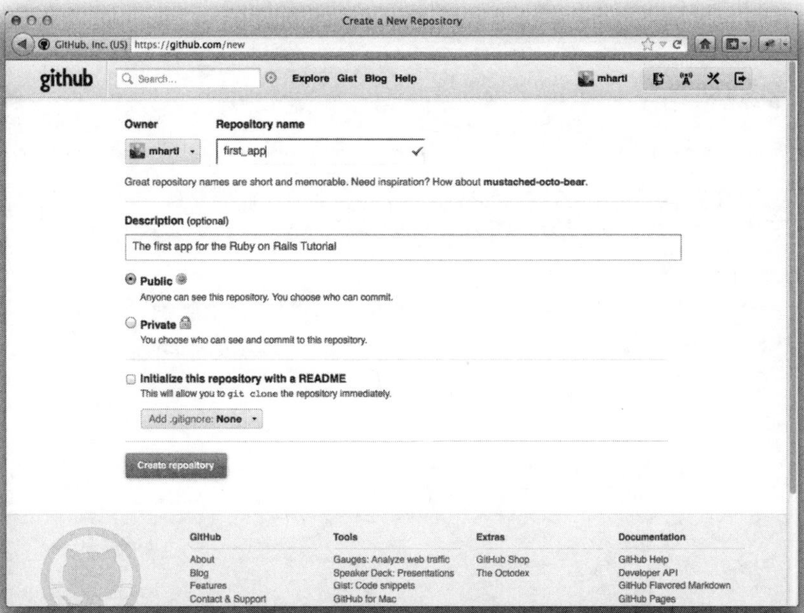

Figure 1.6 Creating the first app repository at GitHub.

GitHub has a variety of paid plans, but for open-source code their services are free, so sign up for a free GitHub account if you don't have one already. (You might have to follow the GitHub tutorial on creating SSH keys first.) After signing up, click on the link to create a repository and fill in the information as in Figure 1.6. (Take care *not* to initialize the repository with a **README** file, as **rails new** creates one of those automatically.) After submitting the form, push up your first application as follows:

```
$ git remote add origin git@github.com:<username>/first_app.git
$ git push -u origin master
```

These commands tell Git that you want to add GitHub as the origin for your main (*master*) branch and then push your repository up to GitHub. (Don't worry about what the -u flag does; if you're curious, do a web search for "git set upstream".) Of course,

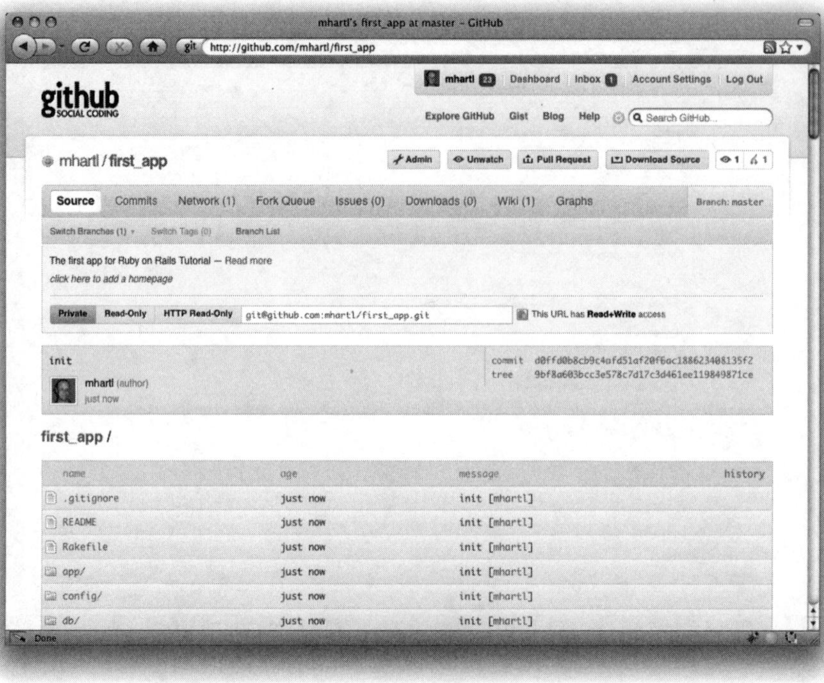

Figure 1.7   A GitHub repository page.

you should replace <username> with your actual username. For example, the command
I ran for the **railstutorial** user was

```
$ git remote add origin git@github.com:railstutorial/first_app.git
```

The result is a page at GitHub for the first application repository, with file browsing,
full commit history, and lots of other goodies (Figure 1.7).

1.3.5 Branch, Edit, Commit, Merge

If you've followed the steps in Section 1.3.4, you might notice that GitHub automatically shows the contents of the **README** file on the main repository page. In our
case, since the project is a Rails application generated using the **rails** command, the
README file is the one that comes with Rails (Figure 1.8). Because of the **.rdoc** extension on the file, GitHub ensures that it is formatted nicely, but the contents aren't

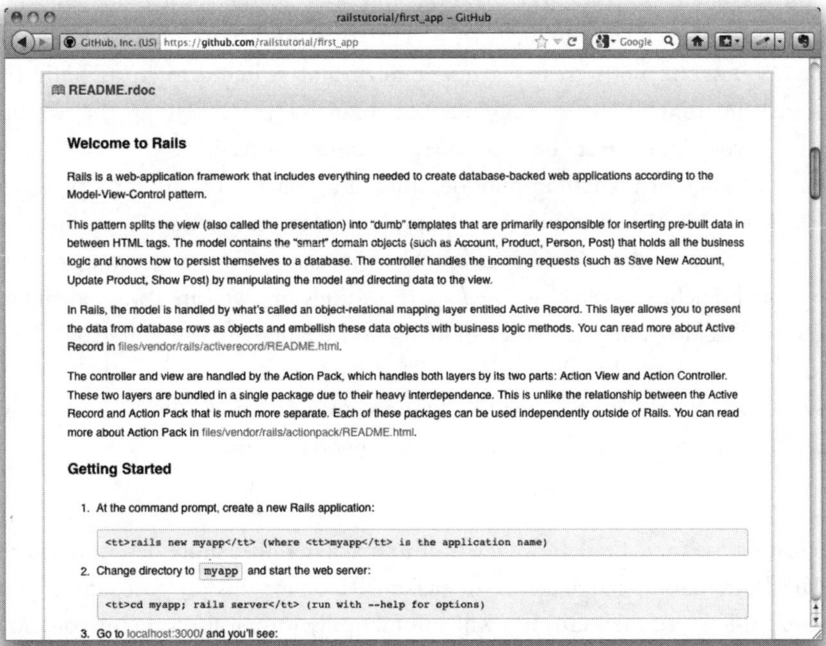

Figure 1.8   The initial (rather useless) **README** file for our project at GitHub.

helpful at all, so in this section we'll make our first edit by changing the **README** to describe our project rather than the Rails framework itself. In the process, we'll see a first example of the branch, edit, commit, merge workflow that I recommend using with Git.

Branch

Git is incredibly good at making *branches*, which are effectively copies of a repository where we can make (possibly experimental) changes without modifying the parent files. In most cases, the parent repository is the *master* branch, and we can create a new topic branch by using **checkout** with the **-b** flag:

```
$ git checkout -b modify-README
Switched to a new branch 'modify-README'
$ git branch
  master
* modify-README
```

Here the second command, `git branch`, just lists all the local branches, and the asterisk `*` identifies which branch we're currently on. Note that `git checkout -b modify-README` both creates a new branch and switches to it, as indicated by the asterisk in front of the **modify-README** branch. (If you set up the `co` alias in Section 1.3, you can use `git co -b modify-README` instead.)

The full value of branching only becomes clear when working on a project with multiple developers,[18] but branches are helpful even for a single-developer tutorial such as this one. In particular, the master branch is insulated from any changes we make to the topic branch, so even if we *really* screw things up, we can always abandon the changes by checking out the master branch and deleting the topic branch. We'll see how to do this at the end of the section.

By the way, for a change as small as this one I wouldn't normally bother with a new branch, but it's never too early to start practicing good habits.

Edit

After creating the topic branch, we'll edit it to make it a little more descriptive. I prefer the Markdown markup language to the default RDoc for this purpose, and if you use the file extension **.md** then GitHub will automatically format it nicely for you. So, first we'll use Git's version of the Unix **mv** ("move") command to change the name, and then fill it in with the contents of Listing 1.8:

```
$ git mv README.rdoc README.md
$ subl README.md
```

Listing 1.8 The new **README** file, **README.md**.

```
# Ruby on Rails Tutorial: first application

This is the first application for
[*Ruby on Rails Tutorial: Learn Rails by Example*](http://railstutorial.org/)
by [Michael Hartl](http://michaelhartl.com/).
```

Commit

With the changes made, we can take a look at the status of our branch:

---

18. See the chapter Git Branching in *Pro Git* for details.

```
$ git status
# On branch modify-README
# Changes to be committed:
#   (use "git reset HEAD <file>..." to unstage)
#
#       renamed:    README.rdoc -> README.md
#
# Changed but not updated:
#   (use "git add <file>..." to update what will be committed)
#   (use "git checkout -- <file>..." to discard changes in working directory)
#
#       modified:   README.md
#
```

At this point, we could use **git add .** as in Section 1.3.2, but Git provides the **-a** flag as a shortcut for the (very common) case of committing all modifications to existing files (or files created using **git mv**, which don't count as new files to Git):

```
$ git commit -a -m "Improve the README file"
2 files changed, 5 insertions(+), 243 deletions(-)
delete mode 100644 README.rdoc
create mode 100644 README.md
```

Be careful about using the **-a** flag improperly; if you have added any new files to the project since the last commit, you still have to tell Git about them using **git add** first.

Note that we write the commit message in the *present* tense. Git models commits as a series of patches, and in this context it makes sense to describe what each commit *does*, rather than what it did. Moreover, this usage matches up with the commit messages generated by Git commands themselves. See the GitHub post Shiny new commit styles for more information.

Merge

Now that we've finished making our changes, we're ready to *merge* the results back into our master branch:

```
$ git checkout master
Switched to branch 'master'
$ git merge modify-README
Updating 34f06b7..2c92bef
Fast forward
README.rdoc      |  243 --------------------------------------------------
```

```
README.md        |   5 +
2 files changed, 5 insertions(+), 243 deletions(-)
delete mode 100644 README.rdoc
create mode 100644 README.md
```

Note that the Git output frequently includes things like **34f06b7**, which are related to Git's internal representation of repositories. Your exact results will differ in these details, but otherwise should essentially match the output shown above.

After you've merged in the changes, you can tidy up your branches by deleting the topic branch using **git branch -d** if you're done with it:

```
$ git branch -d modify-README
Deleted branch modify-README (was 2c92bef).
```

This step is optional, and in fact it's quite common to leave the topic branch intact. This way you can switch back and forth between the topic and master branches, merging in changes every time you reach a natural stopping point.

As mentioned above, it's also possible to abandon your topic branch changes, in this case with **git branch -D**:

```
# For illustration only; don't do this unless you mess up a branch
$ git checkout -b topic-branch
$ <really screw up the branch>
$ git add .
$ git commit -a -m "Major screw up"
$ git checkout master
$ git branch -D topic-branch
```

Unlike the **-d** flag, the **-D** flag will delete the branch even though we haven't merged in the changes.

Push

Now that we've updated the **README**, we can push the changes up to GitHub to see the result. Since we have already done one push (Section 1.3.4), on most systems we can omit **origin master** and simply run **git push**:

```
$ git push
```

As promised, GitHub nicely formats the new file using Markdown (Figure 1.9).

README.markdown

Ruby on Rails Tutorial: first application

This is the first application for *Ruby on Rails Tutorial: Learn Rails by Example* by Michael Hartl.

Figure 1.9 The improved **README** file formatted with Markdown.

1.4 Deploying

Even at this early stage, we're already going to deploy our (still-empty) Rails application to production. This step is optional, but deploying early and often allows us to catch any deployment problems early in our development cycle. The alternative—deploying only after laborious effort sealed away in a development environment—often leads to terrible integration headaches when launch time comes.[19]

Deploying Rails applications used to be a pain, but the Rails deployment ecosystem has matured rapidly in the past few years, and now there are several great options. These include shared hosts or virtual private servers running Phusion Passenger (a module for the Apache and Nginx[20] web servers), full-service deployment companies such as Engine Yard and Rails Machine, and cloud deployment services such as Engine Yard Cloud and Heroku.

My favorite Rails deployment option is Heroku, which is a hosted platform built specifically for deploying Rails and other Ruby web applications.[21] Heroku makes deploying Rails applications ridiculously easy—as long as your source code is under version control with Git. (This is yet another reason to follow the Git setup steps in Section 1.3 if you haven't already.) The rest of this section is dedicated to deploying our first application to Heroku.

1.4.1 Heroku Setup

After signing up for a Heroku account, install the Heroku gem:

```
$ gem install heroku
```

---

19. Though it shouldn't matter for the example applications in the *Rails Tutorial*, if you're worried about accidentally making your app public too soon there are several options; see Section 1.4.4 for one.

20. Pronounced "Engine X."

21. Heroku works with any Ruby web platform that uses Rack middleware, which provides a standard interface between web frameworks and web servers. Adoption of the Rack interface has been extraordinarily strong in the Ruby community, including frameworks as varied as Sinatra, Ramaze, Camping, and Rails, which means that Heroku basically supports any Ruby web app.

As with GitHub (Section 1.3.4), when using Heroku you will need to create SSH keys if you haven't already, and then tell Heroku your public key so that you can use Git to push the sample application repository up to their servers:

```
$ heroku keys:add
```

Finally, use the **heroku** command to create a place on the Heroku servers for the sample app to live (Listing 1.9).

Listing 1.9 Creating a new application at Heroku.

```
$ heroku create --stack cedar
Created http://stormy-cloud-5881.herokuapp.com/ |
git@heroku.com:stormy-cloud-5881.herokuapp.com
Git remote heroku added
```

(The `--stack cedar` argument arranges to use the latest and greatest version of Heroku, called the Celadon Cedar Stack.) Yes, that's it. The **heroku** command creates a new subdomain just for our application, available for immediate viewing. There's nothing there yet, though, so let's get busy deploying.

1.4.2 Heroku Deployment, Step One

To deploy to Heroku, the first step is to use Git to push the application to Heroku:

```
$ git push heroku master
```

1.4.3 Heroku Deployment, Step Two

There is no step two! We're already done (Figure 1.10). To see your newly deployed application, you can visit the address that you saw when you ran **heroku create** (i.e., Listing 1.9, but with the address for your app, not the address for mine). You can also use an argument to the **heroku** command that automatically opens your browser with the right address:

```
$ heroku open
```

Because of the details of their setup, the "About your application's environment" link doesn't work on Heroku. Don't worry; this is normal. The error will go away (in

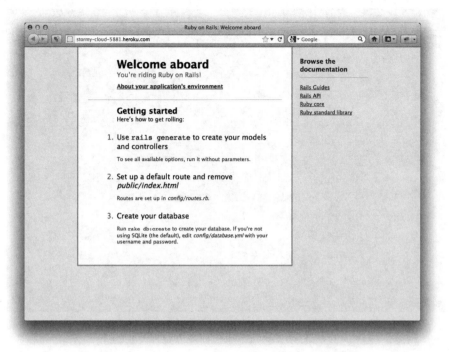

Figure 1.10   The first Rails Tutorial application running on Heroku.

the context of the full sample application) when we remove the default Rails page in Section 5.3.2.

Once you've deployed successfully, Heroku provides a beautiful interface for administering and configuring your application (Figure 1.11).

1.4.4   Heroku Commands

There are many Heroku commands, and we'll barely scratch the surface in this book. Let's take a minute to show just one of them by renaming the application as follows:

```
$ heroku rename railstutorial
```

Don't use this name yourself; it's already taken by me! In fact, you probably shouldn't bother with this step right now; using the default address supplied by Heroku is fine.

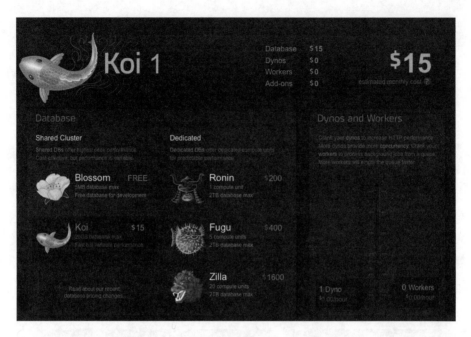

Figure 1.11   The beautiful interface at Heroku.

But if you do want to rename your application, you can arrange for it to be reasonably secure by using a random or obscure subdomain, such as the following:

```
hwpcbmze.heroku.com
seyjhflo.heroku.com
jhyicevg.heroku.com
```

With a random subdomain like this, someone could visit your site only if you gave him or her the address. (By the way, as a preview of Ruby's compact awesomeness, here's the code I used to generate the random subdomains:

```
('a'..'z').to_a.shuffle[0..7].join
```

Pretty sweet.)

In addition to supporting subdomains, Heroku also supports custom domains. (In fact, the Ruby on Rails Tutorial site lives at Heroku; if you're reading this book online, you're looking at a Heroku-hosted site right now!) See the Heroku documentation for more information about custom domains and other Heroku topics.

1.5 Conclusion

We've come a long way in this chapter: installation, development environment setup, version control, and deployment. If you want to share your progress at this point, feel free to send a tweet or Facebook status update with something like this:

> I'm learning Ruby on Rails with @railstutorial! http://railstutorial.org

All that's left is to actually start learning Rails! Let's get to it.

Chapter 2

A Demo App

In this chapter, we'll develop a simple demonstration application to show off some of the power of Rails. The purpose is to get a high-level overview of Ruby on Rails programming (and web development in general) by rapidly generating an application using *scaffold generators*. As discussed in Box 1.1, the rest of the book will take the opposite approach, developing a full application incrementally and explaining each new concept as it arises, but for a quick overview (and some instant gratification) there is no substitute for scaffolding. The resulting demo app will allow us to interact with it through its URIs, giving us insight into the structure of a Rails application, including a first example of the *REST architecture* favored by Rails.

As with the forthcoming sample application, the demo app will consist of *users* and their associated *microposts* (thus constituting a minimalist Twitter-style app). The functionality will be utterly underdeveloped, and many of the steps will seem like magic, but worry not: The full sample app will develop a similar application from the ground up starting in Chapter 3, and I will provide plentiful forward-references to later material. In the meantime, have patience and a little faith—the whole point of this tutorial is to take you *beyond* this superficial, scaffold-driven approach to achieve a deeper understanding of Rails.

2.1 Planning the Application

In this section, we'll outline our plans for the demo application. As in Section 1.2.3, we'll start by generating the application skeleton using the **rails** command:

```
$ cd ~/rails_projects
$ rails new demo_app
$ cd demo_app
```

45

Next, we'll use a text editor to update the **Gemfile** needed by Bundler with the contents of Listing 2.1.

Listing 2.1 A **Gemfile** for the demo app.

```
source 'https://rubygems.org'

gem 'rails', '3.2.13'

group :development do
  gem 'sqlite3', '1.3.5'
end


# Gems used only for assets and not required
# in production environments by default.
group :assets do
  gem 'sass-rails',   '3.2.4'
  gem 'coffee-rails', '3.2.2'

  gem 'uglifier', '1.2.3'
end

gem 'jquery-rails', '2.0.0'

group :production do
  gem 'pg', '0.12.2'
end
```

Note that Listing 2.1 is identical to Listing 1.5 except for the addition of a gem needed in production at Heroku:

```
group :production do
  gem 'pg', '0.12.2'
end
```

The **pg** gem is needed to access PostgreSQL ("post-gres-cue-ell"), the database used by Heroku.

We then install and include the gems using the **bundle install** command:

```
$ bundle install --without production
```

The `--without production` option prevents the installation of the production gems, which in this case is just the PostgreSQL gem `pg`. (If Bundler complains about

```
no such file to load -- readline (LoadError)
```

try adding **gem 'rb-readline'** to your **Gemfile**.)

Finally, we'll put the demo app under version control. Recall that the **rails** command generates a default **.gitignore** file, but depending on your system you may find the augmented file from Listing 1.7 to be more convenient. Then initialize a Git repository and make the first commit:

```
$ git init
$ git add .
$ git commit -m "Initial commit"
```

You can also optionally create a new repository (Figure 2.1) and push it up to GitHub:

```
$ git remote add origin git@github.com:<username>/demo_app.git
$ git push -u origin master
```

(As with the first app, take care *not* to initialize the GitHub repository with a **README** file.)

Now we're ready to start making the app itself. The typical first step when making a web application is to create a *data model*, which is a representation of the structures needed by our application. In our case, the demo app will be a microblog, with only users and short (micro)posts. Thus, we'll begin with a model for *users* of the app (Section 2.1.1), then we'll add a model for *microposts* (Section 2.1.2).

2.1.1   Modeling Demo Users

There are as many choices for a user data model as there are different registration forms on the web; we'll go with a distinctly minimalist approach. Users of our demo app will have a unique **integer** identifier called **id**, a publicly viewable **name** (of type **string**), and an **email** address (also a **string**) that will double as a username. A summary of the data model for users appears in Figure 2.2.

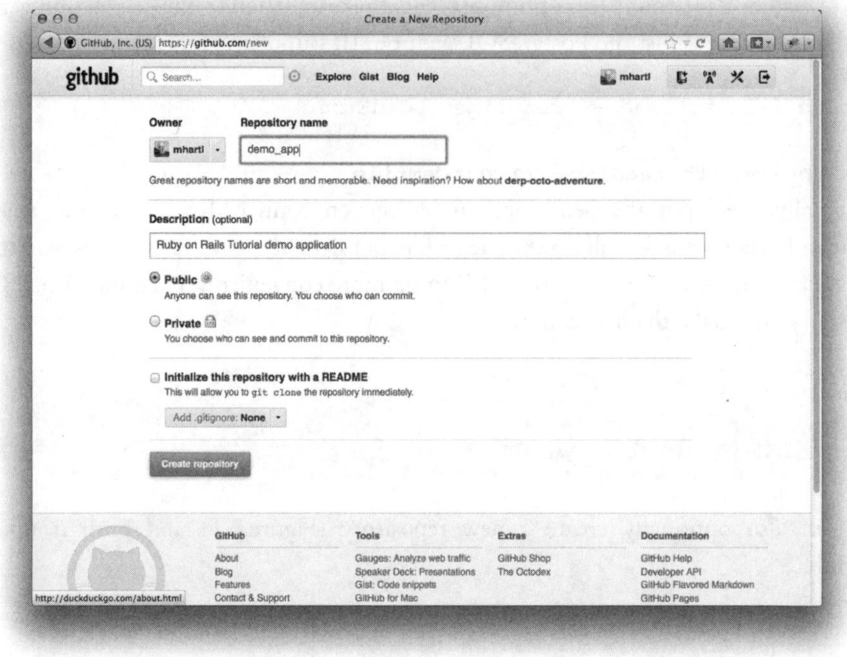

Figure 2.1   Creating a demo app repository at GitHub.

As we'll see starting in Section 6.1.1, the label **users** in Figure 2.2 corresponds to a *table* in a database, and the **id**, **name**, and **email** attributes are *columns* in that table.

2.1.2   Modeling Demo Microposts

The core of the micropost data model is even simpler than the one for users: a micropost has only an **id** and a **content** field for the micropost's text (of type **string**).[1] There's an

users	
id	integer
name	string
email	string

Figure 2.2   The data model for users.

---

1. When modeling longer posts, such as those for a normal (non-micro) blog, you should use the **text** type in place of **string**.

microposts	
id	integer
content	string
user_id	integer

Figure 2.3 The data model for microposts.

additional complication, though: We want to *associate* each micropost with a particular user; we'll accomplish this by recording the **user_id** of the owner of the post. The results are shown in Figure 2.3.

We'll see in Section 2.3.3 (and more fully in Chapter 10) how this **user_id** attribute allows us to succinctly express the notion that a user potentially has many associated microposts.

2.2 The Users Resource

In this section, we'll implement the users data model in Section 2.1.1, along with a web interface to that model. The combination will constitute a *Users resource*, which will allow us to think of users as objects that can be created, read, updated, and deleted through the web via the HTTP protocol. As promised in the introduction, our Users resource will be created by a scaffold generator program, which comes standard with each Rails project. I urge you not to look too closely at the generated code; at this stage, it will only serve to confuse you.

Rails scaffolding is generated by passing the **scaffold** command to the **rails generate** script. The argument of the **scaffold** command is the singular version of the resource name (in this case, **User**), together with optional parameters for the data model's attributes:[2]

```
$ rails generate scaffold User name:string email:string
      invoke  active_record
      create    db/migrate/20111123225336_create_users.rb
      create    app/models/user.rb
      invoke    test_unit
      create      test/unit/user_test.rb
```

---

2. The name of the scaffold follows the convention of *models*, which are singular, rather than resources and controllers, which are plural. Thus, we have **User** instead **Users**.

```
    create      test/fixtures/users.yml
    route    resources :users
   invoke    scaffold_controller
   create       app/controllers/users_controller.rb
   invoke       erb
   create         app/views/users
   create         app/views/users/index.html.erb
   create         app/views/users/edit.html.erb
   create         app/views/users/show.html.erb
   create         app/views/users/new.html.erb
   create         app/views/users/_form.html.erb
   invoke       test_unit
   create          test/functional/users_controller_test.rb
   invoke       helper
   create          app/helpers/users_helper.rb
   invoke         test_unit
   create            test/unit/helpers/users_helper_test.rb
   invoke       assets
   invoke         coffee
   create          app/assets/javascripts/users.js.coffee
   invoke         scss
   create          app/assets/stylesheets/users.css.scss
   invoke    scss
   create       app/assets/stylesheets/scaffolds.css.scss
```

By including **name:string** and **email:string**, we have arranged for the User model to have the form shown in Figure 2.2. (Note that there is no need to include a parameter for **id**; it is created automatically by Rails for use as the *primary key* in the database.)

To proceed with the demo application, we first need to *migrate* the database using *Rake* (Box 2.1):

```
$ bundle exec rake db:migrate
==  CreateUsers: migrating ========================================================
-- create_table(:users)
   -> 0.0017s
==  CreateUsers: migrated (0.0018s) ===============================================
```

This simply updates the database with our new **users** data model. (We'll learn more about database migrations starting in Section 6.1.1.) Note that, in order to ensure that the command uses the version of Rake corresponding to our **Gemfile**, we need to run **rake** using **bundle exec**.

With that, we can run the local web server using **rails s**, which is a shortcut for **rails server**:

```
$ rails s
```

Now the demo application should be ready to go at http://localhost:3000/.

Box 2.1 Rake

In the Unix tradition, the *make* utility has played an important role in building executable programs from source code; many a computer hacker has committed to muscle memory the line

```
$ ./configure && make && sudo make install
```

commonly used to compile code on Unix systems (including Linux and Mac OS X).

Rake is *Ruby make*, a make-like language written in Ruby. Rails uses Rake extensively, especially for the innumerable little administrative tasks necessary when developing database-backed web applications. The **rake db:migrate** command is probably the most common, but there are many others; you can see a list of database tasks using **-T db**:

```
$ bundle exec rake -T db
```

To see all the Rake tasks available, run

```
$ bundle exec rake -T
```

The list is likely to be overwhelming, but don't worry, you don't have to know all (or even most) of these commands. By the end of the *Rails Tutorial*, you'll know all the most important ones.

2.2.1 A User Tour

Visiting the root url http://localhost:3000 shows the same default Rails page shown in Figure 1.3, but in generating the Users resource scaffolding we have also created a large number of pages for manipulating users. For example, the page for listing all users is at /users, and the page for making a new user is at /users/new. The rest of this

Table 2.1   The correspondence between pages and URIs for the Users resource.

URI	Action	Purpose
/users	`index`	page to list all users
/users/1	`show`	page to show user with id **1**
/users/new	`new`	page to make a new user
/users/1/edit	`edit`	page to edit user with id **1**

section is dedicated to taking a whirlwind tour through these user pages. As we proceed, it may help to refer to Table 2.1, which shows the correspondence between pages and URIs.

We start with the page to show all the users in our application, called `index`; as you might expect, initially there are no users at all (Figure 2.4).

To make a new user, we visit the `new` page, as shown in Figure 2.5. (Since the http://localhost:3000 part of the address is implicit whenever we are developing locally, I'll usually omit it from now on.) In Chapter 7, this will become the user signup page.

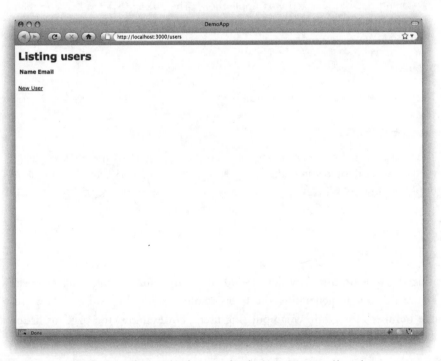

Figure 2.4   The initial index page for the Users resource (/users).

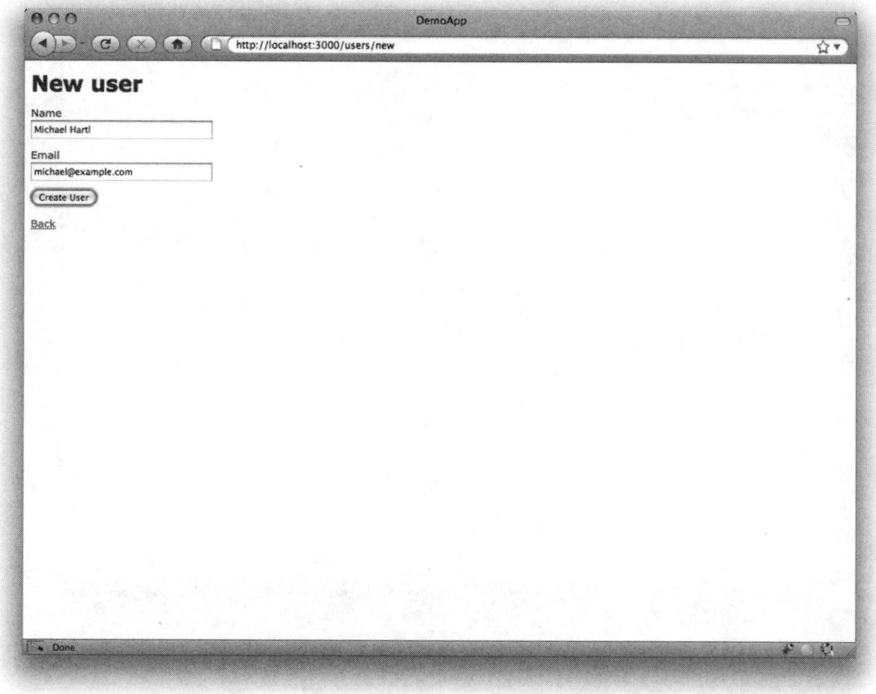

Figure 2.5 The new user page (/users/new).

We can create a user by entering name and email values in the text fields and then clicking the Create User button. The result is the user `show` page, as seen in Figure 2.6. (The green welcome message is accomplished using the *flash*, which we'll learn about in Section 7.4.2.) Note that the URI is /users/1; as you might suspect, the number **1** is simply the user's **id** attribute from Figure 2.2. In Section 7.1, this page will become the user's profile.

To change a user's information, we visit the `edit` page (Figure 2.7). By modifying the user information and clicking the Update User button, we arrange to change the information for the user in the demo application (Figure 2.8). (As we'll see in detail starting in Chapter 6, this user data is stored in a database back-end.) We'll add user edit/update functionality to the sample application in Section 9.1.

Now we'll create a second user by revisiting the `new` page and submitting a second set of user information; the resulting user `index` is shown in Figure 2.9. Section 7.1 will develop the user index into a more polished page for showing all users.

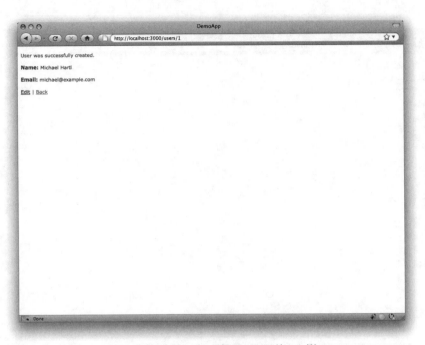

Figure 2.6   The page to show a user (/users/1).

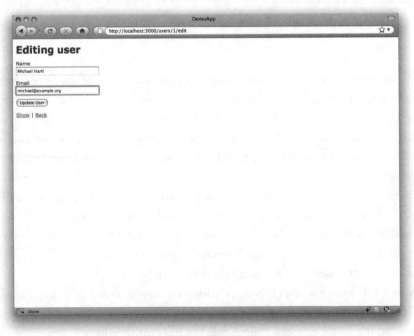

Figure 2.7   The user edit page (/users/1/edit).

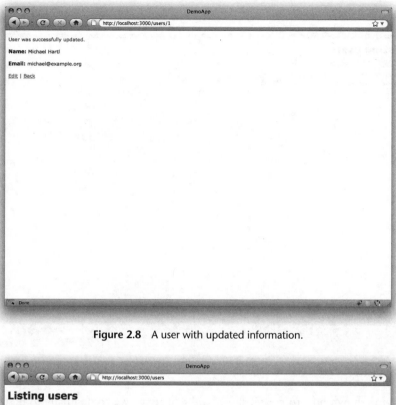

Figure 2.8   A user with updated information.

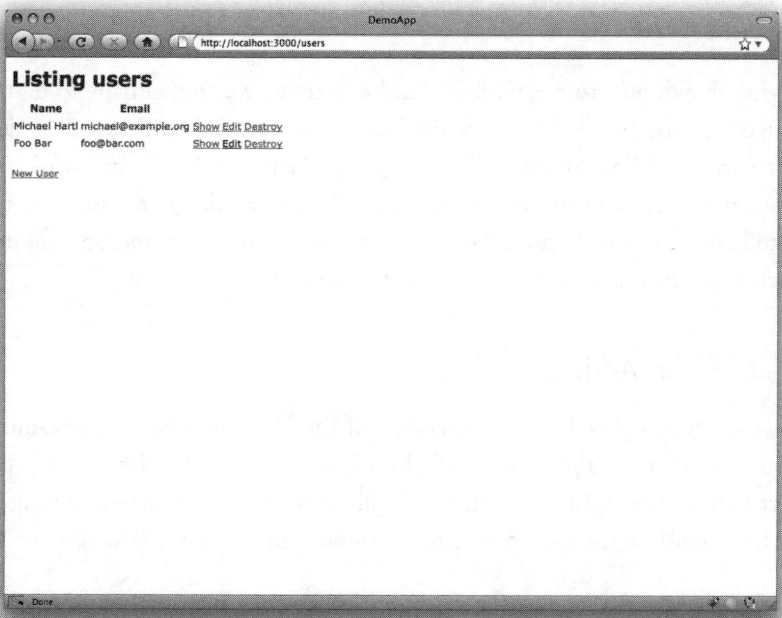

Figure 2.9   The user index page (/users) with a second user.

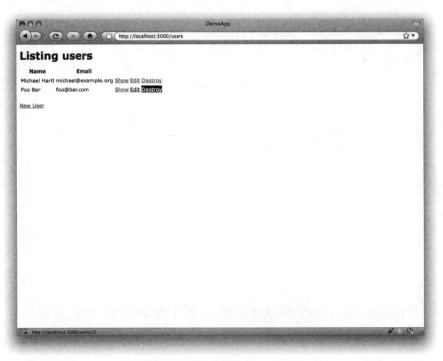

Figure 2.10   Destroying a user.

Having shown how to create, show, and edit users, we come finally to destroying them (Figure 2.10). You should verify that clicking on the link in Figure 2.10 destroys the second user, yielding an index page with only one user. (If it doesn't work, be sure that JavaScript is enabled in your browser; Rails uses JavaScript to issue the request needed to destroy a user.) Section 9.4 adds user deletion to the sample app, taking care to restrict its use to a special class of administrative users.

2.2.2   MVC in Action

Now that we've completed a quick overview of the Users resource, let's examine one particular part of it in the context of the Model-View-Controller (MVC) pattern introduced in Section 1.2.6. Our strategy will be to describe the results of a typical browser hit—a visit to the user index page at /users—in terms of MVC (Figure 2.11).

1. The browser issues a request for the /users URI.
2. Rails routes /users to the **index** action in the Users controller.

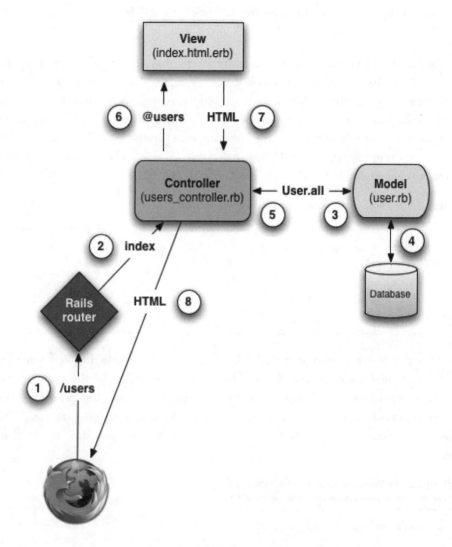

Figure 2.11 A detailed diagram of MVC in Rails.

3. The **index** action asks the User model to retrieve all users (**User.all**).
4. The User model pulls all the users from the database.
5. The User model returns the list of users to the controller.
6. The controller captures the users in the **@users** variable, which is passed to the **index** view.

7. The view uses embedded Ruby to render the page as HTML.
8. The controller passes the HTML back to the browser.[3]

We start with a request issued from the browser—that is, the result of typing a URI in the address bar or clicking on a link (Step 1 in Figure 2.11). This request hits the *Rails router* (Step 2), which dispatches to the proper *controller action* based on the URI (and, as we'll see in Box 3.2, the type of request). The code to create the mapping of user URIs to controller actions for the Users resource appears in Listing 2.2; this code effectively sets up the table of URI/action pairs seen in Table 2.1. (The strange notation **:users** is a *symbol*, which we'll learn about in Section 4.3.3.)

Listing 2.2 The Rails routes, with a rule for the Users resource.
config/routes.rb

```
DemoApp::Application.routes.draw do
  resources :users
  .
  .
  .
end
```

The pages from the tour in Section 2.2.1 correspond to *actions* in the Users *controller*, which is a collection of related actions; the controller generated by the scaffolding is shown schematically in Listing 2.3. Note the notation **class UsersController < ApplicationController**; this is an example of a Ruby *class* with *inheritance*. (We'll discuss inheritance briefly in Section 2.3.4 and cover both subjects in more detail in Section 4.4.)

Listing 2.3 The Users controller in schematic form.
app/controllers/users_controller.rb

```
class UsersController < ApplicationController

  def index
    .
    .
    .
  end
```

---

3. Some references indicate that the view returns the HTML directly to the browser (via a web server such as Apache or Nginx). Regardless of the implementation details, I prefer to think of the controller as a central hub through which all the application's information flows.

```
  def show
    .
    .
    .
  end

  def new
    .
    .
    .
  end

  def create
    .
    .
    .
  end

  def edit
    .
    .
    .
  end

  def update
    .
    .
    .
  end

  def destroy
    .
    .
    .
  end
end
```

You may notice that there are more actions than there are pages; the **index**, **show**, **new**, and **edit** actions all correspond to pages from Section 2.2.1, but there are additional **create**, **update**, and **destroy** actions as well. These actions don't typically render pages (although they sometimes do); instead, their main purpose is to modify information about users in the database. This full suite of controller actions, summarized in Table 2.2, represents the implementation of the REST architecture in Rails (Box 2.2), which is based on the ideas of *representational state transfer* identified and named by

Table 2.2 RESTful routes provided by the Users resource in Listing 2.2.

HTTP request	URI	Action	Purpose
GET	/users	**index**	page to list all users
GET	/users/1	**show**	page to show user with id **1**
GET	/users/new	**new**	page to make a new user
POST	/users	**create**	create a new user
GET	/users/1/edit	**edit**	page to edit user with id **1**
PUT	/users/1	**update**	update user with id **1**
DELETE	/users/1	**destroy**	delete user with id **1**

computer scientist Roy Fielding.[4] Note from Table 2.2 that there is some overlap in the URIs; for example, both the user **show** action and the **update** action correspond to the URI /users/1. The difference between them is the HTTP request method they respond to. We'll learn more about HTTP request methods starting in Section 3.2.1.

Box 2.2 REpresentational State Transfer (REST)

If you read much about Ruby on Rails web development, you'll see a lot of references to "REST," which is an acronym for REpresentational State Transfer. REST is an architectural style for developing distributed, networked systems and software applications such as the World Wide Web and web applications. Although REST theory is rather abstract, in the context of Rails applications REST means that most application components (such as users and microposts) are modeled as *resources* that can be created, read, updated, and deleted—operations that correspond both to the CRUD operations of relational databases and the four fundamental HTTP request methods: POST, GET, PUT, and DELETE. (We'll learn more about HTTP requests in Section 3.2.1 and especially Box 3.2.)

As a Rails application developer, the RESTful style of development helps you make choices about which controllers and actions to write: You simply structure the application using resources that get created, read, updated, and deleted. In the case of users and microposts, this process is straightforward, since they are naturally resources in their own right. In Chapter 11, we'll see an example where REST principles allow us to model a subtler problem, "following users," in a natural and convenient way.

---

4. Fielding, Roy Thomas. *Architectural Styles and the Design of Network-based Software Architectures*. Doctoral dissertation, University of California, Irvine, 2000.

To examine the relationship between the Users controller and the User model, let's focus on a simplified version of the **index** action, shown in Listing 2.4. (The scaffold code is ugly and confusing, so I've suppressed it.)

Listing 2.4 The simplified user **index** action for the demo application.
`app/controllers/users_controller.rb`

```
class UsersController < ApplicationController

  def index
    @users = User.all
  end
  .
  .
  .
end
```

This **index** action has the line **@users = User.all** (Step 3), which asks the User model to retrieve a list of all the users from the database (Step 4), and then places them in the variable **@users** (pronounced "at-users") (Step 5). The User model itself appears in Listing 2.5; although it is rather plain, it comes equipped with a large amount of functionality because of inheritance (Section 2.3.4 and Section 4.4). In particular, by using the Rails library called *Active Record*, the code in Listing 2.5 arranges for **User.all** to return all the users. (We'll learn about the **attr_accessible** line in Section 6.1.2. *Note*: This line will not appear if you are using Rails 3.2.2 or earlier.)

Listing 2.5 The User model for the demo application.
`app/models/user.rb`

```
class User < ActiveRecord::Base
  attr_accessible :email, :name
end
```

Once the **@users** variable is defined, the controller calls the *view* (Step 6), shown in Listing 2.6. Variables that start with the **@** sign, called *instance variables*, are automatically available in the view; in this case, the **index.html.erb** view in Listing 2.6 iterates through the **@users** list and outputs a line of HTML for each one. (Remember, you aren't supposed to understand this code right now. It is shown only for purposes of illustration.)

Listing 2.6 The view for the user index.
`app/views/users/index.html.erb`

```
<h1>Listing users</h1>

<table>
  <tr>
    <th>Name</th>
    <th>Email</th>
    <th></th>
    <th></th>
    <th></th>
  </tr>

<% @users.each do |user| %>
  <tr>
    <td><%= user.name %></td>
    <td><%= user.email %></td>
    <td><%= link_to 'Show', user %></td>
    <td><%= link_to 'Edit', edit_user_path(user) %></td>
    <td><%= link_to 'Destroy', user, confirm: 'Are you sure?',
                                 method: :delete %></td>
  </tr>
<% end %>
</table>

<br />

<%= link_to 'New User', new_user_path %>
```

The view converts its contents to HTML (Step 7), which is then returned by the controller to the browser for display (Step 8).

2.2.3   Weaknesses of this Users Resource

Although good for getting a general overview of Rails, the scaffold Users resource suffers from a number of severe weaknesses.

- **No data validations.** Our User model accepts data such as blank names and invalid email addresses without complaint.

- **No authentication.** We have no notion signing in or out and no way to prevent any user from performing any operation.

- **No tests.** This isn't technically true—the scaffolding includes rudimentary tests—but the generated tests are ugly and inflexible, and they don't test for data validation, authentication, or any other custom requirements.

- **No layout.** There is no consistent site styling or navigation.

- **No real understanding.** If you understand the scaffold code, you probably shouldn't be reading this book.

2.3   The Microposts Resource

Having generated and explored the Users resource, we turn now to the associated Microposts resource. Throughout this section, I recommend comparing the elements of the Microposts resource with the analogous user elements from Section 2.2; you should see that the two resources parallel each other in many ways. The RESTful structure of Rails applications is best absorbed by this sort of repetition of form; indeed, seeing the parallel structure of Users and Microposts even at this early stage is one of the prime motivations for this chapter. (As we'll see, writing applications more robust than the toy example in this chapter takes considerable effort—we won't see the Microposts resource again until Chapter 10—and I didn't want to defer its first appearance quite that far.)

2.3.1   A Micropost Microtour

As with the Users resource, we'll generate scaffold code for the Microposts resource using **rails generate scaffold**, in this case implementing the data model from Figure 2.3:[5]

```
$ rails generate scaffold Micropost content:string user_id:integer
      invoke  active_record
      create    db/migrate/20111123225811_create_microposts.rb
      create    app/models/micropost.rb
      invoke  test_unit
      create      test/unit/micropost_test.rb
      create      test/fixtures/microposts.yml
```

---

5. As with the User scaffold, the scaffold generator for microposts follows the singular convention of Rails models; thus, we have **generate Micropost**.

```
     route   resources :microposts
    invoke   scaffold_controller
    create      app/controllers/microposts_controller.rb
    invoke      erb
    create         app/views/microposts
    create         app/views/microposts/index.html.erb
    create         app/views/microposts/edit.html.erb
    create         app/views/microposts/show.html.erb
    create         app/views/microposts/new.html.erb
    create         app/views/microposts/_form.html.erb
    invoke      test_unit
    create         test/functional/microposts_controller_test.rb
    invoke      helper
    create         app/helpers/microposts_helper.rb
    invoke         test_unit
    create            test/unit/helpers/microposts_helper_test.rb
    invoke      assets
    invoke         coffee
    create            app/assets/javascripts/microposts.js.coffee
    invoke         scss
    create            app/assets/stylesheets/microposts.css.scss
    invoke      scss
 identical      app/assets/stylesheets/scaffolds.css.scss
```

To update our database with the new data model, we need to run a migration as in Section 2.2:

```
$ bundle exec rake db:migrate
==  CreateMicroposts: migrating ================================================
-- create_table(:microposts)
   -> 0.0023s
==  CreateMicroposts: migrated (0.0026s) =======================================
```

Now we are in a position to create microposts in the same way we created users in Section 2.2.1. As you might guess, the scaffold generator has updated the Rails routes file with a rule for Microposts resource, as seen in Listing 2.7.[6] As with users, the **resources :microposts** routing rule maps micropost URIs to actions in the Microposts controller, as seen in Table 2.3.

---

6. The scaffold code may have extra newlines compared to Listing 2.7. This is not a cause for concern, as Ruby ignores extra newlines.

Table 2.3 RESTful routes provided by the Microposts resource in Listing 2.7.

HTTP request	URI	Action	Purpose
GET	/microposts	**index**	page to list all microposts
GET	/microposts/1	**show**	page to show micropost with id **1**
GET	/microposts/new	**new**	page to make a new micropost
POST	/microposts	**create**	create a new micropost
GET	/microposts/1/edit	**edit**	page to edit micropost with id **1**
PUT	/microposts/1	**update**	update micropost with id **1**
DELETE	/microposts/1	**destroy**	delete micropost with id **1**

Listing 2.7 The Rails routes, with a new rule for Microposts resources.
config/routes.rb

```
DemoApp::Application.routes.draw do
  resources :microposts
  resources :users
  .
  .
  .
end
```

The Microposts controller itself appears in schematic form Listing 2.8. Note that, apart from having **MicropostsController** in place of **UsersController**, Listing 2.8 is *identical* to the code in Listing 2.3. This is a reflection of the REST architecture common to both resources.

Listing 2.8 The Microposts controller in schematic form.
app/controllers/microposts_controller.rb

```
class MicropostsController < ApplicationController

  def index
    .
    .
    .
  end

  def show
    .
    .
    .
  end
```

```
  def new
    .
    .
    .
  end

  def create
    .
    .
    .
  end

  def edit
    .
    .
    .
  end

  def update
    .
    .
    .
  end

  def destroy
    .
    .
    .
  end
end
```

To make some actual microposts, we enter information at the new microposts page, /microposts/new, as seen in Figure 2.12.

At this point, go ahead and create a micropost or two, taking care to make sure that at least one has a **user_id** of **1** to match the id of the first user created in Section 2.2.1. The result should look something like Figure 2.13.

2.3.2 Putting the *micro* in Microposts

Any *micro*post worthy of the name should have some means of enforcing the length of the post. Implementing this constraint in Rails is easy with *validations*; to accept

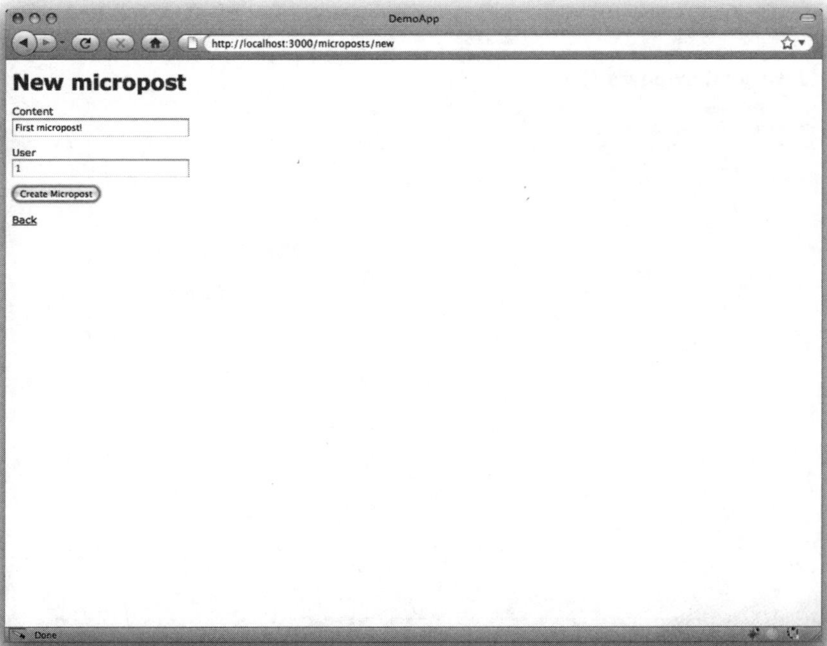

Figure 2.12   The new micropost page (/microposts/new).

microposts with at most 140 characters (à la Twitter), we use a *length* validation. At
this point, you should open the file **app/models/micropost.rb** in your text editor or
IDE and fill it with the contents of Listing 2.9. (The use of **validates** in Listing 2.9 is
characteristic of Rails 3; if you've previously worked with Rails 2.3, you should compare
this to the use of **validates_length_of**.)

Listing 2.9   Constraining microposts to be at most 140 characters.
app/models/micropost.rb

```
class Micropost < ActiveRecord::Base
  attr_accessible :content, :user_id
  validates :content, :length => { :maximum => 140 }
end
```

The code in Listing 2.9 may look rather mysterious—we'll cover validations more
thoroughly starting in Section 6.2—but its effects are readily apparent if we go to the

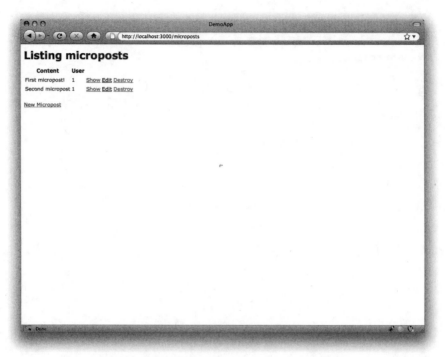

Figure 2.13   The micropost index page (/microposts).

new micropost page and enter more than 140 characters for the content of the post. As
seen in Figure 2.14, Rails renders *error messages* indicating that the micropost's content
is too long. (We'll learn more about error messages in Section 7.3.2.)

2.3.3 A User `has_many` Microposts

One of the most powerful features of Rails is the ability to form *associations* between
different data models. In the case of our User model, each user potentially has many
microposts. We can express this in code by updating the User and Micropost models as
in Listing 2.10 and Listing 2.11.

Listing 2.10 A user has many microposts.
app/models/user.rb

```
class User < ActiveRecord::Base
  attr_accessible :email, :name
  has_many :microposts
end
```

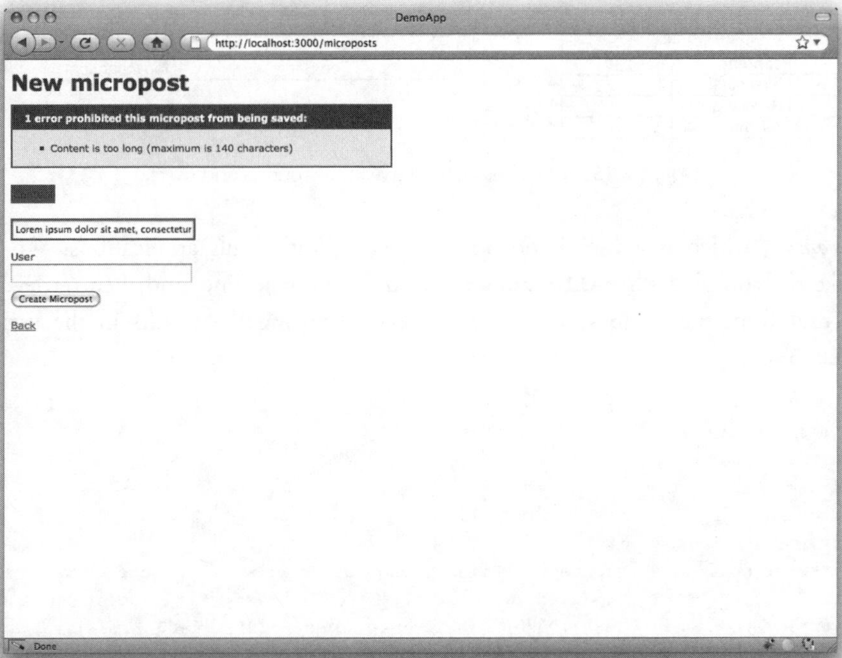

Figure 2.14 Error messages for a failed micropost creation.

Listing 2.11 A micropost belongs to a user.
app/models/micropost.rb

```ruby
class Micropost < ActiveRecord::Base
  attr_accessible :content, :user_id

  belongs_to :user

  validates :content, :length => { :maximum => 140 }
end
```

We can visualize the result of this association in Figure 2.15. Because of the **user_id** column in the **microposts** table, Rails (using Active Record) can infer the microposts associated with each user.

In Chapter 10 and Chapter 11, we will use the association of users and microposts both to display all a user's microposts and to construct a Twitter-like micropost feed. For now, we can examine the implications of the user-micropost association by using

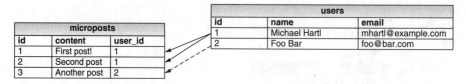

Figure 2.15 The association between microposts and users.

the *console*, which is a useful tool for interacting with Rails applications. We first invoke the console with **rails console** at the command line, and then retrieve the first user from the database using **User.first** (putting the results in the variable **first_user**):[7]

```
$ rails console
>> first_user = User.first
=> #<User id: 1, name: "Michael Hartl", email: "michael@example.org",
created_at: "2011-11-03 02:01:31", updated_at: "2011-11-03 02:01:31">
>> first_user.microposts
=> [#<Micropost id: 1, content: "First micropost!", user_id: 1, created_at:
"2011-11-03 02:37:37", updated_at: "2011-11-03 02:37:37">, #<Micropost id: 2,
content: "Second micropost", user_id: 1, created_at: "2011-11-03 02:38:54",
updated_at: "2011-11-03 02:38:54">]
>> exit
```

(I include the last line just to demonstrate how to exit the console, and on most systems you can Ctrl-d for the same purpose.) Here we have accessed the user's microposts using the code **first_user.microposts**: With this code, Active Record automatically returns all the microposts with **user_id** equal to the id of **first_user** (in this case, **1**). We'll learn much more about the association facilities in Active Record in Chapter 10 and Chapter 11.

2.3.4 Inheritance Hierarchies

We end our discussion of the demo application with a brief description of the controller and model class hierarchies in Rails. This discussion will only make sense if you have some experience with object-oriented programming (OOP); if you haven't studied OOP, feel free to skip this section. In particular, if you are unfamiliar

---

7. Your console prompt might be something like **ruby-1.9.3-head >**, but the examples use >> since Ruby versions will vary.

with *classes* (discussed in Section 4.4), I suggest looping back to this section at a later time.

We start with the inheritance structure for models. Comparing Listing 2.12 and Listing 2.13, we see that both the User model and the Micropost model inherit (via the left angle bracket <) from **ActiveRecord::Base**, which is the base class for models provided by ActiveRecord; a diagram summarizing this relationship appears in Figure 2.16. It is by inheriting from **ActiveRecord::Base** that our model objects gain the ability to communicate with the database, treat the database columns as Ruby attributes, and so on.

Listing 2.12 The **User** class, with inheritance.
app/models/user.rb

```
class User < ActiveRecord::Base
  .
  .
  .
end
```

Listing 2.13 The **Micropost** class, with inheritance.
app/models/micropost.rb

```
class Micropost < ActiveRecord::Base
  .
  .
  .
end
```

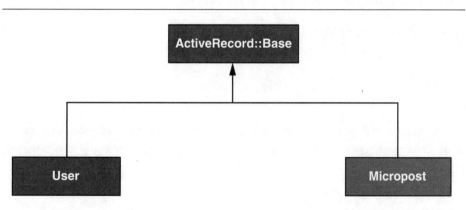

Figure 2.16   The inheritance hierarchy for the User and Micropost models.

The inheritance structure for controllers is only slightly more complicated. Comparing Listing 2.14 and Listing 2.15, we see that both the Users controller and the Microposts controller inherit from the Application controller. Examining Listing 2.16, we see that **ApplicationController** itself inherits from **ActionController::Base**; this is the base class for controllers provided by the Rails library Action Pack. The relationships between these classes is illustrated in Figure 2.17.

Listing 2.14 The **UsersController** class, with inheritance.
app/controllers/users_controller.rb

```
class UsersController < ApplicationController
  .
  .
  .
end
```

Listing 2.15 The **MicropostsController** class, with inheritance.
app/controllers/microposts_controller.rb

```
class MicropostsController < ApplicationController
  .
  .
  .
end
```

Listing 2.16 The **ApplicationController** class, with inheritance.
app/controllers/application_controller.rb

```
class ApplicationController < ActionController::Base
  .
  .
  .
end
```

As with model inheritance, by inheriting ultimately from **ActionController::Base** both the Users and Microposts controllers gain a large amount of functionality,

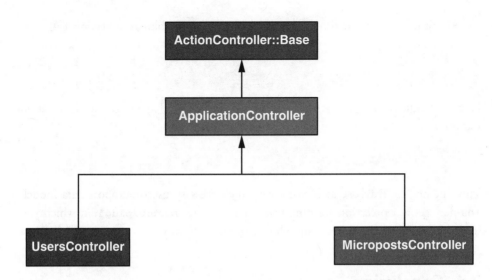

Figure 2.17   The inheritance hierarchy for the Users and Microposts controllers.

such as the ability to manipulate model objects, filter inbound HTTP requests, and render views as HTML. Since all Rails controllers inherit from `ApplicationController`, rules defined in the Application controller automatically apply to every action in the application. For example, in Section 8.2.1 we'll see how to include helpers for signing in and signing out of all of the sample application's controllers.

2.3.5   Deploying the Demo App

With the completion of the Microposts resource, now is a good time to push the repository up to GitHub:

```
$ git add .
$ git commit -m "Finish demo app"
$ git push
```

Ordinarily, you should make smaller, more frequent commits, but for the purposes of this chapter a single big commit at the end is fine.

At this point, you can also deploy the demo app to Heroku as in Section 1.4:

```
$ heroku create --stack cedar
$ git push heroku master
```

Finally, migrate the production database (see below if you get a deprecation warning):

```
$ heroku run rake db:migrate
```

This updates the database at Heroku with the necessary user/micropost data model. You may get a deprecation warning regarding assets in **vendor/plugins**, which you should ignore since there aren't any plugins in that directory.

2.4 Conclusion

We've come now to the end of the 30,000-foot view of a Rails application. The demo app developed in this chapter has several strengths and a host of weaknesses.

Strengths

- High-level overview of Rails
- Introduction to MVC
- First taste of the REST architecture
- Beginning data modeling
- A live, database-backed web application in production

Weaknesses

- No custom layout or styling
- No static pages (like "Home" or "About")
- No user passwords
- No user images
- No signing in

- No security
- No automatic user/micropost association
- No notion of "following" or "followed"
- No micropost feed
- No test-driven development
- **No real understanding**

The rest of this tutorial is dedicated to building on the strengths and eliminating the weaknesses.

CHAPTER 3
Mostly Static Pages

In this chapter, we will begin developing the sample application that will serve as our example throughout the rest of this tutorial. Although the sample app will eventually have users, microposts, and a full login and authentication framework, we will begin with a seemingly limited topic: the creation of static pages. Despite its apparent simplicity, making static pages is a highly instructive exercise, rich in implications—a perfect start for our nascent application.

Although Rails is designed for making database-backed dynamic websites, it also excels at making the kind of static pages we might make with raw HTML files. In fact, using Rails even for static pages yields a distinct advantage: We can easily add just a *small* amount of dynamic content. In this chapter we'll learn how. Along the way, we'll get our first taste of *automated testing*, which will help us be more confident that our code is correct. Moreover, having a good test suite will allow us to *refactor* our code with confidence, changing its form without changing its function.

There's a lot of code in this chapter, especially in Section 3.2 and Section 3.3, and if you're new to Ruby you shouldn't worry about understanding the details right now. As noted in Section 1.1.1, one strategy is to copy-and-paste the tests and use them to verify the application code, without worrying at this point how they work. In addition, Chapter 4 covers Ruby in more depth, so there is plenty of opportunity for these ideas to sink in. Finally, RSpec tests will recur throughout the tutorial, so if you get stuck now I recommend forging ahead; you'll be amazed how, after just a few more chapters, initially inscrutable code will suddenly look simple.

As in Chapter 2, before getting started we need to create a new Rails project, this time called **sample_app**:

```
$ cd ~/rails_projects
$ rails new sample_app --skip-test-unit
$ cd sample_app
```

Here the `--skip-test-unit` option to the **rails** command tells Rails not to generate a **test** directory associated with the default **Test::Unit** framework. This is not because we won't be writing tests; on the contrary, starting in Section 3.2 we will be using an alternate testing framework called *RSpec* to write a thorough test suite.

As in Section 2.1, our next step is to use a text editor to update the **Gemfile** with the gems needed by our application. On the other hand, for the sample application we'll also need two gems we didn't need before: the gem for RSpec and the gem for the RSpec library specific to Rails. The code to include them is shown in Listing 3.1. (*Note*: If you would like to install *all* the gems needed for the sample application, you should use the code in Listing 9.49 at this time.)

Listing 3.1 A **Gemfile** for the sample app.

```
source 'https://rubygems.org'

gem 'rails', '3.2.3'

group :development, :test do
  gem 'sqlite3', '1.3.5'
  gem 'rspec-rails', '2.9.0'
end

# Gems used only for assets and not required
# in production environments by default.
group :assets do
  gem 'sass-rails',   '3.2.4'
  gem 'coffee-rails', '3.2.2'
  gem 'uglifier', '1.2.3'
end

gem 'jquery-rails', '2.0.0'

group :test do
  gem 'capybara', '1.1.2'
end

group :production do
  gem 'pg', '0.12.2'
end
```

This includes `rspec-rails` in development mode so that we have access to RSpec-specific generators, and it includes it in test mode in order to run the tests. We don't have to install RSpec itself because it is a dependency of `rspec-rails` and will thus be installed automatically. We also include the Capybara gem, which allows us to simulate a user's interaction with the sample application using a natural English-like syntax.[1] As in Chapter 2, we also must include the PostgreSQL gem in production for deployment to Heroku:

```
group :production do
  gem 'pg', '0.12.2'
end
```

Heroku recommends against using different databases in development and production, but for the sample application it won't make any difference, and SQLite is *much* easier than PostgreSQL to install and configure. Installing and configuring PostgreSQL on your local machine is left as an exercise (Section 3.5).

To install and include the new gems, we run **bundle install**:

```
$ bundle install --without production
```

As in Chapter 2, we suppress the installation of production gems using the option `--without production`. This is a "remembered option," which means that we don't have to include it in future invocations of Bundler. Instead, we can write simply **bundle install**.[2]

Next, we need to configure Rails to use RSpec in place of **Test::Unit**. This can be accomplished with **rails generate rspec:install**:

```
$ rails generate rspec:install
```

If your system complains about the lack of a JavaScript runtime, visit the execjs page at GitHub for a list of possibilities. I particularly recommend installing Node.js.

---

1. The successor to *Webrat*, Capybara is named after the world's largest rodent.
2. In fact, you can even leave off **install**. The **bundle** command by itself is an alias for **bundle install**.

With that, all we have left is to initialize the Git repository:[3]

```
$ git init
$ git add .
$ git commit -m "Initial commit"
```

As with the first application, I suggest updating the **README** file (located in the root directory of the application) to be more helpful and descriptive, as shown in Listing 3.2.

Listing 3.2 An improved **README** file for the sample app.

```
# Ruby on Rails Tutorial: sample application

This is the sample application for
[*Ruby on Rails Tutorial: Learn Rails by Example*](http://railstutorial.org/)
by [Michael Hartl](http://michaelhartl.com/).
```

Then change it to use the Markdown extension **.md** and commit the changes:

```
$ git mv README.rdoc README.md
$ git commit -a -m "Improve the README"
```

Since we'll be using this sample app throughout the rest of the book, it's a good idea to make a repository at GitHub (Figure 3.1) and push it up:

```
$ git remote add origin git@github.com:<username>/sample_app.git
$ git push -u origin master
```

As a result of my performing this step, you can find the Rails Tutorial sample application code on GitHub (under a slightly different name).[4]

Of course, we can optionally deploy the app to Heroku even at this early stage:

```
$ heroku create --stack cedar
$ git push heroku master
```

---

3. As before, you may find the augmented file from Listing 1.7 to be more convenient depending on your system.

4. https://github.com/railstutorial/sample_app_2nd_ed

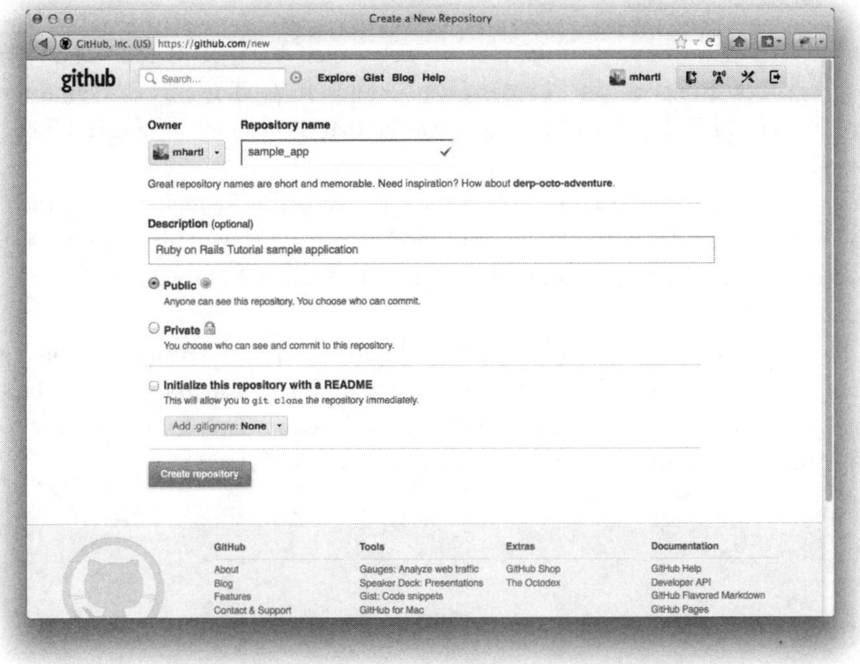

Figure 3.1   Creating the sample app repository at GitHub.

As you proceed through the rest of the book, I recommend pushing and deploying the application regularly:

```
$ git push
$ git push heroku
```

This provides remote backups and lets you catch any production errors as soon as possible. If you run into problems at Heroku, make sure to take a look at the production logs to try to diagnose the problem:

```
$ heroku logs
```

With all the preparation finished, we're finally ready to get started developing the sample application.

3.1   Static Pages

Rails has two main ways of making static web pages. First, Rails can handle *truly* static pages consisting of raw HTML files. Second, Rails allows us to define *views* containing raw HTML, which Rails can *render* so that the web server can send it to the browser.

In order to get our bearings, it's helpful to recall the Rails directory structure from Section 1.2.3 (Figure 1.2). In this section, we'll be working mainly in the **app/controllers** and **app/views** directories. (In Section 3.2, we'll even add a new directory of our own.)

This is the first section where it's useful to be able to open the entire Rails directory in your text editor or IDE. Unfortunately, how to do this is system-dependent, but in many cases you can open the current application directory, represented in Unix by a dot **.**, using the command-line command for your editor of choice:

```
$ cd ~/rails_projects/sample_app
$ <editor name> .
```

For example, to open the sample app in Sublime Text, you type

```
$ subl .
```

For Vim, you type **vim .**, **gvim .**, or **mvim .**, depending on which flavor of Vim you use.

3.1.1   Truly Static Pages

We start with truly static pages. Recall from Section 1.2.5 that every Rails application comes with a minimal working application thanks to the **rails** script, with a default welcome page at the address http://localhost:3000 (Figure 1.3).

To learn where this page comes from, take a look at the file **public/index.html** (Figure 3.2). Because the file contains its own stylesheet information, it's a little messy, but it gets the job done: By default, Rails serves any files in the **public** directory directly to the browser.[5] In the case of the special **index.html** file, you don't even have to indicate the file in the URI, as **index.html** is the default. You can include it if you

---

5. In fact, Rails ensures that requests for such files never hit the main Rails stack; they are delivered directly from the filesystem. (See *The Rails 3 Way* for more details.)

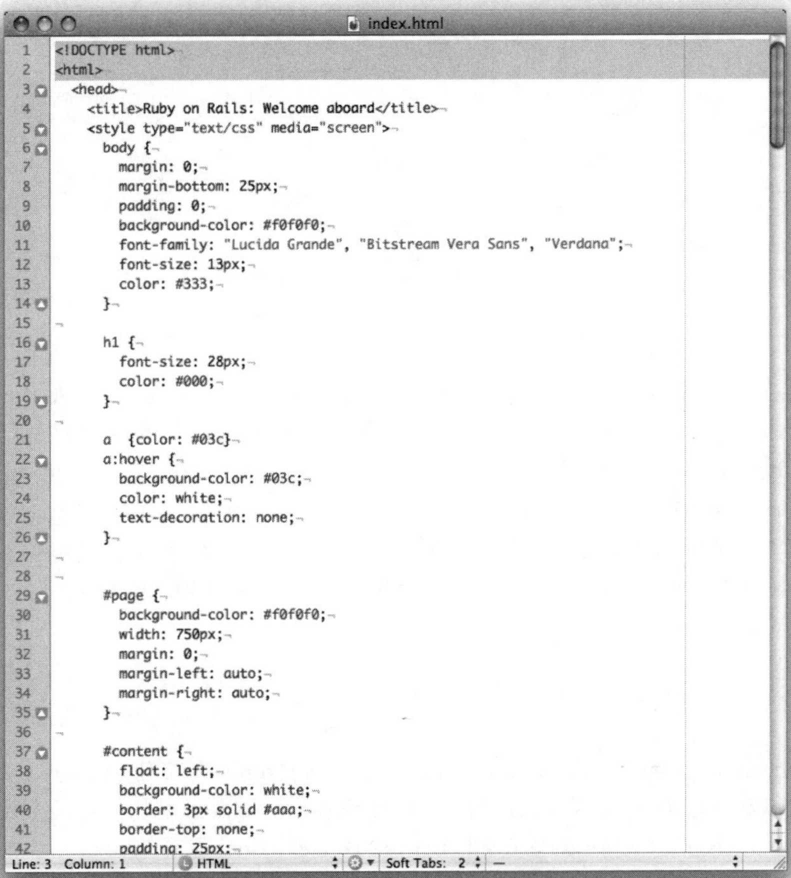

Figure 3.2 The `public/index.html` file.

want, though; the addresses http://localhost:3000 and http://localhost:3000/index.html are equivalent.

As you might expect, if we want we can make our own static HTML files and put them in the same `public` directory as `index.html`. For example, let's create a file with a friendly greeting (Listing 3.3):[6]

```
$ subl public/hello.html
```

---

6. As usual, replace `subl` with the command for your text editor.

Listing 3.3 A typical HTML file, with a friendly greeting.
public/hello.html

```
<!DOCTYPE html>
<html>
  <head>
    <title>Greeting</title>
  </head>
  <body>
    <p>Hello, world!</p>
  </body>
</html>
```

We see in Listing 3.3 the typical structure of an HTML document: A *document type*, or doctype, declaration at the top to tell browsers which version of HTML we're using (in this case, HTML5);[7] a **head** section, in this case with "Greeting" inside a **title** tag; and a **body** section, in this case with "Hello, world!" inside a **p** (paragraph) tag. (The indentation is optional—HTML is not sensitive to whitespace and ignores both tabs and spaces—but it makes the document's structure easier to see.)

Now run a local server using

```
$ rails server
```

and navigate to http://localhost:3000/hello.html. As promised, Rails renders the page straightaway (Figure 3.3). Note that the title displayed at the top of the browser window in Figure 3.3 is just the contents inside the **title** tag, namely, "Greeting."

Since this file is just for demonstration purposes, we don't really want it to be part of our sample application, so it's probably best to remove it once the thrill of creating it has worn off:

```
$ rm public/hello.html
```

---

7. HTML changes with time; by explicitly making a doctype declaration we make it likelier that browsers will render our pages properly in the future. The extremely simple doctype **<!DOCTYPE html>** is characteristic of the latest HTML standard, HTML5.

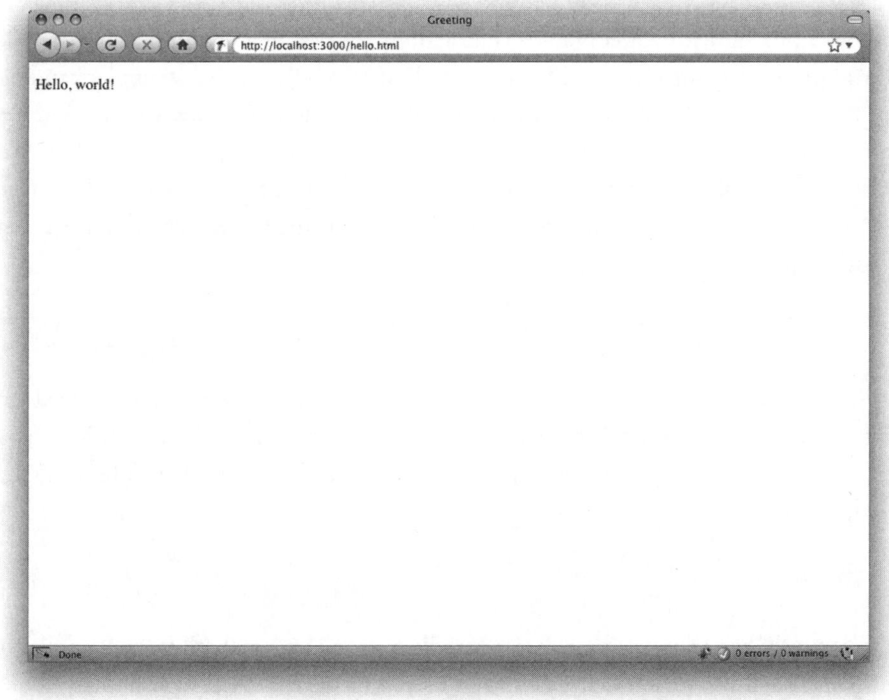

Figure 3.3   A new static HTML file.

We'll leave the `index.html` file alone for now, but of course eventually we should remove it: We don't want the root of our application to be the Rails default page shown in Figure 1.3. We'll see in Section 5.3 how to change the address http://localhost:3000 to point to something other than `public/index.html`.

3.1.2   Static Pages with Rails

The ability to return static HTML files is nice, but it's not particularly useful for making dynamic web applications. In this section, we'll take a first step toward making dynamic pages by creating a set of Rails *actions*, which are a more powerful way to define URIs than static files.[8] Rails actions come bundled together inside *controllers* (the C in MVC from Section 1.2.6), which contain sets of actions related by a common purpose. We got a glimpse of controllers in Chapter 2 and will come to a deeper understanding once we explore the REST architecture more fully (starting in Chapter 6); in essence, a controller is a container for a group of (possibly dynamic) web pages.

To get started, recall from Section 1.3.5 that, when using Git, it's a good practice to do our work on a separate topic branch rather than the master branch. If you're using Git for version control, you should run the following command:

```
$ git checkout -b static-pages
```

Rails comes with a script for making controllers called **generate**; all it needs to work its magic is the controller's name. In order to use **generate** with RSpec, you need to run the RSpec generator command if you didn't run it when following the introduction to this chapter:

```
$ rails generate rspec:install
```

Since we'll be making a controller to handle static pages, we'll call it the StaticPages controller. We'll also plan to make actions for a Home page, a Help page, and an About page. The **generate** script takes an optional list of actions, so we'll include two of the initial actions directly on the command line (Listing 3.4).

Listing 3.4 Generating a StaticPages controller.

```
$ rails generate controller StaticPages home help --no-test-framework
      create  app/controllers/static_pages_controller.rb
       route  get "static_pages/help"
       route  get "static_pages/home"
      invoke  erb
      create    app/views/static_pages
      create    app/views/static_pages/home.html.erb
      create    app/views/static_pages/help.html.erb
```

---

8. Our method for making static pages is probably the simplest, but it's not the only way. The optimal method really depends on your needs; if you expect a *large* number of static pages, using a Static-Pages controller can get quite cumbersome, but in our sample app we'll only need a few. See this blog post on simple pages at has_many :through for a survey of techniques for making static pages with Rails. *Warning:* The discussion is fairly advanced, so you might want to wait a while before trying to understand it.

```
invoke  helper
create    app/helpers/static_pages_helper.rb
invoke  assets
invoke    coffee
create      app/assets/javascripts/static_pages.js.coffee
invoke    scss
create      app/assets/stylesheets/static_pages.css.scss
```

Note that we've used the option `--no-test-framework` to suppress the generation of the default RSpec tests, which we won't be using. Instead, we'll create the tests by hand starting in Section 3.2. We've also intentionally left off the **about** action from the command line arguments in Listing 3.4 so that we can see how to add it using test-driven development, or TDD (Section 3.2).

By the way, if you ever make a mistake when generating code, it's useful to know how to reverse the process. See Box 3.1 for some techniques on how to undo things in Rails.

Box 3.1 Undoing Things

Even when you're very careful, things can sometimes go wrong when developing Rails applications. Happily, Rails has some facilities to help you recover.

One common scenario is wanting to undo code generation—for example, if you change your mind on the name of a controller. When generating a controller, Rails creates many more files than the controller file itself (as seen in Listing 3.4). Undoing the generation means removing not only the principal generated file, but all the ancillary files as well. (In fact, we also want to undo any automatic edits made to the `routes.rb` file.) In Rails, this can be accomplished with `rails destroy`. In particular, these two commands cancel each other out:

```
$ rails generate controller FooBars baz quux
$ rails destroy  controller FooBars baz quux
```

Similarly, in Chapter 6 we'll generate a *model* as follows:

```
$ rails generate model Foo bar:string baz:integer
```

This can be undone using

```
$ rails destroy model Foo
```

(In this case, it turns out we can omit the other command-line arguments. When you get to Chapter 6, see if you can figure out why.)

Another technique related to models involves undoing *migrations*, which we saw briefly in Chapter 2 and will see much more of starting in Chapter 6. Migrations change the state of the database using

```
$ rake db:migrate
```

We can undo a single migration step using

```
$ rake db:rollback
```

To go all the way back to the beginning, we can use

```
$ rake db:migrate VERSION=0
```

As you might guess, substituting any other number for 0 migrates to that version number, where the version numbers come from listing the migrations sequentially.

With these techniques in hand, we are well equipped to recover from the inevitable development snafus.

The StaticPages controller generation in Listing 3.4 automatically updates the *routes* file, called **config/routes.rb**, which Rails uses to find the correspondence between URIs and web pages. This is our first encounter with the **config** directory, so it's helpful to take a quick look at it (Figure 3.4). The **config** directory is where Rails collects files needed for the application configuration—hence the name.

Since we generated **home** and **help** actions, the routes file already has a rule for each one, as seen in Listing 3.5.

Listing 3.5 The routes for the **home** and **help** actions in the StaticPages controller.
config/routes.rb

```
SampleApp::Application.routes.draw do
  get "static_pages/home"
  get "static_pages/help"
  .
  .
  .
end
```

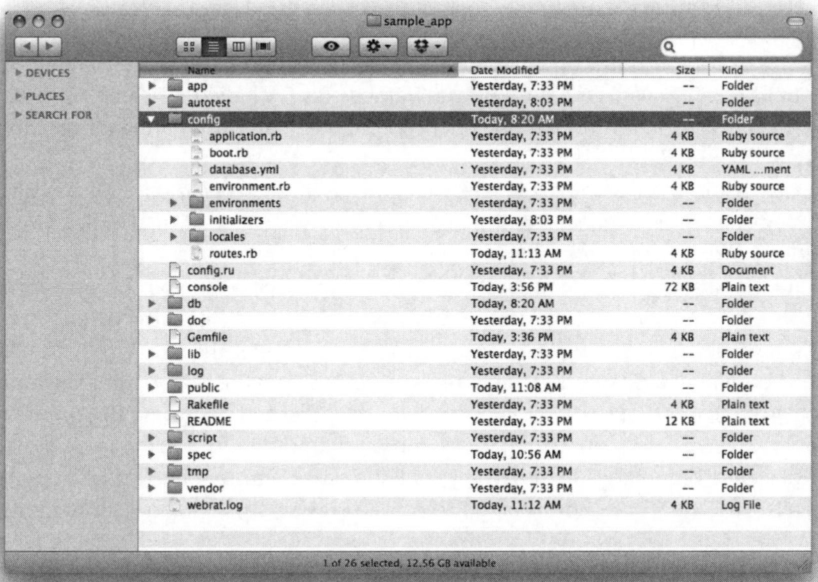

Figure 3.4   Contents of the sample app's **config** directory.

Here, the rule

```
get "static_pages/home"
```

maps requests for the URI /static_pages/home to the **home** action in the StaticPages controller. Moreover, by using **get** we arrange for the route to respond to a GET request, which is one of the fundamental *HTTP verbs* supported by the hypertext transfer protocol (Box 3.2). In our case, this means that when we generate a **home** action inside the StaticPages controller we automatically get a page at the address /static_pages/home. To see the results, navigate to /static_pages/home (Figure 3.5).

Box 3.2 GET, et cetera

The hypertext transfer protocol (HTTP) defines four basic operations, corresponding to the four verbs *get*, *post*, *put*, and *delete*. These refer to operations between a *client* computer (typically running a web browser such as Firefox or Safari) and a *server* (typically running a web server such as Apache or Nginx). (It's important to understand that, when developing Rails applications on a local computer, the client and server are the same physical machine, but in general they are different.) An emphasis on HTTP verbs is typical of web frameworks (including Rails) influenced by the *REST architecture*, which we saw briefly in Chapter 2 and will start learning about more in Chapter 7.

GET is the most common HTTP operation, used for *reading* data on the web; it just means "get a page," and every time you visit a site like google.com or wikipedia.org, your browser is submitting a GET request. POST is the next most common operation; it is the request sent by your browser when you submit a form. In Rails applications, POST requests are typically used for *creating* things (although HTTP also allows POST to perform updates); for example, the POST request sent when you submit a registration form creates a new user on the remote site. The other two verbs, PUT and DELETE, are designed for *updating* and *destroying* things on the remote server. These requests are less common than GET and POST since browsers are incapable of sending them natively, but some web frameworks (including Ruby on Rails) have clever ways of making it *seem* like browsers are issuing such requests.

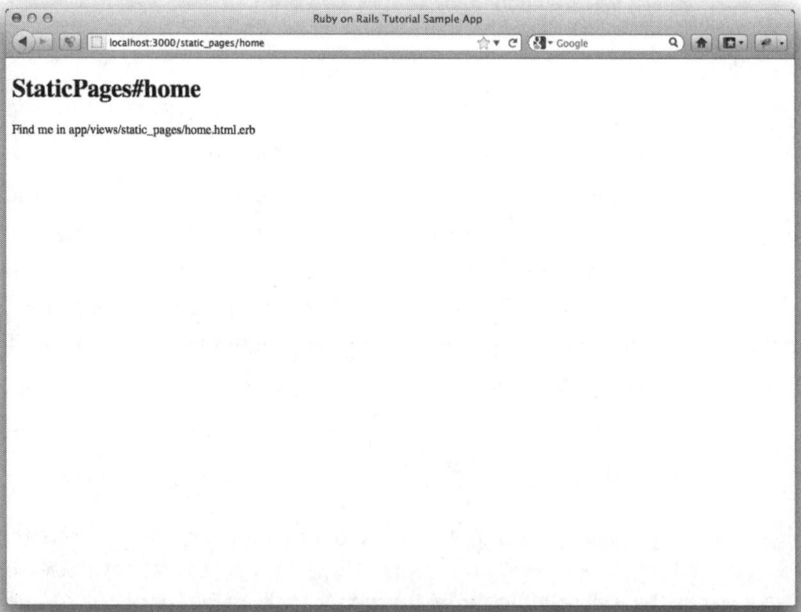

Figure 3.5   The raw home view (/static_pages/home).

To understand where this page comes from, let's start by taking a look at the StaticPages controller in a text editor; you should see something like Listing 3.6. You may note that, unlike the demo Users and Microposts controllers from Chapter 2, the StaticPages controller does not use the standard REST actions. This is normal for a collection of static pages—the REST architecture isn't the best solution to every problem.

Listing 3.6 The StaticPages controller made by Listing 3.4.
`app/controllers/static_pages_controller.rb`

```
class StaticPagesController < ApplicationController

  def home
  end

  def help
  end
end
```

We see from the **class** keyword in Listing 3.6 that **static_pages_controller.rb** defines a *class* called **StaticPagesController**. Classes are simply a convenient way to organize *functions* (also called *methods*) like the **home** and **help** actions, which are defined using the **def** keyword. The angle bracket **<** indicates that **StaticPagesController** *inherits* from the Rails class **ApplicationController**; as we'll see momentarily, this means that our pages come equipped with a large amount of Rails-specific functionality. (We'll learn more about both classes and inheritance in Section 4.4.)

In the case of the StaticPages controller, both its methods are initially empty:

```
def home
end

def help
end
```

In plain Ruby, these methods would simply do nothing. In Rails, the situation is different. **StaticPagesController** is a Ruby class, but because it inherits from **ApplicationController**, the behavior of its methods is specific to Rails. When visiting the URI /static_pages/home, Rails looks in the StaticPages controller and executes the code in the **home** action, and then renders the *view* (the V in MVC from Section 1.2.6) corresponding to the action. In the present case, the **home** action is empty, so all visiting /static_pages/home does is render the view. So, what does a view look like, and how do we find it?

If you take another look at the output in Listing 3.4, you might be able to guess the correspondence between actions and views: An action like **home** has a corresponding view called **home.html.erb**. We'll learn in Section 3.3 what the **.erb** part means; from the **.html** part you probably won't be surprised that it basically looks like HTML (Listing 3.7).

Listing 3.7 The generated view for the Home page.
app/views/static_pages/home.html.erb

```
<h1>StaticPages#home</h1>
<p>Find me in app/views/static_pages/home.html.erb</p>
```

The view for the **help** action is analogous (Listing 3.8).

Listing 3.8 The generated view for the Help page.
app/views/static_pages/help.html.erb

```
<h1>StaticPages#help</h1>
<p>Find me in app/views/static_pages/help.html.erb</p>
```

Both of these views are just placeholders: They have a top-level heading (inside the **h1** tag) and a paragraph (**p** tag) with the full path to the relevant file. We'll add some (very slightly) dynamic content starting in Section 3.3, but as they stand these views underscore an important point: Rails views can simply contain static HTML. As far as the browser is concerned, the raw HTML files from Section 3.1.1 and the controller/action method of delivering pages are indistinguishable: All the browser ever sees is HTML.

In the remainder of this chapter, we'll add some custom content to the Home and Help pages, then add in the About page we left off in Section 3.1.2. Then we'll add a very small amount of dynamic content by changing the title on a per-page basis.

Before moving on, if you're using Git, it's a good idea to add the files for the StaticPages controller to the repository:

```
$ git add .
$ git commit -m "Add a StaticPages controller"
```

3.2 Our First Tests

The *Rails Tutorial* takes an intuitive approach to testing that emphasizes the behavior of the application rather than its precise implementation, a variant of test-driven development (TDD) known as behavior-driven development (BDD). Our main tools will be *integration tests* (starting in this section) and *unit tests* (starting in Chapter 6). Integration tests, known as *request specs* in the context of RSpec, allow us to simulate the actions of a user interacting with our application using a web browser. Together with the natural-language syntax provided by Capybara, integration tests provide a powerful method to test our application's functionality without having to manually check each page with a browser. (Another popular choice for BDD, called Cucumber, is introduced in Section 8.3.)

The defining quality of TDD is writing tests *first*, before the application code. Initially, this might take some getting used to, but the benefits are significant. By writing a *failing* test first and then implementing the application code to get it to pass, we increase our confidence that the test is actually covering the functionality we think it is. Moreover, the fail-implement-pass development cycle induces a flow state, leading to enjoyable coding and high productivity. Finally, the tests act as a *client* for the application code, often leading to more elegant software designs.

It's important to understand that TDD is not always the right tool for the job. There's no reason to dogmatically insist that tests always should be written first, that they should cover every single feature, or that there should necessarily be any tests at all. For example, when you aren't at all sure how to solve a given programming problem, it's often useful to skip the tests and write only application code, just to get a sense of what the solution will look like. (In the language of Extreme Programming [XP], this exploratory step is called a *spike*.) Once you see the general shape of the solution, you can then use TDD to implement a more polished version.

In this section, we'll be running the tests using the **rspec** command supplied by the RSpec gem. This practice is straightforward but not ideal, and if you are a more advanced user I suggest setting up your system as described in Section 3.6.

3.2.1 Test-driven Development

In test-driven development, we first write a *failing* test, represented in many testing tools by the color red. We then implement code to get the test to pass, represented by the color green. Finally, if necessary, we refactor the code, changing its form (by eliminating duplication, for example) without changing its function. This cycle is known as "Red, Green, Refactor."

We'll begin by adding some content to the Home page using test-driven development, including a top-level heading (**<h1>**) with the content **Sample App**. The first step is to generate an integration test (request spec) for our static pages:

```
$ rails generate integration_test static_pages
      invoke  rspec
      create    spec/requests/static_pages_spec.rb
```

This creates the **static_pages_spec.rb** in the **spec/requests** directory. As with most generated code, the result is not pretty, so let's open **static_pages_spec.rb** with a text editor and replace it with the contents of Listing 3.9.

Listing 3.9 Code to test the contents of the Home page.
spec/requests/static_pages_spec.rb

```
require 'spec_helper'

describe "Static pages" do

  describe "Home page" do

    it "should have the content 'Sample App'" do
      visit '/static_pages/home'
      page.should have_content('Sample App')
    end
  end
end
```

The code in Listing 3.9 is pure Ruby, but even if you've studied Ruby before it probably won't look very familiar. This is because RSpec uses the general malleability of Ruby to define a *domain-specific language* (DSL) built just for testing. The important point is that *you do not need to understand RSpec's syntax to be able to use RSpec*. It may seem like magic at first, but RSpec and Capybara are designed to read more or less like English, and if you follow the examples from the **generate** script and the other examples in this tutorial, you'll pick it up fairly quickly.

Listing 3.9 contains a **describe** block with one *example*, i.e., a block starting with **it "..." do**:

```
describe "Home page" do

  it "should have the content 'Sample App'" do
    visit '/static_pages/home'
    page.should have_content('Sample App')
  end
end
```

The first line indicates that we are describing the Home page. This is just a string, and it can be anything you want; RSpec doesn't care, but you and other human readers probably do. Then the spec says that when you visit the Home page at **/static_pages/home**, the content should contain the words "Sample App." As with the first line, what goes inside the quote marks is irrelevant to RSpec and is intended to be descriptive to human readers. Then the line

```
visit '/static_pages/home'
```

uses the Capybara function **visit** to simulate visiting the URI **/static_pages/home** in a browser, while the line

```
page.should have_content('Sample App')
```

uses the **page** variable (also provided by Capybara) to test that the resulting page has the right content.

To run the test, we have several options, including some convenient but rather advanced tools discussed in Section 3.6. For now, we'll use the **rspec** command at the command line (executed with **bundle exec** to ensure that RSpec runs in the environment specified by our **Gemfile**):[9]

```
$ bundle exec rspec spec/requests/static_pages_spec.rb
```

This yields a failing test. The appearance of the result depends on your system; on my system, the red failing test appears as in Figure 3.6.[10] (The screenshot, which predates,

---

9. Running **bundle exec** every time is rather cumbersome; see Section 3.6 for some options to eliminate it.

10. I actually use a dark background for both my terminal and editor, but the light background looks better in the screenshots.

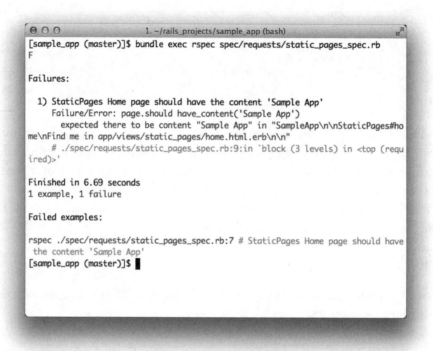

Figure 3.6   A red (failing) test.

the current Git branching strategy, shows work on the `master` branch instead the `static-pages` branch, but this is not cause for concern.)

To get the test to pass, we'll replace the default Home page test with the HTML in Listing 3.10.

Listing 3.10 Code to get a passing test for the Home page.
`app/views/static_pages/home.html.erb`

```
<h1>Sample App</h1>
<p>
  This is the home page for the
  <a href="http://railstutorial.org/">Ruby on Rails Tutorial</a>
  sample application.
</p>
```

This arranges for a top-level heading (**`<h1>`**) with the content **`Sample App`**, which should get the test to pass. We also include an *anchor* tag **a**, which creates links to the given URI (called an "href," or "hypertext reference," in the context of an anchor tag):

```
<a href="http://railstutorial.org/">Ruby on Rails Tutorial</a>
```

Now re-run the test to see the effect:

```
$ bundle exec rspec spec/requests/static_pages_spec.rb
```

On my system, the passing test appears as in Figure 3.7.

Based on the example for the Home page, you can probably guess the analogous test and application code for the Help page. We start by testing for the relevant content, in this case the string **`'Help'`** (Listing 3.11).

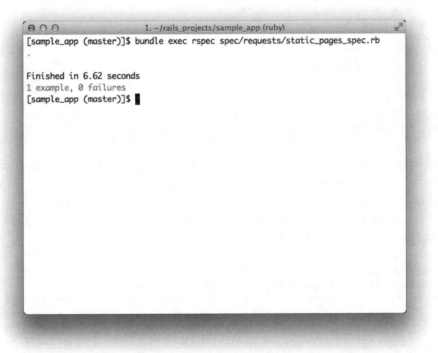

Figure 3.7 A green (passing) test.

Listing 3.11 Adding code to test the contents of the Help page.
`spec/requests/static_pages_spec.rb`

```
require 'spec_helper'

describe "Static pages" do

  describe "Home page" do

    it "should have the content 'Sample App'" do
      visit '/static_pages/home'
      page.should have_content('Sample App')
    end
  end

  describe "Help page" do

    it "should have the content 'Help'" do
      visit '/static_pages/help'
      page.should have_content('Help')
    end
  end
end
```

Then run the tests:

```
$ bundle exec rspec spec/requests/static_pages_spec.rb
```

One test should fail. (Since systems will vary, and since keeping track of how many tests there are at each stage of the tutorial is a maintenance nightmare, I'll omit the RSpec output from now on.)

The application code (which for now is raw HTML) is similar to the code in Listing 3.10, as seen in Listing 3.12.

Listing 3.12 Code to get a passing test for the Help page.
`app/views/static_pages/help.html.erb`

```
<h1>Help</h1>
<p>
  Get help on the Ruby on Rails Tutorial at the
  <a href="http://railstutorial.org/help">Rails Tutorial help page</a>.
  To get help on this sample app, see the
  <a href="http://railstutorial.org/book">Rails Tutorial book</a>.
</p>
```

The tests should now pass:

```
$ bundle exec rspec spec/requests/static_pages_spec.rb
```

3.2.2 Adding a Page

Having seen test-driven development in action in a simple example, we'll use the same technique to accomplish the slightly more complicated task of adding a new page, namely, the About page that we intentionally left off in Section 3.1.2. By writing a test and running RSpec at each step, we'll see how TDD can guide us through the development of our application code.

Red

We'll get to the Red part of the Red-Green cycle by writing a failing test for the About page. Following the models from Listing 3.11, you can probably guess the right test (Listing 3.13).

Listing 3.13 Adding code to test the contents of the About page.
`spec/requests/static_pages_spec.rb`

```ruby
require 'spec_helper'

describe "Static pages" do

  describe "Home page" do

    it "should have the content 'Sample App'" do
      visit '/static_pages/home'
      page.should have_content('Sample App')
    end
  end

  describe "Help page" do

    it "should have the content 'Help'" do
      visit '/static_pages/help'
      page.should have_content('Help')
    end
  end

  describe "About page" do
```

```
   it "should have the content 'About Us'" do
     visit '/static_pages/about'
     page.should have_content('About Us')
   end
 end
end
```

Green

Recall from Section 3.1.2 that we can generate a static page in Rails by creating an action and corresponding view with the page's name. In our case, the About page will first need an action called **about** in the StaticPages controller. Having written a failing test, we can now be confident that, in getting it to pass, we will actually have created a working About page.

If you run the RSpec example using

```
$ bundle exec rspec spec/requests/static_pages_spec.rb
```

the output includes the following complaint:

```
No route matches [GET] "/static_pages/about"
```

This is a hint that we need to add **/static_pages/about** to the routes file, which we can accomplish by following the pattern in Listing 3.5, as shown in Listing 3.14.

Listing 3.14 Adding the **about** route.
`config/routes.rb`

```
SampleApp::Application.routes.draw do
  get "static_pages/home"
  get "static_pages/help"
  get "static_pages/about"
  .
  .
  .
end
```

Now running

```
$ bundle exec rspec spec/requests/static_pages_spec.rb
```

complains that

```
The action 'about' could not be found for StaticPagesController
```

To solve this problem, we follow the model provided by **home** and **help** from Listing 3.6 by adding an **about** action in the StaticPages controller (Listing 3.15).

Listing 3.15 The StaticPages controller with added **about** action.
app/controllers/static_pages_controller.rb

```
class StaticPagesController < ApplicationController

  def home
  end

  def help
  end

  def about
  end
end
```

Now running

```
$ bundle exec rspec spec/requests/static_pages_spec.rb
```

says that we are missing a "template," i.e., a view:

```
ActionView::MissingTemplate:
  Missing template static_pages/about
```

To solve this issue, we add the **about** view. This involves creating a new file called **about.html.erb** in the **app/views/static_pages** directory with the contents shown in Listing 3.16.

Listing 3.16 Code for the About page.
app/views/static_pages/about.html.erb

```
<h1>About Us</h1>
<p>
  The <a href="http://railstutorial.org/">Ruby on Rails Tutorial</a>
  is a project to make a book and screencasts to teach web development
  with <a href="http://rubyonrails.org/">Ruby on Rails</a>. This
  is the sample application for the tutorial.
</p>
```

Running RSpec should now get us back to Green:

```
$ bundle exec rspec spec/requests/static_pages_spec.rb
```

Of course, it's never a bad idea to take a look at the page in a browser to make sure our tests aren't completely crazy (Figure 3.8).

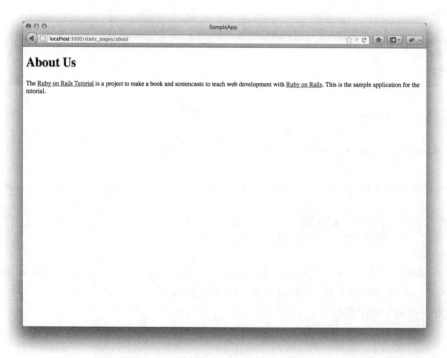

Figure 3.8   The new About page (/static_pages/about).

Refactor

Now that we've gotten to Green, we are free to refactor our code with confidence. Oftentimes code will start to "smell," meaning that it gets ugly, bloated, or filled with repetition. The computer doesn't care, of course, but humans do, so it is important to keep the code base clean by refactoring frequently. Having a good test suite is an invaluable tool in this regard, because it dramatically lowers the probability of introducing bugs while refactoring.

Our sample app is a little too small to refactor right now, but code smell seeps in at every crack, so we won't have to wait long: We'll already get busy refactoring in Section 3.3.4.

3.3 Slightly Dynamic Pages

Now that we've created the actions and views for some static pages, we'll make them *very slightly* dynamic by adding some content that changes on a per-page basis: We'll have the title of each page change to reflect its content. Whether a changing title represents *truly* dynamic content is debatable, but in any case it lays the necessary foundation for unambiguously dynamic content in Chapter 7.

If you skipped the TDD material in Section 3.2, be sure to create an About page at this point using the code from Listing 3.14, Listing 3.15, and Listing 3.16.

3.3.1 Testing a Title Change

Our plan is to edit the Home, Help, and About pages to make page titles that change on each page. This will involve using the `<title>` tag in our page views. Most browsers display the contents of the title tag at the top of the browser window (Google Chrome is an odd exception), and it is also important for search-engine optimization. We'll start by writing tests for the titles, then add the titles themselves, and then use a *layout* file to refactor the resulting pages and eliminate duplication.

You may have noticed that the `rails new` command already created a layout file. We'll learn its purpose shortly, but for now you should rename it before proceeding:

```
$ mv app/views/layouts/application.html.erb foobar    # temporary change
```

(`mv` is a Unix command; on Windows you may need to rename the file using the file browser or the `rename` command.) You wouldn't normally do this in a real application, but it's easier to understand the purpose of the layout file if we start by disabling it.

Table 3.1   The (mostly) static pages for the sample app.

Page	URI	Base title	Variable title
Home	/static_pages/home	`"Ruby on Rails Tutorial Sample App"`	`"Home"`
Help	/static_pages/help	`"Ruby on Rails Tutorial Sample App"`	`"Help"`
About	/static_pages/about	`"Ruby on Rails Tutorial Sample App"`	`"About"`

By the end of this section, all three of our static pages will have titles of the form "Ruby on Rails Tutorial Sample App | Home," where the last part of the title will vary depending on the page (Table 3.1). We'll build on the tests in Listing 3.13, adding title tests following the model in Listing 3.17.

Listing 3.17 A title test.

```
it "should have the right title" do
  visit '/static_pages/home'
  page.should have_selector('title',
                  :text => "Ruby on Rails Tutorial Sample App | Home")
end
```

This uses the **have_selector** method, which checks for an HTML element (the "selector") with the given content. In other words, the code

```
page.should have_selector('title',
                  :text => "Ruby on Rails Tutorial Sample App | Home")
```

checks to see that the content inside the **title** tag is

```
"Ruby on Rails Tutorial Sample App | Home"
```

(We'll learn in Section 4.3.3 that the **:text => "..."** syntax is a *hash* using a *symbol* as the key.) It's worth mentioning that the content need not be an exact match; any substring works as well, so that

```
page.should have_selector('title', :text => " | Home")
```

will also match the full title.

Note that in Listing 3.17 we've broken the material inside **have_selector** into two lines; this tells you something important about Ruby syntax: Ruby doesn't care about newlines.[11] The *reason* I chose to break the code into pieces is that I prefer to keep lines of source code under 80 characters for legibility.[12] As it stands, this code formatting is still rather ugly; Section 3.5 has a refactoring exercise that makes them prettier, and Section 5.3.4 completely rewrites the StaticPages tests to take advantage of the latest features in RSpec.

Adding new tests for each of our three static pages, following the model of Listing 3.17, gives us our new StaticPages test (Listing 3.18).

Listing 3.18 The StaticPages controller spec with title tests.
`spec/requests/static_pages_spec.rb`

```
require 'spec_helper'

describe "Static pages" do

  describe "Home page" do

    it "should have the h1 'Sample App'" do
      visit '/static_pages/home'
      page.should have_selector('h1', :text => 'Sample App')
    end

    it "should have the title 'Home'" do
      visit '/static_pages/home'
      page.should have_selector('title',
                      :text => "Ruby on Rails Tutorial Sample App | Home")
    end
  end
```

---

11. A newline is what comes at the end of a line, thereby starting a new line. In code, it is represented by the character **\n**.

12. Actually *counting* columns could drive you crazy, which is why many text editors have a visual aid to help you. For example, if you take a look back at Figure 1.1, you'll see a small vertical line on the right to help keep code under 80 characters. (It's actually at 78 columns, which gives you a little margin for error.) If you use TextMate, you can find this feature under View > Wrap Column > 78. In Sublime Text, you can use View > Ruler > 78 or View > Ruler > 80.

```
describe "Help page" do

  it "should have the h1 'Help'" do
    visit '/static_pages/help'
    page.should have_selector('h1', :text => 'Help')
  end

  it "should have the title 'Help'" do
    visit '/static_pages/help'
    page.should have_selector('title',
                    :text => "Ruby on Rails Tutorial Sample App | Help")
  end
end

describe "About page" do

  it "should have the h1 'About Us'" do
    visit '/static_pages/about'
    page.should have_selector('h1', :text => 'About Us')
  end

  it "should have the title 'About Us'" do
    visit '/static_pages/about'
    page.should have_selector('title',
                  :text => "Ruby on Rails Tutorial Sample App | About Us")
  end
 end
end
```

Note that we've changed **have_content** to the more specific **have_selector('h1',
...)**. See if you can figure out why. (*Hint:* What would happen if the title contained,
say, 'Help', but the content inside **h1** tag had 'Helf' instead?)

With the tests from Listing 3.18 in place, you should run

```
$ bundle exec rspec spec/requests/static_pages_spec.rb
```

to verify that our code is now Red (failing tests).

3.3.2 Passing Title Tests

Now we'll get our title tests to pass and at the same time add the full HTML structure
needed to make valid web pages. Let's start with the Home page (Listing 3.19), using
the same basic HTML skeleton as in the "hello" page from Listing 3.3.

Listing 3.19 The view for the Home page with full HTML structure.
`app/views/static_pages/home.html.erb`

```
<!DOCTYPE html>
<html>
  <head>
    <title>Ruby on Rails Tutorial Sample App | Home</title>
  </head>
  <body>
    <h1>Sample App</h1>
    <p>
      This is the home page for the
      <a href="http://railstutorial.org/">Ruby on Rails Tutorial</a>
      sample application.
    </p>
  </body>
</html>
```

Listing 3.19 uses the title tested for in Listing 3.18:

```
<title>Ruby on Rails Tutorial Sample App | Home</title>
```

As a result, the tests for the Home page should now pass. We're still Red because of the failing Help and About tests, and we can get to Green with the code in Listing 3.20 and Listing 3.21.

Listing 3.20 The view for the Help page with full HTML structure.
`app/views/static_pages/help.html.erb`

```
<!DOCTYPE html>
<html>
  <head>
    <title>Ruby on Rails Tutorial Sample App | Help</title>
  </head>
  <body>
    <h1>Help</h1>
    <p>
      Get help on the Ruby on Rails Tutorial at the
      <a href="http://railstutorial.org/help">Rails Tutorial help page</a>.
      To get help on this sample app, see the
      <a href="http://railstutorial.org/book">Rails Tutorial book</a>.
    </p>
  </body>
</html>
```

Listing 3.21 The view for the About page with full HTML structure.
`app/views/static_pages/about.html.erb`

```
<!DOCTYPE html>
<html>
  <head>
    <title>Ruby on Rails Tutorial Sample App | About Us</title>
  </head>
  <body>
    <h1>About Us</h1>
    <p>
      The <a href="http://railstutorial.org/">Ruby on Rails Tutorial</a>
      is a project to make a book and screencasts to teach web development
      with <a href="http://rubyonrails.org/">Ruby on Rails</a>. This
      is the sample application for the tutorial.
    </p>
  </body>
</html>
```

3.3.3 Embedded Ruby

We've achieved a lot already in this section, generating three valid pages using Rails controllers and actions, but they are purely static HTML and hence don't show off the power of Rails. Moreover, they suffer from terrible duplication:

- The page titles are almost (but not quite) exactly the same.
- "Ruby on Rails Tutorial Sample App" is common to all three titles.
- The entire HTML skeleton structure is repeated on each page.

This repeated code is a violation of the important "Don't Repeat Yourself" (DRY) principle; in this section and the next we'll "DRY out our code" by removing the repetition.

Paradoxically, we'll take the first step toward eliminating duplication by first adding some more: We'll make the titles of the pages, which are currently quite similar, match *exactly*. This will make it much simpler to remove all the repetition at a stroke.

The technique involves using *Embedded Ruby* in our views. Since the Home, Help, and About page titles have a variable component, we'll use a special Rails function called **provide** to set a different title on each page. We can see how this works by replacing the literal title "Home" in the **home.html.erb** view with the code in Listing 3.22.

Listing 3.22 The view for the Home page with an Embedded Ruby title.
app/views/static_pages/home.html.erb

```
<% provide(:title, 'Home') %>
<!DOCTYPE html>
<html>
  <head>
    <title>Ruby on Rails Tutorial Sample App | <%= yield(:title) %></title>
  </head>
  <body>
    <h1>Sample App</h1>
    <p>
      This is the home page for the
      <a href="http://railstutorial.org/">Ruby on Rails Tutorial</a>
      sample application.
    </p>
  </body>
</html>
```

Listing 3.22 is our first example of Embedded Ruby, also called *ERb*. (Now you know why HTML views have the file extension **.html.erb**.) ERb is the primary template system for including dynamic content in web pages.[13] The code

```
<% provide(:title, 'Home') %>
```

indicates using <% ... %> that Rails should call the **provide** function and associate the string **'Home'** with the label **:title**.[14] Then, in the title, we use the closely related notation <%= ... %> to insert the title into the template using Ruby's **yield** function:[15]

```
<title>Ruby on Rails Tutorial Sample App | <%= yield(:title) %></title>
```

---

13. There is a second popular template system called Haml, which I personally love, but it's not *quite* standard enough yet for use in an introductory tutorial.

14. Experienced Rails developers might have expected the use of **content_for** at this point, but it doesn't work well with the asset pipeline. The **provide** function is its replacement.

15. If you've studied Ruby before, you might suspect that Rails is *yielding* the contents to a block, and your suspicion would be correct. But you don't need to know this to develop applications with Rails.

(The distinction between the two types of embedded Ruby is that `<% ... %>` *executes* the code inside, while `<%= ... %>` executes it and *inserts* the result into the template.) The resulting page is exactly the same as before, only now the variable part of the title is generated dynamically by ERb.

We can verify that all this works by running the tests from Section 3.3.1 and see that they still pass:

```
$ bundle exec rspec spec/requests/static_pages_spec.rb
```

Then we can make the corresponding replacements for the Help and About pages (Listing 3.23 and Listing 3.24).

Listing 3.23 The view for the Help page with an Embedded Ruby title.
app/views/static_pages/help.html.erb

```erb
<% provide(:title, 'Help') %>
<!DOCTYPE html>
<html>
  <head>
    <title>Ruby on Rails Tutorial Sample App | <%= yield(:title) %></title>
  </head>
  <body>
    <h1>Help</h1>
    <p>
      Get help on the Ruby on Rails Tutorial at the
      <a href="http://railstutorial.org/help">Rails Tutorial help page</a>.
      To get help on this sample app, see the
      <a href="http://railstutorial.org/book">Rails Tutorial book</a>.
    </p>
  </body>
</html>
```

Listing 3.24 The view for the About page with an Embedded Ruby title.
app/views/static_pages/about.html.erb

```erb
<% provide(:title, 'About Us') %>
<!DOCTYPE html>
<html>
  <head>
    <title>Ruby on Rails Tutorial Sample App | <%= yield(:title) %></title>
  </head>
```

```
<body>
  <h1>About Us</h1>
  <p>
    The <a href="http://railstutorial.org/">Ruby on Rails Tutorial</a>
    is a project to make a book and screencasts to teach web development
    with <a href="http://rubyonrails.org/">Ruby on Rails</a>. This
    is the sample application for the tutorial.
  </p>
</body>
</html>
```

3.3.4 Eliminating Duplication with Layouts

Now that we've replaced the variable part of the page titles with ERb, each of our pages looks something like this:

```
<% provide(:title, 'Foo') %>
<!DOCTYPE html>
<html>
  <head>
    <title>Ruby on Rails Tutorial Sample App | <%= yield(:title) %></title>
  </head>
  <body>
    Contents
  </body>
</html>
```

In other words, *all* our pages are identical in structure, including the contents of the title tag, with the sole exception of the material inside the **body** tag.

In order to factor out this common structure, Rails comes with a special *layout* file called **application.html.erb**, which we renamed in Section 3.3.1 and which we'll now restore:

```
$ mv foobar app/views/layouts/application.html.erb
```

To get the layout to work, we have to replace the default title with the Embedded Ruby from the examples above:

```
<title>Ruby on Rails Tutorial Sample App | <%= yield(:title) %></title>
```

The resulting layout appears in Listing 3.25.

Listing 3.25 The sample application site layout.
app/views/layouts/application.html.erb

```
<!DOCTYPE html>
<html>
  <head>
    <title>Ruby on Rails Tutorial Sample App | <%= yield(:title) %></title>
    <%= stylesheet_link_tag    "application", :media => "all" %>
    <%= javascript_include_tag "application" %>
    <%= csrf_meta_tags %>
  </head>
  <body>
    <%= yield %>
  </body>
</html>
```

Note here the special line

```
<%= yield %>
```

This code is responsible for inserting the contents of each page into the layout. It's not important to know exactly how this works; what matters is that using this layout ensures that, for example, visiting the page /static_pages/home converts the contents of **home.html.erb** to HTML and then inserts it in place of `<%= yield %>`.

It's also worth noting that the default Rails layout includes several additional lines:

```
<%= stylesheet_link_tag    "application", :media => "all" %>
<%= javascript_include_tag "application" %>
<%= csrf_meta_tags %>
```

This code arranges to include the application stylesheet and JavaScript, which are part of the asset pipeline (Section 5.2.1), together with the Rails method **csrf_meta_tags**, which prevents cross-site request forgery (CSRF), a type of malicious web attack.

Of course, the views in Listing 3.22, Listing 3.23, and Listing 3.24 are still filled with all the HTML structure included in the layout, so we have to remove it, leaving only the interior contents. The resulting cleaned-up views appear in Listing 3.26, Listing 3.27, and Listing 3.28.

Listing 3.26 The Home page with HTML structure removed.
`app/views/static_pages/home.html.erb`

```erb
<% provide(:title, 'Home') %>
<h1>Sample App</h1>
<p>
  This is the home page for the
  <a href="http://railstutorial.org/">Ruby on Rails Tutorial</a>
  sample application.
</p>
```

Listing 3.27 The Help page with HTML structure removed.
`app/views/static_pages/help.html.erb`

```erb
<% provide(:title, 'Help') %>
<h1>Help</h1>
<p>
  Get help on the Ruby on Rails Tutorial at the
  <a href="http://railstutorial.org/help">Rails Tutorial help page</a>.
  To get help on this sample app, see the
  <a href="http://railstutorial.org/book">Rails Tutorial book</a>.
</p>
```

Listing 3.28 The About page with HTML structure removed.
`app/views/static_pages/about.html.erb`

```erb
<% provide(:title, 'About Us') %>
<h1>About Us</h1>
<p>
  The <a href="http://railstutorial.org/">Ruby on Rails Tutorial</a>
  is a project to make a book and screencasts to teach web development
  with <a href="http://rubyonrails.org/">Ruby on Rails</a>. This
  is the sample application for the tutorial.
</p>
```

With these views defined, the Home, Help, and About pages are the same as before, but they have much less duplication. Verifying that the test suite still passes gives us confidence that this code refactoring was successful:

```
$ bundle exec rspec spec/requests/static_pages_spec.rb
```

3.4 Conclusion

Seen from the outside, this chapter hardly accomplished anything: We started with static pages, and ended with . . . *mostly* static pages. But appearances are deceiving: By developing in terms of Rails controllers, actions, and views, we are now in a position to add arbitrary amounts of dynamic content to our site. Seeing exactly how this plays out is the task for the rest of this tutorial.

Before moving on, let's take a minute to commit our changes and merge them into the master branch. Back in Section 3.1.2 we created a Git branch for the development of static pages. If you haven't been making commits as we've been moving along, first make a commit indicating that we've reached a stopping point:

```
$ git add .
$ git commit -m "Finish static pages"
```

Then merge the changes back into the master branch using the same technique as in Section 1.3.5:

```
$ git checkout master
$ git merge static-pages
```

Once you reach a stopping point like this, it's usually a good idea to push your code up to a remote repository (which, if you followed the steps in Section 1.3.4, will be GitHub):

```
$ git push
```

If you like, at this point you can even deploy the updated application to Heroku:

```
$ git push heroku
```

3.5 Exercises

1. Make a Contact page for the sample app. First write a test for the existence of a page at the URI /static_pages/contact. (*Hint*: Test for the right title.) Then write a second test for the title "Ruby on Rails Tutorial Sample App | Contact." Get your

tests to pass, then fill in the Contact page with the content from Listing 3.29. (This exercise is solved as part of Section 5.3.)

2. You may have noticed some repetition in the StaticPages controller spec (Listing 3.18). In particular, the base title, "Ruby on Rails Tutorial Sample App," is the same for every title test. Using the RSpec **let** function, which creates a variable corresponding to its argument, verify that the tests in Listing 3.30 still pass. Listing 3.30 introduces *string interpolation*, which is covered further in Section 4.2.2.

3. **(advanced)** As noted on the Heroku page on using sqlite3 for development, it's a good idea to use the same database in development, test, and production environments to minimize the possibility of subtle incompatibilities. Follow the Heroku instructions for local PostgreSQL installation to install the PostgreSQL database on your local system. Update your **Gemfile** to eliminate the sqlite3 gem and use the pg gem exclusively, as shown in Listing 3.31. You will also have to learn about the **config/database.yml** file and how to run PostgreSQL locally. Your goal should be to create and configure both the development database and the test database to use PostgreSQL. **Warning:** You may find this exercise challenging, and I recommend it only for advanced users. If you get stuck, don't hesitate to skip it; as noted previously, the sample application developed in this tutorial is fully compatible with both SQLite and PostgreSQL.

Listing 3.29 Code for a proposed Contact page.
app/views/static_pages/contact.html.erb

```
<% provide(:title, 'Contact') %>
<h1>Contact</h1>
<p>
  Contact Ruby on Rails Tutorial about the sample app at the
  <a href="http://railstutorial.org/contact">contact page</a>.
</p>
```

Listing 3.30 The StaticPages controller spec with a base title.
spec/requests/static_pages_spec.rb

```
require 'spec_helper'

describe "Static pages" do

  let(:base_title) { "Ruby on Rails Tutorial Sample App" }
```

```ruby
describe "Home page" do

  it "should have the h1 'Sample App'" do
    visit '/static_pages/home'
    page.should have_selector('h1', :text => 'Sample App')
  end

  it "should have the title 'Home'" do
    visit '/static_pages/home'
    page.should have_selector('title', :text => "#{base_title} | Home")
  end
end

describe "Help page" do

  it "should have the h1 'Help'" do
    visit '/static_pages/help'
    page.should have_selector('h1', :text => 'Help')
  end

  it "should have the title 'Help'" do
    visit '/static_pages/help'
    page.should have_selector('title', :text => "#{base_title} | Help")
  end
end

describe "About page" do

  it "should have the h1 'About Us'" do
    visit '/static_pages/about'
    page.should have_selector('h1', :text => 'About Us')
  end

  it "should have the title 'About Us'" do
    visit '/static_pages/about'
    page.should have_selector('title', :text => "#{base_title} | About Us")
  end
end

describe "Contact page" do

  it "should have the h1 'Contact'" do
    visit '/static_pages/contact'
    page.should have_selector('h1', :text => 'Contact')
  end

  it "should have the title 'Contact'" do
    visit '/static_pages/contact'
```

```
      page.should have_selector('title', :text => "#{base_title} | Contact")
    end
  end
end
```

Listing 3.31 The **Gemfile** needed to use PostgreSQL instead of SQLite.

```
source 'https://rubygems.org'

gem 'rails', '3.2.13'
gem 'pg', '0.12.2'

group :development, :test do
  gem 'rspec-rails', '2.9.0'
end

# Gems used only for assets and not required
# in production environments by default.
group :assets do
  gem 'sass-rails',   '3.2.4'
  gem 'coffee-rails', '3.2.2'
  gem 'uglifier', '1.2.3'
end

gem 'jquery-rails', '2.0.0'

group :test do
  gem 'capybara', '1.1.2'
end
```

3.6 Advanced Setup

As mentioned briefly in Section 3.2, using the **rspec** command directly is not ideal. In this section, we'll first discuss a method to eliminate the necessity of typing **bundle exec**, and then set up testing setup to automate the running of the test suite using Guard (Section 3.6.2) and, optionally, Spork (Section 3.6.3). Finally, we'll mention a method for running tests directly inside Sublime Text, a technique especially useful when used in concert with Spork.

This section should only be attempted by fairly advanced users and can be skipped without loss of continuity. Among other things, this material is likely to go out of date faster than the rest of the tutorial, so you shouldn't expect everything on your system to match the examples exactly, and you may have to Google around to get everything to work.

3.6.1 Eliminating `bundle exec`

As mentioned briefly in Section 3.2.1, it is necessary in general to prefix commands such as **rake** or **rspec** with **bundle exec** so that the programs run in the exact gem environment specified by the **Gemfile**. (For technical reasons, the only exception to this is the **rails** command itself.) This practice is rather cumbersome, and in this section we discuss two ways to eliminate its necessity.

RVM Bundler Integration

The first and preferred method is to use the RVM Bundler integration[16] to configure the Ruby Version Manager to include the proper executables automatically in the local environment. The steps are simple if somewhat mysterious. First, run these two commands:

```
$ rvm get head && rvm reload
$ chmod +x $rvm_path/hooks/after_cd_bundler
```

Then run these:

```
$ cd ~/rails_projects/sample_app
$ bundle install --without production --binstubs=./bundler_stubs
```

Together, these commands combine RVM and Bundler magic to ensure that commands such as **rake** and **rspec** are automatically executed in the right environment. Since these files are specific to your local setup, you should add the **bundler_stubs** directory to your **.gitignore** file (Listing 3.32).

Listing 3.32 Adding **bundler_stubs** to the **.gitignore** file.

```
# Ignore bundler config
/.bundle

# Ignore the default SQLite database.
/db/*.sqlite3
```

---

16. www.beginrescueend.com/integration/bundler

```
# Ignore all logfiles and tempfiles.
/log/*.log
/tmp

# Ignore other unneeded files.
doc/
*.swp
*~
.project
.DS_Store
bundler_stubs/
```

If you add another executable (such as **guard** in Section 3.6.2), you should re-run the **bundle install** command:

```
$ bundle install --binstubs=./bundler_stubs
```

binstubs

If you're not using RVM, you can still avoid typing **bundle exec**. Bundler allows the creation of the associated binaries as follows:

```
$ bundle --binstubs
```

(In fact, this step, with a different target directory, is also used when using RVM.) This command creates all the necessary executables in the **bin/** directory of the application, so that we can now run the test suite as follows:

```
$ bin/rspec spec/
```

The same goes for **rake**, etc.:

```
$ bin/rake db:migrate
```

If you add another executable (such as **guard** in Section 3.6.2), you should re-run the bundle --binstubs command.

For the sake of readers who skip this section, the rest of this tutorial will err on the side of caution and explicitly use **bundle exec**, but of course you should feel free to use the more compact version if your system is properly configured.

3.6.2 Automated Tests with Guard

One annoyance associated with using the **rspec** command is having to switch to the command line and run the tests by hand. (A second annoyance, the slow start-up time of the test suite, is addressed in Section 3.6.3.) In this section, we'll show how to use Guard to automate the running of the tests. Guard monitors changes in the filesystem so that, for example, when we change the **static_pages_spec.rb** file only those test get run. Even better, we can configure Guard so that when, say, the **home.html.erb** file is modified, the **static_pages_spec.rb** automatically runs.

First we add **guard-rspec** to the **Gemfile** (Listing 3.33).

Listing 3.33 A **Gemfile** for the sample app, including Guard.

```
source 'https://rubygems.org'

gem 'rails', '3.2.13'

group :development do
  gem 'sqlite3', '1.3.5'
  gem 'rspec-rails', '2.9.0'
  gem 'guard-rspec', '0.5.5'
end

# Gems used only for assets and not required
# in production environments by default.
group :assets do
  gem 'sass-rails',   '3.2.4'
  gem 'coffee-rails', '3.2.2'
  gem 'uglifier', '1.2.3'
end

gem 'jquery-rails', '2.0.0'

group :test do
  gem 'rspec-rails', '2.9.0'
  gem 'capybara', '1.1.2'
  # System-dependent gems
end

group :production do
  gem 'pg', '0.12.2'
end
```

Then we have to replace the comment at the end of the test group with some system-dependent gems (OS X users may have to install Growl and growlnotify as well):

```
# Test gems on Macintosh OS X
group :test do
  gem 'rspec-rails', '2.9.0'
  gem 'capybara', '1.1.2'
  gem 'rb-fsevent', '0.4.3.1', :require => false
  gem 'growl', '1.0.3'
end
```

```
# Test gems on Linux
group :test do
  gem 'rspec-rails', '2.9.0'
  gem 'capybara', '1.1.2'
  gem 'rb-inotify', '0.8.8'
  gem 'libnotify', '0.5.9'
end
```

```
# Test gems on Windows
group :test do
  gem 'rspec-rails', '2.9.0'
  gem 'capybara', '1.1.2'
  gem 'rb-fchange', '0.0.5'
  gem 'rb-notifu', '0.0.4'
  gem 'win32console', '1.3.0'
end
```

We next install the gems by running `bundle install`:

```
$ bundle install
```

Then initialize Guard so that it works with RSpec:

```
$ bundle exec guard init rspec
Writing new Guardfile to /Users/mhartl/rails_projects/sample_app/Guardfile
rspec guard added to Guardfile, feel free to edit it
```

Now edit the resulting **Guardfile** so that Guard will run the right tests when the integration tests and views are updated (Listing 3.34).

Listing 3.34 Additions to the default **Guardfile**.

```
require 'active_support/core_ext'

guard 'rspec', :version => 2, :all_after_pass => false do
  .
  .
  .
  watch(%r{^app/controllers/(.+)_(controller)\.rb$})  do |m|
    ["spec/routing/#{m[1]}_routing_spec.rb",
     "spec/#{m[2]}s/#{m[1]}_#{m[2]}_spec.rb",
     "spec/acceptance/#{m[1]}_spec.rb",
     (m[1][/_pages/] ? "spec/requests/#{m[1]}_spec.rb" :
                       "spec/requests/#{m[1].singularize}_pages_spec.rb")]
  end
  watch(%r{^app/views/(.+)/}) do |m|
    "spec/requests/#{m[1].singularize}_pages_spec.rb"
  end
  .
  .
  .
end
```

Here the line

```
guard 'rspec', :version => 2, :all_after_pass => false do
```

ensures that Guard doesn't run all the tests after a failing test passes (to speed up the Red-Green-Refactor cycle).

We can now start **guard** as follows:

```
$ bundle exec guard
```

To eliminate the need to prefix the command with **bundle exec**, re-follow the steps in Section 3.6.1.

3.6.3 Speeding up Tests with Spork

When running **bundle exec rspec**, you may have noticed that it takes several seconds just to start running the tests, but once they start running they finish quickly. This is because each time RSpec runs the tests it has to reload the entire Rails environment. The Spork test server[17] aims to solve this problem. Spork loads the environment *once*, and then maintains a pool of processes for running future tests. Spork is particularly useful when combined with Guard (Section 3.6.2).

The first step is to add the **spork** gem dependency to the **Gemfile** (Listing 3.35).

Listing 3.35 A **Gemfile** for the sample app.

```
source 'https://rubygems.org'

gem 'rails', '3.2.13'
  .
  .
  .
group :test do
  .
  .
  .
  gem 'guard-spork', '0.3.2'
  gem 'spork', '0.9.0'
end
```

Then install Spork using **bundle install**:

```
$ bundle install
```

Next, bootstrap the Spork configuration:

```
$ bundle exec spork --bootstrap
```

Now we need to edit the RSpec configuration file, located in **spec/spec_helper.rb**, so that the environment gets loaded in a *prefork* block, which arranges for it to be loaded only once (Listing 3.36).

---

17. A *spork* is a combination spoon-fork. The project's name is a pun on Spork's use of POSIX forks.

Listing 3.36 Adding environment loading to the **Spork.prefork** block.
spec/spec_helper.rb

```ruby
require 'rubygems'
require 'spork'

Spork.prefork do
  # Loading more in this block will cause your tests to run faster. However,
  # if you change any configuration or code from libraries loaded here, you'll
  # need to restart spork for it take effect.
  # This file is copied to spec/ when you run 'rails generate rspec:install'
  ENV["RAILS_ENV"] ||= 'test'
  require File.expand_path("../../config/environment", __FILE__)
  require 'rspec/rails'
  require 'rspec/autorun'

  # Requires supporting ruby files with custom matchers and macros, etc,
  # in spec/support/ and its subdirectories.
  Dir[Rails.root.join("spec/support/**/*.rb")].each {|f| require f}

  RSpec.configure do |config|
    # == Mock Framework
    #
    # If you prefer to use mocha, flexmock or RR, uncomment the appropriate line:
    #
    # config.mock_with :mocha
    # config.mock_with :flexmock
    # config.mock_with :rr
    config.mock_with :rspec

    # Remove this line if you're not using ActiveRecord or ActiveRecord fixtures
    config.fixture_path = "#{::Rails.root}/spec/fixtures"

    # If you're not using ActiveRecord, or you'd prefer not to run each of your
    # examples within a transaction, remove the following line or assign false
    # instead of true.
    config.use_transactional_fixtures = true

    # If true, the base class of anonymous controllers will be inferred
    # automatically. This will be the default behavior in future versions of
    # rspec-rails.
    config.infer_base_class_for_anonymous_controllers = false
  end
end

Spork.each_run do
  # This code will be run each time you run your specs.

end
```

Before running Spork, we can get a baseline for the testing overhead by timing our test suite as follows:

```
$ time bundle exec rspec spec/requests/static_pages_spec.rb
......

6 examples, 0 failures

real       0m8.633s
user       0m7.240s
sys        0m1.068s
```

Here the test suite takes more than 7 seconds to run even though the actual tests run in under a tenth of a second. To speed this up, we can open a dedicated terminal window, navigate to the application root directory, and then start a Spork server:

```
$ bundle exec spork
Using RSpec
Loading Spork.prefork block...
Spork is ready and listening on 8989!
```

(To eliminate the need to prefix the command with **bundle exec**, re-follow the steps in Section 3.6.1.) In another terminal window, we can now run our test suite with the --drb ("distributed Ruby") option and verify that the environment-loading overhead is greatly reduced:

```
$ time bundle exec rspec spec/requests/static_pages_spec.rb --drb
......

6 examples, 0 failures

real       0m2.649s
user       0m1.259s
sys        0m0.258s
```

It's inconvenient to have to include the --drb option every time we run **rspec**, so I recommend adding it to the **.rspec** file in the application's root directory, as shown in Listing 3.37.

Listing 3.37 Configuring RSpec to automatically use Spork.
.rspec

```
--colour
--drb
```

One word of advice when using Spork: After changing a file included in the prefork loading (such as **routes.rb**), you will have to restart the Spork server to load the new Rails environment. If your tests are failing when you think they should be passing, quit the Spork server with `Control-C` and restart it:

```
$ bundle exec spork
Using RSpec
Loading Spork.prefork block...
Spork is ready and listening on 8989!
^C
$ bundle exec spork
```

Guard with Spork

Spork is especially useful when used with Guard, which we can arrange as follows:

```
$ bundle exec guard init spork
```

We then need to change the **Guardfile** as in Listing 3.38.

Listing 3.38 The **Guardfile** updated for Spork.
Guardfile

```
guard 'spork', :rspec_env => { 'RAILS_ENV' => 'test' } do
  watch('config/application.rb')
  watch('config/environment.rb')
  watch(%r{^config/environments/.+\.rb$})
  watch(%r{^config/initializers/.+\.rb$})
  watch('Gemfile')
  watch('Gemfile.lock')
  watch('spec/spec_helper.rb')
  watch('test/test_helper.rb')
  watch('spec/support/')
end

guard 'rspec', :version => 2, :all_after_pass => false, :cli => '--drb' do
  .
  .
  .
end
```

Note that we've updated the arguments to **guard** to include `:cli => --drb`, which ensures that Guard uses the command-line interface (cli) to the Spork server. We've also added a command to watch the **spec/support/** directory, which we'll start modifying in Chapter 5.

With that configuration in place, we can start Guard and Spork at the same time with the **guard** command:

```
$ bundle exec guard
```

Guard automatically starts a Spork server, dramatically reducing the overhead each time a test gets run.

A well-configured testing environment with Guard, Spork, and (optionally) test notifications makes test-driven development positively addictive. See the Rails Tutorial screencasts[18] for more information.

3.6.4 Tests inside Sublime Text

If you're using Sublime Text, there is a powerful set of helper commands to run tests directly inside the editor. To get them working, follow the instructions for your platform at Sublime Text 2 Ruby Tests.[19] On my platform (Macintosh OS X), I can install the commands as follows:

```
$ cd ~/Library/Application\ Support/Sublime\ Text\ 2/Packages
$ git clone https://github.com/maltize/sublime-text-2-ruby-tests.git RubyTest
```

You may also want to follow the set-up instructions for Rails Tutorial Sublime Text at this time.[20]

After restarting Sublime Text, the RubyTest package supplies the following commands:

- **Command-Shift-R**: run a single test (if run on an **it** block) or group of tests (if run on a **describe** block)

- **Command-Shift-E**: run the last test(s)

- **Command-Shift-T**: run all the tests in current file

Because test suites can become quite slow even for relatively small projects, being able to run one test (or a small group of tests) at a time can be a huge win. Even a single test requires the same Rails environment overhead, of course, which is why these

---

18. http://railstutorial.org/screencasts

19. https://github.com/maltize/sublime-text-2-ruby-tests

20. https://github.com/mhartl/rails_tutorial_sublime_text

commands are perfectly complemented by Spork: Running a single test eliminates the overhead of running the entire test file, while running Spork eliminates the overhead of starting the test environment. Here is the sequence I recommend:

1. Start Spork in a terminal window.
2. Write a single test or small group of tests.
3. Run Command-Shift-R to verify that the test or test group is red.
4. Write the corresponding application code.
5. Run Command-Shift-E to run the same test/group again, verifying that it's green.
6. Repeat steps 2–5 as necessary.
7. When reaching a natural stopping point (such as before a commit), run `rspec spec/` at the command line to confirm that the entire test suite is still green.

Even with the ability to run tests inside of Sublime Text, I still sometimes prefer using Guard, but at this point my bread-and-butter TDD technique is the one enumerated above.

CHAPTER 4

Rails-Flavored Ruby

Grounded in examples from Chapter 3, this chapter explores some elements of Ruby important for Rails. Ruby is a big language, but fortunately the subset needed to be productive as a Rails developer is relatively small. Moreover, this subset is *different* from the usual approaches to learning Ruby, which is why, if your goal is making dynamic web applications, I recommend learning Rails first, picking up bits of Ruby along the way. To become a Rails *expert*, you need to understand Ruby more deeply, and this book gives you a good foundation for developing that expertise. As noted in Section 1.1.1, after finishing the *Rails Tutorial* I suggest reading a pure Ruby book such as *Beginning Ruby*, *The Well-Grounded Rubyist*, or *The Ruby Way*.

This chapter covers a lot of material, and it's OK not to get it all on the first pass. I'll refer back to it frequently in future chapters.

4.1 Motivation

As we saw in the last chapter, it's possible to develop the skeleton of a Rails application, and even start testing it, with essentially no knowledge of the underlying Ruby language. We did this by relying on the test code provided by the tutorial and addressing each error message until the test suite was passing. This situation can't last forever, though, and we'll open this chapter with an addition to the site that bring us face-to-face with our Ruby limitations.

When we last saw our new application, we had just updated our mostly static pages to use Rails layouts to eliminate duplication in our views (Listing 4.1).

Let's focus on one particular line in Listing 4.1:

```
<%= stylesheet_link_tag "application", :media => "all" %>
```

Listing 4.1 The sample application site layout.
`app/views/layouts/application.html.erb`

```
<!DOCTYPE html>
<html>
  <head>
    <title>Ruby on Rails Tutorial Sample App | <%= yield(:title) %></title>
    <%= stylesheet_link_tag    "application", :media => "all" %>
    <%= javascript_include_tag "application" %>
    <%= csrf_meta_tags %>
  </head>
  <body>
    <%= yield %>
  </body>
</html>
```

This uses the built-in Rails function **`stylesheet_link_tag`** (which you can read more about at the Rails API) to include **`application.css`** for all media types (including computer screens and printers). To an experienced Rails developer, this line looks simple, but there are at least four potentially confusing Ruby ideas: built-in Rails methods, method invocation with missing parentheses, symbols, and hashes. We'll cover all of these ideas in this chapter.

In addition to coming equipped with a large number of built-in functions for use in the views, Rails also allows the creation of new ones. Such functions are called *helpers*; to see how to make a custom helper, let's start by examining the title line from Listing 4.1:

```
Ruby on Rails Tutorial Sample App | <%= yield(:title) %>
```

This relies on the definition of a page title (using **`provide`**) in each view, as in

```
<% provide(:title, 'Home') %>
<h1>Sample App</h1>
<p>
  This is the home page for the
  <a href="http://railstutorial.org/">Ruby on Rails Tutorial</a>
  sample application.
</p>
```

But what if we don't provide a title? It's a good convention to have a *base title* we use on every page, with an optional page title if we want to be more specific. We've *almost* achieved that with our current layout, with one wrinkle: As you can see if you delete the **provide** call in one of the views, in the absence of a page-specific title the full title appears as follows:

```
Ruby on Rails Tutorial Sample App |
```

In other words, there's a suitable base title, but there's also a trailing vertical bar character | at the end.

To solve the problem of a missing page title, we'll define a custom helper called **full_title**. The **full_title** helper returns a base title, "Ruby on Rails Tutorial Sample App," if no page title is defined, and adds a vertical bar followed by the page title if one is defined (Listing 4.2).[1]

Listing 4.2 Defining a **full_title** helper.
app/helpers/application_helper.rb

```ruby
module ApplicationHelper

  # Returns the full title on a per-page basis.
  def full_title(page_title)
    base_title = "Ruby on Rails Tutorial Sample App"
    if page_title.empty?
      base_title
    else
      "#{base_title} | #{page_title}"
    end
  end
end
```

Now that we have a helper, we can use it to simplify our layout by replacing

```erb
<title>Ruby on Rails Tutorial Sample App | <%= yield(:title) %></title>
```

with

```erb
<title><%= full_title(yield(:title)) %></title>
```

as seen in Listing 4.3.

---

1. If a helper is specific to a particular controller, you should put it in the corresponding helper file; for example, helpers for the StaticPages controller generally go in **app/helpers/static_pages_helper.rb**. In our case, we expect the **full_title** helper to be used on all the site's pages, and Rails has a special helper file for this case: **app/helpers/application_helper.rb**.

Listing 4.3 The sample application site layout.
`app/views/layouts/application.html.erb`

```
<!DOCTYPE html>
<html>
  <head>
    <title><%= full_title(yield(:title)) %></title>
    <%= stylesheet_link_tag    "application", :media => "all" %>
    <%= javascript_include_tag "application" %>
    <%= csrf_meta_tags %>
  </head>
  <body>
    <%= yield %>
  </body>
</html>
```

To put our helper to work, we can eliminate the unnecessary word "Home" from the Home page, allowing it to revert to the base title. We do this by first updating our test with the code in Listing 4.4, which updates the previous title test and adds one to test for the absence of the custom `'Home'` string in the title.

Listing 4.4 Updated tests for the Home page's title.
`spec/requests/static_pages_spec.rb`

```
require 'spec_helper'

describe "Static pages" do

  describe "Home page" do

    it "should have the h1 'Sample App'" do
      visit '/static_pages/home'
      page.should have_selector('h1', :text => 'Sample App')
    end

    it "should have the base title" do
      visit '/static_pages/home'
      page.should have_selector('title',
                        :text => "Ruby on Rails Tutorial Sample App")
    end
```

```
it "should not have a custom page title" do
  visit '/static_pages/home'
  page.should_not have_selector('title', :text => '| Home')
end
end
  .
  .
  .
end
```

See if you can figure out why we've added a new test instead of just altering the current one. (*Hint*: The answer is in Section 3.3.1.)

Let's run the test suite to verify that one test fails:

```
$ bundle exec rspec spec/requests/static_pages_spec.rb
```

To get the test suite to pass, we'll remove the **provide** line from the Home page's view, as seen in Listing 4.5.

Listing 4.5 The Home page with no custom page title.
app/views/static_pages/home.html.erb

```
<h1>Sample App</h1>
<p>
  This is the home page for the
  <a href="http://railstutorial.org/">Ruby on Rails Tutorial</a>
  sample application.
</p>
```

At this point the tests should pass:

```
$ bundle exec rspec spec/requests/static_pages_spec.rb
```

As with the line to include the application stylesheet, the code in Listing 4.2 may look simple to the eyes of an experienced Rails developer, but it's *full* of potentially confusing Ruby ideas: modules, comments, local variable assignment, booleans, control flow, string interpolation, and return values. This chapter will cover all of these ideas as well.

4.2 Strings and Methods

Our principal tool for learning Ruby will be the *Rails console*, a command-line tool
for interacting with Rails applications first seen in Section 2.3.3. The console itself is
built on top of interactive Ruby (`irb`), and thus has access to the full power of the
Ruby language. (As we'll see in Section 4.4.4, the console also has access to the Rails
environment.) Start the console at the command line as follows:

```
$ rails console
Loading development environment
>>
```

By default, the console starts in a *development environment*, which is one of three separate
environments defined by Rails (the others are *test* and *production*). This distinction won't
be important in this chapter, but we'll learn more about environments in Section 7.1.1.

   The console is a great learning tool, and you should feel free to explore—don't
worry, you (probably) won't break anything. When using the console, type Ctrl-C if
you get stuck, or Ctrl-D to exit the console altogether. Throughout the rest of this
chapter, you might find it helpful to consult the Ruby API. It's packed (perhaps even
too packed) with information; for example, to learn more about Ruby strings you can
look at the Ruby API entry for the `String` class.

4.2.1 Comments

Ruby *comments* start with the pound sign `#` (also called the "hash mark" or, more
poetically, the "octothorpe") and extend to the end of the line. Ruby ignores comments,
but they are useful for human readers (including, often, the original author!). In
the code

```
# Returns the full title on a per-page basis.
def full_title(page_title)
  .
  .
  .
end
```

the first line is a comment indicating the purpose of the subsequent function definition.

You don't ordinarily include comments in console sessions, but for instructional purposes I'll include some comments in what follows, like this:

```
$ rails console
>> 17 + 42   # Integer addition
=> 59
```

If you follow along in this section typing or copying-and-pasting commands into your own console, you can of course omit the comments if you like; the console will ignore them in any case.

4.2.2 Strings

Strings are probably the most important data structure for web applications, since web pages ultimately consist of strings of characters sent from the server to the browser. Let's start exploring strings with the console, this time started with **rails c**, which is a shortcut for **rails console**:

```
$ rails c
>> ""        # An empty string
=> ""
>> "foo"     # A nonempty string
=> "foo"
```

These are *string literals* (also, amusingly, called *literal strings*), created using the double quote character **"**. The console prints the result of evaluating each line, which in the case of a string literal is just the string itself.

We can also concatenate strings with the **+** operator:

```
>> "foo" + "bar"    # String concatenation
=> "foobar"
```

Here the result of evaluating **"foo"** plus **"bar"** is the string **"foobar"**.[2]

---

2. For more on the origins of "foo" and "bar"—and, in particular, the possible *non*-relation of "foobar" to "FUBAR"—see the Jargon File entry on "foo."

Another way to build up strings is via *interpolation* using the special syntax #{}:[3]

```
>> first_name = "Michael"      # Variable assignment
=> "Michael"
>> "#{first_name} Hartl"       # String interpolation
=> "Michael Hartl"
```

Here we've *assigned* the value **"Michael"** to the variable **first_name** and then interpolated it into the string **"#{first_name} Hartl"**. We could also assign both strings a variable name:

```
>> first_name = "Michael"
=> "Michael"
>> last_name = "Hartl"
=> "Hartl"
>> first_name + " " + last_name      # Concatenation, with a space in between
=> "Michael Hartl"
>> "#{first_name} #{last_name}"      # The equivalent interpolation
=> "Michael Hartl"
```

Note that the final two expressions are equivalent, but I prefer the interpolated version; having to add the single space **" "** seems a bit awkward.

Printing

To *print* a string, the most commonly used Ruby function is **puts** (pronounced "put ess," for "put string"):

```
>> puts "foo"      # put string
foo
=> nil
```

The **puts** method operates as a *side-effect*: the expression **puts "foo"** prints the string to the screen and then returns literally nothing: **nil** is a special Ruby value for "nothing at all." (In what follows, I'll sometimes suppress the **=> nil** part for simplicity.)

---

3. Programmers familiar with Perl or PHP should compare this to the automatic interpolation of dollar sign variables in expressions like **"foo $bar"**.

Using **puts** automatically appends a newline character \n to the output; the related **print** method does not:

```
>> print "foo"     # print string (same as puts, but without the newline)
foo=> nil
>> print "foo\n"  # Same as puts "foo"
foo
=> nil
```

Single-quoted Strings
All the examples so far have used *double-quoted strings*, but Ruby also supports *single-quoted* strings. For many uses, the two types of strings are effectively identical:

```
>> 'foo'          # A single-quoted string
=> "foo"
>> 'foo' + 'bar'
=> "foobar"
```

There's an important difference, though; Ruby won't interpolate into single-quoted strings:

```
>> '#{foo} bar'     # Single-quoted strings don't allow interpolation
=> "\#{foo} bar"
```

Note how the console returns values using double-quoted strings, which requires a backslash to *escape* special characters such as **#**.

If double-quoted strings can do everything that single-quoted strings can do, and interpolate to boot, what's the point of single-quoted strings? They are often useful because they are truly literal and contain exactly the characters you type. For example, the "backslash" character is special on most systems, as in the literal newline \n. If you want a variable to contain a literal backslash, single quotes make it easier:

```
>> '\n'         # A literal 'backslash n' combination
=> "\\n"
```

As with the **#** character in our previous example, Ruby needs to escape the backslash with an additional backslash; inside double-quoted strings, a literal backslash is represented with *two* backslashes. For a small example like this, there's not much savings, but if there are lots of things to escape it can be a real help:

```
>> 'Newlines (\n) and tabs (\t) both use the backslash character \.'
=> "Newlines (\\n) and tabs (\\t) both use the backslash character \\."
```

4.2.3   Objects and Message Passing

Everything in Ruby, including strings and even **nil**, is an *object*. We'll see the technical meaning of this in Section 4.4.2, but I don't think anyone ever understood objects by reading the definition in a book; you have to build up your intuition for objects by seeing lots of examples.

It's easier to describe what objects *do*, which is respond to messages. An object like a string, for example, can respond to the message **length**, which returns the number of characters in the string:

```
>> "foobar".length          # Passing the "length" message to a string
=> 6
```

Typically, the messages that get passed to objects are *methods*, which are functions defined on those objects.[4] Strings also respond to the **empty?** method:

```
>> "foobar".empty?
=> false
>> "".empty?
=> true
```

Note the question mark at the end of the **empty?** method. This is a Ruby convention indicating that the return value is *boolean*: **true** or **false**. Booleans are especially useful for *control flow*:

---

4. Apologies in advance for switching haphazardly between *function* and *method* throughout this chapter; in Ruby, they're the same thing: All methods are functions, and all functions are methods, because everything is an object.

```
>> s = "foobar"
>> if s.empty?
>>    "The string is empty"
>> else
>>    "The string is nonempty"
>> end
=> "The string is nonempty"
```

Booleans can also be combined using the **&&** ("and"), **||** ("or"), and **!** ("not") operators:

```
>> x = "foo"
=> "foo"
>> y = ""
=> ""
>> puts "Both strings are empty" if x.empty? && y.empty?
=> nil
>> puts "One of the strings is empty" if x.empty? || y.empty?
"One of the strings is empty"
=> nil
>> puts "x is not empty" if !x.empty?
"x is not empty"
=> nil
```

Since everything in Ruby is an object, it follows that **nil** is an object, so it too can respond to methods. One example is the **to_s** method that can convert virtually any object to a string:

```
>> nil.to_s
=> ""
```

This certainly appears to be an empty string, as we can verify by *chaining* the messages we pass to **nil**:

```
>> nil.empty?
NoMethodError: You have a nil object when you didn't expect it!
You might have expected an instance of Array.
The error occurred while evaluating nil.empty?
>> nil.to_s.empty?      # Message chaining
=> true
```

We see here that the **nil** object doesn't itself respond to the **empty?** method, but **nil.to_s** does.

There's a special method for testing for **nil**-ness, which you might be able to guess:

```
>> "foo".nil?
=> false
>> "".nil?
=> false
>> nil.nil?
=> true
```

The code

```
puts "x is not empty" if !x.empty?
```

also shows an alternate use of the **if** keyword: Ruby allows you to write a statement that is evaluated only if the statement following **if** is true. There's a complementary **unless** keyword that works the same way:

```
>> string = "foobar"
>> puts "The string '#{string}' is nonempty." unless string.empty?
The string 'foobar' is nonempty.
=> nil
```

It's worth noting that the **nil** object is special, in that it is the *only* Ruby object that is false in a boolean context, apart from **false** itself:

```
>> if nil
>>   true
>> else
>>   false        # nil is false
>> end
=> false
```

In particular, all other Ruby objects are *true*, even 0:

```
>> if 0
>>   true         # 0 (and everything other than nil and false itself) is true
>> else
>>   false
>> end
=> true
```

4.2.4 Method Definitions

The console allows us to define methods the same way we did with the **home** action from Listing 3.6 or the **full_title** helper from Listing 4.2. (Defining methods in the console is a bit cumbersome, and ordinarily you would use a file, but it's convenient for demonstration purposes.) For example, let's define a function **string_message** that takes a single *argument* and returns a message based on whether the argument is empty or not:

```
>> def string_message(string)
>>   if string.empty?
>>     "It's an empty string!"
>>   else
>>     "The string is nonempty."
>>   end
>> end
=> nil
>> puts string_message("")
It's an empty string!
>> puts string_message("foobar")
The string is nonempty.
```

Note that Ruby functions have an *implicit return*, meaning they return the last statement evaluated—in this case, one of the two message strings, depending on whether the method's argument **string** is empty or not. Ruby also has an explicit return option; the following function is equivalent to the one above:

```
>> def string_message(string)
>>   return "It's an empty string!" if string.empty?
>>   return "The string is nonempty."
>> end
```

The alert reader might notice at this point that the second **return** here is actually unnecessary—being the last expression in the function, the string **"The string is nonempty."** will be returned regardless of the **return** keyword, but using **return** in both places has a pleasing symmetry to it.

4.2.5 Back to the Title Helper

We are now in a position to understand the **full_title** helper from Listing 4.2:[5]

```
module ApplicationHelper

  # Returns the full title on a per-page basis.    # Documentation comment
  def full_title(page_title)                       # Method definition
    base_title = "Ruby on Rails Tutorial Sample App"  # Variable assignment
    if page_title.empty?                           # Boolean test
      base_title                                   # Implicit return
    else
      "#{base_title} | #{page_title}"              # String interpolation
    end
  end
end
```

These elements—function definition, variable assignment, boolean tests, control flow, and string interpolation—come together to make a compact helper method for use in our site layout. The final element is **module ApplicationHelper**: Modules give us a way to package together related methods, which can then be *mixed in* to Ruby classes using **include**. When writing ordinary Ruby, you often write modules and include them explicitly yourself, but in the case of a helper module Rails handles the inclusion for us. The result is that the **full_title** method is automagically available in all our views.

4.3 Other Data Structures

Although web apps are ultimately about strings, actually *making* those strings requires using other data structures as well. In this section, we'll learn about some Ruby data structures important for writing Rails applications.

4.3.1 Arrays and Ranges

An array is just a list of elements in a particular order. We haven't discussed arrays yet in the *Rails Tutorial*, but understanding them gives a good foundation for understanding

---

5. Well, there will still be *one* thing left that we don't understand, which is how Rails ties this all together: mapping URIs to actions, making the **full_title** helper available in views, etc. This is an interesting subject, and I encourage you to investigate it further, but knowing exactly *how* Rails works is not necessary when *using* Rails. (For a deeper understanding, I recommend *The Rails 3 Way* by Obie Fernandez.)

hashes (Section 4.3.3) and for aspects of Rails data modeling (such as the **has_many** association seen in Section 2.3.3 and covered more in Section 10.1.3).

So far we've spent a lot of time understanding strings, and there's a natural way to get from strings to arrays using the **split** method:

```
>>  "foo bar      baz".split     # Split a string into a three-element array
=>  ["foo", "bar", "baz"]
```

The result of this operation is an array of three strings. By default, **split** divides a string into an array by splitting on whitespace, but you can split on nearly anything else as well:

```
>> "fooxbarxbazx".split('x')
=> ["foo", "bar", "baz"]
```

As is conventional in most computer languages, Ruby arrays are *zero-offset*, which means that the first element in the array has index 0, the second has index 1, and so on:

```
>> a = [42, 8, 17]
=> [42, 8, 17]
>> a[0]                  # Ruby uses square brackets for array access.
=> 42
>> a[1]
=> 8
>> a[2]
=> 17
>> a[-1]                 # Indices can even be negative!
=> 17
```

We see here that Ruby uses square brackets to access array elements. In addition to this bracket notation, Ruby offers synonyms for some commonly accessed elements:[6]

```
>> a                     # Just a reminder of what 'a' is
=> [42, 8, 17]
>> a.first
=> 42
>> a.second
=> 8
>> a.last
```

---

6. The **second** method used here isn't currently part of Ruby itself, but rather is added by Rails. It works in this case because the Rails console automatically includes the Rails extensions to Ruby.

```
=> 17
>> a.last == a[-1]      # Comparison using ==
=> true
```

This last line introduces the equality comparison operator **==**, which Ruby shares with many other languages, along with the associated **!=** ("not equal"), etc.:

```
>> x = a.length         # Like strings, arrays respond to the 'length' method.
=> 3
>> x == 3
=> true
>> x == 1
=> false
>> x != 1
=> true
>> x >= 1
=> true
>> x < 1
=> false
```

In addition to **length** (seen in the first line above), arrays respond to a wealth of other methods:

```
>> a
=> [42, 8, 17]
>> a.sort
=> [8, 17, 42]
>> a.reverse
=> [17, 8, 42]
>> a.shuffle
=> [17, 42, 8]
>> a
=> [42, 8, 17]
```

Note that none of the methods above changes **a** itself. To *mutate* the array, use the corresponding "bang" methods (so-called because the exclamation point is usually pronounced "bang" in this context):

```
>> a
=> [42, 8, 17]
```

```
>> a.sort!
=> [8, 17, 42]
>> a
=> [8, 17, 42]
```

You can also add to arrays with the **push** method or its equivalent operator, **<<**:

```
>> a.push(6)                 # Pushing 6 onto an array
=> [42, 8, 17, 6]
>> a << 7                    # Pushing 7 onto an array
=> [42, 8, 17, 6, 7]
>> a << "foo" << "bar"       # Chaining array pushes
=> [42, 8, 17, 6, 7, "foo", "bar"]
```

This last example shows that you can chain pushes together and also that, unlike arrays in many other languages, Ruby arrays can contain a mixture of different types (in this case, integers and strings).

Before we saw **split** convert a string to an array. We can also go the other way with the **join** method:

```
>> a
=> [42, 8, 17, 7, "foo", "bar"]
>> a.join                    # Join on nothing
=> "428177foobar"
>> a.join(', ')              # Join on comma-space
=> "42, 8, 17, 7, foo, bar"
```

Closely related to arrays are *ranges*, which can probably most easily be understood by converting them to arrays using the **to_a** method:

```
>> 0..9
=> 0..9
>> 0..9.to_a                 # Oops, call to_a on 9
NoMethodError: undefined method `to_a' for 9:Fixnum
>> (0..9).to_a               # Use parentheses to call to_a on the range
=> [0, 1, 2, 3, 4, 5, 6, 7, 8, 9]
```

Although **0..9** is a valid range, the second expression above shows that we need to add parentheses to call a method on it.

Ranges are useful for pulling out array elements:

```
>> a = %w[foo bar baz quux]              # Use %w to make a string array.
=> ["foo", "bar", "baz", "quux"]
>> a[0..2]
=> ["foo", "bar", "baz"]
```

Ranges also work with characters:

```
>> ('a'..'e').to_a
=> ["a", "b", "c", "d", "e"]
```

4.3.2 Blocks

Both arrays and ranges respond to a host of methods that accept *blocks*, which are simultaneously one of Ruby's most powerful and most confusing features:

```
>> (1..5).each { |i| puts 2 * i }
2
4
6
8
10
=> 1..5
```

This code calls the **each** method on the range **(1..5)** and passes it the block **{ |i| puts 2 * i }**. The vertical bars around the variable name in **|i|** are Ruby syntax for a block variable, and it's up to the method to know what to do with the block. In this case, the range's **each** method can handle a block with a single local variable, which we've called **i**, and it just executes the block for each value in the range.

Curly braces are one way to indicate a block, but there is a second way as well:

```
>> (1..5).each do |i|
?>    puts 2 * i
>> end
2
4
6
8
10
=> 1..5
```

Blocks can be more than one line, and often are. In the *Rails Tutorial* we'll follow the common convention of using curly braces only for short one-line blocks and the **do..end** syntax for longer one-liners and for multi-line blocks:

```
>> (1..5).each do |number|
?>   puts 2 * number
>>   puts '--'
>> end
2
--
4
--
6
--
8
--
10
--
=> 1..5
```

Here I've used **number** in place of **i** just to emphasize that any variable name will do.

Unless you already have a substantial programming background, there is no shortcut to understanding blocks; you just have to see them a lot, and eventually you'll get used to them.[7] Luckily, humans are quite good at making generalizations from concrete examples; here are a few more, including a couple using the **map** method:

```
>> 3.times { puts "Betelgeuse!" }    # 3.times takes a block with no variables.
"Betelgeuse!"
"Betelgeuse!"
"Betelgeuse!"
=> 3
>> (1..5).map { |i| i**2 }           # The ** notation is for 'power'.
=> [1, 4, 9, 16, 25]
>> %w[a b c]                         # Recall that %w makes string arrays.
=> ["a", "b", "c"]
>> %w[a b c].map { |char| char.upcase }
=> ["A", "B", "C"]
>> %w[A B C].map { |char| char.downcase }
=> ["a", "b", "c"]
```

---

7. Programming experts, on the other hand, might benefit from knowing that blocks are *closures*, which are one-shot anonymous functions with data attached.

As you can see, the **map** method returns the result of applying the given block to each element in the array or range.

By the way, we're now in a position to understand the line of Ruby I threw into Section 1.4.4 to generate random subdomains:

```
('a'..'z').to_a.shuffle[0..7].join
```

Let's build it up step-by-step:

```
>> ('a'..'z').to_a              # An alphabet array
=> ["a", "b", "c", "d", "e", "f", "g", "h", "i", "j", "k", "l", "m", "n", "o",
"p", "q", "r", "s", "t", "u", "v", "w", "x", "y", "z"]
>> ('a'..'z').to_a.shuffle          # Shuffle it.
=> ["c", "g", "l", "k", "h", "z", "s", "i", "n", "d", "y", "u", "t", "j", "q",
"b", "r", "o", "f", "e", "w", "v", "m", "a", "x", "p"]
>> ('a'..'z').to_a.shuffle[0..7]        # Pull out the first eight elements.
=> ["f", "w", "i", "a", "h", "p", "c", "x"]
>> ('a'..'z').to_a.shuffle[0..7].join # Join them together to make one string.
=> "mznpybuj"
```

4.3.3 Hashes and Symbols

Hashes are essentially a generalization of arrays: You can think of hashes basically like arrays, but not limited to integer indices. (In fact, some languages, especially Perl, sometimes call hashes *associative arrays* for this reason.) Instead, hash indices, or *keys*, can be almost any object. For example, we can use strings as keys:

```
>> user = {}                    # {} is an empty hash.
=> {}
>> user["first_name"] = "Michael"     # Key "first_name", value "Michael"
=> "Michael"
>> user["last_name"] = "Hartl"        # Key "last_name", value "Hartl"
=> "Hartl"
>> user["first_name"]                 # Element access is like arrays.
=> "Michael"
>> user                          # A literal representation of the hash
=> {"last_name"=>"Hartl", "first_name"=>"Michael"}
```

Hashes are indicated with curly braces containing key-value pairs; a pair of braces with no key-value pairs—i.e., `{}`—is an empty hash. It's important to note that the curly braces for hashes have nothing to do with the curly braces for blocks. (Yes, this can be confusing.) Although hashes resemble arrays, one important difference is that hashes don't generally guarantee keeping their elements in a particular order.[8] If order matters, use an array.

Instead of defining hashes one item at a time using square brackets, it's easy to use a literal representation with keys and values separated by `=>`, called a "hashrocket":

```
>> user = { "first_name" => "Michael", "last_name" => "Hartl" }
=> {"last_name"=>"Hartl", "first_name"=>"Michael"}
```

Here I've used the usual Ruby convention of putting an extra space at the two ends of the hash—a convention ignored by the console output. (Don't ask me why the spaces are conventional; probably some early influential Ruby programmer liked the look of the extra spaces, and the convention stuck.)

So far we've used strings as hash keys, but in Rails it is much more common to use *symbols* instead. Symbols look kind of like strings, but prefixed with a colon instead of surrounded by quotes. For example, **:name** is a symbol. You can think of symbols as basically strings without all the extra baggage:[9]

```
>> "name".split('')
=> ["n", "a", "m", "e"]
>> :name.split('')
NoMethodError: undefined method `split' for :name:Symbol
>> "foobar".reverse
=> "raboof"
>> :foobar.reverse
NoMethodError: undefined method `reverse' for :foobar:Symbol
```

---

8. Ruby 1.9 actually guarantees that hashes keep their elements in the same order entered, but it would be unwise to ever count on a particular ordering.

9. As a result of having less baggage, symbols are easier to compare to each other; strings need to be compared character by character, while symbols can be compared all in one go. This makes them ideal for use as hash keys.

Symbols are a special Ruby data type shared with very few other languages, so they may seem weird at first, but Rails uses them a lot, so you'll get used to them fast.

In terms of symbols as hash keys, we can define a **user** hash as follows:

```
>> user = { :name => "Michael Hartl", :email => "michael@example.com" }
=> {:name=>"Michael Hartl", :email=>"michael@example.com"}
>> user[:name]                    # Access the value corresponding to :name.
=> "Michael Hartl"
>> user[:password]                # Access the value of an undefined key.
=> nil
```

We see here from the last example that the hash value for an undefined key is simply **nil**.

Since it's so common for hashes to use symbols as keys, Ruby 1.9 supports a new syntax just for this special case:

```
>> h1 = { :name => "Michael Hartl", :email => "michael@example.com" }
=> {:name=>"Michael Hartl", :email=>"michael@example.com"}
>> h2 = { name: "Michael Hartl", email: "michael@example.com" }
=> {:name=>"Michael Hartl", :email=>"michael@example.com"}
>> h1 == h2
=> true
```

The second syntax replaces the symbol/hashrocket combination with the name of the key followed by a colon and a value:

```
{ name: "Michael Hartl", email: "michael@example.com" }
```

This construction more closely follows the hash notation in other languages (such as JavaScript) and enjoys growing popularity in the Rails community. Both syntaxes are still in common use, so it's essential to be able to recognize them. Most hashes in the rest of this book use the new notation, which won't work with Ruby 1.8.7 or earlier; if you are using an earlier version of Ruby, you will either have to upgrade to Ruby 1.9 (recommended) or use the old hash notation.

Hash values can be virtually anything, even other hashes, as seen in Listing 4.6.

Listing 4.6 Nested hashes.

```
>> params = {}           # Define a hash called 'params' (short for 'parameters').
=> {}
>> params[:user] = { name: "Michael Hartl", email: "mhartl@example.com" }
=> {:name=>"Michael Hartl", :email=>"mhartl@example.com"}
>> params
=> {:user=>{:name=>"Michael Hartl", :email=>"mhartl@example.com"}}
>> params[:user][:email]
=> "mhartl@example.com"
```

These sorts of hashes-of-hashes, or *nested hashes*, are heavily used by Rails, as we'll see starting in Section 7.3.

As with arrays and ranges, hashes respond to the **each** method. For example, consider a hash named **flash** with keys for two conditions, **:success** and **:error**:

```
>> flash = { success: "It worked!", error: "It failed." }
=> {:success=>"It worked!", :error=>"It failed."}
>> flash.each do |key, value|
?>   puts "Key #{key.inspect} has value #{value.inspect}"
>> end
Key :success has value "It worked!"
Key :error has value "It failed."
```

Note that, while the **each** method for arrays takes a block with only one variable, **each** for hashes takes two, a *key* and a *value*. Thus, the **each** method for a hash iterates through the hash one key-value *pair* at a time.

The last example uses the useful **inspect** method, which returns a string with a literal representation of the object it's called on:

```
>> puts (1..5).to_a         # Put an array as a string.
1
2
3
4
5
>> puts (1..5).to_a.inspect  # Put a literal array.
[1, 2, 3, 4, 5]
```

```
>> puts :name, :name.inspect
name
:name
>> puts "It worked!", "It worked!".inspect
It worked!
"It worked!"
```

By the way, using **inspect** to print an object is common enough that there's a shortcut for it, the **p** function:

```
>> p :name              # Same as 'puts :name.inspect'
:name
```

4.3.4 CSS revisited

It's time now to revisit the line from Listing 4.1 used in the layout to include the cascading style sheets:

```
<%= stylesheet_link_tag "application", :media => "all" %>
```

We are now nearly in a position to understand this. As mentioned briefly in Section 4.1, Rails defines a special function to include stylesheets, and

```
stylesheet_link_tag "application", :media => "all"
```

is a call to this function. But there are two mysteries. First, where are the parentheses? In Ruby, they are optional; these two lines are equivalent:

```
# Parentheses on function calls are optional.
stylesheet_link_tag("application", :media => "all")
stylesheet_link_tag "application", :media => "all"
```

Second, the **:media** argument sure looks like a hash, but where are the curly braces? When hashes are the *last* argument in a function call, the curly braces are optional; these two lines are equivalent:

```
# Curly braces on final hash arguments are optional.
stylesheet_link_tag "application", { :media => "all" }
stylesheet_link_tag "application", :media => "all"
```

So, we see now that the line

```
stylesheet_link_tag "application", :media => "all"
```

calls the **stylesheet_link_tag** function with two arguments: a string, indicating the path to the stylesheet, and a hash, indicating the media type. Because of the <%= %> brackets, the results are inserted into the template by ERb, and if you view the source of the page in your browser you should see the HTML needed to include a stylesheet (Listing 4.7). (You may see some extra things, like **?body=1**, after the CSS filenames. These are inserted by Rails to ensure that browsers reload the CSS when it changes on the server.)

Listing 4.7 The HTML source produced by the CSS includes.

```
<link href="/assets/application.css" media="all" rel="stylesheet"
type="text/css" />
```

If you actually view the CSS file by navigating to http://localhost:3000/assets/application.css, you'll see that (apart from some comments) it is empty. We'll set about changing this in Chapter 5.

4.4 Ruby Classes

We've said before that everything in Ruby is an object, and in this section we'll finally get to define some of our own. Ruby, like many object-oriented languages, uses *classes* to organize methods; these classes are then *instantiated* to create objects. If you're new to object-oriented programming, this may sound like gibberish, so let's look at some concrete examples.

4.4.1 Constructors

We've seen lots of examples of using classes to instantiate objects, but we have yet to do so explicitly. For example, we instantiated a string using the double quote characters, which is a *literal constructor* for strings:

```
>> s = "foobar"        # A literal constructor for strings using double quotes
=> "foobar"
>> s.class
=> String
```

We see here that strings respond to the method **class** and simply return the class they belong to.

Instead of using a literal constructor, we can use the equivalent *named constructor*, which involves calling the **new** method on the class name:[10]

```
>> s = String.new("foobar")    # A named constructor for a string
=> "foobar"
>> s.class
=> String
>> s == "foobar"
=> true
```

This is equivalent to the literal constructor, but it's more explicit about what we're doing.

Arrays work the same way as strings:

```
>> a = Array.new([1, 3, 2])
=> [1, 3, 2]
```

Hashes, in contrast, are different. While the array constructor **Array.new** takes an initial value for the array, **Hash.new** takes a *default* value for the hash, which is the value of the hash for a nonexistent key:

```
>> h = Hash.new
=> {}
>> h[:foo]              # Try to access the value for the nonexistent key :foo.
=> nil
>> h = Hash.new(0)      # Arrange for nonexistent keys to return 0 instead of nil.
=> {}
>> h[:foo]
=> 0
```

When a method gets called on the class itself, as in the case of **new**, it's called a *class method*. The result of calling **new** on a class is an object of that class, also called an *instance* of the class. A method called on an instance, such as **length**, is called an *instance method*.

---

10. These results will vary based on the version of Ruby you are using. This example assumes you are using Ruby 1.9.3.

4.4.2 Class Inheritance

When learning about classes, it's useful to find out the *class hierarchy* using the **superclass** method:

```
>> s = String.new("foobar")
=> "foobar"
>> s.class                    # Find the class of s.
=> String
>> s.class.superclass         # Find the superclass of String.
=> Object
>> s.class.superclass.superclass  # Ruby 1.9 uses a new BasicObject base class
=> BasicObject
>> s.class.superclass.superclass.superclass
=> nil
```

A diagram of this inheritance hierarchy appears in Figure 4.1. We see here that the superclass of **String** is **Object** and the superclass of **Object** is **BasicObject**, but **BasicObject** has no superclass. This pattern is true of every Ruby object: Trace back the class hierarchy far enough and every class in Ruby ultimately inherits from **BasicObject**, which has no superclass itself. This is the technical meaning of "everything in Ruby is an object."

To understand classes a little more deeply, there's no substitute for making one of our own. Let's make a **Word** class with a **palindrome?** method that returns **true** if the word is the same spelled forward and backward:

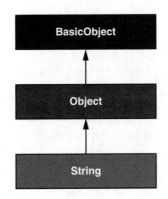

Figure 4.1 The inheritance hierarchy for the **String** class.

```
>> class Word
>>   def palindrome?(string)
>>     string == string.reverse
>>   end
>> end
=> nil
```

We can use it as follows:

```
>> w = Word.new                    # Make a new Word object.
=> #<Word:0x22d0b20>
>> w.palindrome?("foobar")
=> false
>> w.palindrome?("level")
=> true
```

If this example strikes you as a bit contrived, good; this is by design. It's odd to create a new class just to create a method that takes a string as an argument. Since a word *is a* string, it's more natural to have our **Word** class *inherit* from **String**, as seen in Listing 4.8. (You should exit the console and re-enter it to clear out the old definition of **Word**.)

Listing 4.8 Defining a **Word** class in the console.

```
>> class Word < String              # Word inherits from String.
>>   # Returns true if the string is its own reverse.
>>   def palindrome?
>>     self == self.reverse         # self is the string itself.
>>   end
>> end
=> nil
```

Here **Word < String** is the Ruby syntax for inheritance (discussed briefly in Section 3.1.2), which ensures that, in addition to the new **palindrome?** method, words also have all the same methods as strings:

```
>> s = Word.new("level")     # Make a new Word, initialized with "level".
=> "level"
>> s.palindrome?             # Words have the palindrome? method.
=> true
>> s.length                  # Words also inherit all the normal string methods.
=> 5
```

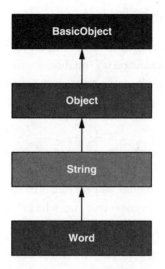

Figure 4.2   The inheritance hierarchy for the (non-built-in) **Word** class from Listing 4.8.

Since the **Word** class inherits from **String**, we can use the console to see the class hierarchy explicitly:

```
>> s.class
=> Word
>> s.class.superclass
=> String
>> s.class.superclass.superclass
=> Object
```

This hierarchy is illustrated in Figure 4.2.

In Listing 4.8, note that checking that the word is its own reverse involves accessing the word inside the **Word** class. Ruby allows us to do this using the **self** keyword: Inside the **Word** class, **self** is the object itself, which means we can use

```
self == self.reverse
```

to check if the word is a palindrome.[11]

---

11. For more on Ruby classes and the **self** keyword, see the RailsTips post "Class and Instance Variables in Ruby."

4.4.3 Modifying Built-in Classes

While inheritance is a powerful idea, in the case of palindromes it might be even more natural to add the **palindrome?** method to the **String** class itself, so that (among other things) we can call **palindrome?** on a string literal, which we currently can't do:

```
>> "level".palindrome?
NoMethodError: undefined method `palindrome?' for "level":String
```

Somewhat amazingly, Ruby lets you do just this; Ruby classes can be *opened* and modified, allowing ordinary mortals such as ourselves to add methods to them:[12]

```
>> class String
>>    # Returns true if the string is its own reverse.
>>    def palindrome?
>>      self == self.reverse
>>    end
>> end
=> nil
>> "deified".palindrome?
=> true
```

(I don't know which is cooler: that Ruby lets you add methods to built-in classes or that **"deified"** is a palindrome.)

Modifying built-in classes is a powerful technique, but with great power comes great responsibility, and it's considered bad form to add methods to built-in classes without having a *really* good reason for doing so. Rails does have some good reasons; for example, in web applications we often want to prevent variables from being *blank*—e.g., a user's name should be something other than spaces and other whitespace—so Rails adds a **blank?** method to Ruby. Since the Rails console automatically includes the Rails extensions, we can see an example here (this won't work in plain **irb**):

```
>> "".blank?
=> true
>> "      ".empty?
=> false
>> "      ".blank?
```

---

12. For those familiar with JavaScript, this functionality is comparable to using a built-in class prototype object to augment the class. (Thanks to reader Erik Eldridge for pointing this out.)

```
=> true
>> nil.blank?
=> true
```

We see that a string of spaces is not *empty*, but it is *blank*. Note also that **nil** is blank; since **nil** isn't a string, this is a hint that Rails actually adds **blank?** to **String**'s base class, which (as we saw at the beginning of this section) is **Object** itself. We'll see some other examples of Rails additions to Ruby classes in Section 8.2.1.

4.4.4 A Controller Class

All this talk about classes and inheritance may have triggered a flash of recognition, because we have seen both before, in the StaticPages controller (Listing 3.15):

```
class StaticPagesController < ApplicationController

  def home
  end

  def help
  end

  def about
  end
end
```

You're now in a position to appreciate, at least vaguely, what this code means: **StaticPagesController** is a class that inherits from **ApplicationController** and comes equipped with **home**, **help**, and **about** methods. Since each Rails console session loads the local Rails environment, we can even create a controller explicitly and examine its class hierarchy:[13]

```
>> controller = StaticPagesController.new
=> #<StaticPagesController:0x22855d0>
>> controller.class
=> StaticPagesController
>> controller.class.superclass
=> ApplicationController
```

---

13. You don't have to know what each class in this hierarchy does. *I* don't know what they all do, and I've been programming in Ruby on Rails since 2005. This means either that (a) I'm grossly incompetent or (b) you can be a skilled Rails developer without knowing all its innards. I hope for both our sakes that it's the latter.

```
>> controller.class.superclass.superclass
=> ActionController::Base
>> controller.class.superclass.superclass.superclass
=> ActionController::Metal
>> controller.class.superclass.superclass.superclass.superclass
=> AbstractController::Base
>> controller.class.superclass.superclass.superclass.superclass.superclass
=> Object
```

A diagram of this hierarchy appears in Figure 4.3.

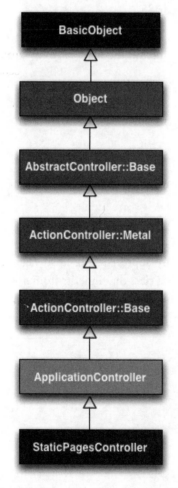

Figure 4.3   The inheritance hierarchy for the StaticPages controller.

We can even call the controller actions inside the console, which are just methods:

```
>> controller.home
=> nil
```

Here the return value is **nil** because the **home** action is blank.

But wait—actions don't have return values, at least not ones that matter. The point of the **home** action, as we saw in Chapter 3, is to render a web page, not to return a value. And I sure don't remember ever calling **StaticPagesController.new** anywhere. What's going on?

What's going on is that Rails is *written in* Ruby, but Rails isn't Ruby. Some Rails classes are used like ordinary Ruby objects, but some are just grist for Rails' magic mill. Rails is *sui generis* and should be studied and understood separately from Ruby. This is why, if your principal programming interest is writing web applications, I recommend learning Rails first, then learning Ruby, then looping back to Rails.

4.4.5 A User Class

We end our tour of Ruby with a complete class of our own, a **User** class that anticipates the User model coming up in Chapter 6.

So far we've entered class definitions at the console, but this quickly becomes tiresome; instead, create the file **example_user.rb** in your application root directory and fill it with the contents of Listing 4.9.

Listing 4.9 Code for an example user.
example_user.rb

```ruby
class User
  attr_accessor :name, :email

  def initialize(attributes = {})
    @name  = attributes[:name]
    @email = attributes[:email]
  end

  def formatted_email
    "#{@name} <#{@email}>"
  end
end
```

There's quite a bit going on here, so let's take it step by step. The first line,

```
attr_accessor :name, :email
```

creates *attribute accessors* corresponding to a user's name and email address. This creates "getter" and "setter" methods that allow us to retrieve (get) and assign (set) **@name** and **@email** *instance variables*, which were mentioned briefly in Section 2.2.2. In Rails, the principal importance of instance variables is that they are automatically available in the views, but in general they are used for variables that need to be available throughout a Ruby class. (We'll have more to say about this in a moment.) Instance variables always begin with an **@** sign, and are **nil** when undefined.

The first method, **initialize**, is special in Ruby: It's the method called when we execute **User.new**. This particular **initialize** takes one argument, **attributes**:

```
def initialize(attributes = {})
  @name  = attributes[:name]
  @email = attributes[:email]
end
```

Here the **attributes** variable has a *default value* equal to the empty hash, so that we can define a user with no name or email address (recall from Section 4.3.3 that hashes return **nil** for nonexistent keys, so **attributes[:name]** will be **nil** if there is no **:name** key, and similarly for **attributes[:email]**).

Finally, our class defines a method called **formatted_email** that uses the values of the assigned **@name** and **@email** variables to build up a nicely formatted version of the user's email address using string interpolation (Section 4.2.2):

```
def formatted_email
  "#{@name} <#{@email}>"
end
```

Because **@name** and **@email** are both instance variables (as indicated with the **@** sign), they are automatically available in the **formatted_email** method.

Let's fire up the console, **require** the example user code, and take our User class out for a spin:

```
>> require './example_user'      # This is how you load the example_user code.
=> ["User"]
>> example = User.new
=> #<User:0x224ceec @email=nil, @name=nil>
>> example.name                  # nil since attributes[:name] is nil
=> nil
>> example.name = "Example User"           # Assign a non-nil name
=> "Example User"
>> example.email = "user@example.com"      # and a non-nil email address
=> "user@example.com"
>> example.formatted_email
=> "Example User <user@example.com>"
```

Here the **'.'** is Unix for "current directory," and **'./example_user'** tells Ruby to look for an example user file relative to that location. The subsequent code creates an empty example user and then fills in the name and email address by assigning directly to the corresponding attributes (assignments made possible by the **attr_accessor** line in Listing 4.9). When we write

```
example.name = "Example User"
```

Ruby is setting the **@name** variable to **"Example User"** (and similarly for the **email** attribute), which we then use in the **formatted_email** method.

Recalling from Section 4.3.4 that we can omit the curly braces for final hash arguments, we can create another user by passing a hash to the **initialize** method to create a user with predefined attributes:

```
>> user = User.new(name: "Michael Hartl", email: "mhartl@example.com")
=> #<User:0x225167c @email="mhartl@example.com", @name="Michael Hartl">
>> user.formatted_email
=> "Michael Hartl <mhartl@example.com>"
```

We will see starting in Chapter 7 that initializing objects using a hash argument is common in Rails applications.

4.5 Conclusion

This concludes our overview of the Ruby language. In Chapter 5, we'll start putting it to good use in developing the sample application.

We won't be using the **example_user.rb** file from Section 4.4.5, so I suggest removing it:

```
$ rm example_user.rb
```

Then commit the other changes to the main source code repository:

```
$ git add .
$ git commit -m "Add a full_title helper"
```

4.6 Exercises

1. By replacing the question marks in Listing 4.10 with the appropriate methods, combine **split**, **shuffle**, and **join** to write a function that shuffles the letters in a given string.
2. Using Listing 4.11 as a guide, add a **shuffle** method to the **String** class.
3. Create three hashes called **person1**, **person2**, and **person3**, with first and last names under the keys **:first** and **:last**. Then create a **params** hash so that **params [:father]** is **person1**, **params[:mother]** is **person2**, and **params[:child]** is **person3**. Verify that, for example, **params[:father][:first]** has the right value.
4. Find an online version of the Ruby API and read about the **Hash** method **merge**.
5. Find and follow the Ruby Koans to reach Ruby enlightenment.

Listing 4.10 Skeleton for a string shuffle function.

```
>> def string_shuffle(s)
>>    s.split('').?.?
>> end
=> nil
>> string_shuffle("foobar")
```

Listing 4.11 Skeleton for a **shuffle** method attached to the **String** class.

```
>> class String
>>   def shuffle
>>     self.split('').?.?
>>   end
>> end
=> nil
>> "foobar".shuffle
```

CHAPTER 5
Filling in the Layout

In the process of taking a brief tour of Ruby in Chapter 4, we learned about including the application stylesheet into the sample application—but, as noted in Section 4.3.4, this stylesheet is currently empty. In this chapter, we'll change this by incorporating the *Bootstrap* framework into our application, and then we'll add some custom styles of our own.[1] We'll also start filling in the layout with links to the pages (such as Home and About) that we've created so far (Section 5.1). Along the way, we'll learn about partials, Rails routes, and the asset pipeline, including an introduction to Sass (Section 5.2). We'll also refactor the tests from Chapter 3 using the latest RSpec techniques. We'll end by taking a first important step toward letting users sign up to our site.

5.1 Adding Some Structure

Rails Tutorial is a book on web development, not web design, but it would be depressing to work on an application that looks like *complete* crap, so in this section we'll add some structure to the layout and give it some minimal styling with CSS. In addition to using some custom CSS rules, we'll make use of Bootstrap, an open-source web design framework from Twitter. We'll also give our *code* some styling, so to speak, using *partials* to tidy up the layout once it gets a little cluttered.

When building web applications, it is often useful to get a high-level overview of the user interface as early as possible. Throughout the rest of this book, I will thus often include *mockups* (in a web context often called *wireframes*), which are rough sketches

---

1. Thanks to reader Colm Tuite for his excellent work in helping to convert the sample application over to Bootstrap.

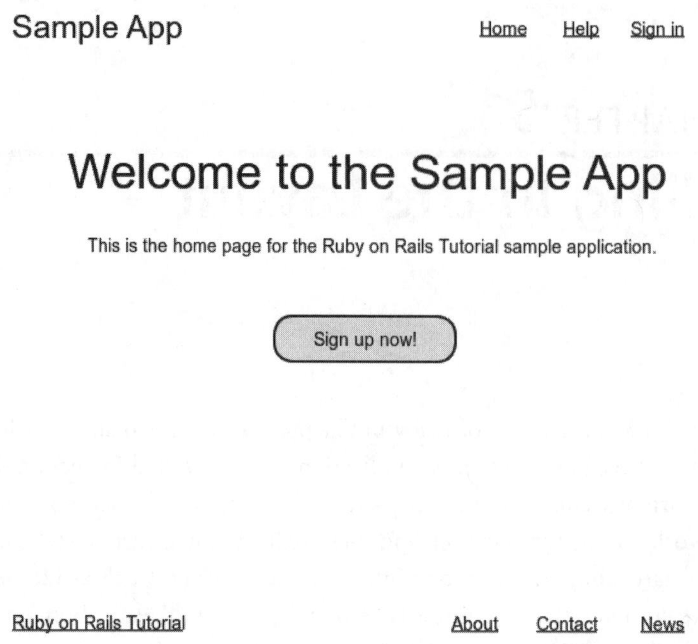

Sample App   Home   Help   Sign in

Welcome to the Sample App

This is the home page for the Ruby on Rails Tutorial sample application.

Sign up now!

Ruby on Rails Tutorial   About   Contact   News

Figure 5.1   A mockup of the sample application's Home page.

of what the eventual application will look like.[2] In this chapter, we will principally be developing the static pages introduced in Section 3.1, including a site logo, a navigation header, and a site footer. A mockup for the most important of these pages, the Home page, appears in Figure 5.1. You can see the final result in Figure 5.7. You'll note that it differs in some details—for example, we'll end up adding a Rails logo on the page—but that's fine, since a mockup need not be exact.

As usual, if you're using Git for version control, now would be a good time to make a new branch:

```
$ git checkout -b filling-in-layout
```

---

2. The mockups in the *Ruby on Rails Tutorial* are made with an excellent online mockup application called Mockingbird.

5.1.1 Site Navigation

As a first step toward adding links and styles to the sample application, we'll update the site layout file **application.html.erb** (last seen in Listing 4.3) with additional HTML structure. This includes some additional divisions, some CSS classes, and the start of our site navigation. The full file is in Listing 5.1; explanations for the various pieces follow immediately thereafter. If you'd rather not delay gratification, you can see the results in Figure 5.2. (*Note:* it's not (yet) very gratifying.)

Listing 5.1 The site layout with added structure.
app/views/layouts/application.html.erb

```erb
<!DOCTYPE html>
<html>
  <head>
    <title><%= full_title(yield(:title)) %></title>
    <%= stylesheet_link_tag    "application", media: "all" %>
    <%= javascript_include_tag "application" %>
    <%= csrf_meta_tags %>
    <!--[if lt IE 9]>
    <script src="http://html5shim.googlecode.com/svn/trunk/html5.js"></script>
    <![endif]-->
  </head>
  <body>
    <header class="navbar navbar-fixed-top">
      <div class="navbar-inner">
        <div class="container">
          <%= link_to "sample app", '#', id: "logo" %>
          <nav>
            <ul class="nav pull-right">
              <li><%= link_to "Home",    '#' %></li>
              <li><%= link_to "Help",    '#' %></li>
              <li><%= link_to "Sign in", '#' %></li>
            </ul>
          </nav>
        </div>
      </div>
    </header>
    <div class="container">
      <%= yield %>
    </div>
  </body>
</html>
```

One thing to note immediately is the switch from Ruby 1.8–style hashes to the new Ruby 1.9 style (Section 4.3.3). That is,

```
<%= stylesheet_link_tag "application", :media => "all" %>
```

has been replaced with

```
<%= stylesheet_link_tag "application", media: "all" %>
```

It's important to note the old hash syntax is deeply entrenched, so it's important to be able to recognize both.

Let's look at the other new elements in Listing 5.1 from top to bottom. As noted briefly in Section 3.1, Rails 3 uses HTML5 by default (as indicated by the doctype **<!DOCTYPE html>**); since the HTML5 standard is relatively new, some browsers (especially older versions Internet Explorer) don't fully support it, so we include some JavaScript code (known as an "HTML5 shim") to work around the issue:

```
<!--[if lt IE 9]>
<script src="http://html5shim.googlecode.com/svn/trunk/html5.js"></script>
<![endif]-->
```

The somewhat odd syntax

```
<!--[if lt IE 9]>
```

includes the enclosed line only if the version of Microsoft Internet Explorer (IE) is less than 9 (**if lt IE 9**). The weird **[if lt IE 9]** syntax is *not* part of Rails; it's actually a conditional comment supported by Internet Explorer browsers for just this sort of situation. It's a good thing, too, because it means we can include the HTML5 shim *only* for IE browsers less than version 9, leaving other browsers such as Firefox, Chrome, and Safari unaffected.

The next section includes a **header** for the site's (plain-text) logo, a couple of divisions (using the **div** tag), and a list of elements with navigation links:

```
<header class="navbar navbar-fixed-top">
  <div class="navbar-inner">
    <div class="container">
      <%= link_to "sample app", '#', id: "logo" %>
      <nav>
        <ul class="nav pull-right">
          <li><%= link_to "Home",     '#' %></li>
```

```
      <li><%= link_to "Help",    '#' %></li>
      <li><%= link_to "Sign in", '#' %></li>
    </ul>
  </nav>
  </div>
  </div>
</header>
```

Here the **header** tag indicates elements that should go at the top of the page. We've given the **header** tag two *CSS classes*,[3] called **navbar** and **navbar-fixed-top**, separated with a space:

```
<header class="navbar navbar-fixed-top">
```

All HTML elements can be assigned both classes and *ids*; these are merely labels and are useful for styling with CSS (Section 5.1.2). The main difference between classes and ids is that classes can be used multiple times on a page, but ids can be used only once. In the present case, both of the **navbar** and **navbar-fixed-top** classes have special meaning to the Bootstrap framework, which we'll install and use in Section 5.1.2.

Inside the **header** tag, we see a couple of **div** tags:

```
<div class="navbar-inner">
  <div class="container">
```

The **div** tag is a generic division; it doesn't do anything apart from dividing the document into distinct parts. In older-style HTML, **div** tags are used for nearly all site divisions, but HTML5 adds the **header**, **nav**, and **section** elements for divisions common to many applications. In this case, each **div** has a CSS class as well. As with the **header** tag's classes, these classes have special meaning to Bootstrap.

After the divs, we encounter some embedded Ruby:

```
<%= link_to "sample app", '#', id: "logo" %>
<nav>
  <ul class="nav pull-right">
    <li><%= link_to "Home",    '#' %></li>
    <li><%= link_to "Help",    '#' %></li>
    <li><%= link_to "Sign in", '#' %></li>
  </ul>
</nav>
```

---

3. These are completely unrelated to Ruby classes.

This uses the Rails helper **link_to** to create links (which we created directly with the anchor tag **a** in Section 3.3.2); the first argument to **link_to** is the link text, while the second is the URI. We'll fill in the URIs with *named routes* in Section 5.3.3, but for now we use the stub URI **'#'** commonly used in web design. The third argument is an options hash, in this case adding the CSS id **logo** to the sample app link. (The other three links have no options hash, which is fine since it's optional.) Rails helpers often take options hashes in this way, giving us the flexibility to add arbitrary HTML options without ever leaving Rails.

The second element inside the divs is a list of navigation links, made using the *unordered list* tag **ul**, together with the *list item* tag **li**:

```
<nav>
  <ul class="nav pull-right">
    <li><%= link_to "Home",    '#' %></li>
    <li><%= link_to "Help",    '#' %></li>
    <li><%= link_to "Sign in", '#' %></li>
  </ul>
</nav>
```

The **nav** tag, though formally unnecessary here, communicates the purpose of the navigation links. The **nav** and **pull-right** classes on the **ul** tag have special meaning to Bootstrap. Once Rails has processed this layout and evaluated the embedded Ruby, the list looks like this:

```
<nav>
  <ul class="nav pull-right">
    <li><a href="#">Home</a></li>
    <li><a href="#">Help</a></li>
    <li><a href="#">Sign in</a></li>
  </ul>
</nav>
```

The final part of the layout is a **div** for the main content:

```
<div class="container">
  <%= yield %>
</div>
```

As before, the **container** class has special meaning to Bootstrap. As we learned in Section 3.3.4, the **yield** method inserts the contents of each page into the site layout.

Apart from the site footer, which we'll add in Section 5.1.3, our layout is now complete, and we can look at the results by visiting the Home page. To take advantage of the upcoming style elements, we'll add some extra elements to the **home.html.erb** view (Listing 5.2).

Listing 5.2 The Home page with a link to the signup page.
app/views/static_pages/home.html.erb

```
<div class="center hero-unit">
  <h1>Welcome to the Sample App</h1>

  <h2>
    This is the home page for the
    <a href="http://railstutorial.org/">Ruby on Rails Tutorial</a>
    sample application.
  </h2>

  <%= link_to "Sign up now!", '#', class: "btn btn-large btn-primary" %>
</div>

<%= link_to image_tag("rails.png", alt: "Rails"), 'http://rubyonrails.org/' %>
```

In preparation for adding users to our site in Chapter 7, the first **link_to** creates a stub link of the form

```
<a href="#" class="btn btn-large btn-primary">Sign up now!</a>
```

In the **div** tag, the **hero-unit** CSS class has a special meaning to Bootstrap, as do the **btn**, **btn-large**, and **btn-primary** classes in the signup button.

The second **link_to** shows off the **image_tag** helper, which takes as arguments the path to an image and an optional options hash, in this case setting the **alt** attribute of the image tag using symbols. To make this clearer, let's look at the HTML this tag produces:[4]

```
<img alt="Rails" src="/assets/rails.png" />
```

---

4. You might notice that the **img** tag, rather than looking like <img>...</img>, instead looks like <img ... />. Tags that follow this form are known as *self-closing* tags.

The **alt** attribute is what will be displayed if there is no image, and it is also what will be displayed by screen readers for the visually impaired. Although people are sometimes sloppy about including the **alt** attribute for images, it is in fact required by the HTML standard. Luckily, Rails includes a default **alt** attribute; if you don't specify the attribute in the call to **image_tag**, Rails just uses the image filename (minus extension). In this case, though, we've set the **alt** text explicitly in order to capitalize "Rails."

Now we're finally ready to see the fruits of our labors (Figure 5.2). Pretty underwhelming, you say? Perhaps so. Happily, though, we've done a good job of giving our HTML elements sensible classes, which puts us in a great position to add style to the site with CSS.

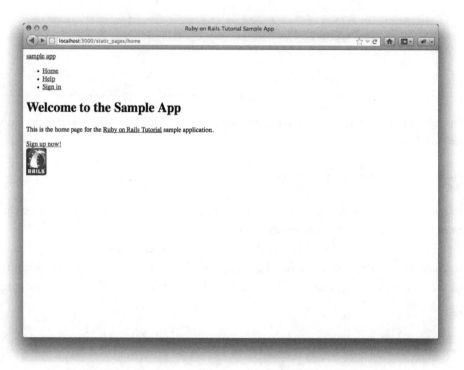

Figure 5.2   The Home page (/static_pages/home) with no custom CSS.

By the way, you might be surprised to discover that the **rails.png** image actually exists. Where did it come from? It's included for free with every new Rails application, and you will find it in **app/assets/images/rails.png**. Because we used the **image_tag** helper, Rails finds it automatically using the asset pipeline (Section 5.2).

5.1.2 Bootstrap and Custom CSS

In Section 5.1.1, we associated many of the HTML elements with CSS classes, which gives us considerable flexibility in constructing a layout based on CSS. As noted in Section 5.1.1, many of these classes are specific to Bootstrap, a framework from Twitter that makes it easy to add nice web design and user interface elements to an HTML5 application. In this section, we'll combine Bootstrap with some custom CSS rules to start adding some style to the sample application.

Our first step is to add Bootstrap, which in Rails applications can be accomplished with the bootstrap-sass gem, as shown in Listing 5.3. The Bootstrap framework natively uses the LESS CSS language for making dynamic stylesheets, but the Rails asset pipeline supports the (very similar) Sass language by default (Section 5.2), so bootstrap-sass converts LESS to Sass and makes all the necessary Bootstrap files available to the current application.[5]

Listing 5.3 Adding the bootstrap-sass gem to the **Gemfile**.

```
source 'https://rubygems.org'

gem 'rails', '3.2.13'
gem 'bootstrap-sass', '2.0.0'
  .
  .
  .
```

To install Bootstrap, we run **bundle install** as usual:

```
$ bundle install
```

---

5. It is also possible to use LESS with the asset pipeline; see the less-rails-bootstrap gem for details.

Then restart the web server to incorporate the changes into the development application.

The first step in adding custom CSS to our application is to create a file to contain it:

```
app/assets/stylesheets/custom.css.scss
```

(Use you text editor or IDE to create the new file.) Here both the directory name and filename are important. The directory

```
app/assets/stylesheets
```

is part of the asset pipeline (Section 5.2), and any stylesheets in this directory will automatically be included as part of the **application.css** file included in the site layout. Furthermore, the filename **custom.css.scss** includes the **.css** extension, which indicates a CSS file, and the **.scss** extension, which indicates a "Sassy CSS" file and arranges for the asset pipeline to process the file using Sass. (We won't be using Sass until Section 5.2.2, but it's needed now for the bootstrap-sass gem to work its magic.)

After creating the file for custom CSS, we can use the **@import** function to include Bootstrap, as shown in Listing 5.4.

Listing 5.4 Adding Bootstrap CSS.
app/assets/stylesheets/custom.css.scss

```
@import "bootstrap";
```

This one line includes the entire Bootstrap CSS framework, with the result shown in in Figure 5.3. The placement of the text isn't good and the logo doesn't have any style, but the colors and signup button look promising.

Next we'll add some CSS that will be used site-wide for styling the layout and each individual page, as shown in Listing 5.5. There are quite a few rules in Listing 5.5; to get a sense of what a CSS rule does, it's often helpful to comment it out using CSS comments, i.e., by putting it inside /* ... */, and seeing what changes. The result of the CSS in Listing 5.5 is shown in Figure 5.4.

Figure 5.3 The sample application with Bootstrap CSS.

Listing 5.5 Adding CSS for some universal styling applying to all pages.
`app/assets/stylesheets/custom.css.scss`

```scss
@import "bootstrap";

/* universal */

html {
  overflow-y: scroll;
}

body {
  padding-top: 60px;
}
```

```
section {
  overflow: auto;
}

textarea {
  resize: vertical;
}

.center {
  text-align: center;
}

.center h1 {
  margin-bottom: 10px;
}
```

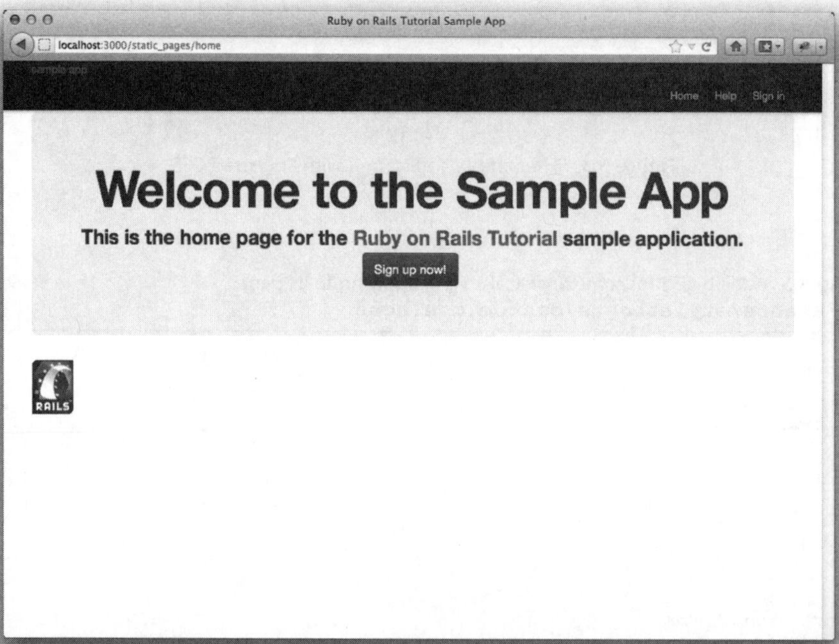

Figure 5.4   Adding some spacing and other universal styling.

Note that the CSS in Listing 5.5 has a consistent form. In general, CSS rules refer either to a class, an id, an HTML tag, or some combination thereof, followed by a list of styling commands. For example,

```
body {
  padding-top: 60px;
}
```

puts 60 pixels of padding at the top of the page. Because of the **navbar-fixed-top** class in the **header** tag, Bootstrap fixes the navigation bar to the top of the page, so the padding serves to separate the main text from the navigation. Meanwhile, the CSS in the rule

```
.center {
  text-align: center;
}
```

associates the **center** class with the **text-align: center** property. In other words, the dot **.** in **.center** indicates that the rule styles a class. (As we'll see in Listing 5.7, the pound sign **#** identifies a rule to style a CSS *id*.) This means that elements inside any tag (such as a **div**) with class **center** will be centered on the page. (We saw an example of this class in Listing 5.2.)

Although Bootstrap comes with CSS rules for nice typography, we'll also add some custom rules for the appearance of the text on our site, as shown in Listing 5.6. (Not all of these rules apply to the Home page, but each rule here will be used at some point in the sample application.) The result of Listing 5.6 is shown in Figure 5.5.

Listing 5.6 Adding CSS for nice typography.
app/assets/stylesheets/custom.css.scss

```
@import "bootstrap";
  .
  .
  .

/* typography */

h1, h2, h3, h4, h5, h6 {
  line-height: 1;
}
```

```
h1 {
  font-size: 3em;
  letter-spacing: -2px;
  margin-bottom: 30px;
  text-align: center;
}

h2 {
  font-size: 1.7em;
  letter-spacing: -1px;
  margin-bottom: 30px;
  text-align: center;
  font-weight: normal;
  color: #999;
}

p {
  font-size: 1.1em;
  line-height: 1.7em;
}
```

Figure 5.5 Adding some typographic styling.

Finally, we'll add some rules to style the site's logo, which simply consists of the text "sample app." The CSS in Listing 5.7 converts the text to uppercase and modifies its size, color, and placement. (We've used a CSS id because we expect the site logo to appear on the page only once, but you could use a class instead.)

Listing 5.7 Adding CSS for the site logo.
`app/assets/stylesheets/custom.css.scss`

```scss
@import "bootstrap";
  .
  .
  .

/* header */

#logo {
  float: left;
  margin-right: 10px;
  font-size: 1.7em;
  color: #fff;
  text-transform: uppercase;
  letter-spacing: -1px;
  padding-top: 9px;
  font-weight: bold;
  line-height: 1;
}

#logo:hover {
  color: #fff;
  text-decoration: none;
}
```

Here `color: #fff` changes the color of the logo to white. HTML colors can be coded with three base-16 (hexadecimal) numbers, one each for the primary colors red, green, and blue (in that order). The code `#ffffff` maxes out all three colors, yielding pure white, and `#fff` is a shorthand for the full `#ffffff`. The CSS standard also defines a large number of synonyms for common HTML colors, including `white` for `#fff`. The result of the CSS in Listing 5.7 is shown in Figure 5.6.

5.1.3 Partials

Although the layout in Listing 5.1 serves its purpose, it's getting a little cluttered. The HTML shim takes up three lines and uses weird IE-specific syntax, so it would be nice

Figure 5.6   The sample app with nicely styled logo.

to tuck it away somewhere on its own. In addition, the header HTML forms a logical unit, so it should all be packaged up in one place. The way to achieve this in Rails is to use a facility called *partials*. Let's first take a look at what the layout looks like after the partials are defined (Listing 5.8).

Listing 5.8   The site layout with partials for the stylesheets and header.
app/views/layouts/application.html.erb

```
<!DOCTYPE html>
<html>
  <head>
    <title><%= full_title(yield(:title)) %></title>
    <%= stylesheet_link_tag    "application", media: "all" %>
    <%= javascript_include_tag "application" %>
    <%= csrf_meta_tags %>
```

```
  <%= render 'layouts/shim' %>
</head>
<body>
  <%= render 'layouts/header' %>
  <div class="container">
    <%= yield %>
  </div>
</body>
</html>
```

In Listing 5.8, we've replaced the HTML shim stylesheet lines with a single call to a Rails helper called **render**:

```
<%= render 'layouts/shim' %>
```

The effect of this line is to look for a file called **app/views/layouts/_shim.html.erb**, evaluate its contents, and insert the results into the view.[6] (Recall that `<%= ... %>` is the embedded Ruby syntax needed to evaluate a Ruby expression and then insert the results into the template.) Note the leading underscore on the filename **_shim.html.erb**; this underscore is the universal convention for naming partials and, among other things, makes it possible to identify all the partials in a directory at a glance.

Of course, to get the partial to work, we have to fill it with some content; in the case of the shim partial, this is just the three lines of shim code from Listing 5.1; the result appears in Listing 5.9.

Listing 5.9 A partial for the HTML shim.
app/views/layouts/_shim.html.erb

```
<!--[if lt IE 9]>
<script src="http://html5shim.googlecode.com/svn/trunk/html5.js"></script>
<![endif]-->
```

Similarly, we can move the header material into the partial shown in Listing 5.10 and insert it into the layout with another call to **render**.

---

6. Many Rails developers use a **shared** directory for partials shared across different views. I prefer to use the **shared** folder for utility partials that are useful on multiple views, while putting partials that are literally on every page (as part of the site layout) in the **layouts** directory. (We'll create the **shared** directory starting in Chapter 7.) That seems to me a logical division, but putting them all in the **shared** folder certainly works fine, too.

Listing 5.10 A partial for the site header.
`app/views/layouts/_header.html.erb`

```
<header class="navbar navbar-fixed-top">
  <div class="navbar-inner">
    <div class="container">
      <%= link_to "sample app", '#', id: "logo" %>
      <nav>
        <ul class="nav pull-right">
          <li><%= link_to "Home",    '#' %></li>
          <li><%= link_to "Help",    '#' %></li>
          <li><%= link_to "Sign in", '#' %></li>
        </ul>
      </nav>
    </div>
  </div>
</header>
```

Now that we know how to make partials, let's add a site footer to go along with the header. By now you can probably guess that we'll call it **_footer.html.erb** and put it in the layouts directory (Listing 5.11).[7]

Listing 5.11 A partial for the site footer.
`app/views/layouts/_footer.html.erb`

```
<footer class="footer">
  <small>
    <a href="http://railstutorial.org/">Rails Tutorial</a>
    by Michael Hartl
  </small>
  <nav>
    <ul>
      <li><%= link_to "About",   '#' %></li>
      <li><%= link_to "Contact", '#' %></li>
      <li><a href="http://news.railstutorial.org/">News</a></li>
    </ul>
  </nav>
</footer>
```

As with the header, in the footer we've used **link_to** for the internal links to the About and Contact pages and stubbed out the URIs with **'#'** for now. (As with **header**, the **footer** tag is new in HTML5.)

---

7. You may wonder why we use both the **footer** tag and **.footer** class. The answer is that the tag has a clear meaning to human readers, and the class is used by Bootstrap. Using a **div** tag in place of **footer** would work as well.

We can render the footer partial in the layout by following the same pattern as the stylesheets and header partials (Listing 5.12).

Listing 5.12 The site layout with a footer partial.
app/views/layouts/application.html.erb

```
<!DOCTYPE html>
<html>
  <head>
    <title><%= full_title(yield(:title)) %></title>
    <%= stylesheet_link_tag    "application", media: "all" %>
    <%= javascript_include_tag "application" %>
    <%= csrf_meta_tags %>
    <%= render 'layouts/shim' %>
  </head>
  <body>
    <%= render 'layouts/header' %>
    <div class="container">
      <%= yield %>
      <%= render 'layouts/footer' %>
    </div>
  </body>
</html>
```

Of course, the footer will be ugly without some styling (Listing 5.13). The results appear in Figure 5.7.

Listing 5.13 Adding the CSS for the site footer.
app/assets/stylesheets/custom.css.scss

```
.
.
.

/* footer */

footer {
  margin-top: 45px;
  padding-top: 5px;
  border-top: 1px solid #eaeaea;
  color: #999;
}

footer a {
  color: #555;
}
```

```
footer a:hover {
  color: #222;
}

footer small {
  float: left;
}

footer ul {
  float: right;
  list-style: none;
}

footer ul li {
  float: left;
  margin-left: 10px;
}
```

Figure 5.7   The Home page (/static_pages/home) with an added footer.

5.2 Sass and the Asset Pipeline

One of the most notable differences between Rails 3.0 and more recent versions is the asset pipeline, which significantly improves the production and management of static assets such as CSS, JavaScript, and images. This section gives a high-level overview of the asset pipeline and then shows how to use a remarkable tool for making CSS called *Sass*, now included by default as part of the asset pipeline.

5.2.1 The Asset Pipeline

The asset pipeline involves lots of changes under Rails' hood, but from the perspective of a typical Rails developer there are three principal features to understand: asset directories, manifest files, and preprocessor engines.[8] Let's consider each in turn.

Asset Directories

In versions of Rails before 3.0 (including 3.0 itself), static assets lived in the **public/** directory, as follows:

- **public/stylesheets**
- **public/javascripts**
- **public/images**

Files in these directories are (even post-3.0) automatically served up via requests to http://example.com/stylesheets, etc.

Starting in Rails 3.1, there are *three* canonical directories for static assets, each with its own purpose:

- **app/assets**: assets specific to the present application
- **lib/assets**: assets for libraries written by your dev team
- **vendor/assets**: assets from third-party vendors

As you might guess, each of these directories has a subdirectory for each asset class, e.g.,

```
$ ls app/assets/
images       javascripts stylesheets
```

---

8. The structure of this section is based on the excellent blog post The Rails 3 Asset Pipeline in (about) 5 Minutes by Michael Erasmus. For more details, see the Rails Guide on the Asset Pipeline.

At this point, we're in a position to understand the motivation behind the location of the **custom.css.scss** file in Section 5.1.2: **custom.css.scss** is specific to the sample application, so it goes in **app/assets/stylesheets**.

Manifest Files

Once you've placed your assets in their logical locations, you can use *manifest files* to tell Rails (via the Sprockets gem) how to combine them to form single files. (This applies to CSS and JavaScript but not to images.) As an example, let's take a look at the default manifest file for app stylesheets (Listing 5.14).

Listing 5.14 The manifest file for app-specific CSS.
app/assets/stylesheets/application.css

```
/*
 * This is a manifest file that'll automatically include all the stylesheets
 * available in this directory and any sub-directories. You're free to add
 * application-wide styles to this file and they'll appear at the top of the
 * compiled file, but it's generally better to create a new file per style
 * scope.
 *= require_self
 *= require_tree .
 */
```

The key lines here are actually CSS comments, but they are used by Sprockets to include the proper files:

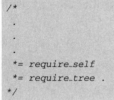

Here

```
*= require_tree .
```

ensures that all CSS files in the **app/assets/stylesheets** directory (including the tree subdirectories) are included into the application CSS. The line

```
*= require_self
```

ensures that CSS in **application.css** is also included.

Rails comes with sensible default manifest files, and in the *Rails Tutorial* we won't need to make any changes, but the Rails Guides entry on the asset pipeline has more detail if you need it.

Preprocessor Engines

After you've assembled your assets, Rails prepares them for the site template by running them through several preprocessing engines and using the manifest files to combine them for delivery to the browser. We tell Rails which processor to use using filename extensions; the three most common cases are **.scss** for Sass, **.coffee** for CoffeeScript, and **.erb** for embedded Ruby (ERb). We first covered ERb in Section 3.3.3, and cover Sass in Section 5.2.2. We won't be needing CoffeeScript in this tutorial, but it's an elegant little language that compiles to JavaScript. (The RailsCast on CoffeeScript basics is a good place to start.)

The preprocessor engines can be chained, so that

foobar.js.coffee

gets run through the CoffeeScript processor, and

foobar.js.erb.coffee

gets run through both CoffeeScript and ERb (with the code running from right to left, i.e., CoffeeScript first).

Efficiency in Production

One of the best things about the asset pipeline is that it automatically results in assets that are optimized to be efficient in a production application. Traditional methods for organizing CSS and JavaScript involve splitting functionality into separate files and using nice formatting (with lots of indentation). While convenient for the programmer, this is inefficient in production; including multiple full-sized files can significantly slow page-load times (one of the most important factors affecting the quality of the user experience). With the asset pipeline, in production all the application stylesheets get rolled into one CSS file (`application.css`), all the application JavaScript code gets rolled into one JavaScript file (`javascripts.js`), and all such files (including those in `lib/assets` and `vendor/assets`) are *minified* to remove the unnecessary whitespace that bloats file size. As a result, we get the best of both worlds: multiple nicely formatted files for programmer convenience, with single optimized files in production.

5.2.2　Syntactically Awesome Stylesheets

Sass is a language for writing stylesheets that improves on CSS in many ways. In this section, we cover two of the most important improvements, *nesting* and *variables*. (A third technique, *mixins*, is introduced in Section 7.1.1.)

As noted briefly in Section 5.1.2, Sass supports a format called SCSS (indicated with a `.scss` filename extension), which is a strict superset of CSS itself; that is, SCSS only *adds* features to CSS, rather than defining an entirely new syntax.[9] This means that every valid CSS file is also a valid SCSS file, which is convenient for projects with existing style rules. In our case, we used SCSS from the start in order to take advantage of Bootstrap. Since the Rails asset pipeline automatically uses Sass to process files with the `.scss` extension, the `custom.css.scss` file will be run through the Sass preprocessor before being packaged up for delivery to the browser.

Nesting

A common pattern in stylesheets is having rules that apply to nested elements. For example, in Listing 5.5 we have rules both for `.center` and for `.center h1`:

```scss
.center {
  text-align: center;
}

.center h1 {
  margin-bottom: 10px;
}
```

---

9. The older `.sass` format, also supported by Sass, defines a new language that is less verbose (and has fewer curly braces) but is less convenient for existing projects and is harder to learn for those already familiar with CSS.

We can replace this in Sass with

```
.center {
  text-align: center;
  h1 {
    margin-bottom: 10px;
  }
}
```

Here the nested **h1** rule automatically inherits the **.center** context.

There's a second candidate for nesting that requires a slightly different syntax. In Listing 5.7, we have the code

```
#logo {
  float: left;
  margin-right: 10px;
  font-size: 1.7em;
  color: #fff;
  text-transform: uppercase;
  letter-spacing: -1px;
  padding-top: 9px;
  font-weight: bold;
  line-height: 1;
}

#logo:hover {
  color: #fff;
  text-decoration: none;
}
```

Here the logo id **#logo** appears twice, once by itself and once with the **hover** attribute (which controls its appearance when the mouse pointer hovers over the element in question). In order to nest the second rule, we need to reference the parent element **#logo**; in SCSS, this is accomplished with the ampersand character **&** as follows:

```
#logo {
  float: left;
  margin-right: 10px;
  font-size: 1.7em;
  color: #fff;
```

```
    text-transform: uppercase;
    letter-spacing: -1px;
    padding-top: 9px;
    font-weight: bold;
    line-height: 1;
    &:hover {
      color: #fff;
      text-decoration: none;
    }
}
```

Sass changes **&:hover** into **#logo:hover** as part of converting from SCSS to CSS.

Both of these nesting techniques apply to the footer CSS in Listing 5.13, which can be transformed into the following:

```
footer {
    margin-top: 45px;
    padding-top: 5px;
    border-top: 1px solid #eaeaea;
    color: #999;
    a {
      color: #555;
      &:hover {
        color: #222;
      }
    }
    small {
      float: left;
    }
    ul {
      float: right;
      list-style: none;
      li {
        float: left;
        margin-left: 10px;
      }
    }
}
```

Converting Listing 5.13 by hand is a good exercise, and you should verify that the CSS still works properly after the conversion.

Variables

Sass allows us to define *variables* to eliminate duplication and write more expressive code. For example, looking at Listing 5.6 and Listing 5.13, we see that there are repeated references to the same color:

```
h2 {
  .
  .
  .
  color: #999;
}
.
.
.
footer {
  .
  .
  .
  color: #999;
}
```

In this case, **#999** is a light gray, and we can give it a name by defining a variable as follows:

```
$lightGray: #999;
```

This allows us to rewrite our SCSS like this:

```
$lightGray: #999;
.
.
.
h2 {
  .
  .
  .
  color: $lightGray;
}
.
.
.
```

```
footer {
  .
  .
  .
  color: $lightGray;
}
```

Because variable names such as **$lightGray** are more descriptive than **#999**, it's often useful to define variables even for values that aren't repeated. Indeed, the Bootstrap framework defines a large number of variables for colors, available online on the Bootstrap page of LESS variables. That page defines variables using LESS, not Sass, but the `bootstrap-sass` gem provides the Sass equivalents. It is not difficult to guess the correspondence; where LESS uses an "at" sign **@**, Sass uses a dollar sign **$**. Looking the Bootstrap variable page, we see that there is a variable for light gray:

```
@grayLight: #999;
```

This means that, via the `bootstrap-sass` gem, there should be a corresponding SCSS variable **$grayLight**. We can use this to replace our custom variable, **$lightGray**, which gives

```
h2 {
  .
  .
  .
  color: $grayLight;
}
  .
  .
  .
footer {
  .
  .
  .
  color: $grayLight;
}
```

Applying the Sass nesting and variable definition features to the full SCSS file gives the file in Listing 5.15. This uses both Sass variables (as inferred from the Bootstrap LESS variable page) and built-in named colors (i.e., **white** for **#fff**). Note in particular the dramatic improvement in the rules for the **footer** tag.

Listing 5.15 The initial SCSS file converted to use nesting and variables.
`app/assets/stylesheets/custom.css.scss`

```scss
@import "bootstrap";

/* mixins, variables, etc. */

$grayMediumLight: #eaeaea;

/* universal */

html {
  overflow-y: scroll;
}

body {
  padding-top: 60px;
}

section {
  overflow: auto;
}

textarea {
  resize: vertical;
}

.center {
  text-align: center;
  h1 {
    margin-bottom: 10px;
  }
}

/* typography */

h1, h2, h3, h4, h5, h6 {
  line-height: 1;
}

h1 {
  font-size: 3em;
  letter-spacing: -2px;
  margin-bottom: 30px;
  text-align: center;
}
```

```scss
h2 {
  font-size: 1.7em;
  letter-spacing: -1px;
  margin-bottom: 30px;
  text-align: center;
  font-weight: normal;
  color: $grayLight;
}


p {
  font-size: 1.1em;
  line-height: 1.7em;
}


/* header */

#logo {
  float: left;
  margin-right: 10px;
  font-size: 1.7em;
  color: white;
  text-transform: uppercase;
  letter-spacing: -1px;
  padding-top: 9px;
  font-weight: bold;
  line-height: 1;
  &:hover {
    color: white;
    text-decoration: none;
  }
}

/* footer */

footer {
  margin-top: 45px;
  padding-top: 5px;
  border-top: 1px solid $grayMediumLight;
  color: $grayLight;
  a {
    color: $gray;
    &:hover {
      color: $grayDarker;
    }
  }
  small {
    float: left;
  }
```

```
ul {
  float: right;
  list-style: none;
  li {
    float: left;
    margin-left: 10px;
  }
}
}
```

Sass gives us even more ways to simplify our stylesheets, but the code in Listing 5.15 uses the most important features and gives us a great start. See the Sass website for more details.

5.3 Layout Links

Now that we've finished a site layout with decent styling, it's time to start filling in the links we've stubbed out with '#'. Of course, we could hard-code links like

```
<a href="/static_pages/about">About</a>
```

but that isn't the Rails Way. For one, it would be nice if the URI for the About page were /about rather than /static_pages/about; moreover, Rails conventionally uses *named routes*, which involves code like

```
<%= link_to "About", about_path %>
```

This way the code has a more transparent meaning, and it's also more flexible since we can change the definition of **about_path** and have the URI change everywhere **about_path** is used.

The full list of our planned links appears in Table 5.1, along with their mapping to URIs and routes. We'll implement all but the last one by the end of this chapter. (We'll make the last one in Chapter 8.)

Before moving on, let's add a Contact page (left as an exercise in Chapter 3). The test appears as in Listing 5.16, which simply follows the model last seen in Listing 3.18. Note that, as in the application code, in Listing 5.16 we've switched to Ruby 1.9–style hashes.

Table 5.1 Route and URI mapping for site links.

Page	URI	Named route
Home	/	`root_path`
About	/about	`about_path`
Help	/help	`help_path`
Contact	/contact	`contact_path`
Sign up	/signup	`signup_path`
Sign in	/signin	`signin_path`

Listing 5.16 Tests for a Contact page.
`spec/requests/static_pages_spec.rb`

```
require 'spec_helper'

describe "Static pages" do
  .
  .
  .
  describe "Contact page" do

    it "should have the h1 'Contact'" do
      visit '/static_pages/contact'
      page.should have_selector('h1', text: 'Contact')
    end

    it "should have the title 'Contact'" do
      visit '/static_pages/contact'
      page.should have_selector('title',
                  text: "Ruby on Rails Tutorial Sample App | Contact")
    end
  end
end
```

You should verify that these tests fail:

```
$ bundle exec rspec spec/requests/static_pages_spec.rb
```

The application code parallels the addition of the About page in Section 3.2.2: first we update the routes (Listing 5.17), then we add a **contact** action to the StaticPages controller (Listing 5.18), and finally we create a Contact view (Listing 5.19).

Listing 5.17 Adding a route for the Contact page.
config/routes.rb

```
SampleApp::Application.routes.draw do
  get "static_pages/home"
  get "static_pages/help"
  get "static_pages/about"
  get "static_pages/contact"
  .
  .
  .
end
```

Listing 5.18 Adding an action for the Contact page.
app/controllers/static_pages_controller.rb

```
class StaticPagesController < ApplicationController
  .
  .
  .
  def contact
  end
end
```

Listing 5.19 The view for the Contact page.
app/views/static_pages/contact.html.erb

```
<% provide(:title, 'Contact') %>
<h1>Contact</h1>
<p>
  Contact Ruby on Rails Tutorial about the sample app at the
  <a href="http://railstutorial.org/contact">contact page</a>.
</p>
```

Now make sure that the tests pass:

```
$ bundle exec rspec spec/requests/static_pages_spec.rb
```

5.3.1 Route Tests

With the work we've done writing integration test for the static pages, writing tests for the routes is simple: We just replace each occurrence of a hard-coded address with the desired named route from Table 5.1. In other words, we change

```
visit '/static_pages/about'
```

to

```
visit about_path
```

and so on for the other pages. The result appears in Listing 5.20.

Listing 5.20 Tests for the named routes.
spec/requests/static_pages_spec.rb

```ruby
require 'spec_helper'

describe "Static pages" do

  describe "Home page" do

    it "should have the h1 'Sample App'" do
      visit root_path
      page.should have_selector('h1', text: 'Sample App')
    end

    it "should have the base title" do
      visit root_path
      page.should have_selector('title',
                    text: "Ruby on Rails Tutorial Sample App")
    end

    it "should not have a custom page title" do
      visit root_path
      page.should_not have_selector('title', text: '| Home')
    end
  end

  describe "Help page" do
```

```
    it "should have the h1 'Help'" do
      visit help_path
      page.should have_selector('h1', text: 'Help')
    end

    it "should have the title 'Help'" do
      visit help_path
      page.should have_selector('title',
                      text: "Ruby on Rails Tutorial Sample App | Help")
    end
  end

  describe "About page" do

    it "should have the h1 'About'" do
      visit about_path
      page.should have_selector('h1', text: 'About Us')
    end

    it "should have the title 'About Us'" do
      visit about_path
      page.should have_selector('title',
                      text: "Ruby on Rails Tutorial Sample App | About Us")
    end
  end

  describe "Contact page" do

    it "should have the h1 'Contact'" do
      visit contact_path
      page.should have_selector('h1', text: 'Contact')
    end

    it "should have the title 'Contact'" do
      visit contact_path
      page.should have_selector('title',
                      text: "Ruby on Rails Tutorial Sample App | Contact")
    end
  end
end
```

As usual, you should check that the tests are now red:

```
$ bundle exec rspec spec/requests/static_pages_spec.rb
```

By the way, if the code in Listing 5.20 strikes you as repetitive and verbose, you're not alone. We'll refactor this mess into a beautiful jewel in Section 5.3.4.

5.3.2 Rails Routes

Now that we have tests for the URIs we want, it's time to get them to work. As noted in Section 3.1.2, the file Rails uses for URI mappings is **config/routes.rb**. If you take a look at the default routes file, you'll see that it's quite a mess, but it's a useful mess—full of commented-out example route mappings. I suggest reading through it at some point, and I also suggest taking a look at the Rails Guides article "Rails Routing from the outside in" for a much more in-depth treatment of routes.

To define the named routes, we need to replace rules such as

```
get 'static_pages/help'
```

with

```
match '/help', to: 'static_pages#help'
```

This arranges both for a valid page at **/help** and a named route called **help_path** that returns the path to that page. (Actually, using **get** in place of **match** gives the same named routes, but using **match** is more conventional.)

Applying this pattern to the other static pages gives Listing 5.21. The only exception is the Home page, which we'll take care of in Listing 5.23.

Listing 5.21 Routes for static pages.
config/routes.rb

```
SampleApp::Application.routes.draw do
  match '/help',    to: 'static_pages#help'
  match '/about',   to: 'static_pages#about'
  match '/contact', to: 'static_pages#contact'
  .
  .
  .
end
```

If you read the code in Listing 5.21 carefully, you can probably figure out what it does; for example, you can see that

```
match '/about', to: 'static_pages#about'
```

matches **`/about`** and routes it to the **about** action in the StaticPages controller. Before, this was more explicit: We used

```
get 'static_pages/about'
```

to get to the same place, but **/about** is more succinct. In addition, as mentioned above, the code **match '/about'** also automatically creates *named routes* for use in the controllers and views:

```
about_path => '/about'
about_url  => 'http://localhost:3000/about'
```

Note that **about_url** is the *full* URI http://localhost:3000/about (with **localhost:3000** being replaced with the domain name, such as **example.com**, for a fully deployed site). As discussed in Section 5.3, to get just /about, you use **about_path**. (The *Rails Tutorial* uses the **path** form for consistency, but the difference rarely matters in practice.)

With these routes now defined, the tests for the Help, About, and Contact pages should pass:

```
$ bundle exec rspec spec/requests/static_pages_spec.rb
```

This leaves the test for the Home page as the last one to fail.

To establish the route mapping for the Home page, we *could* use code like this:

```
match '/', to: 'static_pages#home'
```

This is unnecessary, though; Rails has special instructions for the root URI / ("slash") located lower down in the file (Listing 5.22).

Listing 5.22 The commented-out hint for defining the root route.
`config/routes.rb`

```
SampleApp::Application.routes.draw do
  .

  .

  # You can have the root of your site routed with "root"
  # just remember to delete public/index.html.
  # root :to => "welcome#index"
  .

  .

  .
end
```

Using Listing 5.22 as a model, we arrive at Listing 5.23 to route the root URI / to the Home page.

Listing 5.23 Adding a mapping for the root route.
`config/routes.rb`

```
SampleApp::Application.routes.draw do
  root to: 'static_pages#home'

  match '/help',    to: 'static_pages#help'
  match '/about',   to: 'static_pages#about'
  match '/contact', to: 'static_pages#contact'
  .

  .

  .
end
```

This code maps the root URI / to /static_pages/home, and also gives URI helpers as follows:

```
root_path => '/'
root_url  => 'http://localhost:3000/'
```

We should also heed the comment in Listing 5.22 and delete `public/index.html` to prevent Rails from rendering the default page (Figure 1.3) when we visit /. You can of course simply remove the file by trashing it, but if you're using Git for version control there's a way to tell Git about the removal at the same time using **git rm**:

```
$ git rm public/index.html
```

With that, all of the routes for static pages are working, and the tests should pass:

```
$ bundle exec rspec spec/requests/static_pages_spec.rb
```

Now we just have to fill in the links in the layout.

5.3.3 Named Routes

Let's put the named routes created in Section 5.3.2 to work in our layout. This will entail filling in the second arguments of the **link_to** functions with the proper named routes. For example, we'll convert

```
<%= link_to "About", '#' %>
```

to

```
<%= link_to "About", about_path %>
```

and so on.

We'll start in the header partial, **_header.html.erb** (Listing 5.24), which has links to the Home and Help pages. While we're at it, we'll follow a common web convention and link the logo to the Home page as well.

Listing 5.24 Header partial with links.
app/views/layouts/_header.html.erb

```
<header class="navbar navbar-fixed-top">
  <div class="navbar-inner">
    <div class="container">
```

```erb
    <%= link_to "sample app", root_path, id: "logo" %>
    <nav>
      <ul class="nav pull-right">
        <li><%= link_to "Home",    root_path %></li>
        <li><%= link_to "Help",    help_path %></li>
        <li><%= link_to "Sign in", '#' %></li>
      </ul>
    </nav>
  </div>
</div>
</header>
```

We won't have a named route for the "Sign in" link until Chapter 8, so we've left it as `'#'` for now.

The other place with links is the footer partial, **_footer.html.erb**, which has links for the About and Contact pages (Listing 5.25).

Listing 5.25 Footer partial with links.
app/views/layouts/_footer.html.erb

```erb
<footer class="footer">
  <small>
    <a href="http://railstutorial.org/">Rails Tutorial</a>
    by Michael Hartl
  </small>
  <nav>
    <ul>
      <li><%= link_to "About",   about_path %></li>
      <li><%= link_to "Contact", contact_path %></li>
      <li><a href="http://news.railstutorial.org/">News</a></li>
    </ul>
  </nav>
</footer>
```

With that, our layout has links to all the static pages created in Chapter 3, so that, for example, /about goes to the About page (Figure 5.8).

By the way, it's worth noting that, although we haven't actually tested for the presence of the links on the layout, our tests will fail if the routes aren't defined. You can check this by commenting out the routes in Listing 5.21 and running your test suite. For a testing method that actually makes sure the links go to the right places, see Section 5.6.

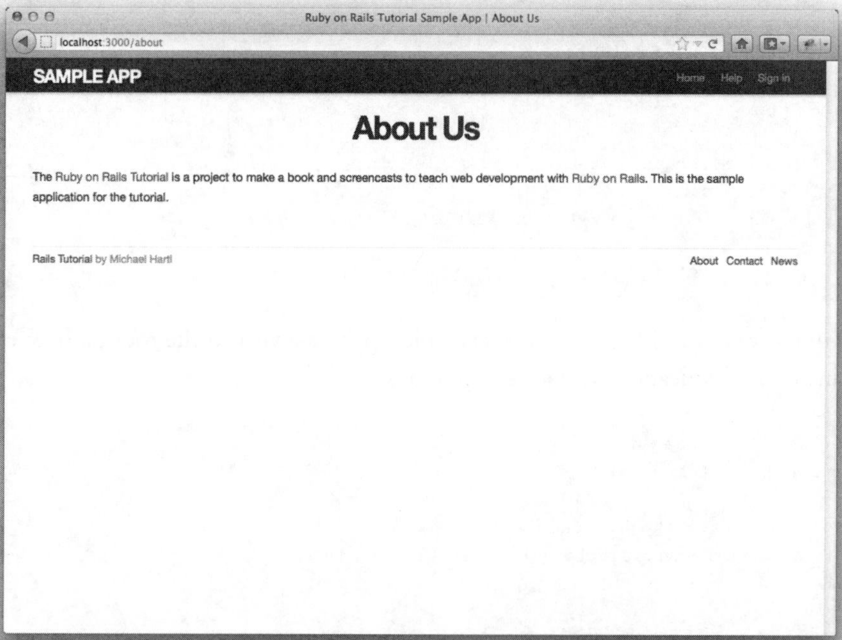

Figure 5.8 The About page at /about.

5.3.4 Pretty RSpec

We noted in Section 5.3.1 that the tests for the static pages are getting a little verbose and repetitive (Listing 5.20). In this section we'll make use of the latest features of RSpec to make our tests more compact and elegant.

Let's take a look at a couple of the examples to see how they can be improved:

```
describe "Home page" do

  it "should have the h1 'Sample App'" do
    visit root_path
    page.should have_selector('h1', text: 'Sample App')
  end
```

```
    it "should have the base title" do
      visit root_path
      page.should have_selector('title',
                          text: "Ruby on Rails Tutorial Sample App")
    end

    it "should not have a custom page title" do
      visit root_path
      page.should_not have_selector('title', text: '| Home')
    end
  end
```

One thing we notice is that all three examples include a visit to the root path. We can
eliminate this duplication with a **before** block:

```
describe "Home page" do
  before { visit root_path }

  it "should have the h1 'Sample App'" do
    page.should have_selector('h1', text: 'Sample App')
  end

  it "should have the base title" do
    page.should have_selector('title',
                        text: "Ruby on Rails Tutorial Sample App")
  end

  it "should not have a custom page title" do
    page.should_not have_selector('title', text: '| Home')
  end
end
```

This uses the line

```
before { visit root_path }
```

to visit the root path before each example. (The **before** method can also be invoked
with **before(:each)**, which is a synonym.)

Another source of duplication appears in each example; we have both

```
it "should have the h1 'Sample App'" do
```

and

```
page.should have_selector('h1', text: 'Sample App')
```

which say essentially the same thing. In addition, both examples reference the **page** variable. We can eliminate these sources of duplication by telling RSpec that **page** is the *subject* of the tests using

```
subject { page }
```

and then using a variant of the **it** method to collapse the code and description into one line:

```
it { should have_selector('h1', text: 'Sample App') }
```

Because of **subject { page }**, the call to **should** automatically uses the **page** variable supplied by Capybara (Section 3.2.1).

Applying these changes gives much more compact tests for the Home page:

```
subject { page }

describe "Home page" do
  before { visit root_path }

  it { should have_selector('h1', text: 'Sample App') }
  it { should have_selector 'title',
                      text: "Ruby on Rails Tutorial Sample App" }
  it { should_not have_selector 'title', text: '| Home' }
end
```

This code looks nicer, but the title test is still a bit long. Indeed, most of the title tests in Listing 5.20 have long title text of the form

```
"Ruby on Rails Tutorial Sample App | About"
```

An exercise in Section 3.5 proposes eliminating some of this duplication by defining a **base_title** variable and using string interpolation (Listing 3.30). We can do even better by defining a **full_title**, which parallels the **full_title** helper from Listing 4.2.

We do this by creating both a **spec/support** directory and a **utilities.rb** file for RSpec utilities (Listing 5.26).

Listing 5.26 A file for RSpec utilities with a **full_title** function.
spec/support/utilities.rb

```
def full_title(page_title)
  base_title = "Ruby on Rails Tutorial Sample App"
  if page_title.empty?
    base_title
  else
    "#{base_title} | #{page_title}"
  end
end
```

Of course, this is essentially a duplicate of the helper in Listing 4.2, but having two independent methods allows us to catch any typos in the base title. This is dubious design though, and a better (slightly more advanced) approach, which tests the original **full_title** helper directly, appears in the exercises (Section 5.6).

Files in the **spec/support** directory are automatically included by RSpec, which means that we can write the Home tests as follows:

```
subject { page }

describe "Home page" do
  before { visit root_path }

  it { should have_selector('h1',    text: 'Sample App') }
  it { should have_selector('title', text: full_title('')) }
end
```

We can now simplify the tests for the Help, About, and Contact pages using the same methods used for the Home page. The results appear in Listing 5.27.

Listing 5.27 Prettier tests for the static pages.
spec/requests/static_pages_spec.rb

```
require 'spec_helper'

describe "Static pages" do

  subject { page }

  describe "Home page" do
```

```
    before { visit root_path }

    it { should have_selector('h1',    text: 'Sample App') }
    it { should have_selector('title', text: full_title('')) }
    it { should_not have_selector 'title', text: '| Home' }
  end

  describe "Help page" do
    before { visit help_path }

    it { should have_selector('h1',    text: 'Help') }
    it { should have_selector('title', text: full_title('Help')) }
  end

  describe "About page" do
    before { visit about_path }

    it { should have_selector('h1',    text: 'About') }
    it { should have_selector('title', text: full_title('About Us')) }
  end

  describe "Contact page" do
    before { visit contact_path }

    it { should have_selector('h1',    text: 'Contact') }
    it { should have_selector('title', text: full_title('Contact')) }
  end
end
```

You should now verify that the tests still pass:

```
$ bundle exec rspec spec/requests/static_pages_spec.rb
```

This RSpec style in Listing 5.27 is much pithier than the style in Listing 5.20—indeed, it can be made even pithier (Section 5.6). We will use this more compact style whenever possible when developing the rest of the sample application.

5.4 User Signup: A First Step

As a capstone to our work on the layout and routing, in this section we'll make a route for the signup page, which will mean creating a second controller along the way. This is a first important step toward allowing users to register for our site; we'll take the next step, modeling users, in Chapter 6, and we'll finish the job in Chapter 7.

5.4.1 Users Controller

It's been a while since we created our first controller, the StaticPages controller, way back in Section 3.1.2. It's time to create a second one, the Users controller. As before, we'll use **generate** to make the simplest controller that meets our present needs, namely, one with a stub signup page for new users. Following the conventional REST architecture favored by Rails, we'll call the action for new users **new** and pass it as an argument to **generate controller** to create it automatically (Listing 5.28).

Listing 5.28 Generating a Users controller (with a **new** action).

```
$ rails generate controller Users new --no-test-framework
      create  app/controllers/users_controller.rb
       route  get "users/new"
      invoke  erb
      create    app/views/users
      create    app/views/users/new.html.erb
      invoke  helper
      create    app/helpers/users_helper.rb
      invoke  assets
      invoke    coffee
      create      app/assets/javascripts/users.js.coffee
      invoke    scss
      create      app/assets/stylesheets/users.css.scss
```

This creates a Users controller with a **new** action (Listing 5.29) and a stub user view (Listing 5.30).

Listing 5.29 The initial Users controller, with a **new** action.
app/controllers/users_controller.rb

```
class UsersController < ApplicationController
  def new
  end

end
```

Listing 5.30 The initial **new** action for Users.
app/views/users/new.html.erb

```
<h1>Users#new</h1>
<p>Find me in app/views/users/new.html.erb</p>
```

5.4.2 Signup URI

With the code from Section 5.4.1, we already have a working page for new users at /users/new, but recall from Table 5.1 that we want the URI to be /signup instead. As in Section 5.3, we'll first write some integration tests, which we'll now generate:

```
$ rails generate integration_test user_pages
```

Then, following the model of the static pages spec in Listing 5.27, we'll fill in the user pages test with code to test for the contents of the **h1** and **title** tags, as seen in Listing 5.31.

Listing 5.31 The initial spec for users, with a test for the signup page.
spec/requests/user_pages_spec.rb

```ruby
require 'spec_helper'

describe "User pages" do

  subject { page }

  describe "signup page" do
    before { visit signup_path }

    it { should have_selector('h1',    text: 'Sign up') }
    it { should have_selector('title', text: full_title('Sign up')) }
  end
end
```

We can run these tests using the **rspec** command as usual:

```
$ bundle exec rspec spec/requests/user_pages_spec.rb
```

It's worth noting that we can also run all the request specs by passing the whole directory instead of just one file:

```
$ bundle exec rspec spec/requests/
```

Based on this pattern, you may be able to guess how to run *all* the specs:

```
$ bundle exec rspec spec/
```

For completeness, we'll usually use this method to run the tests through the rest of the tutorial. By the way, it's worth noting (since you may see other people use it) that you can also run the test suite using the **spec** Rake task:

```
$ bundle exec rake spec
```

(In fact, you can just type **rake** by itself; the default behavior of **rake** is to run the test suite.)

By construction, the Users controller already has a **new** action, so to get the test to pass all we need is the right route and the right view content. We'll follow the examples from Listing 5.21 and add a **match '/signup'** rule for the signup URI (Listing 5.32).

Listing 5.32 A route for the signup page.
config/routes.rb

```
SampleApp::Application.routes.draw do
  get "users/new"

  root to: 'static_pages#home'

  match '/signup',  to: 'users#new'

  match '/help',    to: 'static_pages#help'
  match '/about',   to: 'static_pages#about'
  match '/contact', to: 'static_pages#contact'
  .
  .
  .
end
```

Note that we have kept the rule **get "users/new"**, which was generated automatically by the Users controller generation in Listing 5.28. Currently, this rule is necessary for the **'users/new'** routing to work, but it doesn't follow the proper REST conventions (Table 2.2), and we will eliminate it in Section 7.1.2.

To get the tests to pass, all we need now is a view with the title and heading "Sign up" (Listing 5.33).

Listing 5.33 The initial (stub) signup page.
app/views/users/new.html.erb

```
<% provide(:title, 'Sign up') %>
<h1>Sign up</h1>
<p>Find me in app/views/users/new.html.erb</p>
```

At this point, the signup test in Listing 5.31 should pass. All that's left is to add the proper link to the button on the Home page. As with the other routes, **match** **'/signup'** gives us the named route **signup_path**, which we put to use in Listing 5.34.

Listing 5.34 Linking the button to the Signup page.
app/views/static_pages/home.html.erb

```
<div class="center hero-unit">
  <h1>Welcome to the Sample App</h1>

  <h2>
    This is the home page for the
    <a href="http://railstutorial.org/">Ruby on Rails Tutorial</a>
    sample application.
  </h2>

  <%= link_to "Sign up now!", signup_path, class: "btn btn-large btn-primary" %>
</div>

<%= link_to image_tag("rails.png", alt: "Rails"), 'http://rubyonrails.org/' %>
```

With that, we're done with the links and named routes, at least until we add a route for signing in (Chapter 8). The resulting new user page (at the URI /signup) appears in Figure 5.9.

At this point the tests should pass:

```
$ bundle exec rspec spec/
```

5.5 Conclusion

In this chapter, we've hammered our application layout into shape and polished up the routes. The rest of the book is dedicated to fleshing out the sample application: first, by adding users who can sign up, sign in, and sign out; next, by adding user microposts; and, finally, by adding the ability to follow other users.

At this point, if you are using Git you should merge the changes back into the master branch:

```
$ git add .
$ git commit -m "Finish layout and routes"
$ git checkout master
$ git merge filling-in-layout
```

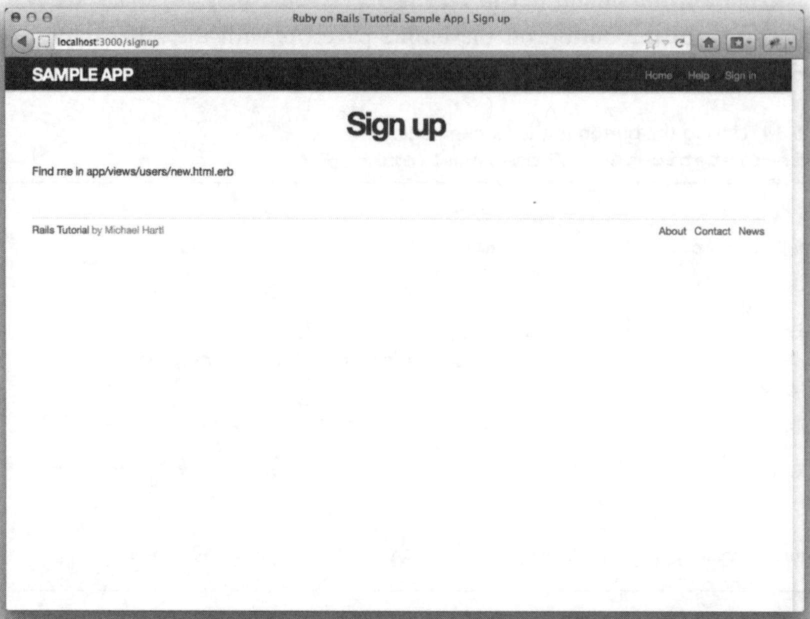

Figure 5.9 The new signup page at /signup.

You can also push up to GitHub:

```
$ git push
```

Finally, you can deploy to Heroku:

```
$ git push heroku
```

The result should be a working sample application on the production server:

```
$ heroku open
```

If you run into trouble, try running

```
$ heroku logs
```

to debug the error using the Heroku logfile.

5.6 Exercises

1. The code in Listing 5.27 for testing static pages is compact but is still a bit repetitive. RSpec supports a facility called *shared examples* to eliminate the kind of duplication. By following the example in Listing 5.35, fill in the missing tests for the Help, About, and Contact pages. Note that the **let** command, introduced briefly in Listing 3.30, creates a local variable with the given value on demand (i.e., when the variable is used), in contrast to an instance variable, which is created upon assignment.

2. You may have noticed that our tests for the layout links test the routing but don't actually check that the links on the layout go to the right pages. One way to implement these tests is to use **visit** and **click_link** inside the RSpec integration test. Fill in the code in Listing 5.36 to verify that all the layout links are properly defined.

3. Eliminate the need for the **full_title** test helper in Listing 5.26 by writing tests for the original helper method, as shown in Listing 5.37. (You will have to create both the **spec/helpers** directory and the **application_helper_spec.rb** file.) Then **include** it into the test using the code in Listing 5.38. Verify by running the test suite that the new code is still valid. *Note*: Listing 5.37 uses *regular expressions*, which we'll learn more about in Section 6.2.4. (Thanks to Alex Chaffee for the suggestion and code used in this exercise.)

Listing 5.35 Using an RSpec shared example to eliminate test duplication.
spec/requests/static_pages_spec.rb

```
require 'spec_helper'

describe "Static pages" do

  subject { page }

  shared_examples_for "all static pages" do
    it { should have_selector('h1',    text: heading) }
    it { should have_selector('title', text: full_title(page_title)) }
  end

  describe "Home page" do
    before { visit root_path }
    let(:heading)    { 'Sample App' }
    let(:page_title) { '' }

    it_should_behave_like "all static pages"
```

```
      it { should_not have_selector 'title', text: '| Home' }
  end

  describe "Help page" do
    .
    .
    .
  end

  describe "About page" do
    .
    .
    .
  end

  describe "Contact page" do
    .
    .
    .
  end
end
```

Listing 5.36 A test for the links on the layout.
spec/requests/static_pages_spec.rb

```
require 'spec_helper'

describe "Static pages" do
  .
  .
  .
  it "should have the right links on the layout" do
    visit root_path
    click_link "About"
    page.should have_selector 'title', text: full_title('About Us')
    click_link "Help"
    page.should # fill in
    click_link "Contact"
    page.should # fill in
    click_link "Home"
    click_link "Sign up now!"
    page.should # fill in
    click_link "sample app"
    page.should # fill in
  end
end
```

Listing 5.37 Tests for the **full_title** helper.
spec/helpers/application_helper_spec.rb

```
require 'spec_helper'

describe ApplicationHelper do

  describe "full_title" do
    it "should include the page title" do
      full_title("foo").should =~ /foo/
    end

    it "should include the base title" do
      full_title("foo").should =~ /^Ruby on Rails Tutorial Sample App/
    end

    it "should not include a bar for the home page" do
      full_title("").should_not =~ /\|/
    end
  end
end
```

Listing 5.38 Replacing the **full_title** test helper with a simple **include**.
spec/support/utilities.rb

```
include ApplicationHelper
```

CHAPTER 6
Modeling Users

In Chapter 5, we ended with a stub page for creating new users (Section 5.4); over the course of the next four chapters, we'll fulfill the promise implicit in this incipient signup page. The first critical step is to create a *data model* for users of our site, together with a way to store that data. In Chapter 7, we'll give users the ability to sign up for our site and create a user profile page. Once users can sign up, we'll let them sign in and sign out as well (Chapter 8), and in Chapter 9 (Section 9.2.1) we'll learn how to protect pages from improper access. Taken together, the material in Chapter 6 through Chapter 9 develops a full Rails login and authentication system. As you may know, there are various pre-built authentication solutions for Rails; Box 6.1 explains why, at least at first, it's probably a better idea to roll your own.

This is a long and action-packed chapter, and you may find it unusually challenging, especially if you are new to data modeling. By the end of it, though, we will have created an industrial-strength system for validating, storing, and retrieving user information.

Box 6.1 Roll Your Own Authentication System

Virtually all web applications require a login and authentication system of some sort. As a result, most web frameworks have a plethora of options for implementing such systems, and Rails is no exception. Examples of authentication and authorization systems include Clearance, Authlogic, Devise, and CanCan (as well as non-Rails-specific solutions built on top of OpenID or OAuth). It's reasonable to ask why we should reinvent the wheel. Why not just use an off-the-shelf solution instead of rolling our own?

For one, practical experience that authentication on most sites requires extensive customization and modifying a third-party product is often more work than writing

---

the system from scratch. In addition, off-the-shelf systems are "black boxes," with potentially mysterious innards; when you write your own system, you are far more likely to understand it. Moreover, recent additions to Rails (Section 6.3) make it easy to write a custom authentication system. Finally, if you do end up using a third-party system later on, you'll be in a much better position to understand and modify it if you've first built one yourself.

As usual, if you're following along using Git for version control, now would be a good time to make a topic branch for modeling users:

```
$ git checkout master
$ git checkout -b modeling-users
```

(The first line here is just to make sure that you start on the master branch, so that the **modeling-users** topic branch is based on **master**. You can skip that command if you're already on the master branch.)

6.1 User Model

Although the ultimate goal of the next three chapters is to make a signup page for our site (mocked up in Figure 6.1), it would do little good now to accept information for new users: We don't currently have any place to put it. Thus, the first step in signing up users is to make a data structure to capture and store their information.

In Rails, the default data structure for a data model is called, naturally enough, a *model* (the M in MVC from Section 1.2.6). The default Rails solution to the problem of persistence is to use a *database* for long-term data storage, and the default library for interacting with the database is called *Active Record*.[1] Active Record comes with a host of methods for creating, saving, and finding data objects, all without having to use the structured query language (SQL)[2] used by relational databases. Moreover, Rails has a feature called *migrations* to allow data definitions to be written in pure Ruby, without having to learn an SQL data definition language (DDL). The effect is that Rails

---

1. The name comes from the "active record pattern," identified and named in *Patterns of Enterprise Application Architecture* by Martin Fowler.

2. Pronounced "ess-cue-ell," although the alternate pronunciation "sequel" is also common.

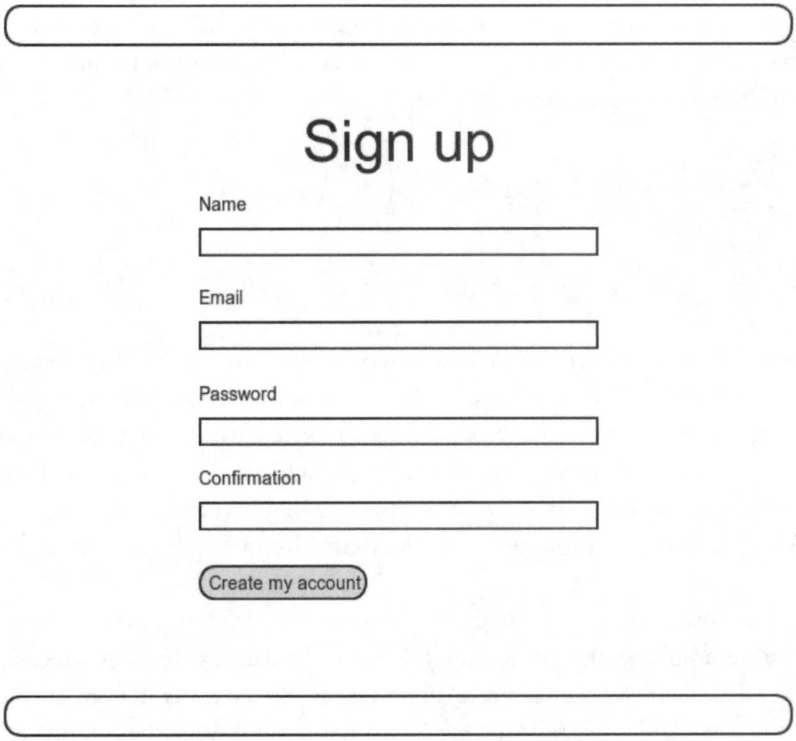

Figure 6.1 A mockup of the user signup page.

insulates you almost entirely from the details of the data store. In this book, by using SQLite for development and PostgreSQL (via Heroku) for deployment (Section 1.4), we have developed this theme even further, to the point where we barely ever have to think about how Rails stores data, even for production applications.

6.1.1 Database Migrations

You may recall from Section 4.4.5 that we have already encountered, via a custom-built `User` class, user objects with `name` and `email` attributes. That class served as a useful example, but it lacked the critical property of *persistence*: When we created a User object at the Rails console, it disappeared as soon as we exited. Our goal in this section is to create a model for users that won't disappear quite so easily.

As with the User class in Section 4.4.5, we'll start by modeling a user with two attributes, a **name** and an **email** address, the latter of which we'll use as a unique username.[3] (We'll add an attribute for passwords in Section 6.3.) In Listing 4.9, we did this with Ruby's **attr_accessor** method:

```
class User
  attr_accessor :name, :email
  .
  .
  .
end
```

In contrast, when using Rails to model users, we don't need to identify the attributes explicitly. As noted briefly above, to store data Rails uses a relational database by default, which consists of *tables* composed of data *rows*, where each row has *columns* of data attributes. For example, to store users with names and email addresses, we'll create a **users** table with **name** and **email** columns (with each row corresponding to one user). By naming the columns in this way, we'll let Active Record figure out the User object attributes for us.

Let's see how this works. (If this discussion gets too abstract for your taste, be patient; the console examples starting in Section 6.1.3 and the database browser screenshots in Figure 6.3 and Figure 6.6 should make things clearer.) You may recall from Listing 5.28 that we created a Users controller (along with a **new** action) using the command

```
$ rails generate controller Users new --no-test-framework
```

There is an analogous command for making a model: **generate model**. Listing 6.1 shows the command to generate a User model with two attributes, **name** and **email**.

Listing 6.1 Generating a User model.

```
$ rails generate model User name:string email:string
      invoke  active_record
      create    db/migrate/[timestamp]_create_users.rb
      create    app/models/user.rb
      invoke  rspec
      create      spec/models/user_spec.rb
```

---

3. By using an email address as the username, we open the theoretical possibility of communicating with our users at a future date.

(Note that, in contrast to the plural convention for controller names, model names are singular: a Users controller, but a User model.) By passing the optional parameters **name:string** and **email:string**, we tell Rails about the two attributes we want, along with what types those attributes should be (in this case, **string**). Compare this with including the action names in Listing 3.4 and Listing 5.28.

One of the results of the **generate** command in Listing 6.1 is a new file called a *migration*. Migrations provide a way to alter the structure of the database incrementally, so that our data model can adapt to changing requirements. In the case of the User model, the migration is created automatically by the model generation script; it creates a **users** table with two columns, **name** and **email**, as shown in Listing 6.2. (We'll see in Section 6.2.5 and again in Section 6.3 how to make a migration from scratch.)

Listing 6.2 Migration for the User model (to create a **users** table).
db/migrate/[timestamp]_create_users.rb

```
class CreateUsers < ActiveRecord::Migration
  def change
    create_table :users do |t|
      t.string :name
      t.string :email

      t.timestamps
    end
  end
end
```

Note that the name of the migration file is prefixed by a *timestamp* based on when the migration was generated. In the early days of migrations, the filenames were prefixed with incrementing integers, which caused conflicts for collaborating teams if multiple programmers had migrations with the same number. Barring the improbable scenario of migrations generated the same second, using timestamps conveniently avoids such collisions.

The migration itself consists of a **change** method that determines the change to be made to the database. In the case of Listing 6.2, **change** uses a Rails method called **create_table** to create a *table* in the database for storing users. The **create_table** method accepts a block (Section 4.3.2) with one block variable, in this case called **t** (for "table"). Inside the block, the **create_table** method uses the **t** object to create **name**

users	
id	integer
name	string
email	string
created_at	datetime
updated_at	datetime

Figure 6.2   The users data model produced by Listing 6.2.

and **email** columns in the database, both of type **string**.[4] Here the table name is plural (**users**) even though the model name is singular (User), which reflects a linguistic convention followed by Rails: A model represents a single user, whereas a database table consists of many users. The final line in the block, **t.timestamps**, is a special command that creates two *magic columns* called **created_at** and **updated_at**, which are timestamps that automatically record when a given user is created and updated. (We'll see concrete examples of the magic columns starting in Section 6.1.3.) The full data model represented by this migration is shown in Figure 6.2.

We can run the migration, known as "migrating up," using the **rake** command (Box 2.1) as follows:

```
$ bundle exec rake db:migrate
```

(You may recall that we ran this command once before, in Section 2.2.) The first time **db:migrate** is run, it creates a file called **db/development.sqlite3**, which is an SQLite[5] database. We can see the structure of the database using the excellent SQLite Database Browser to open the **db/development.sqlite3** file (Figure 6.3); compare with the diagram in Figure 6.2. You might note that there's one column in Figure 6.3 not accounted for in the migration: the **id** column. As noted briefly in Section 2.2, this column is created automatically and is used by Rails to identify each row uniquely.

---

4. Don't worry about exactly how the **t** object manages to do this; the beauty of *abstraction layers* is that we don't have to know. We can just trust the **t** object to do its job.

5. Officially pronounced "ess-cue-ell-ite," although the (mis)pronunciation "sequel-ite" is also common.

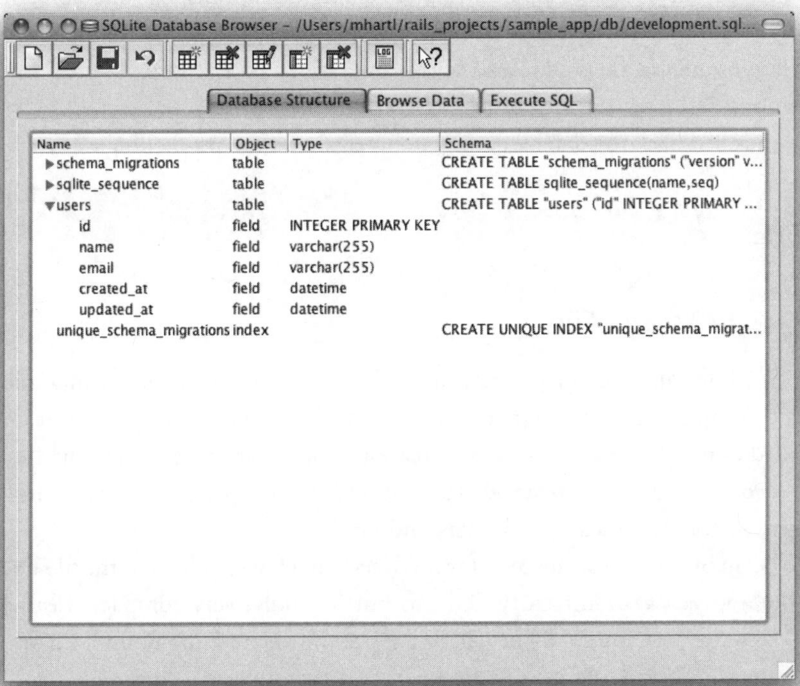

Figure 6.3   The SQLite Database Browser with our new **users** table.

Most migrations, including all the ones in the *Rails Tutorial*, are *reversible*, which means we can "migrate down" and undo them with a single Rake task, called **db:rollback**:

```
$ bundle exec rake db:rollback
```

(See Box 3.1 for another technique useful for reversing migrations.) Under the hood, this command executes the **drop_table** command to remove the users table from the database. The reason this works is that the **change** method knows that **drop_table** is the inverse of **create_table**, which means that the rollback migration can be easily inferred. In the case of an irreversible migration, such as one to remove a database column, it is necessary to define separate **up** and **down** methods in place of the single **change** method. Read about migrations in the Rails Guides for more information.

If you rolled back the database, migrate up again before proceeding:

```
$ bundle exec rake db:migrate
```

6.1.2 The Model File

We've seen how the User model generation in Listing 6.1 generated a migration file (Listing 6.2), and we saw in Figure 6.3 the results of running this migration: It updated a file called **development.sqlite3** by creating a table **users** with columns **id**, **name**, **email**, **created_at**, and **updated_at**. Listing 6.1 also created the model itself; the rest of this section is dedicated to understanding it.

We begin by looking at the code for the User model, which lives in the file **user.rb** inside the **app/models/** directory. It is, to put it mildly, very compact (Listing 6.3). (*Note*: The **attr_accessible** line will not appear if you are using Rails 3.2.2 or earlier. In this case, you should add it in Section 6.1.2.)

Listing 6.3 The brand new User model.
app/models/user.rb

```
class User < ActiveRecord::Base
  attr_accessible :name, :email
end
```

Recall from Section 4.4.2 that the syntax **class User < ActiveRecord::Base** means that the **User** class *inherits* from **ActiveRecord::Base**, so that the User model automatically has all the functionality of the **ActiveRecord::Base** class. Of course, knowledge of this inheritance doesn't do any good unless we know what **ActiveRecord::Base** contains, and we'll get a first look momentarily. Before we move on, though, there are two tasks to complete.

Model Annotation

Although it's not strictly necessary, you might find it convenient to *annotate* your Rails models using the **annotate** gem (Listing 6.4).

Listing 6.4 Adding the **annotate** gem to the **Gemfile**.

```
source 'https://rubygems.org'
.
.
.
group :development do
  gem 'sqlite3', '1.3.5'
  gem 'rspec-rails', '2.9.0'
  gem 'annotate', '~> 2.4.1.beta'

group :test do
  .
  .
  .
end
```

(We place the **annotate** gem in a **group :development** block (analogous to **group :test**) because the annotations aren't needed in production applications.) We next install it with **bundle install**:

```
$ bundle install
```

This gives us a command called **annotate**, which simply adds comments containing the data model to the model file:

```
$ bundle exec annotate --position before
Annotated (1): User
```

The results appear in Listing 6.5.

Listing 6.5 The annotated User model.
app/models/user.rb

```
# == Schema Information
#
# Table name: users
#
#  id         :integer          not null, primary key
#  name       :string(255)
#  email      :string(255)
#  created_at :datetime
```

```
#   updated_at :datetime
#

class User < ActiveRecord::Base
  attr_accessible :name, :email
end
```

I find that having the data model visible in the model files helps remind me which attributes the model has, but future code listings will omit the annotations for brevity. (Note that, if you want your annotations to be up-to-date, you'll have to run **annotate** again any time the data model changes.)

Accessible Attributes

Let's revisit the User model, focusing now on the **attr_accessible** line (Listing 6.6). This line tells Rails which attributes of the model are *accessible*, that is, which attributes can be modified automatically by outside users (such as users submitting requests with web browsers).

Listing 6.6 Making the **name** and **email** attributes accessible.
app/models/user.rb

```
class User < ActiveRecord::Base
  attr_accessible :name, :email
end
```

The code in Listing 6.6 doesn't do quite what you might think. By default, *all* model attributes are accessible. What Listing 6.6 does is to ensure that the **name** and **email** attributes—and *only* the **name** and **email** attributes—are automatically accessible to outside users. We'll see why this is important in Chapter 9: using **attr_accessible** is important for preventing a *mass assignment* vulnerability, a distressingly common and often serious security hole in many Rails applications.

6.1.3 Creating User Objects

We've done some good prep work, and now it's time to cash in and learn about Active Record by playing with our newly created User model. As in Chapter 4, our tool of choice is the Rails console. Since we don't (yet) want to make any changes to our database, we'll start the console in a *sandbox*:

```
$ rails console --sandbox
Loading development environment in sandbox
Any modifications you make will be rolled back on exit
>>
```

As indicated by the helpful message "Any modifications you make will be rolled back on exit," when started in a sandbox the console will "roll back" (i.e., undo) any database changes introduced during the session.

In the console session in Section 4.4.5, we created a new user object with **User.new**, which we had access to only after requiring the example user file in Listing 4.9. With models, the situation is different; as you may recall from Section 4.4.4, the Rails console automatically loads the Rails environment, which includes the models. This means that we can make a new user object without any further work:

```
>> User.new
=> #<User id: nil, name: nil, email: nil, created_at: nil, updated_at: nil>
```

We see here the default console representation of a user object, which prints out the same attributes shown in Figure 6.2 and Listing 6.5.

When called with no arguments, **User.new** returns an object with all **nil** attributes. In Section 4.4.5, we designed the example User class to take an *initialization hash* to set the object attributes; that design choice was motivated by Active Record, which allows objects to be initialized in the same way:

```
>> user = User.new(name: "Michael Hartl", email: "mhartl@example.com")
=> #<User id: nil, name: "Michael Hartl", email: "mhartl@example.com",
created_at: nil, updated_at: nil>
```

Here we see that the name and email attributes have been set as expected.

If you've been tailing the development log, you may have noticed that no new lines have shown up yet. This is because calling **User.new** doesn't touch the database; it simply creates a new Ruby object in memory. To save the user object to the database, we call the **save** method on the **user** variable:

```
>> user.save
=> true
```

The **save** method returns **true** if it succeeds and **false** otherwise. (Currently, all saves should succeed; we'll see cases in Section 6.2 when some will fail.) As soon as you save, you should see a line in the development log with the SQL command to **INSERT INTO "users"**. Because of the many methods supplied by Active Record, we won't ever need raw SQL in this book, and I'll omit discussion of the SQL commands from now on. But you can learn a lot by watching the log.

You may have noticed that the new user object had **nil** values for the **id** and the magic columns **created_at** and **updated_at** attributes. Let's see if our **save** changed anything:

```
>> user
=> #<User id: 1, name: "Michael Hartl", email: "mhartl@example.com",
created_at: "2011-12-05 00:57:46", updated_at: "2011-12-05 00:57:46">
```

We see that the **id** has been assigned a value of **1**, while the magic columns have been assigned the current time and date.[6] Currently, the created and updated timestamps are identical; we'll see them differ in Section 6.1.5.

As with the User class in Section 4.4.5, instances of the User model allow access to their attributes using a dot notation:[7]

```
>> user.name
=> "Michael Hartl"
>> user.email
=> "mhartl@example.com"
>> user.updated_at
=> Tue, 05 Dec 2011 00:57:46 UTC +00:00
```

---

6. In case you're curious about **"2011-12-05 00:57:46"**, I'm not writing this after midnight; the timestamps are recorded in Coordinated Universal Time (UTC), which for most practical purposes is the same as Greenwich Mean Time. From the NIST Time and Frequency FAQ: **Q:** Why is UTC used as the acronym for Coordinated Universal Time instead of CUT? **A:** In 1970 the Coordinated Universal Time system was devised by an international advisory group of technical experts within the International Telecommunication Union (ITU). The ITU felt it was best to designate a single abbreviation for use in all languages in order to minimize confusion. Since unanimous agreement could not be achieved on using either the English word order, CUT, or the French word order, TUC, the acronym UTC was chosen as a compromise.

7. Note the value of **user.updated_at**. told you the timestamp was in UTC.

As we'll see in Chapter 7, it's often convenient to make and save a model in two steps as we have above, but Active Record also lets you combine them into one step with **User.create**:

```
>> User.create(name: "A Nother", email: "another@example.org")
#<User id: 2, name: "A Nother", email: "another@example.org", created_at:
"2011-12-05 01:05:24", updated_at: "2011-12-05 01:05:24">
>> foo = User.create(name: "Foo", email: "foo@bar.com")
#<User id: 3, name: "Foo", email: "foo@bar.com", created_at: "2011-12-05
01:05:42", updated_at: "2011-12-05 01:05:42">
```

Note that **User.create**, rather than returning **true** or **false**, returns the User object itself, which we can optionally assign to a variable (such as **foo** in the second command above).

The inverse of **create** is **destroy**:

```
>> foo.destroy
=> #<User id: 3, name: "Foo", email: "foo@bar.com", created_at: "2011-12-05
01:05:42", updated_at: "2011-12-05 01:05:42">
```

Oddly, **destroy**, like **create**, returns the object in question, although I can't recall ever having used the return value of **destroy**. Even odder, perhaps, is that the **destroy**ed object still exists in memory:

```
>> foo
=> #<User id: 3, name: "Foo", email: "foo@bar.com", created_at: "2011-12-05
01:05:42", updated_at: "2011-12-05 01:05:42">
```

How do we know if we really destroyed an object? And for saved and non-destroyed objects, how can we retrieve users from the database? It's time to learn how to use Active Record to find user objects.

6.1.4   Finding User Objects

Active Record provides several options for finding objects. Let's use them to find the first user we created while verifying that the third user (**foo**) has been destroyed. We'll start with the existing user:

```
>> User.find(1)
=> #<User id: 1, name: "Michael Hartl", email: "mhartl@example.com",
created_at: "2011-12-05 00:57:46", updated_at: "2011-12-05 00:57:46">
```

Here we've passed the id of the user to **User.find**; Active Record returns the user with that id.

Let's see if the user with an **id** of **3** still exists in the database:

```
>> User.find(3)
ActiveRecord::RecordNotFound: Couldn't find User with ID=3
```

Since we destroyed our third user in Section 6.1.3, Active Record can't find it in the database. Instead, **find** raises an *exception*, which is a way of indicating an exceptional event in the execution of a program—in this case, a nonexistent Active Record id, which causes **find** to raise an **ActiveRecord::RecordNotFound** exception.[8]

In addition to the generic **find**, Active Record also allows us to find users by specific attributes:

```
>> User.find_by_email("mhartl@example.com")
=> #<User id: 1, name: "Michael Hartl", email: "mhartl@example.com",
created_at: "2011-12-05 00:57:46", updated_at: "2011-12-05 00:57:46">
```

The **find_by_email** method is automatically created by Active Record based on the **email** attribute in the **users** table. (As you might guess, Active Record creates a **find_by_name** method as well.) Since we will be using email addresses as usernames, this sort of **find** will be useful when we learn how to let users sign in to our site (Chapter 7). If you're worried that **find_by_email** will be inefficient if there are a large number of users, you're ahead of the game; we'll cover this issue, and its solution via database indices, in Section 6.2.5.

We'll end with a couple of more general ways of finding users. First, there's **first**:

```
>> User.first
=> #<User id: 1, name: "Michael Hartl", email: "mhartl@example.com",
created_at: "2011-12-05 00:57:46", updated_at: "2011-12-05 00:57:46">
```

Naturally, **first** just returns the first user in the database. There's also **all**:

```
>> User.all
=> [#<User id: 1, name: "Michael Hartl", email: "mhartl@example.com",
created_at: "2011-12-05 00:57:46", updated_at: "2011-12-05 00:57:46">,
#<User id: 2, name: "A Nother", email: "another@example.org", created_at:
"2011-12-05 01:05:24", updated_at: "2011-12-05 01:05:24">]
```

---

8. Exceptions and exception handling are somewhat advanced Ruby subjects, and we won't need them much in this book. They are important, though, and I suggest learning about them using one of the Ruby books recommended in Section 1.1.1.

No prizes for inferring that **all** returns an array (Section 4.3.1) of all users in the database.

6.1.5 Updating User Objects

Once we've created objects, we often want to update them. There are two basic ways to do this. First, we can assign attributes individually, as we did in Section 4.4.5:

```
>> user            # Just a reminder about our user's attributes
=> #<User id: 1, name: "Michael Hartl", email: "mhartl@example.com",
created_at: "2011-12-05 00:57:46", updated_at: "2011-12-05 00:57:46">
>> user.email = "mhartl@example.net"
=> "mhartl@example.net"
>> user.save
=> true
```

Note that the final step is necessary to write the changes to the database. We can see what happens without a save by using **reload**, which reloads the object based on the database information:

```
>> user.email
=> "mhartl@example.net"
>> user.email = "foo@bar.com"
=> "foo@bar.com"
>> user.reload.email
=> "mhartl@example.net"
```

Now that we've updated the user, the magic columns differ, as promised in Section 6.1.3:

```
>> user.created_at
=> "2011-12-05 00:57:46"
>> user.updated_at
=> "2011-12-05 01:37:32"
```

The second way to update attributes is to use **update_attributes**:

```
>> user.update_attributes(name: "The Dude", email: "dude@abides.org")
=> true
>> user.name
=> "The Dude"
>> user.email
=> "dude@abides.org"
```

The `update_attributes` method accepts a hash of attributes, and on success performs both the update and the save in one step (returning `true` to indicate that the save went through). It's worth noting that, once you have defined some attributes as accessible using `attr_accessible` (Section 6.1.2), *only* those attributes can be modified using `update_attributes`. If you ever find that your models mysteriously start refusing to update certain columns, check to make sure that those columns are included in the call to `attr_accessible`.

6.2 User Validations

The User model we created in Section 6.1 now has working `name` and `email` attributes, but they are completely generic: Any string (including an empty one) is currently valid in either case. And yet, names and email addresses are more specific than this. For example, `name` should be non-blank, and `email` should match the specific format characteristic of email addresses. Moreover, since we'll be using email addresses as unique usernames when users sign in, we shouldn't allow email duplicates in the database.

In short, we shouldn't allow `name` and `email` to be just any strings; we should enforce certain constraints on their values. Active Record allows us to impose such constraints using *validations*. In this section, we'll cover several of the most common cases, validating *presence*, *length*, *format*, and *uniqueness*. In Section 6.3.4 we'll add a final common validation, *confirmation*. And we'll see in Section 7.3 how validations give us convenient error messages when users make submissions that violate them.

6.2.1 Initial User Tests

As with the other features of our sample app, we'll add User model validations using test-driven development. Because we didn't pass the

```
--no-test-framework
```

flag when we generated the User model (unlike, e.g., Listing 5.28), the command in Listing 6.1 produces an initial spec for testing users, but in this case it's practically blank (Listing 6.7).

Listing 6.7 The practically blank default User spec.
spec/models/user_spec.rb

```
require 'spec_helper'

describe User do
  pending "add some examples to (or delete) #{__FILE__}"
end
```

This simply uses the **pending** method to indicate that we should fill the spec with something useful. We can see its effect by running the User model spec:

```
$ bundle exec rspec spec/models/user_spec.rb
*

Finished in 0.01999 seconds
1 example, 0 failures, 1 pending

Pending:
  User add some examples to (or delete)
  /Users/mhartl/rails_projects/sample_app/spec/models/user_spec.rb
  (Not Yet Implemented)
```

On many systems, pending specs will be displayed in yellow to indicate that they are in between passing (green) and failing (red).

We'll follow the advice of the default spec by filling it in with some RSpec examples, shown in Listing 6.8.

Listing 6.8 Testing for the **:name** and **:email** attributes.
spec/models/user_spec.rb

```
require 'spec_helper'

describe User do

  before { @user = User.new(name: "Example User", email: "user@example.com") }

  subject { @user }

  it { should respond_to(:name) }
  it { should respond_to(:email) }
end
```

The **before** block, which we saw in Listing 5.27, runs the code inside the block before each example—in this case, creating a new **@user** instance variable using **User.new** and a valid initialization hash. Then

```
subject { @user }
```

makes **@user** the default subject of the test example, as seen before in the context of the **page** variable in Section 5.3.4.

The two examples in Listing 6.8 test for the existence of **name** and **email** attributes:

```
it { should respond_to(:name) }
it { should respond_to(:email) }
```

These examples implicitly use the Ruby method **respond_to?**, which accepts a symbol and returns **true** if the object responds to the given method or attribute and **false** otherwise:

```
$ rails console --sandbox
>> user = User.new
>> user.respond_to?(:name)
=> true
>> user.respond_to?(:foobar)
=> false
```

(Recall from Section 4.2.3 that Ruby uses a question mark to indicate such true/false boolean methods.) The tests themselves rely on the *boolean convention* used by RSpec: the code

```
@user.respond_to?(:name)
```

can be tested using the RSpec code

```
@user.should respond_to(:name)
```

Because of **subject { @user }**, we can leave off **@user** in the test, yielding

```
it { should respond_to(:name) }
```

These kinds of tests allow us to use TDD to add new attributes and methods to our User model, and as a side effect we get a nice specification for the methods that all **User** objects should respond to.

You should verify at this point that the tests fail:

```
$ bundle exec rspec spec/
```

Even though we created a development database with **rake db:migrate** in Section 6.1.1, the tests fail because the *test database* doesn't yet know about the data model (indeed, it doesn't yet exist at all). We can create a test database with the correct structure, and thereby get the tests to pass, using the **db:test:prepare** Rake task:

```
$ bundle exec rake db:test:prepare
```

This just ensures that the data model from the development database, **db/development .sqlite3**, is reflected in the test database, **db/test.sqlite3**. Failure to run this Rake task after a migration is a common source of confusion. In addition, sometimes the test database gets corrupted and needs to be reset. If your test suite is mysteriously breaking, be sure to try running **rake db:test:prepare** to see if that fixes the problem.

6.2.2   Validating Presence

Perhaps the most elementary validation is *presence*, which simply verifies that a given attribute is present. For example, in this section we'll ensure that both the name and email fields are present before a user gets saved to the database. In Section 7.3.2, we'll see how to propagate this requirement up to the signup form for creating new users.

We'll start with a test for the presence of a **name** attribute. Although the first step in TDD is to write a *failing* test (Section 3.2.1), in this case we don't yet know enough about validations to write the proper test, so we'll write the validation first, using the console to understand it. Then we'll comment out the validation, write a failing test, and verify that uncommenting the validation gets the test to pass. This procedure may seem pedantic for such a simple test, but I have seen many "simple" tests that actually test the wrong thing; being meticulous about TDD is simply the *only* way to be confident that we're testing the right thing. (This comment-out technique is also useful when rescuing an application whose application code is already written but—*quelle horreur!*—has no tests.)

The way to validate the presence of the name attribute is to use the **validates** method with argument **presence: true**, as shown in Listing 6.9. The **presence: true** argument is a one-element *options hash*; recall from Section 4.3.4 that curly braces are optional when passing hashes as the final argument in a method. (As noted in Section 5.1.1, the use of options hashes is a recurring theme in Rails.)

Listing 6.9 Validating the presence of a **name** attribute.
app/models/user.rb

```
class User < ActiveRecord::Base
  attr_accessible :name, :email

  validates :name, presence: true
end
```

Listing 6.9 may look like magic, but **validates** is just a method, as indeed is **attr_accessible**. An equivalent formulation of Listing 6.9 using parentheses is as follows:

```
class User < ActiveRecord::Base
  attr_accessible(:name, :email)

  validates(:name, presence: true)
end
```

Let's drop into the console to see the effects of adding a validation to our User model:[9]

```
$ rails console --sandbox
>> user = User.new(name: "", email: "mhartl@example.com")
>> user.save
=> false
>> user.valid?
=> false
```

Here **user.save** returns **false**, indicating a failed save. In the final command, we use the **valid?** method, which returns **false** when the object fails one or more validations,

9. I'll omit the output of console commands when they are not particularly instructive—for example, the results of **User.new**.

and **true** when all validations pass. In this case, we only have one validation, so we
know which one failed, but it can still be helpful to check using the **errors** object
generated on failure:

```
>> user.errors.full_messages
=> ["Name can't be blank"]
```

(The error message is a hint that Rails validates the presence of an attribute using the
blank? method, which we saw at the end of Section 4.4.3.)

   Now for the failing test. To ensure that our incipient test will fail, let's comment
out the validation at this point (Listing 6.10).

Listing 6.10 Commenting out a validation to ensure a failing test.
app/models/user.rb

```
class User < ActiveRecord::Base
  attr_accessible :name, :email

  # validates :name, presence: true
end
```

   The initial validation tests then appear as in Listing 6.11.

Listing 6.11 A failing test for validation of the **name** attribute.
spec/models/user_spec.rb

```
require 'spec_helper'

describe User do

  before do
    @user = User.new(name: "Example User", email: "user@example.com")
  end

  subject { @user }

  it { should respond_to(:name) }
  it { should respond_to(:email) }

  it { should be_valid }

  describe "when name is not present" do
    before { @user.name = " " }
    it { should_not be_valid }
  end
end
```

The first new example is just a sanity check, verifying that the **@user** object is initially valid:

```
it { should be_valid }
```

This is another example of the RSpec boolean convention we saw in Section 6.2.1: Whenever an object responds to a boolean method **foo?**, there is a corresponding test method called **be_foo**. In this case, we can test the result of calling

```
@user.valid?
```

with

```
@user.should be_valid
```

As before, **subject { @user }** lets us leave off **@user**, yielding

```
it { should be_valid }
```

The second test first sets the user's name to an invalid (blank) value, and then tests to see that the resulting **@user** object is invalid:

```
describe "when name is not present" do
  before { @user.name = " " }
  it { should_not be_valid }
end
```

This uses a **before** block to set the user's name to an invalid (blank) value and then checks that the resulting user object is not valid.

You should verify that the tests fail at this point:

```
$ bundle exec rspec spec/models/user_spec.rb
...F
4 examples, 1 failure
```

Now uncomment the validation (i.e., revert Listing 6.10 back to Listing 6.9) to get the tests to pass:

```
$ bundle exec rspec spec/models/user_spec.rb
....
4 examples, 0 failures
```

Of course, we also want to validate the presence of email addresses. The test (Listing 6.12) is analogous to the one for the **name** attribute.

Listing 6.12 A test for presence of the **email** attribute.
`spec/models/user_spec.rb`

```
require 'spec_helper'

describe User do

  before do
    @user = User.new(name: "Example User", email: "user@example.com")
  end
  .
  .
  .
  describe "when email is not present" do
    before { @user.email = " " }
    it { should_not be_valid }
  end
end
```

The implementation is also virtually the same, as seen in Listing 6.13.

Listing 6.13 Validating the presence of the **name** and **email** attributes.
`app/models/user.rb`

```
class User < ActiveRecord::Base
  attr_accessible :name, :email

  validates :name,  presence: true
  validates :email, presence: true
end
```

Now all the tests should pass, and the presence validations are complete.

6.2.3 Length Validation

We've constrained our User model to require a name for each user, but we should go further: The users' names will be displayed on the sample site, so we should enforce some limit on their length. With all the work we did in Section 6.2.2, this step is easy.

We start with a test. There's no science to picking a maximum length; we'll just pull **50** out of thin air as a reasonable upper bound, which means verifying that names of **51** characters are too long (Listing 6.14).

Listing 6.14 A test for **name** length validation.
spec/models/user_spec.rb

```
require 'spec_helper'

describe User do

  before do
    @user = User.new(name: "Example User", email: "user@example.com")
  end
  .
  .
  .
  describe "when name is too long" do
    before { @user.name = "a" * 51 }
    it { should_not be_valid }
  end
end
```

For convenience, we've used "string multiplication" in Listing 6.14 to make a string 51 characters long. We can see how this works using the console:

```
>> "a" * 51
=> "aaaaaaaaaaaaaaaaaaaaaaaaaaaaaaaaaaaaaaaaaaaaaaaaaaa"
>> ("a" * 51).length
=> 51
```

The test in Listing 6.14 should fail. To get it to pass, we need to know about the validation argument to constrain length, **:length**, along with the **:maximum** parameter to enforce the upper bound (Listing 6.15).

Listing 6.15 Adding a length validation for the **name** attribute.
app/models/user.rb

```
class User < ActiveRecord::Base
  attr_accessible :name, :email

  validates :name,  presence: true, length: { maximum: 50 }
  validates :email, presence: true
end
```

Now the tests should pass. With our test suite passing again, we can move on to a more challenging validation: email format.

6.2.4 Format Validation

Our validations for the **name** attribute enforce only minimal constraints—any non-blank name under 51 characters will do—but of course the **email** attribute must satisfy more stringent requirements. So far we've only rejected blank email addresses; in this section, we'll require email addresses to conform to the familiar pattern **user@example.com**.

Neither the tests nor the validation will be exhaustive, just good enough to accept most valid email addresses and reject most invalid ones. We'll start with a couple tests involving collections of valid and invalid addresses. To make these collections, it's worth knowing about the useful **%w[]** technique for making arrays of strings, as seen in this console session:

```
>> %w[foo bar baz]
=> ["foo", "bar", "baz"]
>> addresses = %w[user@foo.COM THE_US-ER@foo.bar.org first.last@foo.jp]
=> ["user@foo.COM", "THE_US-ER@foo.bar.org", "first.last@foo.jp"]
>> addresses.each do |address|
?>   puts address
>> end
user@foo.COM
THE_US-ER@foo.bar.org
first.last@foo.jp
```

Here we've iterated over the elements of the **addresses** array using the **each** method (Section 4.3.2). With this technique in hand, we're ready to write some basic email format validation tests (Listing 6.16).

Listing 6.16 Tests for email format validation.
spec/models/user_spec.rb

```
require 'spec_helper'

describe User do

  before do
    @user = User.new(name: "Example User", email: "user@example.com")
  end
  .
  .
  .
  describe "when email format is invalid" do
    it "should be invalid" do
      addresses = %w[user@foo,com user_at_foo.org example.user@foo.
                     foo@bar_baz.com foo@bar+baz.com]
```

```
          addresses.each do |invalid_address|
            @user.email = invalid_address
            @user.should_not be_valid
          end
        end
    end

    describe "when email format is valid" do
      it "should be valid" do
        addresses = %w[user@foo.COM A_US-ER@f.b.org frst.lst@foo.jp a+b@baz.cn]
        addresses.each do |valid_address|
          @user.email = valid_address
          @user.should be_valid
        end
      end
    end
end
```

As noted above, these are far from exhaustive, but we do check the common valid
email forms **user@foo.COM**, **THE_US-ER@foo.bar.org** (uppercase, underscores, and
compound domains), and **first.last@foo.jp** (the standard corporate username
first.last, with a two-letter top-level domain **jp**), along with several invalid forms.

The application code for email format validation uses a *regular expression* (or *regex*)
to define the format, along with the **:format** argument to the **validates** method
(Listing 6.17).

Listing 6.17 Validating the email format with a regular expression.
app/models/user.rb

```
class User < ActiveRecord::Base
  attr_accessible :name, :email

  validates :name,  presence: true, length: { maximum: 50 }
  VALID_EMAIL_REGEX = /\A[\w+\-.]+@[a-z\d\-.]+\.[a-z]+\z/i
  validates :email, presence: true, format: { with: VALID_EMAIL_REGEX }
end
```

Here the regex **VALID_EMAIL_REGEX** is a *constant*, indicated in Ruby by a name starting
with a capital letter. The code

```
VALID_EMAIL_REGEX = /\A[\w+\-.]+@[a-z\d\-.]+\.[a-z]+\z/i
validates :email, presence: true, format: { with: VALID_EMAIL_REGEX }
```

Table 6.1   Breaking down the email regex from Listing 6.17.

Expression	Meaning
`/\A[\w+\-.]+@[a-z\d\-.]+\.[a-z]+\z/i`	full regex
`/`	start of regex
`\A`	match start of a string
`[\w+\-.]+`	at least one word character, plus, hyphen, or dot
`@`	literal "at sign"
`[a-z\d\-.]+`	at least one letter, digit, hyphen, or dot
`\.`	literal dot
`[a-z]+`	at least one letter
`\z`	match end of a string
`/`	end of regex
`i`	case insensitive

ensures that only email addresses that match the pattern will be considered valid. (Because it starts with a capital letter, **VALID_EMAIL_REGEX** is a Ruby *constant*, so its value can't change.)

So, where does the pattern come from? Regular expressions consist of a terse (some would say unreadable) language for matching text patterns; learning to construct regexes is an art, and to get you started I've broken **VALID_EMAIL_REGEX** into bite-sized pieces (Table 6.1).[10] To really learn about regular expressions, though, I consider the amazing Rubular regular expression editor (Figure 6.4) to be simply essential.[11] The Rubular website has a beautiful interactive interface for making regular expressions, along with a handy regex quick reference. I encourage you to study Table 6.1 with a browser window open to Rubular—no amount of reading about regular expressions can replace a couple of hours playing with Rubular. (Note: If you use the regex from Listing 6.17 in Rubular, you should leave off the \A and \z characters.)

---

10. Note that, in Table 6.1, "letter" really means "lower-case letter," but the **i** at the end of the regex enforces case-insensitive matching.

11. If you find it as useful as I do, I encourage you to donate to Rubular to reward developer Michael Lovitt for his wonderful work.

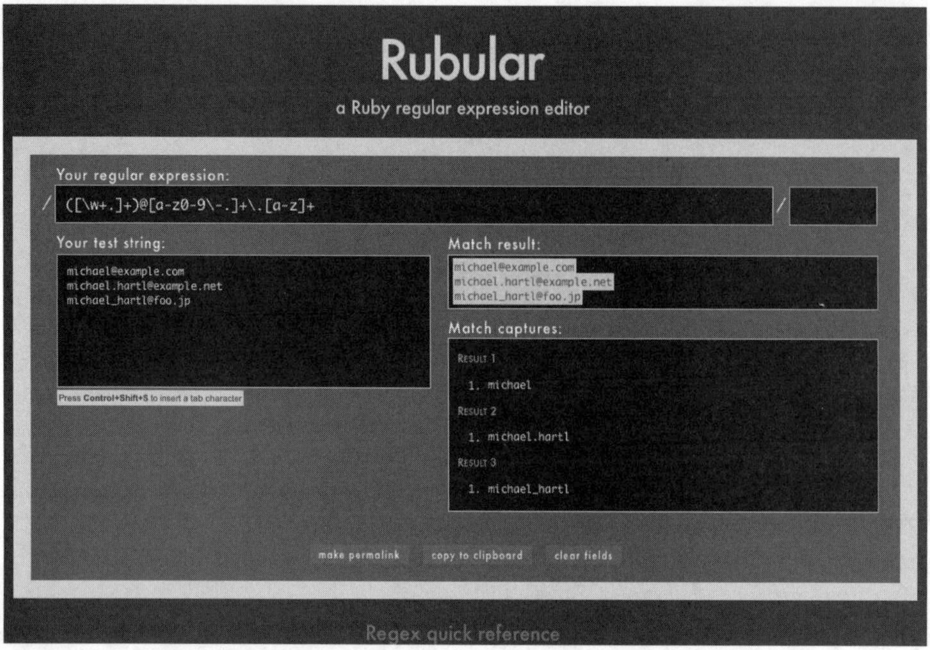

Figure 6.4   The awesome Rubular regular expression editor.

By the way, there actually exists a full regex for matching email addresses according to the official standard, but it's really not worth the trouble. The one in Listing 6.17 is fine, maybe even better than the official one.[12]

The tests should all be passing now. (In fact, the tests for valid email addresses should have been passing all along; since regexes are notoriously error-prone, the valid email tests are there mainly as a sanity check on **VALID_EMAIL_REGEX**.) This means that there's only one constraint left: enforcing the email addresses to be unique.

---

12. Did you know that **"Michael Hartl"@example.com**, with quotation marks and a space in the middle, is a valid email address according to the standard? Incredibly, it is—but it's absurd. If you don't have an email address that contains only letters, numbers, underscores, and dots, then I recommend getting one. N.B. The regex in Listing 6.17 allows plus signs, too, because Gmail (and possibly other email services) does something useful with them: To filter email from example.com, you can use username+example@gmail.com, which will go to the Gmail address username@gmail.com, allowing you to filter on the string example.

6.2.5 Uniqueness Validation

To enforce uniqueness of email addresses (so that we can use them as usernames), we'll be using the **:unique** option to the **validates** method. But be warned: There's a *major* caveat, so don't just skim this section—read it carefully.

We'll start, as usual, with our tests. In our previous model tests, we've mainly used **User.new**, which just creates a Ruby object in memory, but for uniqueness tests we actually need to put a record into the database.[13] The (first) duplicate email test appears in Listing 6.18.

Listing 6.18 A test for the rejection of duplicate email addresses.
spec/models/user_spec.rb

```
require 'spec_helper'

describe User do

  before do
    @user = User.new(name: "Example User", email: "user@example.com")
  end
  .

  .

  .

  describe "when email address is already taken" do
    before do
      user_with_same_email = @user.dup
      user_with_same_email.save
    end

    it { should_not be_valid }
  end
end
```

The method here is to make a user with the same email address as **@user**, which we accomplish using **@user.dup**, which creates a duplicate user with the same attributes. Since we then save that user, the original **@user** has an email address that already exists in the database, and hence should not be valid.

---

13. As noted briefly in the introduction to this section, there is a dedicated test database, **db/test.sqlite3**, for this purpose.

We can get the new test in Listing 6.18 to pass with the code in Listing 6.19.

Listing 6.19 Validating the uniqueness of email addresses.
app/models/user.rb

```
class User < ActiveRecord::Base
  .
  .

  .
  validates :email, presence: true, format: { with: VALID_EMAIL_REGEX },
                    uniqueness: true
end
```

We're not quite done, though. Email addresses are case-insensitive—**foo@bar.com** goes to the same place as **FOO@BAR.COM** or **FoO@BAr.coM**—so our validation should cover this case as well. We test for this with the code in Listing 6.20.

Listing 6.20 A test for the rejection of duplicate email addresses, insensitive to case.
spec/models/user_spec.rb

```
require 'spec_helper'

describe User do

  before do
    @user = User.new(name: "Example User", email: "user@example.com")
  end
  .
  .

  .
  describe "when email address is already taken" do
    before do
      user_with_same_email = @user.dup
      user_with_same_email.email = @user.email.upcase
      user_with_same_email.save
    end

    it { should_not be_valid }
  end
end
```

Here we are using the **upcase** method on strings (seen briefly in Section 4.3.2). This test does the same thing as the first duplicate email test, but with an upper-case email address instead. If this test feels a little abstract, go ahead and fire up the console:

```
$ rails console --sandbox
>> user = User.create(name: "Example User", email: "user@example.com")
>> user.email.upcase
=> "USER@EXAMPLE.COM"
>> user_with_same_email = user.dup
>> user_with_same_email.email = user.email.upcase
>> user_with_same_email.valid?
=> true
```

Of course, **user_with_same_email.valid?** is **true**, because the uniqueness validation is currently case-sensitive, but we want it to be **false**. Fortunately, **:uniqueness** accepts an option, **:case_sensitive**, for just this purpose (Listing 6.21).

Listing 6.21 Validating the uniqueness of email addresses, ignoring case.
app/models/user.rb

```
class User < ActiveRecord::Base
  .
  .
  .
  validates :email, presence: true, format: { with: VALID_EMAIL_REGEX },
                    uniqueness: { case_sensitive: false }
end
```

Note that we have simply replaced **true** with **case_sensitive: false**; Rails infers in this case that **:uniqueness** should be **true**. At this point, our application—with an important caveat—enforces email uniqueness, and our test suite should pass.

The Uniqueness Caveat

There's just one small problem, the caveat alluded to above:

Using validates :uniqueness does not guarantee uniqueness.

D'oh! But what can go wrong? Here's what:

1. Alice signs up for the sample app, with address alice@wonderland.com.
2. Alice accidentally clicks on "Submit" *twice*, sending two requests in quick succession.
3. The following sequence occurs: request 1 creates a user in memory that passes validation, request 2 does the same, request 1's user gets saved, request 2's user gets saved.
4. Result: two user records with the exact same email address, despite the uniqueness validation.

If the above sequence seems implausible, believe me, it isn't: It can happen on any Rails website with significant traffic. Luckily, the solution is straightforward to implement; we just need to enforce uniqueness at the database level as well. Our method is to create a database *index* on the email column, and then require that the index be unique.

The email index represents an update to our data modeling requirements, which (as discussed in Section 6.1.1) is handled in Rails using migrations. We saw in Section 6.1.1 that generating the User model automatically created a new migration (Listing 6.2); in the present case, we are adding structure to an existing model, so we need to create a migration directly using the **migration** generator:

```
$ rails generate migration add_index_to_users_email
```

Unlike the migration for users, the email uniqueness migration is not pre-defined, so we need to fill in its contents with Listing 6.22.[14]

Listing 6.22 The migration for enforcing email uniqueness.
db/migrate/[timestamp]_add_index_to_users_email.rb

```
class AddIndexToUsersEmail < ActiveRecord::Migration
  def change
    add_index :users, :email, unique: true
  end
end
```

This uses a Rails method called **add_index** to add an index on the **email** column of the **users** table. The index by itself doesn't enforce uniqueness, but the option **unique: true** does.

The final step is to migrate the database:

```
$ bundle exec rake db:migrate
```

(If this fails, try exiting any running sandbox console sessions, which can lock the database and prevent migrations.) If you're interested in seeing the practical effect

---

14. Of course, we could just edit the migration file for the **users** table in Listing 6.2, but that would require rolling back and then migrating back up. The Rails Way is to use migrations every time we discover that our data model needs to change.

of this, take a look at the file **db/schema.rb**, which should now include a line like this:

```
add_index "users", ["email"], :name => "index_users_on_email", :unique => true
```

Unfortunately, there's one more change we need to make to be assured of email uniqueness, which is to make sure that the email address is all lowercase before it gets saved to the database. The reason is that not all database adapters use case-sensitive indices.[15] The way to do this is with a *callback*, which is a method that gets invoked at a particular point in the lifetime of an Active Record object (see the Rails API entry on callbacks). In the present case, we'll use a **before_save** callback to force Rails to downcase the email attribute before saving the user to the database, as shown in Listing 6.23.

Listing 6.23 Ensuring email uniqueness by downcasing the email attribute.
app/models/user.rb

```
class User < ActiveRecord::Base
  attr_accessible :name, :email

  before_save { |user| user.email = email.downcase }
  .
  .
  .
end
```

The code in Listing 6.23 passes a block to the **before_save** callback and sets the user's email address to a lowercase version of its current value using the **downcase** string method. This code is a little advanced, and at this point I suggest you simply trust that it works; if you're skeptical, comment out the uniqueness validation from Listing 6.19 and try to create users with identical email addresses to see the error that results. (We'll see this technique again in Section 8.2.1.)

Now the Alice scenario above will work fine: The database will save a user record based on the first request and will reject the second save for violating the uniqueness constraint. (An error will appear in the Rails log, but that doesn't do any harm. You can actually catch the **ActiveRecord::StatementInvalid** exception that gets

---

15. Direct experimentation with SQLite on my system and PostgreSQL on Heroku show that this step is, in fact, necessary.

raised—see Insoshi for an example—but in this tutorial we won't bother with this step.) Adding this index on the email attribute accomplishes a second goal, alluded to briefly in Section 6.1.4: It fixes an efficiency problem in `find_by_email` (Box 6.2).

Box 6.2 Database Indices

When creating a column in a database, it is important to consider whether we will need to *find* records by that column. Consider, for example, the `email` attribute created by the migration in Listing 6.2. When we allow users to sign in to the sample app starting in Chapter 7, we will need to find the user record corresponding to the submitted email address; unfortunately, based on the naïve data model, the only way to find a user by email address is to look through *each* user row in the database and compare its email attribute to the given email. This is known in the database business as a *full-table scan*, and for a real site with thousands of users, it is a Bad Thing.

Putting an index on the email column fixes the problem. To understand a database index, it's helpful to consider the analogy of a book index. In a book, to find all the occurrences of a given string, say "foobar," you would have to scan each page for "foobar." With a book index, on the other hand, you can just look up "foobar" in the index to see all the pages containing "foobar." A database index works essentially the same way.

6.3 Adding a Secure Password

In this section we'll add the last of the basic User attributes: a secure password used to authenticate users of the sample application. The method is to require each user to have a password (with a password confirmation), and then store an encrypted version of the password in the database. We'll also add a way to *authenticate* a user based on a given password, a method we'll use in Chapter 8 to allow users to sign in to the site.

The method for authenticating users will be to take a submitted password, encrypt it, and compare the result to the encrypted value stored in the database. If the two match, then the submitted password is correct and the user is authenticated. By comparing encrypted values instead of raw passwords, we will be able to authenticate users without storing the passwords themselves, thereby avoiding a serious security hole.

users	
id	integer
name	string
email	string
password_digest	string
created_at	datetime
updated_at	datetime

Figure 6.5 The User model with an added **password_digest** attribute.

6.3.1 An Encrypted Password

We'll start with the necessary change to the data model for users, which involves adding a **password_digest** column to the **users** table (Figure 6.5). The name *digest* comes from the terminology of cryptographic hash functions, and the exact name **password_digest** is necessary for the implementation in Section 6.3.4 to work. By encrypting the password properly, we'll ensure that an attacker won't be able to sign in to the site even if he manages to obtain a copy of the database.

We'll use the state-of-the-art hash function called bcrypt to irreversibly encrypt the password to form the password hash. To use bcrypt in the sample application, we need to add the **bcrypt-ruby** gem to our **Gemfile** (Listing 6.24).

Listing 6.24 Adding **bcrypt-ruby** to the **Gemfile**.

```
source 'https://rubygems.org'

gem 'rails', '3.2.13'
gem 'bootstrap-sass', '2.0.0'
gem 'bcrypt-ruby', '3.0.1'
.
.
.
```

Then run **bundle install**:

```
$ bundle install
```

Since we want users to have a password digest column, a user object should respond to **password_digest**, which suggests the test shown in Listing 6.25.

Listing 6.25 Ensuring that a User object has a **password_digest** column.
spec/models/user_spec.rb

```
require 'spec_helper'

describe User do

  before do
    @user = User.new(name: "Example User", email: "user@example.com")
  end

  subject { @user }

  it { should respond_to(:name) }
  it { should respond_to(:email) }
  it { should respond_to(:password_digest) }
  .

  .
  .

end
```

To get the test to pass, we first generate an appropriate migration for the **password_ digest** column:

```
$ rails generate migration add_password_digest_to_users password_digest:string
```

Here the first argument is the migration name, and we've also supplied a second argument with the name and type of attribute we want to create. (Compare this to the original generation of the **users** table in Listing 6.1.) We can choose any migration name we want, but it's convenient to end the name with **_to_users**, since in this case Rails automatically constructs a migration to add columns to the **users** table. Moreover, by including the second argument, we've given Rails enough information to construct the entire migration for us, as seen in Listing 6.26.

Listing 6.26 The migration to add a **password_digest** column to the **users** table.
db/migrate/[ts]_add_password_digest_to_users.rb

```
class AddPasswordDigestToUsers < ActiveRecord::Migration
  def change
    add_column :users, :password_digest, :string
  end
end
```

This code uses the **add_column** method to add a **password_digest** column to the **users** table.

We can get the failing test from Listing 6.25 to pass by migrating the development database and preparing the test database:

```
$ bundle exec rake db:migrate
$ bundle exec rake db:test:prepare
$ bundle exec rspec spec/
```

6.3.2 Password and Confirmation

As seen in the mockup in Figure 6.1, we expect to have users confirm their passwords, a common practice on the web meant to minimize typos. We could enforce this at the controller layer, but it's conventional to put it in the model and use Active Record to enforce the constraint. The method is to add **password** and **password_confirmation** attributes to the User model and then require that the two attributes match before the record is saved to the database. Unlike the other attributes we've seen so far, the password attributes will be *virtual*—they will only exist temporarily in memory and will not be persisted to the database.

We'll start with **respond_to** tests for a password and its confirmation, as seen in Listing 6.27.

Listing 6.27 Testing for the **password** and **password_confirmation** attributes.
spec/models/user_spec.rb

```
require 'spec_helper'

describe User do

  before do
    @user = User.new(name: "Example User", email: "user@example.com",
                     password: "foobar", password_confirmation: "foobar")
  end

  subject { @user }

  it { should respond_to(:name) }
  it { should respond_to(:email) }
  it { should respond_to(:password_digest) }
  it { should respond_to(:password) }
  it { should respond_to(:password_confirmation) }
```

```
it { should be_valid }
    .
    .
    .
end
```

Note that we've added **:password** and **:password_confirmation** to the initialization hash for **User.new**:

```
before do
  @user = User.new(name: "Example User", email: "user@example.com",
                   password: "foobar", password_confirmation: "foobar")
end
```

We definitely don't want users to enter a blank password, so we'll add another test to validate password presence:

```
describe "when password is not present" do
  before { @user.password = @user.password_confirmation = " " }
  it { should_not be_valid }
end
```

Since we'll be testing password mismatch in a moment, here we make sure to test the *presence* validation by setting both the password and its confirmation to a blank string. This uses Ruby's ability to make more than one assignment in a line. For example, in the console we can set both **a** and **b** to **3** as follows:

```
>> a = b = 3
>> a
=> 3
>> b
=> 3
```

In the present case, we use it to set both password attributes to **" "**:

```
@user.password = @user.password_confirmation = " "
```

We also want to ensure that the password and confirmation match. The case where they *do* match is already covered by **it { should be_valid }**, so we only need to test the case of a mismatch:

```
describe "when password doesn't match confirmation" do
  before { @user.password_confirmation = "mismatch" }
  it { should_not be_valid }
end
```

In principle, we are now done, but there is one case that doesn't quite work. What if the password confirmation is blank? If it is empty or consist of whitespace but the password is valid, then the two don't match and the confirmation validation will catch it. If both the password and its confirmation are empty or consist of whitespace, then the password presence validation will catch it. Unfortunately, there's one more possibility, which is that the password confirmation is *nil*. This can never happen through the web, but it can at the console:

```
$ rails console
>> User.create(name: "Michael Hartl", email: "mhartl@example.com",
?>          password: "foobar", password_confirmation: nil)
```

When the confirmation is **nil**, Rails doesn't run the confirmation validation, which means that we can create users at the console without password confirmations. (Of course, right *now* we haven't added the validations yet, so the code above will work in any case.) To prevent this, we'll add a test to catch this case:

```
describe "when password confirmation is nil" do
  before { @user.password_confirmation = nil }
  it { should_not be_valid }
end
```

(This behavior strikes me as a minor bug in Rails, and perhaps it will be fixed in a future version, and in any case adding the validation does no harm.)

Putting everything together gives the (failing) tests in Listing 6.28. We'll get them to pass in Section 6.3.4.

Listing 6.28 Test for the password and password confirmation.
spec/models/user_spec.rb

```
require 'spec_helper'

describe User do

  before do
    @user = User.new(name: "Example User", email: "user@example.com",
                     password: "foobar", password_confirmation: "foobar")
  end

  subject { @user }

  it { should respond_to(:name) }
  it { should respond_to(:email) }
  it { should respond_to(:password_digest) }
```

```
it { should respond_to(:password) }
it { should respond_to(:password_confirmation) }

it { should be_valid }
.
.
.
describe "when password is not present" do
  before { @user.password = @user.password_confirmation = " " }
  it { should_not be_valid }
end

describe "when password doesn't match confirmation" do
  before { @user.password_confirmation = "mismatch" }
  it { should_not be_valid }
end

describe "when password confirmation is nil" do
  before { @user.password_confirmation = nil }
  it { should_not be_valid }
end
end
```

6.3.3 User Authentication

The final piece of our password machinery is a method to retrieve users based on their email and passwords. This divides naturally into two parts: first, find a user by email address; second, authenticate the user with a given password.

The first step is simple; as we saw in Section 6.1.4, we can find a user with a given email address using the **find_by_email** method:

```
user = User.find_by_email(email)
```

The second step is then to use an **authenticate** method to verify that the user has the given password. In Chapter 8, we'll retrieve the current (signed-in) user using code something like this:

```
current_user = user.authenticate(password)
```

If the given password matches the user's password, it should return the user; otherwise, it should return **false**.

As usual, we can express the requirement for **authenticate** using RSpec. The resulting tests are more advanced than the others we've seen, so let's break them down into pieces; if you're new to RSpec, you might want to read this section a couple of times. We start by requiring a User object to respond to **authenticate**:

```
it { should respond_to(:authenticate) }
```

We then cover the two cases of password match and mismatch:

```
describe "return value of authenticate method" do
  before { @user.save }
  let(:found_user) { User.find_by_email(@user.email) }

  describe "with valid password" do
    it { should == found_user.authenticate(@user.password) }
  end

  describe "with invalid password" do
    let(:user_for_invalid_password) { found_user.authenticate("invalid") }

    it { should_not == user_for_invalid_password }
    specify { user_for_invalid_password.should be_false }
  end
end
```

The **before** block saves the user to the database so that it can be retrieved using **find_by_email**, which we accomplish using the **let** method:

```
let(:found_user) { User.find_by_email(@user.email) }
```

We've used **let** in a couple of exercises, but this is the first time we've seen it in the body of the tutorial. Box 6.3 covers **let** in more detail.

The two **describe** blocks cover the case where **@user** and **found_user** should be the same (password match) and different (password mismatch); they use the "double equals" **==** test for object equivalence (Section 4.3.1). Note that the tests in

```
describe "with invalid password" do
  let(:user_for_invalid_password) { found_user.authenticate("invalid") }

  it { should_not == user_for_invalid_password }
  specify { user_for_invalid_password.should be_false }
end
```

use **let** a second time and also use the **specify** method. This is just a synonym for **it** and can be used when writing **it** would sound unnatural. In this case, it sounds good to say "it [i.e., the user] should not equal wrong user," but it sounds strange to say "user: user with invalid password should be false"; saying "specify: user with invalid password should be false" sounds better.

Box 6.3 Using `let`

RSpec's `let` method provides a convenient way to create local variables inside tests. The syntax might look a little strange, but its effect is similar to variable assignment. The argument of `let` is a symbol, and it takes a block whose return value is assigned to a local variable with the symbol's name. In other words,

```
let(:found_user) { User.find_by_email(@user.email) }
```

creates a `found_user` variable whose value is equal to the result of `find_by_email`. We can then use this variable in any of the `before` or `it` blocks throughout the rest of the test. One advantage of `let` is that it *memoizes* its value, which means that it remembers the value from one invocation to the next. (Note that *memoize* is a technical term; in particular, it's *not* a misspelling of "memorize.") In the present case, because `let` memoizes the `found_user` variable, the `find_by_email` method will only be called once whenever the User model specs are run.

Finally, as a security precaution, we'll test for a length validation on passwords, requiring that they be at least six characters long:

```
describe "with a password that's too short" do
  before { @user.password = @user.password_confirmation = "a" * 5 }
  it { should be_invalid }
end
```

Putting together all the tests above gives Listing 6.29.

Listing 6.29 Test for the **authenticate** method.
spec/models/user_spec.rb

```
require 'spec_helper'

describe User do

  before do
    @user = User.new(name: "Example User", email: "user@example.com",
                     password: "foobar", password_confirmation: "foobar")
  end
```

```
subject { @user }
.
.
.
it { should respond_to(:authenticate) }
.
.
.
describe "with a password that's too short" do
  before { @user.password = @user.password_confirmation = "a" * 5 }
  it { should be_invalid }
end

describe "return value of authenticate method" do
  before { @user.save }
  let(:found_user) { User.find_by_email(@user.email) }

  describe "with valid password" do
    it { should == found_user.authenticate(@user.password) }
  end

  describe "with invalid password" do
    let(:user_for_invalid_password) { found_user.authenticate("invalid") }

    it { should_not == user_for_invalid_password }
    specify { user_for_invalid_password.should be_false }
  end
end
end
```

As noted in Box 6.3, **let** memoizes its value, so that the first nested **describe** block in Listing 6.29 invokes **let** to retrieve the user from the database using **find_by_email**, but the second **describe** block doesn't hit the database a second time.

6.3.4 User Has Secure Password

In previous versions of Rails, adding a secure password was difficult and time-consuming, as seen in the Rails 3.0 version of the *Rails Tutorial*,[16] which covers the creation of an authentication system from scratch. But web developers' understanding of how best to authenticate users has matured enough that it now comes bundled with the latest version of Rails. As a result, we'll complete the implementation of secure passwords (and get to a green test suite) using only a few lines of code.

---

16. http://railstutorial.org/book?version=3.0

First, we need to make the **password** and **password_confirmation** columns accessible (Section 6.1.2) so that we can instantiate new users with an initialization hash:

```
@user = User.new(name: "Example User", email: "user@example.com",
                 password: "foobar", password_confirmation: "foobar")
```

Following the model in Listing 6.6, we do this by adding the appropriate symbols to the list of accessible attributes:

```
attr_accessible :name, :email, :password, :password_confirmation
```

Second, we need presence and length validations for the password, the latter of which uses the **:minimum** key in analogy with the **:maximum** key from Listing 6.15:

```
validates :password, presence: true, length: { minimum: 6 }
```

Next, we need to add **password** and **password_confirmation** attributes, require the presence of the password, require that they match, and add an **authenticate** method to compare an encrypted password to the **password_digest** to authenticate users. This is the only nontrivial step, and in the latest version of Rails all these features come for free with one method, **has_secure_password**:

```
has_secure_password
```

As long as there is a **password_digest** column in the database, adding this one method to our model gives us a secure way to create and authenticate new users. (If **has_secure_password** seems a bit too magical for your taste, I suggest taking a look at the source code for secure_password.rb, which is well-documented and quite readable. You'll see that, among other things, it automatically includes a validation for the **password_digest** attribute. In Chapter 7, we'll see that this is a mixed blessing.)

Finally, we need a presence validation for the password confirmation:

```
validates :password_confirmation, presence: true
```

Putting these three elements together yields the User model shown in Listing 6.30, which completes the implementation of secure passwords.

Listing 6.30 The complete implementation for secure passwords.
app/models/user.rb

```
class User < ActiveRecord::Base
  attr_accessible :name, :email, :password, :password_confirmation
  has_secure_password

  before_save { |user| user.email = email.downcase }

  validates :name, presence: true, length: { maximum: 50 }
  VALID_EMAIL_REGEX = /\A[\w+\-.]+@[a-z\d\-.]+\.[a-z]+\z/i
  validates :email, presence:    true,
                    format:      { with: VALID_EMAIL_REGEX },
                    uniqueness: { case_sensitive: false }
  validates :password, presence: true, length: { minimum: 6 }
  validates :password_confirmation, presence: true
end
```

You should confirm at this point that the test suite passes:

```
$ bundle exec rspec spec/
```

6.3.5 Creating a User

Now that the basic User model is complete, we'll create a user in the database as preparation for making a page to show the user's information in Section 7.1. This also gives us a chance to make the work from the previous sections feel more concrete; merely getting the test suite to pass may seem anti-climactic, and it will be gratifying to see an actual user record in the development database.

Since we can't yet sign up through the web—that's the goal of Chapter 7—we'll use the Rails console to create a new user by hand. In contrast to Section 6.1.3, in this section we'll take care *not* to start in a sandbox, since this time the whole point is to save a record to the database:

```
$ rails console
>> User.create(name: "Michael Hartl", email: "mhartl@example.com",
?>              password: "foobar", password_confirmation: "foobar")
=> #<User id: 1, name: "Michael Hartl", email: "mhartl@example.com",
created_at: "2011-12-07 03:38:14", updated_at: "2011-12-07 03:38:14",
password_digest: "$2a$10$P9OnzpdCON80yuMVk3jGr.LMA16VwOExJgjlw0G4f21y...">
```

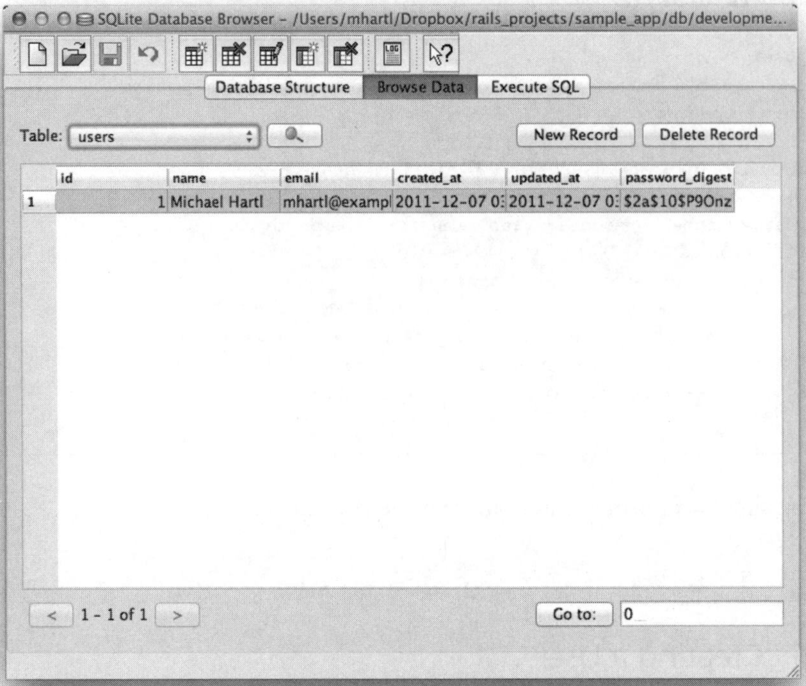

Figure 6.6   A user row in the SQLite database `db/development.sqlite3`.

To check that this worked, let's look at the row in the development database (`db/development.sqlite3`) using the SQLite Database Browser (Figure 6.6). Note that the columns correspond to the attributes of the data model defined in Figure 6.5.

Returning to the console, we can see the effect of `has_secure_password` from Listing 6.30 by looking at the `password_digest` attribute:

```
>> user = User.find_by_email("mhartl@example.com")
>> user.password_digest
=> "$2a$10$P9OnzpdCON80yuMVk3jGr.LMA16VwOExJgjlw0G4f21yZIMSH/xoy"
```

This is the encrypted version of the password (**"foobar"**) used to initialize the user object. We can also verify that the **authenticate** command is working by first using an invalid password and then a valid one:

```
>> user.authenticate("invalid")
=> false
>> user.authenticate("foobar")
=> #<User id: 1, name: "Michael Hartl", email: "mhartl@example.com",
created_at: "2011-12-07 03:38:14", updated_at: "2011-12-07 03:38:14",
password_digest: "$2a$10$P9OnzpdCON80yuMVk3jGr.LMA16VwOExJgjlw0G4f21y...">
```

As required, **authenticate** returns **false** if the password is invalid and the user itself if the password is valid.

6.4 Conclusion

Starting from scratch, in this chapter we created a working User model with **name**, **email**, and various password attributes, together with validations enforcing several important constraints on their values. In addition, we can securely authenticate users using a given password. In previous versions of Rails, such a feat would have taken more than twice as much code, but because of the compact **validates** method and **has_secure_password**, we were able to build a complete User model in only ten source lines of code.

In the next chapter, Chapter 7, we'll make a working signup form to create new users, together with a page to display each user's information. In Chapter 8, we'll use the authentication machinery from Section 6.3 to let users sign into the site.

If you're using Git, now would be a good time to commit if you haven't done so in a while:

```
$ git add .
$ git commit -m "Make a basic User model (including secure passwords)"
```

Then merge back into the master branch:

```
$ git checkout master
$ git merge modeling-users
```

6.5 Exercises

1. Add a test for the email downcasing from Listing 6.23, as shown in Listing 6.31. By commenting out the **before_save** line, verify that Listing 6.31 tests the right thing.
2. By running the test suite, verify that the **before_save** callback can be written as shown in Listing 6.32.
3. Read through the Rails API entry for **ActiveRecord::Base** to get a sense of its capabilities.
4. Study the entry in the Rails API for the **validates** method to learn more about its capabilities and options.
5. Spend a couple of hours playing with Rubular.

Listing 6.31 A test for the email downcasing from Listing 6.23.
spec/models/user_spec.rb

```
require 'spec_helper'

describe User do
  .
  .
  .
  describe "email address with mixed case" do
    let(:mixed_case_email) { "Foo@ExAMPle.CoM" }

    it "should be saved as all lower-case" do
      @user.email = mixed_case_email
      @user.save
      @user.reload.email.should == mixed_case_email.downcase
    end
  end
  .
  .
  .
end
```

Listing 6.32 An alternate implementation of the **before_save** callback.
app/models/user.rb

```
class User < ActiveRecord::Base
  attr_accessible :name, :email, :password, :password_confirmation
  has_secure_password

  before_save { self.email.downcase! }
  .
  .
  .
end
```

CHAPTER 7
Sign Up

Now that we have a working User model, it's time to add an ability few websites can live without: letting users sign up for the site. We'll use an HTML *form* to submit user signup information to our application in Section 7.2, which will then be used to create a new user and save its attributes to the database in Section 7.4. At the end of the signup process, it's important to render a profile page with the newly created user's information, so we'll begin by making a page for *showing* users, which will serve as the first step toward implementing the REST architecture for users (Section 2.2.2). As usual, we'll write tests as we develop, extending the theme of using RSpec and Capybara to write succinct and expressive integration tests.

In order to make a user profile page, we need to have a user in the database, which introduces a chicken-and-egg problem: How can the site have a user before there is a working signup page? Happily, this problem has already been solved: In Section 6.3.5, we created a User record by hand using the Rails console. If you skipped that section, you should go there now and complete it before proceeding.

If you're following along with version control, make a topic branch as usual:

```
$ git checkout master
$ git checkout -b sign-up
```

7.1 Showing Users

In this section, we'll take the first steps toward the final profile by making a page to display a user's name and profile photo, as indicated by the mockup in Figure 7.1.[1] Our

---

1. Mockingbird doesn't support custom images like the profile photo in Figure 7.1; I put that in by hand using Adobe Fireworks.

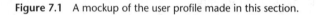

Huckleberry

Figure 7.1   A mockup of the user profile made in this section.

eventual goal for the user profile pages is to show the user's profile image, basic user data, and a list of microposts, as mocked up in Figure 7.2.[2] (Figure 7.2 has our first example of *lorem ipsum* text, which has a fascinating story that you should definitely read about some time.) We'll complete this task, and with it the sample application, in Chapter 11.

7.1.1   Debug and Rails Environments

The profiles in this section will be the first truly dynamic pages in our application. Although the view will exist as a single page of code, each profile will be customized using information retrieved from the site's database. As preparation for adding dynamic pages to our sample application, now is a good time to add some debug information to our site layout (Listing 7.1). This displays some useful information about each page using the built-in `debug` method and `params` variable (which we'll learn more about in Section 7.1.2).

---

2. The hippo here is from http://www.flickr.com/photos/43803060@N00/24308857/.

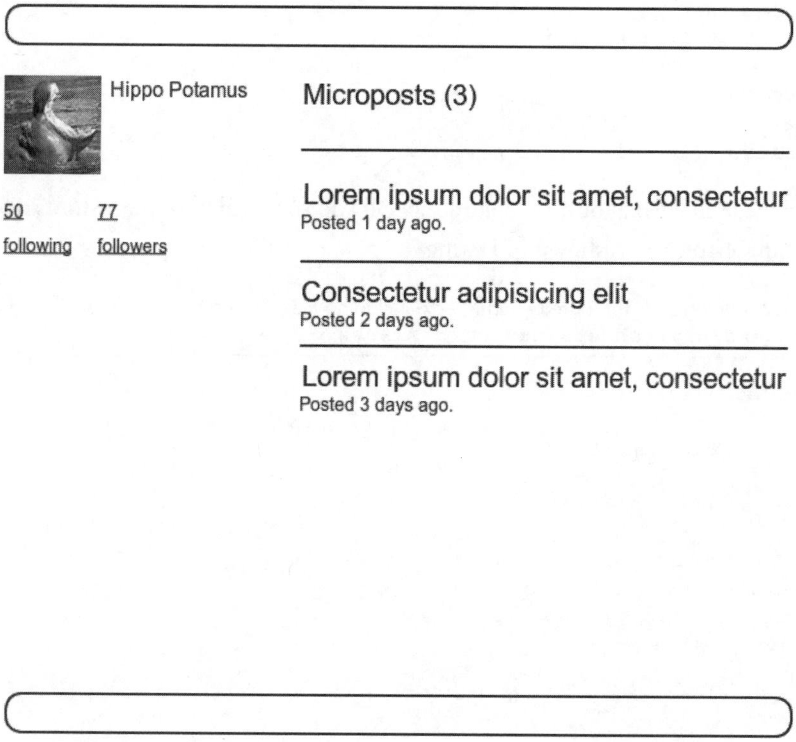

Figure 7.2   A mockup of our best guess at the final profile page.

Listing 7.1 Adding some debug information to the site layout.
app/views/layouts/application.html.erb

```
<!DOCTYPE html>
<html>
    .
    .
    .
  <body>
    <%= render 'layouts/header' %>
    <div class="container">
      <%= yield %>
```

```
      <%= render 'layouts/footer' %>
      <%= debug(params) if Rails.env.development? %>
    </div>
  </body>
</html>
```

To make the debug output look nice, we'll add some rules to the custom stylesheet created in Chapter 5, as shown in Listing 7.2.

Listing 7.2 Adding code for a pretty debug box, including a Sass mixin.
app/assets/stylesheets/custom.css.scss

```
@import "bootstrap";

/* mixins, variables, etc. */

$grayMediumLight: #eaeaea;

@mixin box_sizing {
  -moz-box-sizing: border-box;
  -webkit-box-sizing: border-box;
  box-sizing: border-box;
}
    .
    .
    .


/* miscellaneous */

.debug_dump {
  clear: both;
  float: left;
  width: 100%;
  margin-top: 45px;
  @include box_sizing;
}
```

This introduces the Sass *mixin* facility, in this case called **box_sizing**. A mixin allows a group of CSS rules to be packaged up and used for multiple elements, converting

```
.debug_dump {
    .
    .
    .
  @include box_sizing;
}
```

to

```
.debug_dump {
  .
  .
  .
  -moz-box-sizing: border-box;
  -webkit-box-sizing: border-box;
  box-sizing: border-box;
}
```

We'll put this mixin to use again in Section 7.2.2. The result in the case of the debug box is shown in Figure 7.3.

The debug output in Figure 7.3 gives potentially useful information about the page being rendered:

```
---
controller: static_pages
action: home
```

Figure 7.3   The sample application Home page (/) with debug information.

This is a YAML[3] representation of **params**, which is basically a hash, and in this case identifies the controller and action for the page. We'll see another example in Section 7.1.2

Since we don't want to display debug information to users of a deployed application, Listing 7.1 uses

```
if Rails.env.development?
```

to restrict the debug information to the *development environment*, which is one of three environments defined by default in Rails (Box 7.1).[4] In particular, **Rails.env.development?** is **true** only in a development environment, so the Embedded Ruby

```
<%= debug(params) if Rails.env.development? %>
```

won't be inserted into production applications or tests. (Inserting the debug information into tests probably wouldn't do any harm, but it probably wouldn't do any good, either, so it's best to restrict the debug display to development only.)

Box 7.1 Rails Environments

Rails comes equipped with three environments: test, development, and production. The default environment for the Rails console is development:

```
$ rails console
Loading development environment
>> Rails.env
=> "development"
>> Rails.env.development?
=> true
>> Rails.env.test?
=> false
```

---

3. The Rails **debug** information is shown as YAML (a recursive acronym standing for "YAML Ain't Markup Language"), which is a friendly data format designed to be both machine- *and* human-readable.

4. You can define your own custom environments as well; see the RailsCast on adding an environment for details.

As you can see, Rails provides a `Rails` object with an `env` attribute and associated environment boolean methods, so that, for example, `Rails.env.test?` returns `true` in a test environment and `false` otherwise.

If you ever need to run a console in a different environment (to debug a test, for example), you can pass the environment as a parameter to the `console` script:

```
$ rails console test
Loading test environment
>> Rails.env
=> "test"
>> Rails.env.test?
=> true
```

As with the console, `development` is the default environment for the local Rails server, but you can also run it in a different environment:

```
$ rails server --environment production
```

If you view your app running in production, it won't work without a production database, which we can create by running `rake db:migrate` in production:

```
$ bundle exec rake db:migrate RAILS_ENV=production
```

(I find it confusing that the console, server, and migrate commands specify non-default environments in three mutually incompatible ways, which is why I bothered showing all three.)

By the way, if you have deployed your sample app to Heroku, you can see its environment using the `heroku` command, which provides its own (remote) console:

```
$ heroku run console
Ruby console for yourapp.herokuapp.com
>> Rails.env
=> "production"
>> Rails.env.production?
=> true
```

Naturally, since Heroku is a platform for production sites, it runs each application in a production environment.

7.1.2 A Users Resource

At the end of Chapter 6, we created a new user in the database. As seen in Section 6.3.5, this user has id **1**, and our goal now is to make a page to display this user's information. We'll follow the conventions of the REST architecture favored in Rails applications (Box 2.2), which means representing data as *resources* that can be created, shown, updated, or destroyed—four actions corresponding to the four fundamental operations POST, GET, PUT, and DELETE defined by the HTTP standard (Box 3.2).

When following REST principles, resources are typically referenced using the resource name and a unique identifier. What this means in the context of users—which we're now thinking of as a Users *resource*—is that we should view the user with id **1** by issuing a GET request to the URI /users/1. Here the **show** action is *implicit* in the type of request—when Rails' REST features are activated, GET requests are automatically handled by the **show** action.

We saw in Section 2.2.1 that the page for a user with id **1** has URI /users/1. Unfortunately, visiting that URI right now just gives an error (Figure 7.4).

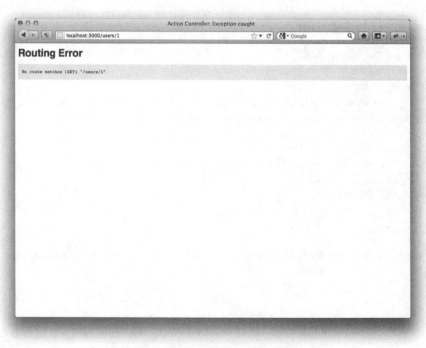

Figure 7.4 The error page for /users/1.

We can get the REST-style URI to work by adding a single line to our routes file (**config/routes.rb**):

```
resources :users
```

The result appears in Listing 7.3.

Listing 7.3 Adding a Users resource to the routes file.
config/routes.rb

```
SampleApp::Application.routes.draw do
  resources :users

  root to: 'static_pages#home'
  .
  .
  .
end
```

You might have noticed that Listing 7.3 removes the line

```
get "users/new"
```

last seen in Listing 5.32. This is because **resources :users** doesn't just add a working /users/1 URI; it endows our sample application with *all* the actions needed for a RESTful Users resource,[5] along with a large number of named routes (Section 5.3.3) for generating user URIs. The resulting correspondence of URIs, actions, and named routes is shown in Table 7.1. (Compare to Table 2.2.) Over the course of the next three chapters, we'll cover all of the other entries in Table 7.1 as we fill in all the actions necessary to make Users a fully RESTful resource.

With the code in Listing 7.3, the routing works, but there's still no page there (Figure 7.5). To fix this, we'll begin with a minimalist version of the profile page, which we'll flesh out in Section 7.1.4.

We'll use the standard Rails location for showing a user, which is **app/views/users/show.html.erb**. Unlike the **new.html.erb** view, which we created with the generator in Listing 5.28, the **show.html.erb** file doesn't currently exist, so you'll have to create it by hand, filling it with the content shown in Listing 7.4.

---

5. This means that the *routing* works, but the corresponding pages don't necessarily work at this point. For example, /users/1/edit gets routed properly to the **edit** action of the Users controller, but since the **edit** action doesn't exist yet actually hitting that URI will return an error.

Table 7.1 RESTful routes provided by the Users resource in Listing 7.3.

HTTP request	URI	Action	Named route	Purpose
GET	/users	**index**	`users_path`	page to list all users
GET	/users/1	**show**	`user_path(user)`	page to show user
GET	/users/new	**new**	`new_user_path`	page to make a new user (signup)
POST	/users	**create**	`users_path`	create a new user
GET	/users/1/edit	**edit**	`edit_user_path(user)`	page to edit user with id **1**
PUT	/users/1	**update**	`user_path_code`	update user
DELETE	/users/1	**destroy**	`user_path(user)`	delete user

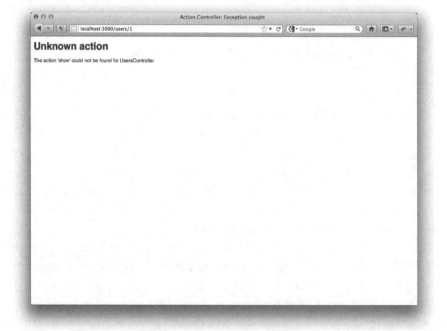

Figure 7.5 The URI /users/1 with routing but no page.

Listing 7.4 A stub view for showing user information.
`app/views/users/show.html.erb`

```
<%= @user.name %>, <%= @user.email %>
```

This view uses Embedded Ruby to display the user's name and email address, assuming the existence of an instance variable called **@user**. Of course, eventually the real user show page will look very different, and won't display the email address publicly.

In order to get the user show view to work, we need to define an **@user** variable in the corresponding **show** action in the Users controller. As you might expect, we use the **find** method on the User model (Section 6.1.4) to retrieve the user from the database, as shown in Listing 7.5.

Listing 7.5 The Users controller with a **show** action.
app/controllers/users_controller.rb

```
class UsersController < ApplicationController

  def show
    @user = User.find(params[:id])
  end

  def new
  end
end
```

Here we've used **params** to retrieve the user id. When we make the appropriate request to the Users controller, **params[:id]** will be the user id 1, so the effect is the same as the **find** method

```
User.find(1)
```

we saw in Section 6.1.4. (Technically, **params[:id]** is the string **"1"**, but **find** is smart enough to convert this to an integer.)

With the user view and action defined, the URI /users/1 works perfectly (Figure 7.6). Note that the debug information in Figure 7.6 confirms the value of **params[:id]**:

```
---
action: show
controller: users
id: '1'
```

This is why the code

```
User.find(params[:id])
```

in Listing 7.5 finds the user with id 1.

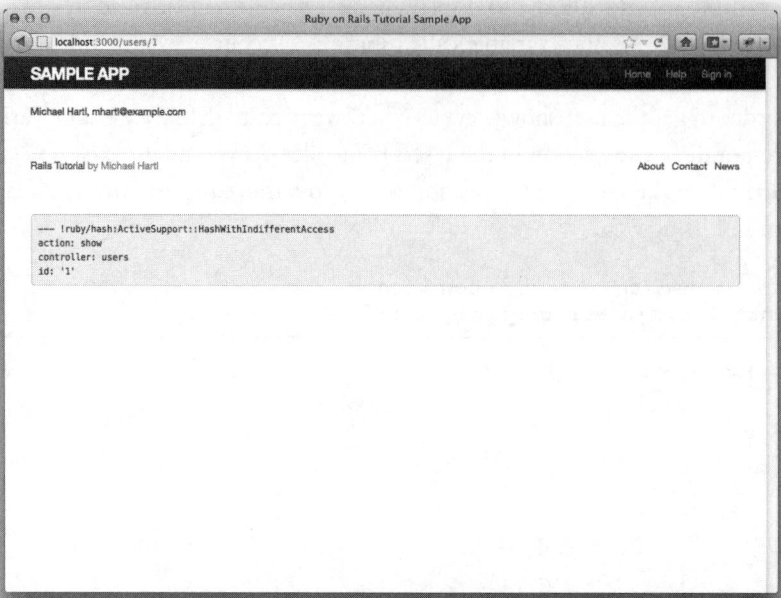

Figure 7.6 The user show page at /users/1 after adding a Users resource.

7.1.3 Testing the User Show Page (with Factories)

Now that we have a minimal working profile, it's time to start working on the version mocked up in Figure 7.1. As with the creation of static pages (Chapter 3) and the User model (Chapter 6), we'll proceed using test-driven development.

Recall from Section 5.4.2 that we have elected to use integration tests for the pages associated with the Users resource. In the case of the signup page, our test first visits the `signup_path` and then checks for the right `h1` and `title` tags, as seen in Listing 5.31 and reproduced in Listing 7.6. (Note that we've omitted the `full_title` helper from Section 5.3.4 since the full title is already adequately tested there.)

Listing 7.6 A recap of the initial User pages spec.
`spec/requests/user_pages_spec.rb`

```
require 'spec_helper'

describe "User pages" do

  subject { page }
```

```
  describe "signup page" do
    before { visit signup_path }

    it { should have_selector('h1',    text: 'Sign up') }
    it { should have_selector('title', text: 'Sign up') }
  end
end
```

To test the user show page, we'll need a User model object so that the code in the **show** action (Listing 7.5) has something to find:

```
describe "profile page" do
  # Code to make a user variable
  before { visit user_path(user) }

  it { should have_selector('h1',    text: user.name) }
  it { should have_selector('title', text: user.name) }
end
```

where we need to fill in the comment with the appropriate code. This uses the **user_path** named route (Table 7.1) to generate the path to the show page for the given user. It then tests that the **h1** and **title** tags both contain the user's name.

In order to make the necessary User model object, we could use Active Record to create a user with **User.create**, but experience shows that user *factories* are a more convenient way to define user objects and insert them in the database. We'll be using the factories generated by Factory Girl,[6] a Ruby gem produced by the good people at thoughtbot. As with RSpec, Factory Girl defines a domain-specific language in Ruby, in this case specialized for defining Active Record objects. The syntax is simple, relying on Ruby blocks and custom methods to define the attributes of the desired object. For cases such as the one in this chapter, the advantage over Active Record may not be obvious, but we'll use more advanced features of factories in future chapters. For example, in Section 9.3.3 it will be important to create a sequence of users with unique email addresses, and factories make it easy to do this.

As with other Ruby gems, we can install Factory Girl by adding a line to the **Gemfile** used by Bundler (Listing 7.7). (Since Factory Girl is only needed in the tests, we've put it in the **:test** group.)

---

6. Presumably "Factory Girl" is a reference to the movie of the same name.

Listing 7.7 Adding Factory Girl to the **Gemfile**.

```
source 'https://rubygems.org'
  .
  .
  .
  group :test do
    .
    .
    .
    gem 'factory_girl_rails', '1.4.0'
  end
  .
  .
  .
end
```

Then install as usual:

```
$ bundle install
```

We'll put all our Factory Girl factories in the file **spec/factories.rb**, which automatically gets loaded by RSpec. The code needed to make a User factory appears in Listing 7.8.

Listing 7.8 A factory to simulate User model objects.
spec/factories.rb

```
FactoryGirl.define do
  factory :user do
    name     "Michael Hartl"
    email    "michael@example.com"
    password "foobar"
    password_confirmation "foobar"
  end
end
```

By passing the symbol **:user** to the **factory** command, we tell Factory Girl that the subsequent definition is for a User model object.

With the definition in Listing 7.8, we can create a User factory in the tests using the **let** command (Box 6.3) and the **FactoryGirl** method supplied by Factory Girl:

```
let(:user) { FactoryGirl.create(:user) }
```

The final result appears in Listing 7.9.

Listing 7.9 A test for the user show page.
`spec/requests/user_pages_spec.rb`

```ruby
require 'spec_helper'

describe "User pages" do

  subject { page }

  describe "profile page" do
    let(:user) { FactoryGirl.create(:user) }
    before { visit user_path(user) }

    it { should have_selector('h1',    text: user.name) }
    it { should have_selector('title', text: user.name) }
  end
  .
  .
  .
end
```

You should verify at this point that the test suite is red:

```
$ bundle exec rspec spec/
```

We can get the tests to green with the code in Listing 7.10.

Listing 7.10 Adding a title and heading for the user profile page.
`app/views/users/show.html.erb`

```erb
<% provide(:title, @user.name) %>
<h1><%= @user.name %></h1>
```

Running the tests again should confirm that the test in Listing 7.9 is passing:

```
$ bundle exec rspec spec/
```

One thing you will quickly notice when running tests with Factory Girl is that they are *slow*. The reason is not Factory Girl's fault, and in fact it is a *feature*, not a bug. The issue is that the BCrypt algorithm used in Section 6.3.1 to create a secure password hash is slow by design: BCrypt's slow speed is part of what makes it so hard to attack. Unfortunately, this means that creating users can bog down the test suite; happily, there is an easy fix. BCrypt uses a *cost factor* to control how computationally costly it is to create the secure hash. The default value is designed for security, not for speed, which is perfect for production applications, but in tests our needs are reversed: We want *fast* tests and don't care at all about the security of the test users' password hashes. The solution is to add a few lines to the test configuration file, **config/environments/test.rb**, redefining the cost factor from its secure default value to its fast minimum value, as shown in Listing 7.11. Even for a small test suite, the gains in speed from this step can be considerable, and I strongly recommend including Listing 7.11 in your **test.rb**.

Listing 7.11 Redefining the BCrypt cost factor in a test environment.
config/environments/test.rb

```
SampleApp::Application.configure do
  .
  .
  .
  # Speed up tests by lowering BCrypt's cost function.
  require 'bcrypt'
  silence_warnings do
    BCrypt::Engine::DEFAULT_COST = BCrypt::Engine::MIN_COST
  end
end
```

7.1.4 A Gravatar Image and a Sidebar

Having defined a basic user page in the previous section, we'll now flesh it out a little with a profile image for each user and the first cut of the user sidebar. When making views, we'll focus on the visual appearance and not worry too much about the exact structure of the page, which means that (at least for now) we won't be writing tests. When we come to more error-prone aspects of view, such as pagination (Section 9.3.3), we'll resume test-driven development.

We'll start by adding a "globally recognized avatar," or Gravatar, to the user profile.[7] Originally created by Tom Preston-Werner (cofounder of GitHub) and later acquired by Automattic (the makers of WordPress), Gravatar is a free service that allows users to upload images and associate them with email addresses they control. Gravatars are a convenient way to include user profile images without going through the trouble of managing image upload, cropping, and storage; all we need to do is construct

---

7. In Hinduism, an avatar is the manifestation of a deity in human or animal form. By extension, the term *avatar* is commonly used to mean some kind of personal representation, especially in a virtual environment. But you've seen the movie, so you already knew this.

the proper Gravatar image URI using the user's email address and the corresponding Gravatar image will automatically appear.[8]

Our plan is to define a **gravatar_for** helper function to return a Gravatar image for a given user, as shown in Listing 7.12.

Listing 7.12 The user show view with name and Gravatar.
app/views/users/show.html.erb

```
<% provide(:title, @user.name) %>
<h1>
  <%= gravatar_for @user %>
  <%= @user.name %>
</h1>
```

You can verify at this point that the test suite is failing:

```
$ bundle exec rspec spec/
```

Because the **gravatar_for** method is undefined, the user show view is currently broken. (Catching errors of this nature is perhaps the most useful aspect of view specs. This is why having *some* test of the view, even a minimalist one, is so important.)

By default, methods defined in any helper file are automatically available in any view, but for convenience we'll put the **gravatar_for** method in the file for helpers associated with the Users controller. As noted at the Gravatar home page, Gravatar URIs are based on an MD5 hash of the user's email address. In Ruby, the MD5 hashing algorithm is implemented using the **hexdigest** method, which is part of the **Digest** library:

```
>> email = "MHARTL@example.COM".
>> Digest::MD5::hexdigest(email.downcase)
=> "1fda4469bcbec3badf5418269ffc5968"
```

Since email addresses are case-insensitive (Section 6.2.4) but MD5 hashes are not, we've used the **downcase** method to ensure that the argument to **hexdigest** is all lower-case. The resulting **gravatar_for** helper appears in Listing 7.13.

---

8. If your application does need to handle custom images or other file uploads, I recommend the Paperclip gem.

Listing 7.13 Defining a **gravatar_for** helper method.
app/helpers/users_helper.rb

```ruby
module UsersHelper

  # Returns the Gravatar (http://gravatar.com/) for the given user.
  def gravatar_for(user)
    gravatar_id = Digest::MD5::hexdigest(user.email.downcase)
    gravatar_url = "https://secure.gravatar.com/avatars/#{gravatar_id}.png"
    image_tag(gravatar_url, alt: user.name, class: "gravatar")
  end
end
```

The code in Listing 7.13 returns an image tag for the Gravatar with a **"gravatar"** class and alt text equal to the user's name (which is especially convenient for sight-impaired browsers using a screen reader). You can confirm that the test suite is now passing:

```
$ bundle exec rspec spec/
```

The profile page appears as in Figure 7.7, which shows the default Gravatar image, which appears because **user@example.com** is an invalid email address (the example.com domain is reserved for examples).

To get our application to display a custom Gravatar, we'll use **update_attributes** (Section 6.1.5) to update the user in the database:

```
$ rails console
>> user = User.first
>> user.update_attributes(name: "Example User",
?>                        email: "example@railstutorial.org",
?>                        password: "foobar",
?>                        password_confirmation: "foobar")
=> true
```

Here we've assigned the user the email address **example@railstutorial.org**, which I've associated with the Rails Tutorial logo, as seen in Figure 7.8.

The last element needed to complete the mockup from Figure 7.1 is the initial version of the user sidebar. We'll implement it using the **aside** tag, which is used for

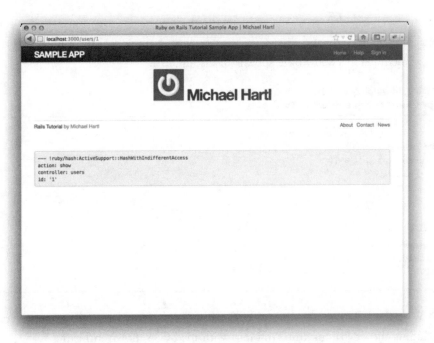

Figure 7.7 The user profile page /users/1 with the default Gravatar.

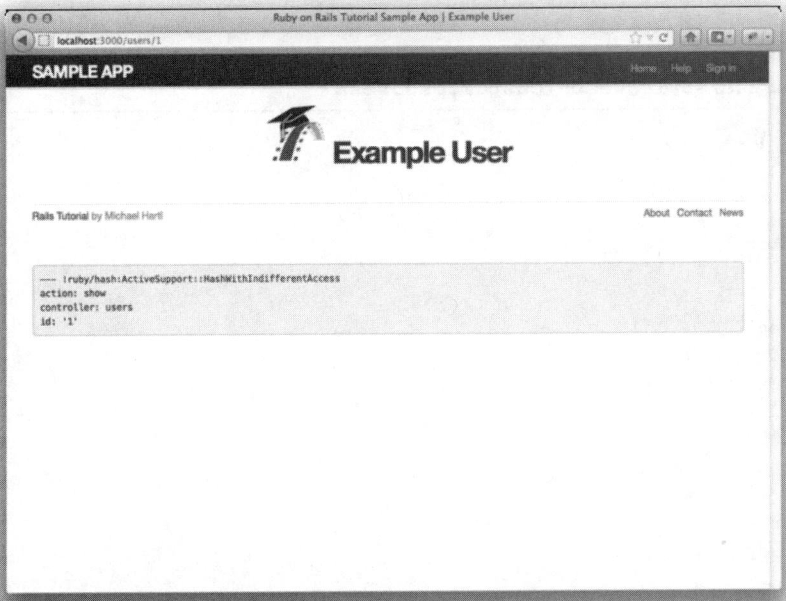

Figure 7.8 The user show page with a custom Gravatar.

content (such as sidebars) that complements the rest of the page but can also stand alone. We include **row** and **span4** classes, which are both part of Bootstrap. The code for the modified user show page appears in Listing 7.14.

Listing 7.14 Adding a sidebar to the user **show** view.
`app/views/users/show.html.erb`

```
<% provide(:title, @user.name) %>
<div class="row">
  <aside class="span4">
    <section>
      <h1>
        <%= gravatar_for @user %>
        <%= @user.name %>
      </h1>
    </section>
  </aside>
</div>
```

With the HTML elements and CSS classes in place, we can style the profile page (including the sidebar and the Gravatar) with the SCSS shown in Listing 7.15. (Note the nesting of the table CSS rules, which works only because of the Sass engine used by the asset pipeline.) The resulting page is shown in Figure 7.9.

Listing 7.15 SCSS for styling the user show page, including the sidebar.
`app/assets/stylesheets/custom.css.scss`

```
.
.
.

/* sidebar */

aside {
  section {
    padding: 10px 0;
    border-top: 1px solid $grayLighter;
    &:first-child {
      border: 0;
      padding-top: 0;
    }
    span {
      display: block;
```

```
        margin-bottom: 3px;
        line-height: 1;
      }
    h1 {
        font-size: 1.6em;
        text-align: left;
        letter-spacing: -1px;
        margin-bottom: 3px;
      }
    }
  }

.gravatar {
  float: left;
  margin-right: 10px;
}
```

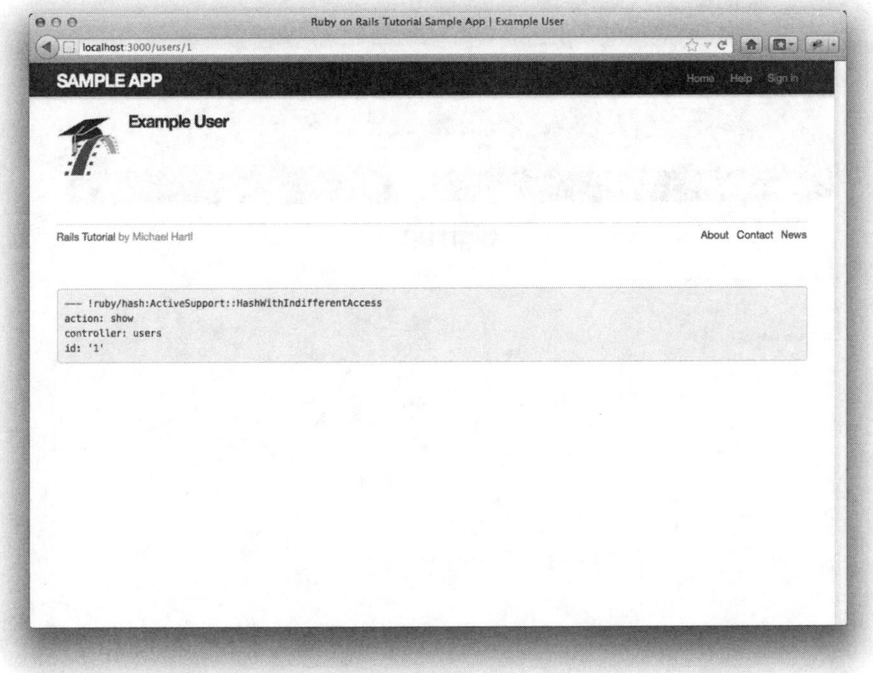

Figure 7.9   The user show page /users/1 with a sidebar and CSS.

7.2 Signup Form

Now that we have a working (although not yet complete) user profile page, we're ready to make a signup form for our site. We saw in Figure 5.9 (shown again in Figure 7.10) that the signup page is currently blank: useless for signing up new users. The goal of this section is to start changing this sad state of affairs by producing the signup form mocked up in Figure 7.11.

Since we're about to add the ability to create new users through the web, let's remove the user created at the console in Section 6.3.5. The cleanest way to do this is to reset the database with the **db:reset** Rake task:

```
$ bundle exec rake db:reset
```

After resetting the database, on some systems the test database needs to be re-prepared as well:

```
$ bundle exec rake db:test:prepare
```

Figure 7.10   The current state of the signup page /signup.

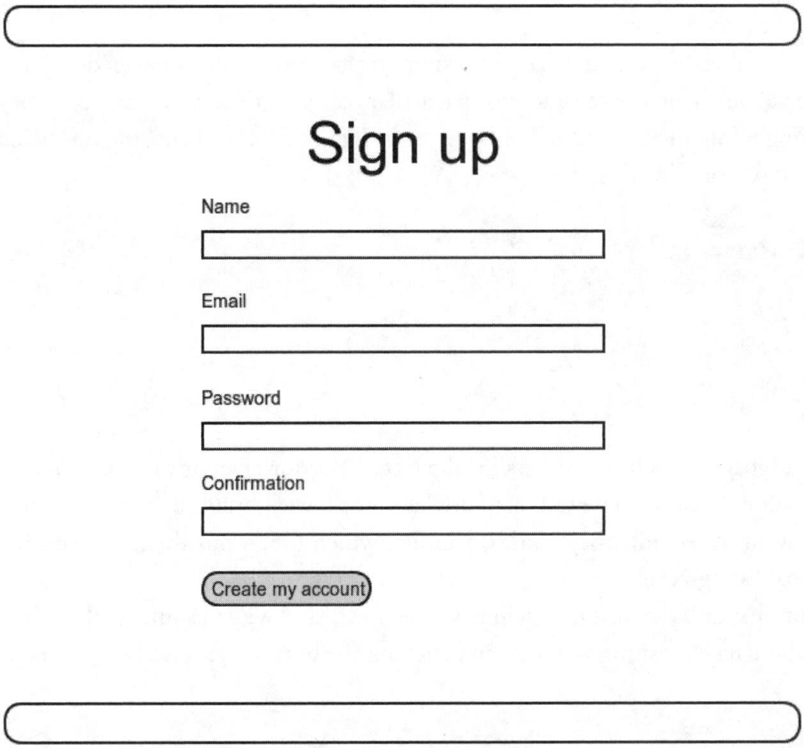

Sign up

Name

Email

Password

Confirmation

Create my account

Figure 7.11 A mockup of the user signup page.

Finally, on some systems you might have to restart the web server for the changes to take effect.[9]

7.2.1 Tests for User Signup

In the days before powerful web frameworks with full testing capabilities, testing was often painful and error-prone. For example, to test a signup page manually, we would have to visit the page in a browser and then submit alternately invalid and valid data, verifying in each case that the application's behavior was correct. Moreover, we would have to remember to repeat the process any time the application changed. With RSpec

---

9. Weird, right? I don't get it either.

and Capybara, we will be able to write expressive tests to automate tasks that used to have to be done by hand.

We've already seen how Capybara supports an intuitive web-navigation syntax. So far, we've mostly used **visit** to visit particular pages, but Capybara can do a lot more, including filling in the kind of fields we see in Figure 7.11 and clicking on the button. The syntax looks like this:

```
visit signup_path
fill_in "Name", with: "Example User"
.
.
.
click_button "Create my account"
```

Our goal now is to write tests for the right behavior given invalid and valid signup information. Because these tests are fairly advanced, we'll build them up piece by piece. If you want to see how they work (including which file to put them in), you can skip ahead to Listing 7.16.

Our first task is to test for a failing signup form, and we can simulate the submission of invalid data by visiting the page and clicking the button using **click_button**:

```
visit signup_path
click_button "Create my account"
```

This is equivalent to visiting the signup page and submitting blank signup information (which is invalid). Similarly, to simulate the submission of valid data, we fill in valid information using **fill_in**:

```
visit signup_path
fill_in "Name",         with: "Example User"
fill_in "Email",        with: "user@example.com"
fill_in "Password",     with: "foobar"
fill_in "Confirmation", with: "foobar"
click_button "Create my account"
```

The purpose of our tests is to verify that clicking the "Create my account" button results in the correct behavior, creating a new user when the information is valid and not creating a user when it's invalid. The way to do this is to check the *count* of users, and

under the hood our tests will use the **count** method available on every Active Record
class, including **User**:

```
$ rails console
>> User.count
=> 0
```

Here **User.count** is **0** because we reset the database at the beginning of this section.

When submitting invalid data, we expect the user count not to change; when
submitting valid data, we expect it to change by 1. We can express this in RSpec by
combining the **expect** method with either the **to** method or the **not_to** method.
We'll start with the invalid case since it is simpler; we visit the signup path and click the
button, and we expect it *not to* change the user count:

```
visit signup_path
expect { click_button "Create my account" }.not_to change(User, :count)
```

Note that, as indicated by the curly braces, **expect** wraps **click_button** in a block
(Section 4.3.2). This is for the benefit of the **change** method, which takes as arguments
an object and a symbol and then calculates the result of calling that symbol as a method
on the object both before and after the block. In other words, the code

```
expect { click_button "Create my account" }.not_to change(User, :count)
```

calculates

```
User.count
```

before and after the execution of

```
click_button "Create my account"
```

In the present case, we want the given code *not* to change the count, which we express
using the **not_to** method. In effect, by enclosing the button click in a block we are able
to replace

```
initial = User.count
click_button "Create my account"
final = User.count
initial.should == final
```

with the single line

```
expect { click_button "Create my account" }.not_to change(User, :count)
```

which reads like natural language and is much more compact.

The case of valid data is similar, but instead of verifying that the user count doesn't change, we check that clicking the button changes the count by 1:

```
visit signup_path
fill_in "Name",          with: "Example User"
fill_in "Email",         with: "user@example.com"
fill_in "Password",      with: "foobar"
fill_in "Confirmation", with: "foobar"
expect do
  click_button "Create my account"
end.to change(User, :count).by(1)
```

This uses the **to** method because we expect a click on the signup button with valid data *to* change the user count by one.

Combining the two cases with the appropriate **describe** blocks and pulling the common code into **before** blocks yields good basic tests for signing up users, as shown in Listing 7.16. Here we've factored out the common text for the submit button using the **let** method to define a **submit** variable.

Listing 7.16 Good basic tests for signing up users.
spec/requests/user_pages_spec.rb

```
require 'spec_helper'

describe "User pages" do

  subject { page }
  .
  .
  .
  describe "signup" do

    before { visit signup_path }

    let(:submit) { "Create my account" }
```

```
    describe "with invalid information" do
      it "should not create a user" do
        expect { click_button submit }.not_to change(User, :count)
      end
    end

    describe "with valid information" do
      before do
        fill_in "Name",         with: "Example User"
        fill_in "Email",        with: "user@example.com"
        fill_in "Password",     with: "foobar"
        fill_in "Confirmation", with: "foobar"
      end

      it "should create a user" do
        expect { click_button submit }.to change(User, :count).by(1)
      end
    end
  end
end
```

We'll add a few more tests as needed in the sections that follow, but the basic tests in Listing 7.16 already cover an impressive amount of functionality. To get them to pass, we have to create a signup page with just the right elements, arrange for the page's submission to be routed to the right place, and successfully create a new user in the database only if the resulting user data is valid.

Of course, at this point the tests should fail:

```
$ bundle exec rspec spec/
```

7.2.2 Using `form_for`

Now that we have good failing tests for user signup, we'll start getting them to pass by making a *form* for signing up users. We can accomplish this in Rails with the **form_for** helper method, which takes in an Active Record object and constructs a form using the object's attributes. The result appears in Listing 7.17. (Readers familiar with Rails 2.x should note that **form_for** uses the "percent-equals" ERb syntax for inserting content; that is, where Rails 2.x used <% form_for ... %>, Rails 3 uses <%= form_for ... %> instead.)

Listing 7.17 A form to sign up new users.
`app/views/users/new.html.erb`

```erb
<% provide(:title, 'Sign up') %>
<h1>Sign up</h1>

<div class="row">
  <div class="span6 offset3">
    <%= form_for(@user) do |f| %>

      <%= f.label :name %>
      <%= f.text_field :name %>

      <%= f.label :email %>
      <%= f.text_field :email %>

      <%= f.label :password %>
      <%= f.password_field :password %>

      <%= f.label :password_confirmation, "Confirmation" %>
      <%= f.password_field :password_confirmation %>

      <%= f.submit "Create my account", class: "btn btn-large btn-primary" %>
    <% end %>
  </div>
</div>
```

Let's break this down into pieces. The presence of the **do** keyword indicates that
form_for takes a block with one variable, which we've called **f** for "form":

```erb
<%= form_for(@user) do |f| %>
  .
  .
  .
<% end %>
```

As is usually the case with Rails helpers, we don't need to know any details about the
implementation, but what we *do* need to know is what the **f** object does: When called
with a method corresponding to an HTML form element—such as a text field, radio
button, or password field—it returns code for that element specifically designed to set
an attribute of the **@user** object. In other words,

```erb
<%= f.label :name %>
<%= f.text_field :name %>
```

creates the HTML needed to make a labeled text field element appropriate for setting the **name** attribute of a User model. (We'll take a look at the HTML itself in Section 7.2.3.)

To see this in action, we need to drill down and look at the actual HTML produced by this form, but here we have a problem: The page currently breaks, because we have not set the **@user** variable—like all undefined instance variables (Section 4.4.5), **@user** is currently **nil**. Appropriately, if you run your test suite at this point, you'll see that the tests for the structure of the signup page from Listing 7.6 (i.e., the **h1** and the **title**) now fail:

```
$ bundle exec rspec spec/requests/user_pages_spec.rb -e "signup page"
```

(The **-e** here arranges to run just the examples whose description strings match **"signup page"**. Note in particular that this is *not* the substring **"signup"**, which would run all the test in Listing 7.16.) To get these tests to pass again and to get our form to render, we must define an **@user** variable in the controller action corresponding to **new.html.erb**, i.e., the **new** action in the Users controller. The **form_for** helper expects **@user** to be a User object, and since we're creating a *new* user we simply use **User.new**, as seen in Listing 7.18.

Listing 7.18 Adding an **@user** variable to the **new** action.
app/controllers/users_controller.rb

```ruby
class UsersController < ApplicationController
  .
  .
  .
  def new
    @user = User.new
  end
end
```

With the **@user** variable so defined, the test for the signup page should be passing again:

```
$ bundle exec rspec spec/requests/user_pages_spec.rb -e "signup page"
```

At this point, the form (with the styling from Listing 7.19) appears as in Figure 7.12. Note the reuse of the **box_sizing** mixin from Listing 7.2.

Listing 7.19 CSS for the signup form.
`app/assets/stylesheets/custom.css.scss`

```
.
.
.

/* forms */

input, textarea, select, .uneditable-input {
  border: 1px solid #bbb;
  width: 100%;
  padding: 10px;
  height: auto;
  margin-bottom: 15px;
  @include box_sizing;
}
```

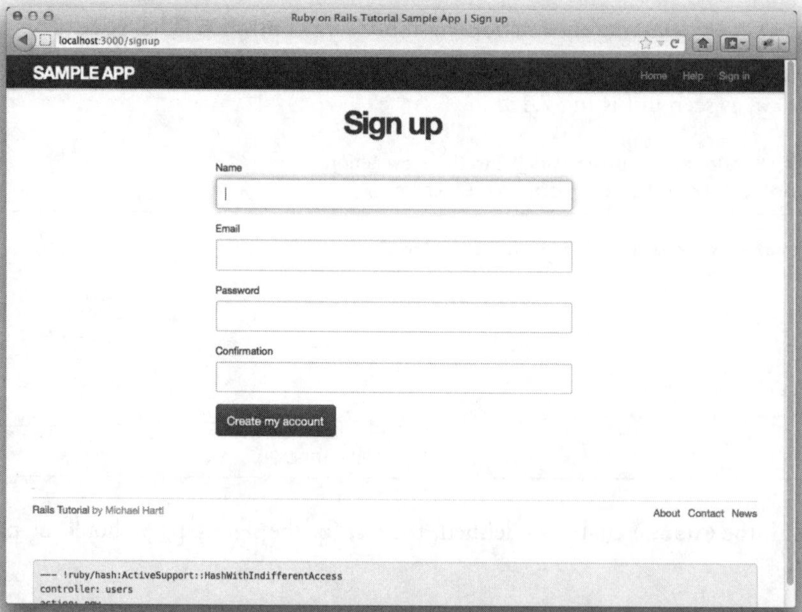

Figure 7.12 The signup form /signup for new users.

7.2.3 The Form HTML

As indicated by Figure 7.12, the signup page now renders properly, indicating that the **form_for** code in Listing 7.17 is producing valid HTML. If you look at the HTML for the generated form (using either Firebug or the "view page source" feature of your browser), you should see markup as in Listing 7.20. Although many of the details are irrelevant for our purposes, let's take a moment to highlight the most important parts of its structure.

Listing 7.20 The HTML for the form in Figure 7.12.

```
<form accept-charset="UTF-8" action="/users" class="new_user"
    id="new_user" method="post">

  <label for="user_name">Name</label>
  <input id="user_name" name="user[name]" size="30" type="text" />

  <label for="user_email">Email</label>
  <input id="user_email" name="user[email]" size="30" type="text" />

  <label for="user_password">Password</label>
  <input id="user_password" name="user[password]" size="30"
      type="password" />

  <label for="user_password_confirmation">Confirmation</label>
  <input id="user_password_confirmation"
      name="user[password_confirmation]" size="30" type="password" />

  <input class="btn btn-large btn-primary" name="commit" type="submit"
      value="Create my account" />
</form>
```

(Here I've omitted some HTML related to the *authenticity token*, which Rails automatically includes to thwart a particular kind of attack called a *cross-site request forgery* (CSRF). See the Stack Overflow entry on the Rails authenticity token if you're interested in the details of how this works and why it's important.)

We'll start with the internal structure of the document. Comparing Listing 7.17 with Listing 7.20, we see that the Embedded Ruby

```
<%= f.label :name %>
<%= f.text_field :name %>
```

produces the HTML

```
<label for="user_name">Name</label>
<input id="user_name" name="user[name]" size="30" type="text" />
```

and

```
<%= f.label :password %>
<%= f.password_field :password %>
```

produces the HTML

```
<label for="user_password">Password</label><br />
<input id="user_password" name="user[password]" size="30" type="password" />
```

As seen in Figure 7.13, text fields (`type="text"`) simply display their contents, whereas password fields (`type="password"`) obscure the input for security purposes, as seen in Figure 7.13.

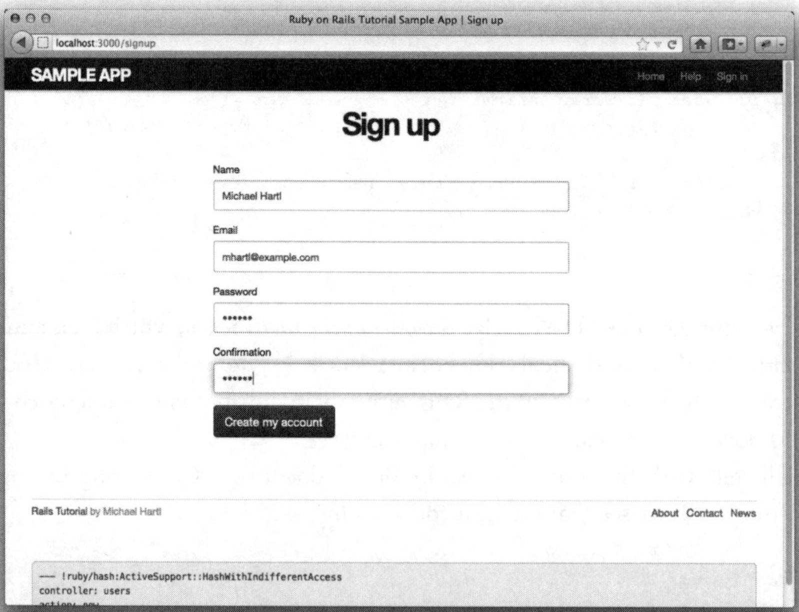

Figure 7.13 A filled-in form with **text** and **password** fields.

As we'll see in Section 7.4, the key to creating a user is the special **name** attribute in each **input**:

```
<input id="user_name" name="user[name]" - - - />
.
.
.
<input id="user_password" name="user[password]" - - - />
```

These **name** values allow Rails to construct an initialization hash (via the **params** variable) for creating users using the values entered by the user, as we'll see in Section 7.3.

The second important element is the **form** tag itself. Rails creates the **form** tag using the **@user** object: because every Ruby object knows its own class (Section 4.4.1), Rails figures out that **@user** is of class **User**; moreover, since **@user** is a *new* user, Rails knows to construct a form with the **post** method, which is the proper verb for creating a new object (Box 3.2):

```
<form action="/users" class="new_user" id="new_user" method="post">
```

Here the **class** and **id** attributes are largely irrelevant; what's important is **action= "/users"** and **method="post"**. Together, these constitute instructions to issue an HTTP POST request to the /users URI. We'll see in the next two sections what effects this has.

7.3 Signup Failure

Although we've briefly examined the HTML for the form in Figure 7.12 (shown in Listing 7.20), it's best understood in the context of *signup failure*. In this section, we'll create a signup form that accepts an invalid submission and re-renders the signup page with a list of errors, as mocked up in Figure 7.14.

7.3.1 A Working Form

Our first step is to eliminate the error that currently results when submitting the signup form, as you can verify in your browser or by running the test for signup with invalid information:

```
$ bundle exec rspec spec/requests/user_pages_spec.rb \
-e "signup with invalid information"
```

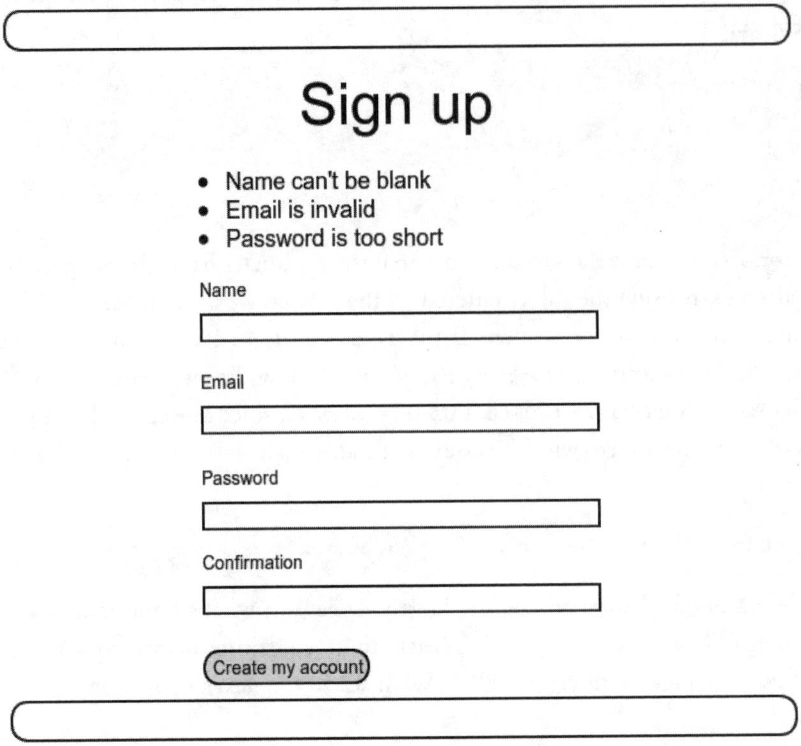

Sign up

- Name can't be blank
- Email is invalid
- Password is too short

Name

Email

Password

Confirmation

Create my account

Figure 7.14   A mockup of the signup failure page.

Recall from Section 7.1.2 that adding **resources :users** to the **routes.rb** file (Listing 7.3) automatically ensures that our Rails application responds to the RESTful URIs from Table 7.1. In particular, it ensures that a POST request to /users is handled by the **create** action. Our strategy for the **create** action is to use the form submission to make a new user object using **User.new**, try (and fail) to save that user, then render the signup page for possible resubmission. Let's get started by reviewing the code for the signup form:

```
<form action="/users" class="new_user" id="new_user" method="post">
```

As noted in Section 7.2.3, this HTML issues a POST request to the /users URI.

We can get the test for invalid information from Listing 7.16 to pass with the code in Listing 7.21. This listing includes a second use of the **render** method, which

we first saw in the context of partials (Section 5.1.3); as you can see, **render** works
in controller actions as well. Note that we've taken this opportunity to introduce an
if-else branching structure, which allows us to handle the cases of failure and success
separately based on the value of **@user.save**, which (as we saw in Section 6.1.3) is
either **true** or **false** depending on whether the save succeeds.

Listing 7.21 A **create** action that can handle signup failure (but not success).
app/controllers/users_controller.rb

```
class UsersController < ApplicationController
  .
  .
  .
  def create
    @user = User.new(params[:user])
    if @user.save
      # Handle a successful save.
    else
      render 'new'
    end
  end
end
```

The best way to understand how the code in Listing 7.21 works is to *submit* the
form with some invalid signup data; the result appears in Figure 7.15, and the full
debug information appears in Figure 7.16.

To get a clearer picture of how Rails handles the submission, let's take a closer look
at the **params** hash from the debug information (Figure 7.16):

```
---
user:
  name: Foo Bar
  password_confirmation: foo
  password: bar
  email: foo@invalid
commit: Create my account
action: create
controller: users
```

We saw starting in Section 7.1.2 that the **params** hash contains information about
each request; in the case of a URI like /users/1, the value of **params[:id]** is the **id** of
the corresponding user (**1** in this example). In the case of posting to the signup form,

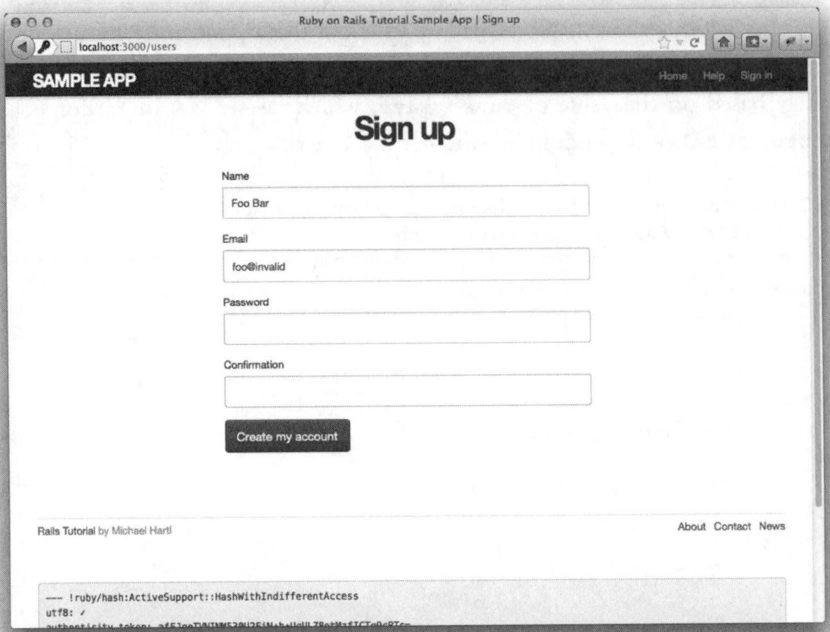

Figure 7.15   Signup failure.

params instead contains a hash of hashes, a construction we first saw in Section 4.3.3, which introduced the strategically named **params** variable in a console session. The debug information above shows that submitting the form results in a **user** hash with attributes corresponding to the submitted values, where the keys come from the **name** attributes of the **input** tags seen in Listing 7.17; for example, the value of

```
<input id="user_email" name="user[email]" size="30" type="text" />
```

with name **"user[email]"** is precisely the **email** attribute of the **user** hash.

Although the hash keys appear as strings in the debug output, internally Rails uses symbols, so that **params[:user]** is the hash of user attributes—in fact, exactly the attributes needed as an argument to **User.new**, as first seen in Section 4.4.5 and appearing in Listing 7.21. This means that the line

```
@user = User.new(params[:user])
```

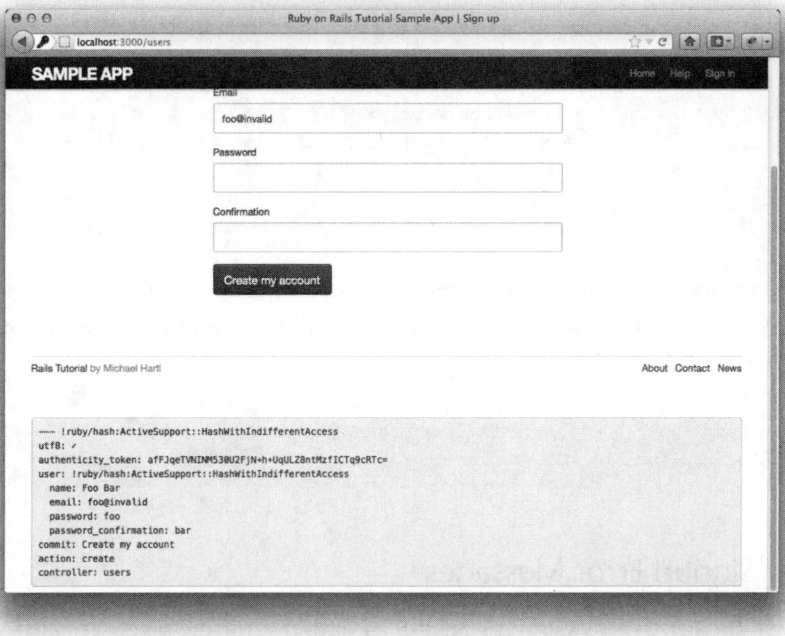

Figure 7.16   Signup failure debug information.

is equivalent to

```
@user = User.new(name: "Foo Bar", email: "foo@invalid",
                 password: "foo", password_confirmation: "bar")
```

Of course, instantiating such a variable has implications for successful signup—as we'll see in Section 7.4, once **@user** is defined properly, calling **@user.save** is all that's needed to complete the registration—but it has consequences even in the failed signup considered here. Note in Figure 7.15 that the fields are *pre-filled* with the data from the failed submission. This is because **form_for** automatically fills in the fields with the attributes of the **@user** object, so that, for example, if **@user.name** is **"Foo"** then

```
<%= form_for(@user) do |f| %>
  <%= f.label :name %>
  <%= f.text_field :name %>
  .
  .
  .
```

will produce the HTML

```
<form action="/users" class="new_user" id="new_user" method="post">

  <label for="user_name">Name</label><br />
  <input id="user_name" name="user[name]" size="30" type="text" value="Foo"/>
  .
  .
  .
```

Here the **value** of the **input** tag is **"Foo"**, so that's what appears in the text field.

As you might guess, now that we can submit a form without generating an error, the test for invalid submission should pass:

```
$ bundle exec rspec spec/requests/user_pages_spec.rb \
-e "signup with invalid information"
```

7.3.2 Signup Error Messages

Although not strictly necessary, it's helpful to output error messages on failed signup to indicate the problems that prevented successful user registration. Rails provides just such messages based on the User model validations. For example, consider trying to save a user with an invalid email address and with a password that's too short:

```
$ rails console
>> user = User.new(name: "Foo Bar", email: "foo@invalid",
?>                 password: "dude", password_confirmation: "dude")
>> user.save
=> false
>> user.errors.full_messages
=> ["Email is invalid", "Password is too short (minimum is 6 characters)"]
```

Here the **errors.full_messages** object (which we saw briefly in Section 6.2.2) contains an array of error messages.

As in the console session above, the failed save in Listing 7.21 generates a list of error messages associated with the **@user** object. To display the messages in the browser, we'll render an error-messages partial on the user **new** page, as shown in Listing 7.22. (Writing a test for the error messages first is a good idea and is left as an exercise; see Section 7.6.) It's worth noting that this error messages partial is only a first attempt; the final version appears in Section 10.3.2.

Listing 7.22 Code to display error messages on the signup form.
`app/views/users/new.html.erb`

```
<% provide(:title, 'Sign up') %>
<h1>Sign up</h1>

<%= form_for(@user) do |f| %>
  <%= render 'shared/error_messages' %>
  .
  .
  .
<% end %>
```

Notice here that we **render** a partial called **`'shared/error_messages'`**; this reflects the common Rails convention of using a dedicated **shared/** directory for partials expected to be used in views across multiple controllers. (We'll see this expectation fulfilled in Section 9.1.1.) This means that we have to create both the new **app/views/shared** directory and the **_error_messages.html.erb** partial file. The partial itself appears in Listing 7.23.

Listing 7.23 A partial for displaying form submission error messages.
`app/views/shared/_error_messages.html.erb`

```
<% if @user.errors.any? %>
  <div id="error_explanation">
    <div class="alert alert-error">
      The form contains <%= pluralize(@user.errors.count, "error") %>.
    </div>
    <ul>
    <% @user.errors.full_messages.each do |msg| %>
      <li>* <%= msg %></li>
    <% end %>
    </ul>
  </div>
<% end %>
```

This partial introduces several new Rails and Ruby constructs, including two methods for Rails objects. The first method is **count**, which simply returns the number of errors:

```
>> user.errors.count
=> 2
```

The other new method is **any?**, which (together with **empty?**) is one of a pair of complementary methods:

```
>> user.errors.empty?
 => false
>> user.errors.any?
 => true
```

We see here that the **empty?** method, which we first saw in Section 4.2.3 in the context of strings, also works on Rails error objects, returning **true** for an empty object and **false** otherwise. The **any?** method is just the opposite of **empty?**, returning **true** if there are any elements present and **false** otherwise. (By the way, all of these methods—**count**, **empty?**, and **any?**—work on Ruby arrays as well. We'll put this fact to good use starting in Section 10.2.)

The other new idea is the **pluralize** text helper. It isn't available in the console by default, but we can include it explicitly through the **ActionView::Helpers:: TextHelper** module:[10]

```
>> include ActionView::Helpers::TextHelper
>> pluralize(1, "error")
=> "1 error"
>> pluralize(5, "error")
=> "5 errors"
```

We see here that **pluralize** takes an integer argument and then returns the number with a properly pluralized version of its second argument. Underlying this method is a powerful *inflector* that knows how to pluralize a large number of words, including many with irregular plurals:

```
>> pluralize(2, "woman")
=> "2 women"
>> pluralize(3, "erratum")
=> "3 errata"
```

As a result of its use of **pluralize**, the code

```
<%= pluralize(@user.errors.count, "error") %>
```

returns **"0 errors"**, **"1 error"**, **"2 errors"**, and so on, depending on how many errors there are, thereby avoiding ungrammatical phrases such as **"1 errors"** (a distressingly common mistake on teh interwebs).

---

10. I figured this out by looking up **pluralize** in the Rails API.

Note that Listing 7.23 includes the CSS id **error_explanation** for use in styling the error messages. (Recall from Section 5.1.2 that CSS uses the pound sign **#** to style ids.) In addition, on error pages Rails automatically wraps the fields with errors in **div**s with the CSS class **field_with_errors**. These labels then allow us to style the error messages with the SCSS shown in Listing 7.24, which makes use of Sass's **@extend** function to include the functionality of two Bootstrap classes **control-group** and **error**. As a result, on failed submission the error messages appear surrounded by red, as seen in Figure 7.17. Because the messages are generated by the model validations, they will automatically change if you ever change your mind about, say, the format of email addresses, or the minimum length of passwords.

Listing 7.24 CSS for styling error messages.
app/assets/stylesheets/custom.css.scss

```
.
.
.

/* forms */
.
.
.

#error_explanation {
  color: #f00;
  ul {
    list-style: none;
    margin: 0 0 18px 0;
  }
}

.field_with_errors {
  @extend .control-group;
  @extend .error;
}
```

To see the results of our work in this section, we'll recapitulate the steps in the failed signup test from Listing 7.16 by visiting the signup page and clicking "Create my account" with blank input fields. The result is shown in Figure 7.18. As you might guess from the working page, at this point the corresponding test should also pass:

```
$ bundle exec rspec spec/requests/user_pages_spec.rb \
> -e "signup with invalid information"
```

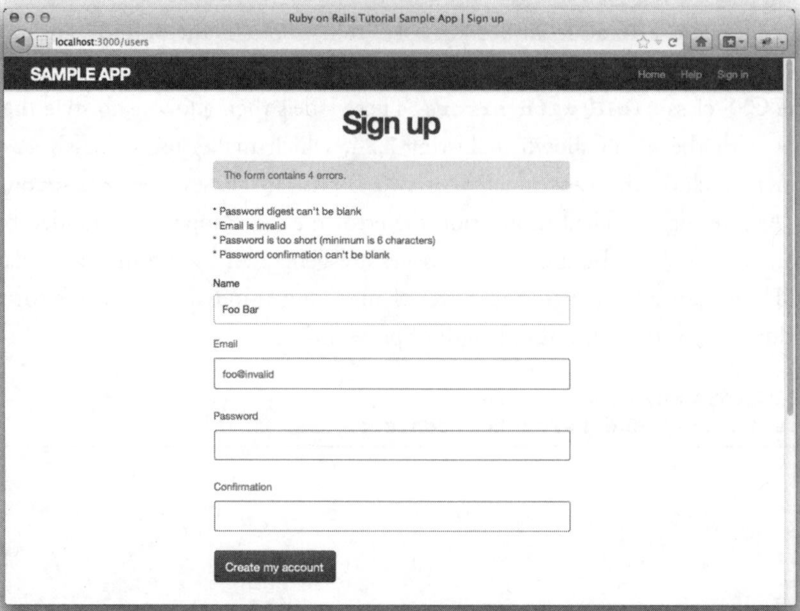

Figure 7.17   Failed signup with error messages.

Unfortunately, there's a minor blemish in the error messages shown in Figure 7.18: The error for a missing password reads as "Password digest can't be blank" instead of the more sensible "Password can't be blank." This is due to the password digest presence validation hiding in `has_secure_password`, as mentioned briefly in Section 6.3.4. Fixing this problem is left as an exercise (Section 7.6).

7.4 Signup Success

Having handled invalid form submissions, now it's time to complete the signup form by actually saving a new user (if valid) to the database. First, we try to save the user; if the save succeeds, the user's information gets written to the database automatically, and we then *redirect* the browser to show the user's profile (together with a friendly greeting), as mocked up in Figure 7.19. If it fails, we simply fall back on the behavior developed in Section 7.3.

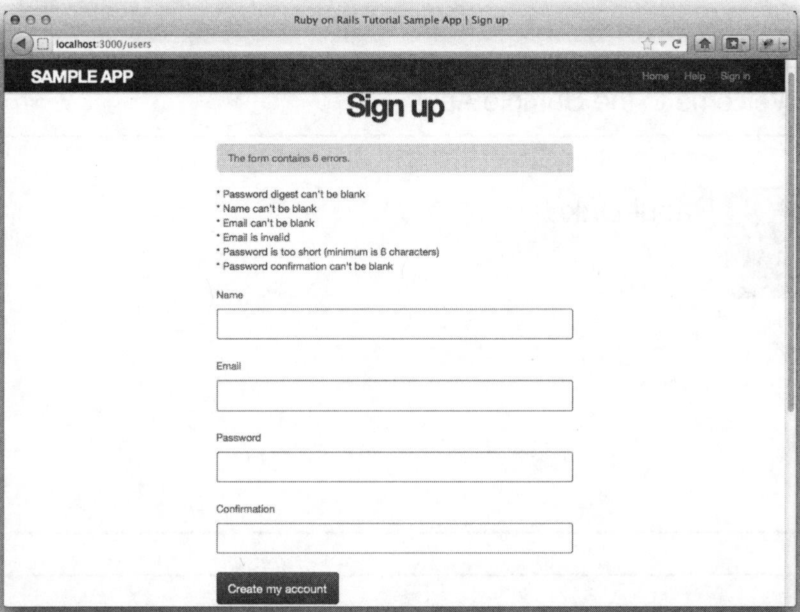

Figure 7.18 The result of visiting /signup and just clicking "Create my account."

7.4.1 The Finished Signup Form

To complete a working signup form, we need to fill in the commented-out section in Listing 7.21 with the appropriate behavior. Currently, the test for valid submission should be failing:

```
$ bundle exec rspec spec/requests/user_pages_spec.rb \
> -e "signup with valid information"
```

This is because the default behavior for a Rails action is to render the corresponding view, but there is not (nor should there be) a view template corresponding to the `create` action. Instead, we need to redirect to a different page, and it makes sense for that page to be the newly created user's profile. Testing that the proper page gets rendered is left as an exercise (Section 7.6); the application code appears in Listing 7.25.

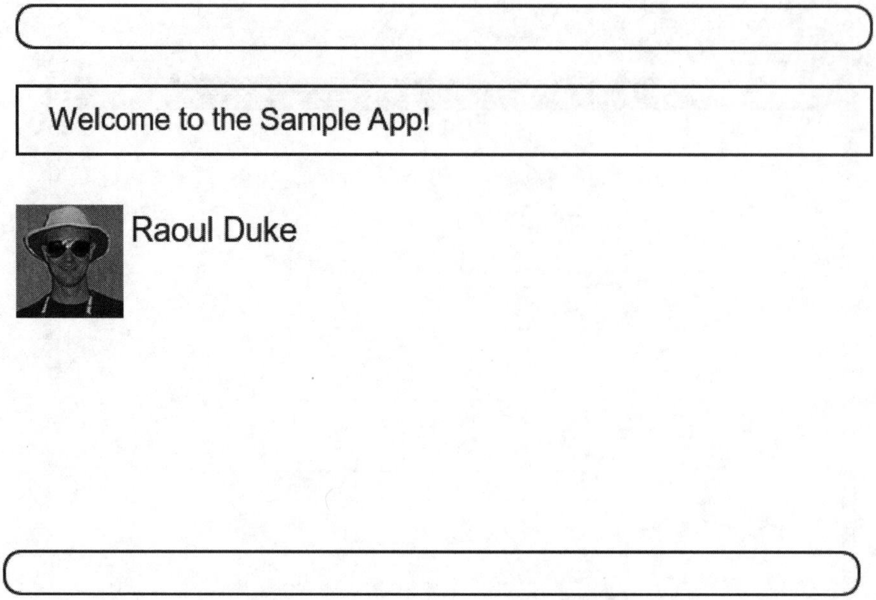

Welcome to the Sample App!

 Raoul Duke

Figure 7.19   A mockup of successful signup.

Listing 7.25   The user **create** action with a save and a redirect.
app/controllers/users_controller.rb

```ruby
class UsersController < ApplicationController
  .
  .
  .
  def create
    @user = User.new(params[:user])
    if @user.save
      redirect_to @user
    else
      render 'new'
    end
  end
end
```

Note that we can omit the **user_path** in the redirect, writing simply **redirect_to**
@user to redirect to the user show page.

With the code in Listing 7.25, our signup form is working, as you can verify by running the test suite:

```
$ bundle exec rspec spec/
```

7.4.2 The Flash

Before submitting a valid registration in a browser, we're going to add a bit of polish common in web applications: a message that appears on the subsequent page (in this case, welcoming our new user to the application) and then disappears upon visiting a second page or on page reload. The Rails way to accomplish this is to use a special variable called the *flash*, which operates like flash memory in that it stores its data temporarily. The **flash** variable is effectively a hash; you may even recall the console example in Section 4.3.3, where we saw how to iterate through a hash using a strategically named **flash** hash:

```
$ rails console
>> flash = { success: "It worked!", error: "It failed." }
=> {:success=>"It worked!", error: "It failed."}
>> flash.each do |key, value|
?>   puts "#{key}"
?>   puts "#{value}"
>> end
success
It worked!
error
It failed.
```

We can arrange to display the contents of the flash site-wide by including it in our application layout, as in Listing 7.26. (This code is a particularly ugly combination of HTML and ERb; an exercise in Section 7.6 shows how to make it prettier.)

Listing 7.26 Adding the contents of the **flash** variable to the site layout.
app/views/layouts/application.html.erb

```
<!DOCTYPE html>
<html>
  .
  .
  .
```

```
<body>
  <%= render 'layouts/header' %>
  <div class="container">
    <% flash.each do |key, value| %>
      <div class="alert alert-<%= key %>"><%= value %></div>
    <% end %>
    <%= yield %>
    <%= render 'layouts/footer' %>
    <%= debug(params) if Rails.env.development? %>
  </div>
    .
    .
    .
  </body>
</html>
```

The code in Listing 7.26 arranges to insert a **div** tag for each element in the flash, with a CSS class indicating the type of message. For example, if **flash[:success] = "Welcome to the Sample App!"**, then the code

```
<% flash.each do |key, value| %>
  <div class="alert alert-<%= key %>"><%= value %></div>
<% end %>
```

will produce this HTML:

```
<div class="alert alert-success">Welcome to the Sample App!</div>
```

(Note that the key **:success** is a symbol, but Embedded Ruby automatically converts it to the string **"success"** before inserting it into the template.) The reason we iterate through all possible key/value pairs is so that we can include other kinds of flash messages. For example, in Section 8.1.5 we'll see **flash[:error]** used to indicate a failed signin attempt.[11]

Writing a test for the right flash message is left as an exercise (Section 7.6), and we can get the test to pass by assigning **flash[:success]** a welcome message in the **create** action, as shown in Listing 7.27.

---

11. Actually, we'll use the closely related **flash.now**, but we'll defer that subtlety until we need it.

Listing 7.27 Adding a flash message to user signup.
`app/controllers/users_controller.rb`

```
class UsersController < ApplicationController
  .
  .
  .
  def create
    @user = User.new(params[:user])
    if @user.save
      flash[:success] = "Welcome to the Sample App!"
      redirect_to @user
    else
      render 'new'
    end
  end
end
```

7.4.3 The First Signup

We can see the result of all this work by signing up our first user under the name "Rails Tutorial" and email address "example@railstutorial.org". The resulting page (Figure 7.20) shows a friendly message upon successful signup, including nice green styling for the **success** class, which comes included with the Bootstrap CSS framework from Section 5.1.2. (If instead you get an error message indicating that the email address has already been taken, be sure to run the **db:reset** Rake task as indicated in Section 7.2.) Then, upon reloading the user show page, the flash message disappears as promised (Figure 7.21).

We can now check our database just to be double sure that the new user was actually created:

```
$ rails console
>> User.find_by_email("example@railstutorial.org")
=> #<User id: 1, name: "Rails Tutorial", email: "example@railstutorial.org",
created_at: "2011-12-13 05:51:34", updated_at: "2011-12-13 05:51:34",
password_digest: "$2a$10$A58/j7wwh3aAffGkMAO9Q.jjh3jshd.6akhDKtchAz/R...">
```

7.4.4 Deploying to Production with SSL

Having developed the User model and the signup functionality, now is a good time to deploy the sample application to production. (If you didn't follow the setup steps in the

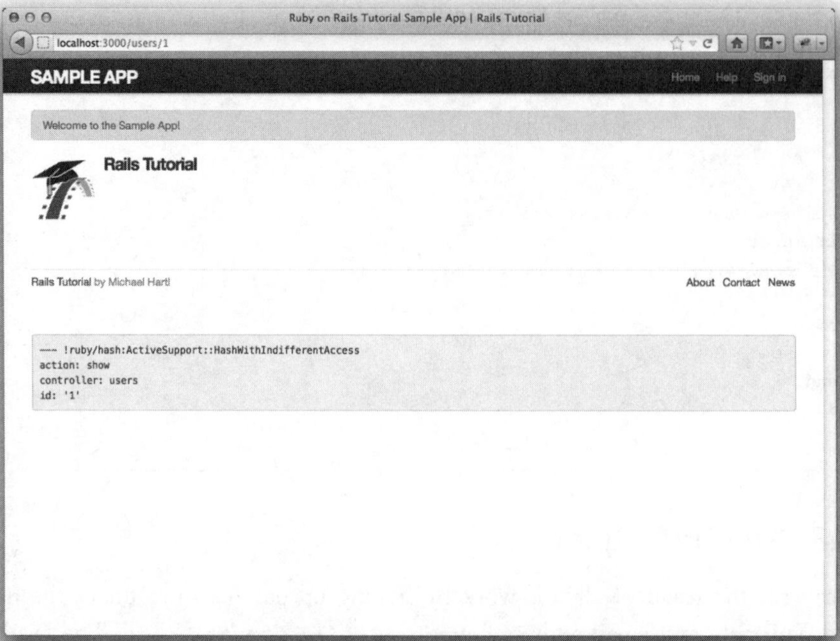

Figure 7.20 The results of a successful user signup, with flash message.

introduction to Chapter 3, you should go back and do them now.) As part of this, we will add Secure Sockets Layer (SSL)[12] to the production application, thereby making signup secure. Since we'll implement SSL site-wide, the sample application will also be secure during user signin (Chapter 8) and will also be immune to the *session hijacking* vulnerability (Section 8.2.2).

As preparation for the deployment, you should merge your changes into the **master** branch at this point:

```
$ git add .
$ git commit -m "Finish user signup"
$ git checkout master
$ git merge sign-up
```

---

12. Technically, SSL is now TLS, for Transport Layer Security, but everyone I know still says "SSL."

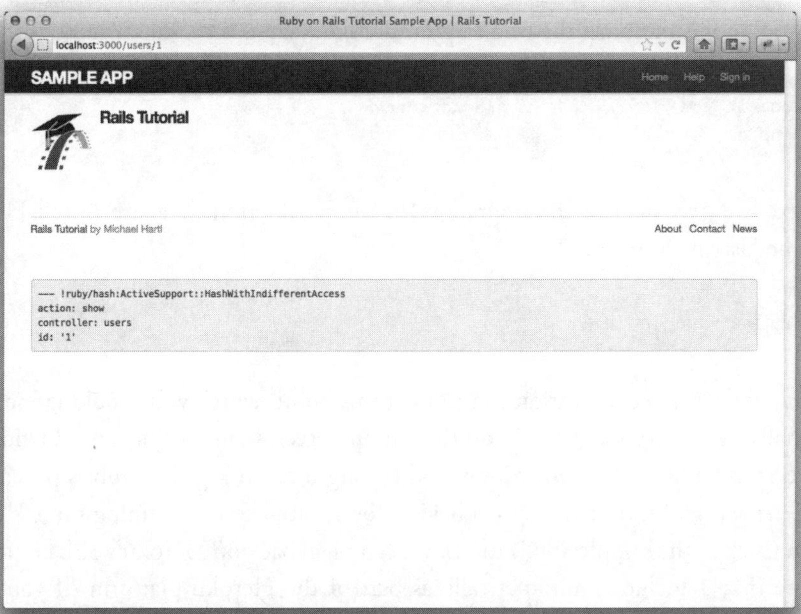

Figure 7.21   The flash-less profile page after a browser reload.

To get the deployment to work, we first need to add a line forcing the use of SSL in production. The result, which involves editing the production configuration file **config/environments/production.rb**, appears in Listing 7.28.

Listing 7.28 Configuring the application to use SSL in production.
config/environments/production.rb

```
SampleApp::Application.configure do
  .
  .
  .
  # Force all access to the app over SSL, use Strict-Transport-Security,
  # and use secure cookies.
  config.force_ssl = true
  .
  .
  .
end
```

To get the production site working, we have to commit the change to the configuration file and push the result up to Heroku:

```
$ git commit -a -m "Add SSL in production"
$ git push heroku
```

Next, we need to run the migration on the production database to tell Heroku about the User data model:[13]

```
$ heroku run rake db:migrate
```

(You might see some deprecation warnings at this point, which you should ignore.)

Finally, we need to set up SSL on the remote server. Configuring a production site to use SSL is painful and error-prone, and among other things it involves purchasing an *SSL certificate* for your domain. Luckily, for an application running on a Heroku domain (such as the sample application), we can piggyback on Heroku's SSL certificate, a feature that is included automatically as part of the Heroku platform. If you want to run SSL on a custom domain, such as **example.com**, you'll have no choice but to endure some pain, which you can read about on Heroku's page on SSL.

The result of all this work is a working signup form on the production server (Figure 7.22):

```
$ heroku open
```

Note in Figure 7.22 the `https://` in place of the usual `http://`. The extra "s" is an indication that SSL is working.

You should feel free to visit the signup page and create a new user at this time. If you have trouble, try running

```
$ heroku logs
```

to debug the error using the Heroku logfile.

---

13. Readers interested in using Heroku for real-life production applications might be interested in Kumade, which handles things like database migrations automatically.

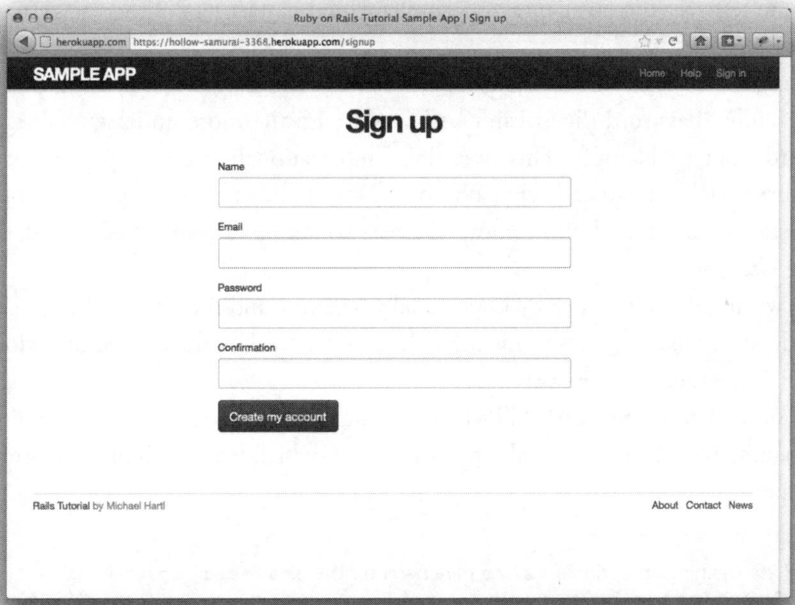

Figure 7.22 A working signup page on the live Web.

7.5 Conclusion

Being able to sign up users is a major milestone for our application. Although the sample app has yet to accomplish anything useful, we have laid an essential foundation for all future development. In Chapter 8, we will complete our authentication machinery by allowing users to sign in and out of the application. In Chapter 9, we will allow all users to update their account information. We will also allow site administrators to delete users, thereby completing the full suite of the Users resource REST actions from Table 7.1. Finally, we'll add authorization methods to our actions to enforce a site security model.

7.6 Exercises

1. Verify that the code in Listing 7.29 allows the `gravatar_for` helper defined in Section 7.1.4 to take an optional `size` parameter, allowing code like `gravatar_for user, size: 40` in the view.

2. Write tests for the error messages implemented in Listing 7.22. A suggested start appears in Listing 7.31.

3. Using the code in Listing 7.30, replace the error message for a missing password, currently "Password digest can't be blank", with the more understandable "Password can't be blank". (This uses Rails' internationalization support to produce a functional but rather hacky solution.) Note that, to avoid duplication of error messages, you should also remove the password's **presence: true** validation in the User model.

4. By writing the test first or by intentionally breaking and then fixing the application code, verify that the tests in Listing 7.32 correctly specify the desired behavior after saving the user in the **create** action.

5. As noted before, the flash HTML in Listing 7.26 is ugly. Verify by running the test suite that the cleaner code in Listing 7.33, which uses the Rails **content_tag** helper, also works.

Listing 7.29 Defining an optional **:size** parameter for the **gravatar_for** helper.
app/helpers/users_helper.rb

```
module UsersHelper

  # Returns the Gravatar (http://gravatar.com/) for the given user.
  def gravatar_for(user, options = { size: 50 })
    gravatar_id = Digest::MD5::hexdigest(user.email.downcase)
    size = options[:size]
    gravatar_url = "https://secure.gravatar.com/avatars/#{gravatar_id}.png?s=
                     #{size}"
    image_tag(gravatar_url, alt: user.name, class: "gravatar")
  end
end
```

Listing 7.30 Hacking a better error message for missing passwords.
config/locales/en.yml

```
en:
  activerecord:
    attributes:
      user:
        password_digest: "Password"
```

Listing 7.31 Suggested error messages tests.
`spec/requests/user_pages_spec.rb`

```
  .
  .
  .
describe "signup" do

  before { visit signup_path }
    .
    .
  describe "with invalid information" do
    .
    .
    describe "after submission" do
      before { click_button submit }

      it { should have_selector('title', text: 'Sign up') }
      it { should have_content('error') }
    end
    .
    .
    .
```

Listing 7.32 Tests for the post-save behavior in the **create** action.
`spec/requests/user_pages_spec.rb`

```
    .
    .
    .
  describe "with valid information" do
    .
    .
    .
    describe "after saving the user" do
      before { click_button submit }
      let(:user) { User.find_by_email('user@example.com') }

      it { should have_selector('title', text: user.name) }
      it { should have_selector('div.alert.alert-success', text: 'Welcome') }
    end
    .
    .
    .
```

Listing 7.33 The **flash** ERb in the site layout using **content_tag**.
app/views/layouts/application.html.erb

```
<!DOCTYPE html>
<html>
    .
    .
    .
    <% flash.each do |key, value| %>
      <%= content_tag(:div, value, class: "alert alert-#{key}") %>
    <% end %>
    .
    .
    .
</html>
```

CHAPTER 8

Sign In, Sign Out

Now that new users can sign up for our site (Chapter 7), it's time to give registered users the ability to sign in and sign out. This will allow us to add customizations based on signin status and based on the identity of the current user. For example, in this chapter we'll update the site header with signin/signout links and a profile link. In Chapter 10, we'll use the identity of a signed-in user to create microposts associated with that user, and in Chapter 11 we'll allow the current user to follow other users of the application (thereby receiving a feed of their microposts).

Having users sign in will also allow us to implement a security model, restricting access to particular pages based on the identity of the signed-in user. For instance, as we'll see in Chapter 9, only signed-in users will be able to access the page used to edit user information. The signin system will also make possible special privileges for administrative users, such as the ability (also introduced in Chapter 9) to delete users from the database.

After implementing the core authentication machinery, we'll take a short detour to investigate *Cucumber*, a popular system for behavior-driven development (Section 8.3). In particular, we'll re-implement a couple of the RSpec integration tests in Cucumber to see how the two methods compare.

As in previous chapters, we'll do our work on a topic branch and merge in the changes at the end:

```
$ git checkout -b sign-in-out
```

8.1 Sessions and Signin Failure

A *session* is a semi-permanent connection between two computers, such as a client computer running a web browser and a server running Rails. We'll be using sessions to implement the common pattern of signing in, and in this context there are several different models for session behavior common on the web: "forgetting" the session on browser close, using an optional "remember me" checkbox for persistent sessions, and automatically remembering sessions until the user explicitly signs out.[1] We'll opt for the final of these options: When users sign in, we will remember their signin status "forever," clearing the session only when the user explicitly signs out. (We'll see in Section 8.2.1 just how long "forever" is.)

It's convenient to model sessions as a RESTful resource: We'll have a signin page for *new* sessions, signing in will *create* a session, and signing out will *destroy* it. Unlike the Users resource, which uses a database back-end (via the User model) to persist data, the Sessions resource will use a *cookie*, which is a small piece of text placed on the user's browser. Much of the work involved in signin comes from building this cookie-based authentication machinery. In this section and the next, we'll prepare for this work by constructing a Sessions controller, a signin form, and the relevant controller actions. We'll then complete user signin in Section 8.2 by adding the necessary cookie-manipulation code.

8.1.1 Sessions Controller

The elements of signing in and out correspond to particular REST actions of the Sessions controller: The signin form is handled by the **new** action (covered in this section), actually signing in is handled by sending a POST request to the **create** action (Section 8.1 and Section 8.2), and signing out is handled by sending a DELETE request to the **destroy** action (Section 8.2.6). (Recall the association of HTTP verbs with REST actions from Table 7.1.) To get started, we'll generate a Sessions controller and an integration test for the authentication machinery:

```
$ rails generate controller Sessions --no-test-framework
$ rails generate integration_test authentication_pages
```

Following the model from Section 7.2 for the signup page, we'll create a signin form for creating new sessions, as mocked up in Figure 8.1.

The signin page will live at the URI given by **signin_path** (defined momentarily), and as usual we'll start with a minimalist test, as shown in Listing 8.1. (Compare to the analogous code for the signup page in Listing 7.6.)

---

1. Another common model is to expire the session after a certain amount of time. This is especially appropriate on sites containing sensitive information, such as banking and financial trading accounts.

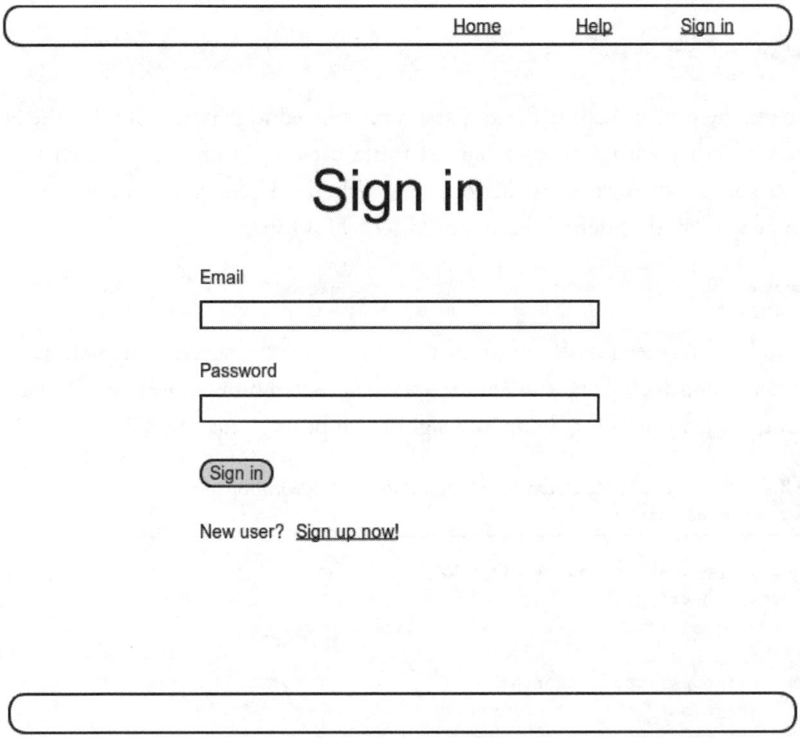

Figure 8.1   A mockup of the signin form.

Listing 8.1 Tests for the **new** session action and view.
`spec/requests/authentication_pages_spec.rb`

```ruby
require 'spec_helper'

describe "Authentication" do

  subject { page }

  describe "signin page" do
    before { visit signin_path }

    it { should have_selector('h1',    text: 'Sign in') }
    it { should have_selector('title', text: 'Sign in') }
  end
end
```

The tests initially fail, as required:

```
$ bundle exec rspec spec/
```

To get the tests in Listing 8.1 to pass, we first need to define routes for the Sessions resource, together with a custom named route for the signin page (which we'll map to the Session controller's **new** action). As with the Users resource, we can use the **resources** method to define the standard RESTful routes:

```
resources :sessions, only: [:new, :create, :destroy]
```

Since we have no need to show or edit sessions, we've restricted the actions to **new**, **create**, and **destroy** using the **:only** option accepted by **resources**. The full result, including named routes for signin and signout, appears in Listing 8.2.

Listing 8.2 Adding a resource to get the standard RESTful actions for sessions.
config/routes.rb

```
SampleApp::Application.routes.draw do
  resources :users
  resources :sessions, only: [:new, :create, :destroy]

  match '/signup',  to: 'users#new'
  match '/signin',  to: 'sessions#new'
  match '/signout', to: 'sessions#destroy', via: :delete
  .
  .
  .
end
```

Note the use of **via: :delete** for the signout route, which indicated that it should be invoked using an HTTP DELETE request.

The resources defined in Listing 8.2 provide URIs and actions similar to those for users (Table 7.1), as shown in Table 8.1. Note that the routes for signin and signout are custom, but the route for creating a session is simply the default (i.e., **[resource name]_path**).

The next step to get the tests in Listing 8.1 to pass is to add a **new** action to the Sessions controller, as shown in Listing 8.3 (which also defines the **create** and **destroy** actions for future reference).

Table 8.1   RESTful routes provided by the sessions rules in Listing 8.2.

HTTP request	URI	Named route	Action	Purpose
GET	/signin	**signin_path**	**new**	page for a new session (signin)
POST	/sessions	**sessions_path**	**create**	create a new session
DELETE	/signout	**signout_path**	**destroy**	delete a session (sign out)

Listing 8.3 The initial Sessions controller.
app/controllers/sessions_controller.rb

```ruby
class SessionsController < ApplicationController

  def new
  end

  def create
  end

  def destroy
  end
end
```

The final step is to define the initial version of the signin page. Note that, since it is the page for a new session, the signin page lives in the file **app/views/sessions/new.html.erb**, which we have to create. The contents, which for now only define the page title and top-level heading, appear as in Listing 8.4.

Listing 8.4 The initial signin view.
app/views/sessions/new.html.erb

```erb
<% provide(:title, "Sign in") %>
<h1>Sign in</h1>
```

With that, the tests in Listing 8.1 should be passing, and we're ready to make the actual signin form.

```
$ bundle exec rspec spec/
```

8.1.2 Signin Tests

Comparing Figure 8.1 with Figure 7.11, we see that the signin form (or, equivalently, the new session form) is similar in appearance to the signup form, except with two fields (email and password) in place of four. As with the signup form, we can test the signin form by using Capybara to fill in the form values and then click the button.

In the process of writing the tests, we'll be forced to design aspects of the application, which is one of the nice side effects of test-driven development. We'll start with invalid signin, as mocked up in Figure 8.2.

As seen in Figure 8.2, when the signin information is invalid we want to re-render the signin page and display an error message. We'll render the error as a flash message, which we can test for as follows:

```
it { should have_selector('div.alert.alert-error', text: 'Invalid') }
```

Figure 8.2 A mockup of signin failure.

(We saw similar code in Listing 7.32 from the exercises in Chapter 7.) Here the selector element (i.e., the tag) we're looking for is

```
div.alert.alert-error
```

Recalling that the dot means "class" in CSS (Section 5.1.2), you might be able to guess that this tests for a **div** tag with the classes **"alert"** and **"alert-error"**. We also test that the error message contains the text **"Invalid"**. Putting these together, the test looks for an element of the following form:

```
<div class="alert alert-error">Invalid...</div>
```

Combining the title and flash tests gives the code in Listing 8.5. As we'll see, these tests miss an important subtlety, which we'll address in Section 8.1.5.

Listing 8.5 The tests for signin failure.
spec/requests/authentication_pages_spec.rb

```
require 'spec_helper'

describe "Authentication" do
    .
    .
    .
  describe "signin" do
    before { visit signin_path }

    describe "with invalid information" do
      before { click_button "Sign in" }

      it { should have_selector('title', text: 'Sign in') }
      it { should have_selector('div.alert.alert-error', text: 'Invalid') }
    end
  end
end
```

Having written tests for signin failure, we now turn to signin success. The changes we'll test for are the rendering of the user's profile page (as determined by the page title, which should be the user's name), together with three planned changes to the site navigation:

1. The appearance of a link to the profile page
2. The appearance of a "Sign out" link
3. The disappearance of the "Sign in" link

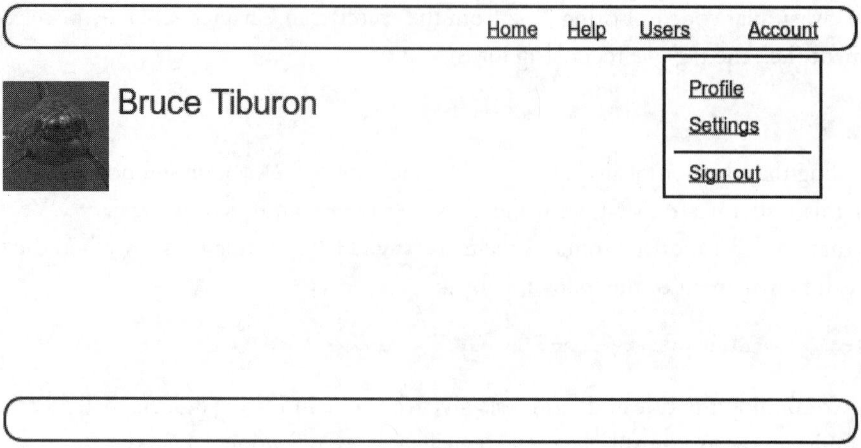

Figure 8.3   A mockup of the user profile after a successful signin.

(We'll defer the test for the "Settings" link to Section 9.1 and for the "Users" link to Section 9.3.) A mockup of these changes appears in Figure 8.3.[2] Note that the signout and profile links appear in a dropdown "Account" menu; in Section 8.2.4, we'll see how to make such a menu with Bootstrap.

The test code for signin success appears in Listing 8.6.

Listing 8.6 Test for signin success.
spec/requests/authentication_pages_spec.rb

```
require 'spec_helper'

describe "Authentication" do
  .
  .
  .
  describe "signin" do
    before { visit signin_path }
    .
    .
    .
```

_____

2. Image from www.flickr.com/photos/hermanusbackpackers/3343254977/.

```
    describe "with valid information" do
      let(:user) { FactoryGirl.create(:user) }
      before do
        fill_in "Email",    with: user.email
        fill_in "Password", with: user.password
        click_button "Sign in"
      end

      it { should have_selector('title', text: user.name) }
      it { should have_link('Profile', href: user_path(user)) }
      it { should have_link('Sign out', href: signout_path) }
      it { should_not have_link('Sign in', href: signin_path) }
    end
  end
end
```

Here we've used the **have_link** method. It takes as arguments the text of the link and an optional **:href** parameter, so that

```
it { should have_link('Profile', href: user_path(user)) }
```

ensures that the anchor tag **a** has the right **href** (URI) attribute—in this case, a link to the user's profile page.

8.1.3   Signin Form

With our tests in place, we're ready to start developing the signin form. Recall from Listing 7.17 that the signup form uses the **form_for** helper, taking as an argument the user instance variable **@user**:

```
<%= form_for(@user) do |f| %>
  .
  .
  .
<% end %>
```

The main difference between this and the signin form is that we have no Session model, hence no analogue for the **@user** variable. This means that, in constructing the new session form, we have to give **form_for** slightly more information; in particular, whereas

```
form_for(@user)
```

allows Rails to infer that the **action** of the form should be to POST to the URI /users, in the case of sessions we need to indicate the *name* of the resource and the corresponding URI:

```
form_for(:session, url: sessions_path)
```

(A second option is to use **form_tag** in place of **form_for**; this might be more even idiomatically correct Rails, but it has less in common with the signup form, and at this stage I want to emphasize the parallel structure. Making a working form with **form_tag** is left as an exercise [Section 8.5].)

With the proper **form_for** in hand, it's easy to make a signin form to match the mockup in Figure 8.1 using the signup form (Listing 7.17) as a model, as shown in Listing 8.7.

Listing 8.7 Code for the signin form.
app/views/sessions/new.html.erb

```erb
<% provide(:title, "Sign in") %>
<h1>Sign in</h1>

<div class="row">
  <div class="span6 offset3">
    <%= form_for(:session, url: sessions_path) do |f| %>

      <%= f.label :email %>
      <%= f.text_field :email %>

      <%= f.label :password %>
      <%= f.password_field :password %>

      <%= f.submit "Sign in", class: "btn btn-large btn-primary" %>
    <% end %>

    <p>New user? <%= link_to "Sign up now!", signup_path %></p>
  </div>
</div>
```

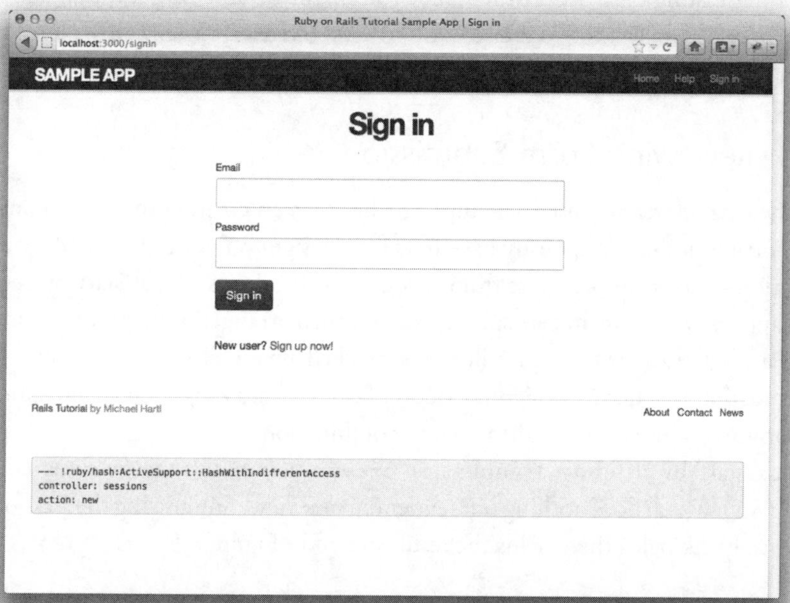

Figure 8.4   The signin form (/signin).

Note that we've added a link to the signup page for convenience. With the code in Listing 8.7, the signin form appears as in Figure 8.4.

Though you'll soon get out of the habit of looking at the HTML generated by Rails (instead trusting the helpers to do their job), for now let's take a look at it (Listing 8.8).

Listing 8.8   HTML for the signin form produced by Listing 8.7.

```
<form accept-charset="UTF-8" action="/sessions" method="post">
  <div>
    <label for="session_email">Email</label>
    <input id="session_email" name="session[email]" size="30" type="text" />
  </div>
  <div>
    <label for="session_password">Password</label>
    <input id="session_password" name="session[password]" size="30"
        type="password" />
  </div>
  <input class="btn btn-large btn-primary" name="commit" type="submit"
      value="Sign in" />
</form>
```

Comparing Listing 8.8 with Listing 7.20, you might be able to guess that submitting this form will result in a `params` hash where `params[:session][:email]` and `params[:session][:password]` correspond to the email and password fields.

8.1.4   Reviewing Form Submission

As in the case of creating users (signup), the first step in creating sessions (signin) is to handle *invalid* input. We already have tests for the signup failure (Listing 8.5), and the application code is simple apart from a couple of subtleties. We'll start by reviewing what happens when a form gets submitted, and then arrange for helpful error messages to appear in the case of signin failure (as mocked up in Figure 8.2.) Then we'll lay the foundation for successful signin (Section 8.2) by evaluating each signin submission based on the validity of its email/password combination.

Let's start by defining a minimalist `create` action for the Sessions controller (Listing 8.9), which does nothing but render the **new** view. Submitting the /sessions/new form with blank fields then yields the result shown in Figure 8.5.

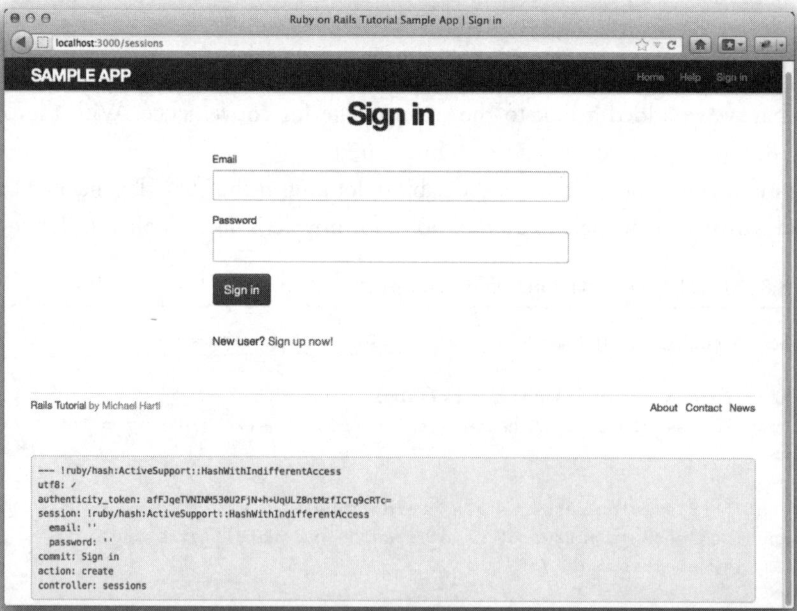

Figure 8.5   The initial failed signin, with `create` as in Listing 8.9.

Listing 8.9 A preliminary version of the Sessions **create** action.
`app/controllers/sessions_controller.rb`

```ruby
class SessionsController < ApplicationController
  .
  .
  .
  def create
    render 'new'
  end
  .
  .
  .
end
```

Carefully inspecting the debug information in Figure 8.5 shows that, as hinted at the end of Section 8.1.3, the submission results in a **params** hash containing the email and password under the key **:session**:

```
---
session:
  email: ''
  password: ''
commit: Sign in
action: create
controller: sessions
```

As with the case of user signup (Figure 7.15) these parameters form a *nested* hash like the one we saw in Listing 4.6. In particular, **params** contains a nested hash of the form

```
{ session: { password: "", email: "" } }
```

This means that

```
params[:session]
```

is itself a hash:

```
{ password: "", email: "" }
```

As a result,

```
params[:session][:email]
```

is the submitted email address and

```
params[:session][:password]
```

is the submitted password.

In other words, inside the **create** action the **params** hash has all the information needed to authenticate users by email and password. Not coincidentally, we already have exactly the methods we need: the **User.find_by_email** method provided by Active Record (Section 6.1.4) and the **authenticate** method provided by **has_secure_password** (Section 6.3.3). Recalling that **authenticate** returns **false** for an invalid authentication, our strategy for user signin can be summarized as follows:

```
def create
  user = User.find_by_email(params[:session][:email])
  if user && user.authenticate(params[:session][:password])
    # Sign the user in and redirect to the user's show page.
  else
    # Create an error message and re-render the signin form.
  end
end
```

The first line here pulls the user out of the database using the submitted email address. The next line is common in idiomatic Ruby:

```
user && user.authenticate(params[:session][:password])
```

This uses **&&** (logical *and*) to determine if the resulting user is valid. Taking into account that any object other than **nil** and **false** itself is **true** in a boolean context (Section 4.2.3), the possibilities appear as in Table 8.2. We see from Table 8.2 that the **if** statement is **true** only if a user with the given email both exists in the database and has the given password, exactly as required.

Table 8.2 Possible results of **user && user.authenticate(...)**.

User	Password	a && b
nonexistent	*anything*	**nil && [anything] == false**
valid user	wrong password	**true && false == false**
valid user	right password	**true && true == true**

8.1.5 Rendering with a Flash Message

Recall from Section 7.3.2 that we displayed signup errors using the User model error messages. These errors are associated with a particular Active Record object, but this strategy won't work here because the session isn't an Active Record model. Instead, we'll put a message in the flash to be displayed upon failed signin. A first, slightly incorrect, attempt appears in Listing 8.10.

Listing 8.10 An (unsuccessful) attempt at handling failed signin.
app/controllers/sessions_controller.rb

```ruby
class SessionsController < ApplicationController

  def new
  end

  def create
    user = User.find_by_email(params[:session][:email])
    if user && user.authenticate(params[:session][:password])
      # Sign the user in and redirect to the user's show page.
    else
      flash[:error] = 'Invalid email/password combination' # Not quite right!
      render 'new'
    end
  end

  def destroy
  end
end
```

Because of the flash message display in the site layout (Listing 7.26), the **flash[:error]** message automatically gets displayed; because of the Bootstrap CSS, it automatically gets nice styling (Figure 8.6).

Unfortunately, as noted in the text and in the comment in Listing 8.10, this code isn't quite right. The page looks fine, though, so what's the problem? The issue is that the contents of the flash persist for one *request*, but—unlike a redirect, which we used in Listing 7.27—re-rendering a template with **render** doesn't count as a request. The result is that the flash message persists one request longer than we want. For example, if we submit invalid information, the flash is set and gets displayed on the signin page (Figure 8.6); if we then click on another page, such as the Home page, that's the first request since the form submission, and the flash gets displayed again (Figure 8.7).

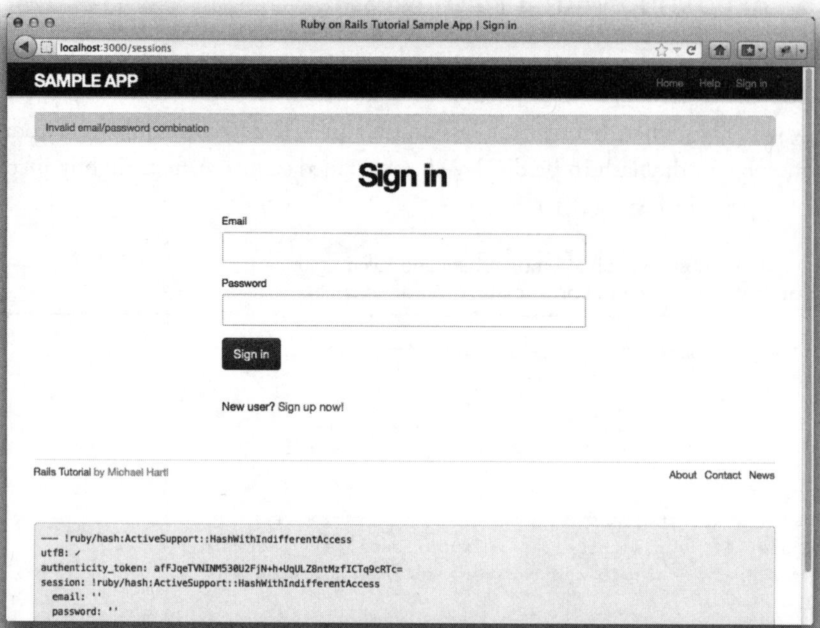

Figure 8.6   The flash message for a failed signin.

This flash persistence is a bug in our application, and before proceeding with a fix, it is a good idea to write a test catching the error. In particular, the signin failure tests are currently passing:

```
$ bundle exec rspec spec/requests/authentication_pages_spec.rb \
> -e "signin with invalid information"
```

But the tests should never pass when there is a known bug, so we should add a failing test to catch it. Fortunately, dealing with a problem like flash persistence is one of many areas where integration tests really shine; they let us say exactly what we mean:

```
describe "after visiting another page" do
  before { click_link "Home" }
  it { should_not have_selector('div.alert.alert-error') }
end
```

Figure 8.7 An example of the flash persisting.

After submitting invalid signin data, this test follows the Home link in the site layout and then requires that the flash error message not appear. The updated code, with the modified flash test, is shown in Listing 8.11.

Listing 8.11 Correct tests for signin failure.
spec/requests/authentication_pages_spec.rb

```
require 'spec_helper'

describe "Authentication" do
  .
  .
  .
  describe "signin" do

    before { visit signin_path }

    describe "with invalid information" do
      before { click_button "Sign in" }
```

```
    it { should have_selector('title', text: 'Sign in') }
    it { should have_selector('div.alert.alert-error', text: 'Invalid') }

    describe "after visiting another page" do
      before { click_link "Home" }
      it { should_not have_selector('div.alert.alert-error') }
    end
  end
  .
  .
  .
  end
end
```

The new test fails, as required:

```
$ bundle exec rspec spec/requests/authentication_pages_spec.rb \
> -e "signin with invalid information"
```

To get the failing test to pass, instead of **flash** we use **flash.now**, which is specifically designed for displaying flash messages on rendered pages; unlike the contents of **flash**, its contents disappear as soon as there is an additional request. The corrected application code appears in Listing 8.12.

Listing 8.12 Correct code for failed signin.
app/controllers/sessions_controller.rb

```
class SessionsController < ApplicationController

  def new
  end

  def create
    user = User.find_by_email(params[:session][:email])
    if user && user.authenticate(params[:session][:password])
      # Sign the user in and redirect to the user's show page.
    else
      flash.now[:error] = 'Invalid email/password combination'
      render 'new'
    end
  end

  def destroy
  end
end
```

Now the test suite for users with invalid information should be green:

```
$ bundle exec rspec spec/requests/authentication_pages_spec.rb \
> -e "with invalid information"
```

8.2 Signin Success

Having handled a failed signin, we now need to actually sign a user in. Getting there will require some of the most challenging Ruby programming so far in this tutorial, so hang in there through the end and be prepared for a little heavy lifting. Happily, the first step is easy—completing the Sessions controller **create** action is a snap. Unfortunately, it's also a cheat.

Filling in the area now occupied by the signin comment (Listing 8.12) is simple: Upon successful signin, we sign the user in using the **sign_in** function, and then redirect to the profile page (Listing 8.13). We see now why this is a cheat: Alas, **sign_in** doesn't currently exist. Writing it will occupy the rest of this section.

Listing 8.13 The completed Sessions controller **create** action (not yet working).
app/controllers/sessions_controller.rb

```ruby
class SessionsController < ApplicationController
  .
  .
  .
  def create
    user = User.find_by_email(params[:session][:email])
    if user && user.authenticate(params[:session][:password])
      sign_in user
      redirect_to user
    else
      flash.now[:error] = 'Invalid email/password combination'
      render 'new'
    end
  end
  .
  .
  .
end
```

8.2.1 Remember Me

We're now in a position to start implementing our signin model, namely, remembering user signin status "forever" and clearing the session only when the user explicitly signs out. The signin functions themselves will end up crossing the traditional Model-View-Controller lines; in particular, several signin functions will need to be available in both controllers and views. You may recall from Section 4.2.5 that Ruby provides a *module* facility for packaging functions together and including them in multiple places, and that's the plan for the authentication functions. We could make an entirely new module for authentication, but the Sessions controller already comes equipped with a module, namely, **SessionsHelper**. Moreover, such helpers are automatically included in Rails views, so all we need to do to use the Sessions helper functions in controllers is to include the module into the Application controller (Listing 8.14).

Listing 8.14 Including the Sessions helper module into the Application controller.
`app/controllers/application_controller.rb`

```
class ApplicationController < ActionController::Base
  protect_from_forgery
  include SessionsHelper
end
```

By default, all the helpers are available in the views but not in the controllers. We need the methods from the Sessions helper in both places, so we have to include it explicitly.

Because HTTP is a *stateless protocol*, web applications requiring user signin must implement a way to track each user's progress from page to page. One technique for maintaining the user signin status is to use a traditional Rails session (via the special **session** function) to store a *remember token* equal to the user's id:

```
session[:remember_token] = user.id
```

This **session** object makes the user id available from page to page by storing it in a cookie that expires upon browser close. On each page, the application could simply call

```
User.find(session[:remember_token])
```

to retrieve the user. Because of the way Rails handles sessions, this process is secure; if a malicious user tries to spoof the user id, Rails will detect a mismatch based on a special *session id* generated for each session.

For our application's design choice, which involves *persistent* sessions—that is, signin status that lasts even after browser close—we need to use a *permanent* identifier for the signed-in user. To accomplish this, we'll generate a unique, secure remember token for each user and store it as a *permanent* cookie rather than one that expires on browser close.

The remember token needs to be associated with a user and stored for future use, so we'll add it as an attribute to the User model as shown in Figure 8.8. We start with a small addition to the User model specs (Listing 8.15).

Listing 8.15 A first test for the remember token.
spec/models/user_spec.rb

```
require 'spec_helper'

describe User do
  .
  .
  .
  it { should respond_to(:password_confirmation) }
  it { should respond_to(:remember_token) }
  it { should respond_to(:authenticate) }
  .
  .
  .
end
```

We can get this test to pass by generating a remember token at the command line:

```
$ rails generate migration add_remember_token_to_users
```

Next we fill in the resulting migration with the code from Listing 8.16. Note that, because we expect to retrieve users by remember token, we've added an index (Box 6.2) to the **remember_token** column.

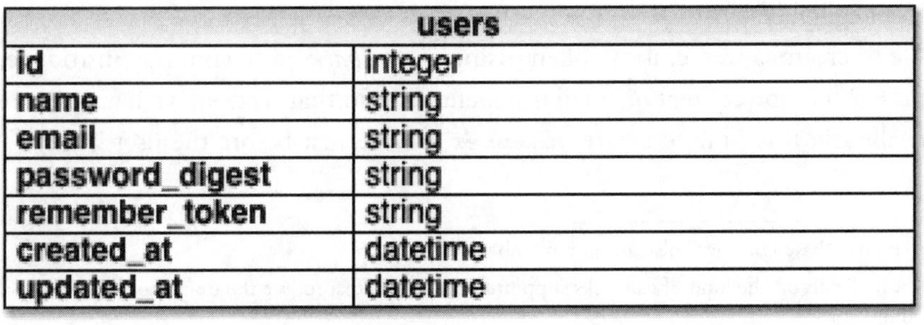

users	
id	integer
name	string
email	string
password_digest	string
remember_token	string
created_at	datetime
updated_at	datetime

Figure 8.8   The User model with an added **remember_token** attribute.

Listing 8.16 A migration to add a **remember_token** to the **users** table. **db/migrate/[timestamp]_add_remember_token_to_users.rb**

```
class AddRememberTokenToUsers < ActiveRecord::Migration
  def change
    add_column :users, :remember_token, :string
    add_index  :users, :remember_token
  end
end
```

Next we update the development and test databases as usual:

```
$ bundle exec rake db:migrate
$ bundle exec rake db:test:prepare
```

At this point the User model specs should be passing:

```
$ bundle exec rspec spec/models/user_spec.rb
```

Now we have to decide what to use as a remember token. There are many mostly equivalent possibilities—essentially, any large random string will do just fine. In principle, since the user passwords are securely encrypted, we could use each user's **password_hash** attribute, but it seems like a terrible idea to unnecessarily expose our users' passwords to potential attackers. We'll err on the side of caution and make a custom remember token using the **urlsafe_base64** method from the **SecureRandom** module in the Ruby standard library, which creates a Base64 string safe for use in URIs (and hence safe for use in cookies as well).[3] As of this writing, **SecureRandom.urlsafe_base64** returns a random string of length 16 composed of the characters A–Z, a–z, 0–9, "-", and "_" (for a total of 64 possibilities). This means that the probability of two remember tokens being the same is $1/64^{16} = 2^{-96} \approx 10^{-29}$, which is negligible.

We'll create a remember token using a *callback*, a technique introduced in Section 6.2.5 in the context of email uniqueness. As in that section, we'll use a **before_save** callback, this time to create **remember_token** just before the user is saved.[4] To

---

3. This choice is based on the RailsCast on remember me.

4. For more details on the kind of callbacks supported by Active Record, see the discussion of callbacks at the Rails Guides.

test for this, we first save the test user and then check that the user's **remember_token** attribute isn't blank. This gives us sufficient flexibility to change the random string if we ever need to. The result appears in Listing 8.17.

Listing 8.17 A test for a valid (nonblank) remember token.
spec/models/user_spec.rb

```
require 'spec_helper'

describe User do

  before do
    @user = User.new(name: "Example User", email: "user@example.com",
                     password: "foobar", password_confirmation: "foobar")
  end

  subject { @user }
  .
  .
  .
  describe "remember token" do
    before { @user.save }
    its(:remember_token) { should_not be_blank }
  end
end
```

Listing 8.17 introduces the **its** method, which is like **it** but applies the subsequent test to the given attribute rather than the subject of the test. In other words,

```
its(:remember_token) { should_not be_blank }
```

is equivalent to

```
it { @user.remember_token.should_not be_blank }
```

The application code introduces several new elements. First, we add a callback method to create the remember token:

```
before_save :create_remember_token
```

This arranges for Rails to look for a method called **create_remember_token** and run it before saving the user. Second, the method itself is only used internally by the User model, so there's no need to expose it to outside users. The Ruby way to accomplish this is to use the **private** keyword:

```
private

  def create_remember_token
    # Create the token.
  end
```

All methods defined in a class after **private** are automatically hidden, so that

```
$ rails console
>> User.first.create_remember_token
```

will raise a **NoMethodError** exception.

Finally, the **create_remember_token** method needs to *assign* to one of the user attributes, and in this context it is necessary to use the **self** keyword in front of **remember_token**:

```
def create_remember_token
  self.remember_token = SecureRandom.urlsafe_base64
end
```

(*Note:* If you are using Ruby 1.8.7, you should use **SecureRandom.hex** here instead.) Because of the way Active Record synthesizes attributes based on database columns, without **self** the assignment would create a *local* variable called **remember_token**, which isn't what we want at all. Using **self** ensures that assignment sets the user's **remember_token** so that it will be written to the database along with the other attributes when the user is saved.

Putting this all together yields the User model shown in Listing 8.18.

Listing 8.18 A **before_save** callback to create **remember_token**.
app/models/user.rb

```
class User < ActiveRecord::Base
  attr_accessible :name, :email, :password, :password_confirmation
  has_secure_password

  before_save { |user| user.email = email.downcase }
  before_save :create_remember_token
  .
  .
  .
  private
```

```
    def create_remember_token
      self.remember_token = SecureRandom.urlsafe_base64
    end
end
```

By the way, the extra level of indentation on **create_remember_token** is there to make it visually apparent which methods are defined after **private**.

Since the **SecureRandom.urlsafe_base64** string is definitely *not* blank, the tests for the User model should now be passing:

```
$ bundle exec rspec spec/models/user_spec.rb
```

8.2.2 A Working **sign_in** Method

Now we're ready to write the first signin element, the **sign_in** function itself. As noted above, our desired authentication method is to place a remember token as a cookie on the user's browser, and then use the token to find the user record in the database as the user moves from page to page (implemented in Section 8.2.3). The result, Listing 8.19, introduces two new ideas: the **cookies** hash and **current_user**.

Listing 8.19 The complete (but not-yet-working) **sign_in** function. **app/helpers/sessions_helper.rb**

```
module SessionsHelper

  def sign_in(user)
    cookies.permanent[:remember_token] = user.remember_token
    self.current_user = user
  end
end
```

Listing 8.19 introduces the **cookies** utility supplied by Rails. We can use **cookies** as if it were a hash; each element in the cookie is itself a hash of two elements, a **value** and an optional **expires** date. For example, we could implement user signin by placing a cookie with value equal to the user's remember token that expires 20 years from now:

```
cookies[:remember_token] = { value:   user.remember_token,
                             expires: 20.years.from_now.utc }
```

(This uses one of the convenient Rails time helpers, as discussed in Box 8.1.)

Box 8.1 Cookies Expire `20.years.from_now`

You may recall from Section 4.4.2 that Ruby lets you add methods to *any* class, even built-in ones. In that section, we added a `palindrome?` method to the `String` class (and discovered as a result that `"deified"` is a palindrome), and we also saw how Rails adds a `blank?` method to class `Object` (so that `"".blank?`, `" ".blank?`, and `nil.blank?` are all `true`). The cookie code in Listing 8.19 (which internally sets a cookie that expires `20.years.from_now`) gives yet another example of this practice through one of Rails' *time helpers*, which are methods added to `Fixnum` (the base class for numbers):

```
$ rails console
>> 1.year.from_now
=> Sun, 13 Mar 2011 03:38:55 UTC +00:00
>> 10.weeks.ago
=> Sat, 02 Jan 2010 03:39:14 UTC +00:00
```

Rails adds other helpers, too:

```
>> 1.kilobyte
=> 1024
>> 5.megabytes
=> 5242880
```

These are useful for upload validations, making it easy to restrict, say, image uploads to `5.megabytes`.

Although it must be used with caution, the flexibility to add methods to built-in classes allows for extraordinarily natural additions to plain Ruby. Indeed, much of the elegance of Rails ultimately derives from the malleability of the underlying Ruby language.

This pattern of setting a cookie that expires 20 years in the future became so common that Rails added a special **permanent** method to implement it, so that we can simply write

```
cookies.permanent[:remember_token] = user.remember_token
```

Under the hood, using **permanent** causes Rails to set the expiration to **20.years. from_now** automatically.

After the cookie is set, on subsequent page views we can retrieve the user with code like

```
User.find_by_remember_token(cookies[:remember_token])
```

Of course, **cookies** isn't *really* a hash, since assigning to **cookies** actually *saves* a piece of text on the browser, but part of the beauty of Rails is that it lets you forget about that detail and concentrate on writing the application.

You may be aware that storing authentication cookies on a user's browser and transmitting them over the network exposes an application to a *session hijacking* attack, which involves copying the remember token and using it to sign in as the corresponding user. This attack was publicized by the Firesheep application, which showed that many high-profile sites (including Facebook and Twitter) were vulnerable. The solution is to use site-wide SSL as described in Section 7.4.4.

8.2.3 Current User

Having discussed how to store the user's remember token in a cookie for later use, we now need to learn how to retrieve the user on subsequent page views. Let's look again at the **sign_in** function to see where we are:

```
module SessionsHelper

  def sign_in(user)
    cookies.permanent[:remember_token] = user.remember_token
    self.current_user = user
  end
end
```

Our focus now is the second line:

```
self.current_user = user
```

The purpose of this line is to create **current_user**, accessible in both controllers and views, which will allow constructions such as

```
<%= current_user.name %>
```

and

```
redirect_to current_user
```

The use of **self** is necessary in this context for the same essential reason noted in the discussion leading up to Listing 8.18: without **self**, Ruby would simply create a local variable called **current_user**.

To start writing the code for **current_user**, note that the line

```
self.current_user = user
```

is an *assignment*, which we must define. Ruby has a special syntax for defining such an assignment function, shown in Listing 8.20.

Listing 8.20 Defining assignment to **current_user**.
app/helpers/sessions_helper.rb

```
module SessionsHelper

  def sign_in(user)
    .
    .
    .
  end

  def current_user=(user)
    @current_user = user
  end
end
```

This might look confusing—most languages don't let you use the equals sign in a method definition—but it simply defines a method **current_user=** expressly designed to handle assignment to **current_user**. In other words, the code

```
self.current_user = ...
```

is automatically converted to

```
current_user=(...)
```

thereby invoking the **current_user=** method. Its one argument is the right-hand side of the assignment, in this case the user to be signed in. The one-line method body just sets an instance variable **@current_user**, effectively storing the user for later use.

In ordinary Ruby, we could define a second method, **current_user**, designed to return the value of **@current_user**, as shown in Listing 8.21.

Listing 8.21   A tempting but useless definition for **current_user**.

```ruby
module SessionsHelper

  def sign_in(user)
    .
    .
    .
  end

  def current_user=(user)
    @current_user = user
  end

  def current_user
    @current_user      # Useless! Don't use this line.
  end
end
```

If we did this, we would effectively replicate the functionality of **attr_accessor**, which we saw in Section 4.4.5.[5] The problem is that it utterly fails to solve our problem: With the code in Listing 8.21, the user's signin status would be forgotten. As soon as the user went to another page—*poof!*—the session would end and the user would be automatically signed out. To avoid this problem, we can find the user corresponding to the remember token created by the code in Listing 8.19, as shown in Listing 8.22.

Listing 8.22   Finding the current user using the **remember_token**.
app/helpers/sessions_helper.rb

```ruby
module SessionsHelper
  .
  .
  .
  def current_user=(user)
    @current_user = user
  end

  def current_user
    @current_user ||= User.find_by_remember_token(cookies[:remember_token])
  end
end
```

---

5. In fact, the two are exactly equivalent; **attr_accessor** is merely a convenient way to create just such getter/setter methods automatically.

Listing 8.22 uses the common but initially obscure ||= ("or equals") assignment operator (Box 8.2). Its effect is to set the **@current_user** instance variable to the user corresponding to the remember token, but only if **@current_user** is undefined.[6] In other words, the construction

```
@current_user ||= User.find_by_remember_token(cookies[:remember_token])
```

calls the **user_from_remember_token** method the first time **current_user** is called, but on subsequent invocations returns **@current_user** without hitting the database.[7] This is only useful if **current_user** is used more than once for a single user request; in any case, **find_by_remember_token** will be called at least once every time a user visits a page on the site.

Box 8.2 What the *$@! Is ||= ?

The ||= construction is very Rubyish—that is, it is highly characteristic of the Ruby language—and hence important to learn if you plan on doing much Ruby programming. Although at first it may seem mysterious, *or equals* is easy to understand by analogy.

We start by noting a common idiom for changing a currently defined variable. Many computer programs involve incrementing a variable, as in

```
x = x + 1
```

Most languages provide a syntactic shortcut for this operation; in Ruby (and in C, C++, Perl, Python, Java, etc.), it appears as follows:

```
x += 1
```

Analogous constructs exist for other operators as well:

```
$ rails console
>> x = 1
=> 1
>> x += 1
=> 2
```

---

6. Typically, this means assigning to variables that are initially **nil**, but note that **false** values will also be overwritten by the ||= operator.

7. This is an example of *memoization*, which we discussed before in Box 6.3.

```
>> x *= 3
=> 6
>> x -= 7
=> -1
```

In each case, the pattern is that x = x O y and x O= y are equivalent for any operator O.

Another common Ruby pattern is assigning to a variable if it's `nil` but otherwise leaving it alone. Recalling the *or* operator || seen in Section 4.2.3, we can write this as follows:

```
>> @user
=> nil
>> @user = @user || "the user"
=> "the user"
>> @user = @user || "another user"
=> "the user"
```

Since `nil` is false in a boolean context, the first assignment is `nil || "the user"`, which evaluates to `"the user"`; similarly, the second assignment is `"the user" || "another user"`, which also evaluates to `"the user"`—since strings are `true` in a boolean context, the series of || expressions terminates after the first expression is evaluated. (This practice of evaluating || expressions from left to right and stopping on the first true value is known as *short-circuit evaluation*.)

Comparing the console sessions for the various operators, we see that `@user = @user || value` follows the x = x O y pattern with || in the place of O, which suggests the following equivalent construction:

```
>> @user ||= "the user"
=> "the user"
```

Voilà !

8.2.4 Changing the Layout Links

We come finally to a practical application of all our signin/out work: We'll change the layout links based on signin status. In particular, as seen in the Figure 8.3 mockup, we'll arrange for the links to change when users sign in or sign out, and we'll also add links for listing all users and user settings (to be completed in Chapter 9) and one for the current user's profile page. In doing so, we'll get the tests in Listing 8.6 to pass, which means our test suite will be green for the first time since the beginning of the chapter.

The way to change the links in the site layout involves using an if-else branching structure inside of Embedded Ruby:

```
<% if signed_in? %>
  # Links for signed-in users
<% else %>
  # Links for non-signed-in-users
<% end %>
```

This kind of code requires the existence of a **signed_in?** boolean, which we'll now define.

A user is signed in if there is a current user in the session, i.e., if **current_user** is non-**nil**. This requires the use of the "not" operator, written using an exclamation point **!** and usually read as "bang." In the present context, a user is signed in if **current_user** is *not* **nil**, as shown in Listing 8.23.

Listing 8.23 The **signed_in?** helper method.
app/helpers/sessions_helper.rb

```
module SessionsHelper

  def sign_in(user)
    cookies.permanent[:remember_token] = user.remember_token
    self.current_user = user
  end

  def signed_in?
    !current_user.nil?
  end
  .
  .
  .
end
```

With the **signed_in?** method in hand, we're ready to finish the layout links. There are four new links, two of which are stubbed out (to be completed in Chapter 9):

```
<%= link_to "Users", '#' %>
<%= link_to "Settings", '#' %>
```

The signout link, meanwhile, uses the signout path defined in Listing 8.2:

```
<%= link_to "Sign out", signout_path, method: "delete" %>
```

(Notice that the signout link passes a hash argument indicating that it should submit with an HTTP DELETE request.[8]) Finally, we'll add a profile link as follows:

```
<%= link_to "Profile", current_user %>
```

Here we could write

```
<%= link_to "Profile", user_path(current_user) %>
```

but Rails allows us to link directly to the user, in this context automatically converting **current_user** into **user_path(current_user)**.

In the process of putting the new links into the layout, we'll take advantage of Bootstrap's ability to make dropdown menus, which you can read more about on the Bootstrap components page. The full result appears in Listing 8.24. Note in particular the CSS ids and classes related to the Bootstrap dropdown menu.

Listing 8.24 Changing the layout links for signed-in users.
app/views/layouts/_header.html.erb

```erb
<header class="navbar navbar-fixed-top">
  <div class="navbar-inner">
    <div class="container">
      <%= link_to "sample app", root_path, id: "logo" %>
      <nav>
        <ul class="nav pull-right">
          <li><%= link_to "Home", root_path %></li>
          <li><%= link_to "Help", help_path %></li>
          <% if signed_in? %>
            <li><%= link_to "Users", '#' %></li>
            <li id="fat-menu" class="dropdown">
              <a href="#" class="dropdown-toggle" data-toggle="dropdown">
              Account <b class="caret"></b>
              </a>
              <ul class="dropdown-menu">
                <li><%= link_to "Profile", current_user %></li>
                <li><%= link_to "Settings", '#' %></li>
                <li class="divider"></li>
                <li>
                  <%= link_to "Sign out", signout_path, method: "delete" %>
                </li>
              </ul>
            </li>
```

---

8. Web browsers can't actually issue DELETE requests; Rails fakes it with JavaScript.

```
      <% else %>
        <li><%= link_to "Sign in", signin_path %></li>
      <% end %>
    </ul>
  </nav>
 </div>
 </div>
</header>
```

The dropdown menu requires the use of Bootstrap's JavaScript library, which we can include using the Rails asset pipeline by editing the application JavaScript file, as shown in Listing 8.25.

Listing 8.25 Adding the Bootstrap JavaScript library to **`application.js`**. **`app/assets/javascripts/application.js`**

```
//= require jquery
//= require jquery_ujs
//= require bootstrap
//= require_tree .
```

This uses the Sprockets library to include the Bootstrap JavaScript, which in turn is available thanks to the `bootstrap-sass` gem from Section 5.1.2.

With the code in Listing 8.24, all the tests should be passing:

```
$ bundle exec rspec spec/
```

Unfortunately, if you actually examine the application in the browser, you'll see that it doesn't yet work. This is because the "remember me" functionality requires the user to have a remember token, but the current user doesn't have one: We created the first user back in Section 7.4.3, long before implementing the callback that sets the remember token. To fix this, we need to save each user to invoke the **`before_save`** callback defined in Listing 8.18, which creates a remember token as a side effect:

```
$ rails console
>> User.first.remember_token
=> nil
>> User.all.each { |user| user.save(validate: false) }
>> User.first.remember_token
=> "Im9POkWtZvD0RdyiK9UHtg"
```

Here we've iterated over all the users in case you added more than one while playing with the signup form. Note that we've passed an option to the **save** method; as currently written, **save** by itself wouldn't work because we haven't included the password or its confirmation. Indeed, for a real site we wouldn't even know any of the passwords, but we would still want to be able to save the users. The solution is to pass **validate: false** to tell Active Record skip the validations (Rails API `save`).

With that change, a signed-in user now sees the new links and dropdown menu defined by Listing 8.24, as shown in Figure 8.9.

At this point, you should verify that you can sign in, close the browser, and then still be signed in when you visit the sample application. If you want, you can even inspect the browser cookies to see the result directly (Figure 8.10).

8.2.5   Signin upon Signup

In principle, although we are now done with authentication, newly registered users might be confused, as they are not signed in by default. Implementing this is the last bit

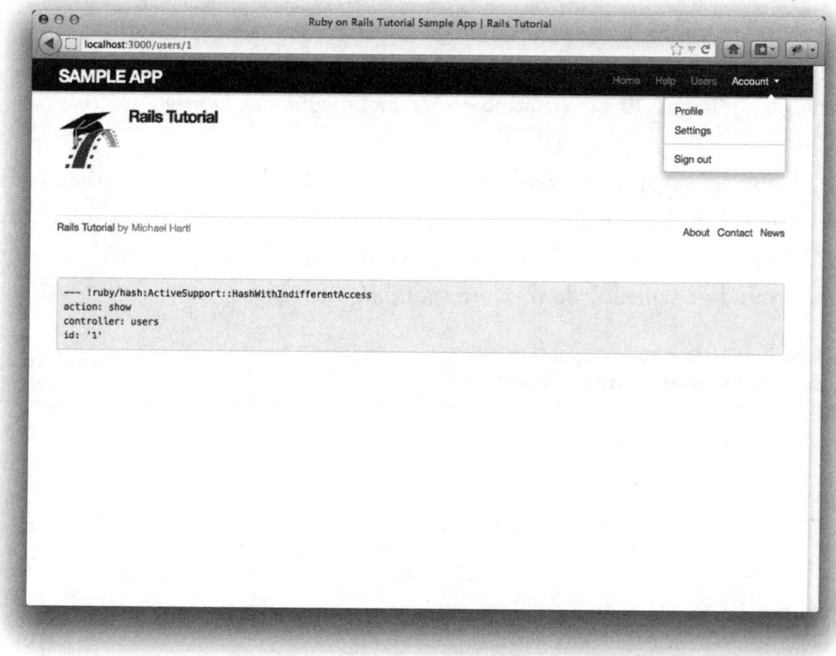

Figure 8.9   A signed-in user with new links and a dropdown menu.

Figure 8.10 The remember token cookie in the local browser.

of polish before letting users sign out. We'll start by adding a line to the authentication tests (Listing 8.26). This includes the "after saving the user" **describe** block from Listing 7.32 from the Chapter 7 exercises (Section 7.6), which you should add to the test now if you didn't already do the corresponding exercise.

Listing 8.26 Testing that newly signed-up users are also signed in.
spec/requests/user_pages_spec.rb

```
require 'spec_helper'

describe "User pages" do
  .
  .

  describe "with valid information" do
    .
    .
```

```
        describe "after saving the user" do
          .
          .
          .
          it { should have_link('Sign out') }
        end
      end
    end
  end
end
```

Here we've tested the appearance of the signout link to verify that the user was successfully signed in after signing up.

With the **sign_in** method from Section 8.2, getting this test to pass by actually signing in the user is easy: Just add **sign_in @user** right after saving the user to the database (Listing 8.27).

Listing 8.27 Signing in the user upon signup.
app/controllers/users_controller.rb

```
class UsersController < ApplicationController
  .
  .
  .
  def create
    @user = User.new(params[:user])
    if @user.save
      sign_in @user
      flash[:success] = "Welcome to the Sample App!"
      redirect_to @user
    else
      render 'new'
    end
  end
end
```

8.2.6   Signing Out

As discussed in Section 8.1, our authentication model is to keep users signed in until they sign out explicitly. In this section, we'll add this necessary signout capability.

So far, the Sessions controller actions have followed the RESTful convention of using **new** for a signin page and **create** to complete the signin. We'll continue this theme by using a **destroy** action to delete sessions, i.e., to sign out. To test this, we'll click on the "Sign out" link and then look for the reappearance of the signin link (Listing 8.28).

Listing 8.28 A test for signing out a user.
spec/requests/authentication_pages_spec.rb

```
require 'spec_helper'

describe "Authentication" do
  .
  .
  .
  describe "signin" do
    .
    .
    .
    describe "with valid information" do
      .
      .
      .
      describe "followed by signout" do
        before { click_link "Sign out" }
        it { should have_link('Sign in') }
      end
    end
  end
end
```

As with user signin, which relied on the **sign_in** function, user signout just defers to a **sign_out** function (Listing 8.29).

Listing 8.29 Destroying a session (user signout).
app/controllers/sessions_controller.rb

```
class SessionsController < ApplicationController
  .
  .
  .
  def destroy
    sign_out
    redirect_to root_path
  end
end
```

As with the other authentication elements, we'll put **sign_out** in the Sessions helper module. The implementation is simple: We set the current user to **nil** and use the **delete** method on cookies to remove the remember token from the session (Listing 8.30). (Setting the current user to **nil** isn't currently necessary because of the immediate redirect in the **destroy** action, but it's a good idea in case we ever want to use **sign_out** without a redirect.)

Listing 8.30 The **sign_out** method in the Sessions helper module.
`app/helpers/sessions_helper.rb`

```ruby
module SessionsHelper

  def sign_in(user)
    cookies.permanent[:remember_token] = user.remember_token
    self.current_user = user
  end
  .
  .
  .
  def sign_out
    self.current_user = nil
    cookies.delete(:remember_token)
  end
end
```

This completes the signup/signin/signout triumvirate, and the test suite should pass:

```
$ bundle exec rspec spec/
```

It's worth noting that our test suite covers most of the authentication machinery, but not all of it. For instance, we don't test how long the "remember me" cookie lasts or whether it gets set at all. It is possible to do so, but experience shows that direct tests of cookie values are brittle and have a tendency to rely on implementation details that sometimes change from one Rails release to the next. The result is breaking tests for application code that still works fine. By focusing on high-level functionality—verifying that users can sign in, stay signed in from page to page, and can sign out—we test the core application code without focusing on less important details.

8.3 Introduction to Cucumber (Optional)

Having finished the foundation of the sample application's authentication system, we're going to take this opportunity to show how to write signin tests using Cucumber, a popular tool for behavior-driven development that enjoys significant popularity in the Ruby community. This section is optional and can be skipped without loss of continuity.

Cucumber allows the definition of plain-text *stories* describing application behavior. Many Rails programmers find Cucumber especially convenient when doing client work; since they can be read even by non-technical users, Cucumber tests can be shared with (and can sometimes even be written by) the client. Of course, using a testing framework that isn't pure Ruby has a downside, and I find that the plain-text stories can be a bit verbose. Nevertheless, Cucumber does have a place in the Ruby testing toolkit, and I especially like its emphasis on high-level behavior over low-level implementation.

Since the emphasis in this book is on RSpec and Capybara, the presentation that follows is necessarily superficial and incomplete and will be a bit light on explanation. Its purpose is just to give you a taste of Cucumber (crisp and juicy, no doubt)—if it strikes your fancy, there are entire books on the subject waiting to satisfy your appetite. (I particularly recommend *The RSpec Book* by David Chelimsky and *Rails 3 in Action* by Ryan Bigg and Yehuda Katz, and *The Cucumber Book* by Matt Wynne and Aslak Hellesøy.)

8.3.1 Installation and Setup

To install Cucumber, first add the `cucumber-rails` gem and a utility gem called `database_cleaner` to the `:test` group in the **Gemfile** (Listing 8.31).

Listing 8.31 Adding the `cucumber-rails` gem to the **Gemfile**.

```
    .
    .
    .
group :test do
    .
    .
    .
  gem 'cucumber-rails', '1.2.1', require: false
  gem 'database_cleaner', '0.7.0'
end
    .
    .
    .
```

Then install as usual:

```
$ bundle install
```

To set up the application to use Cucumber, we next generate some necessary support files and directories:

```
$ rails generate cucumber:install
```

This creates a **features/** directory where the files associated with Cucumber will live.

8.3.2 Features and Steps

Cucumber features are descriptions of expected behavior using a plain-text language called Gherkin. Gherkin tests read much like well-written RSpec examples, but because they are plain-text they are more accessible to those more comfortable reading English than Ruby code.

Our Cucumber features will implement a subset of the signin examples in Listing 8.5 and Listing 8.6. To get started, we'll create a file in the **features/** directory called **signing_in.feature**.

Cucumber features start with a short description of the feature, as follows:

```
Feature: Signing in
```

Then they add individual *scenarios*. For example, to test unsuccessful signin, we could write the following scenario:

```
Scenario: Unsuccessful signin
  Given a user visits the signin page
  When he submits invalid signin information
  Then he should see an error message
```

Similarly, to test successful signin, we could add this:

```
Scenario: Successful signin
  Given a user visits the signin page
    And the user has an account
    And the user submits valid signin information
  Then he should see his profile page
    And he should see a signout link
```

Collecting these together yields the Cucumber feature file shown in Listing 8.32.

Listing 8.32 Cucumber features to test user signin.
`features/signing_in.feature`

```
Feature: Signing in

  Scenario: Unsuccessful signin
    Given a user visits the signin page
    When he submits invalid signin information
    Then he should see an error message

  Scenario: Successful signin
    Given a user visits the signin page
      And the user has an account
      And the user submits valid signin information
    Then he should see his profile page
      And he should see a signout link
```

To run the features, we use the **cucumber** executable:

```
$ bundle exec cucumber features/
```

Compare this to

```
$ bundle exec rspec spec/
```

In this context, it's worth noting that, like RSpec, Cucumber can be invoked using a Rake task:

```
$ bundle exec rake cucumber
```

(For reasons that escape me, this is sometimes written as **rake cucumber:ok**.)

All we've done so far is write some plain text, so it shouldn't be surprising that the Cucumber scenarios aren't yet passing. To get the test suite to green, we need to add a *step* file that maps the plain-text lines to Ruby code. The step file goes in the **features/step_definitions** directory; we'll call it **authentication_steps.rb**.

The **Feature** and **Scenario** lines are mainly for documentation, but each of the other lines needs some corresponding Ruby. For example, the line

```
Given a user visits the signin page
```

in the feature file gets handled by the step definition

```
Given /^a user visits the signin page$/ do
  visit signin_path
end
```

In the feature, **Given** is just a string, but in the step file **Given** is a *method* that takes a regular expression and a block. The regex matches the text of the line in the scenario, and the contents of the block are the Ruby code needed to implement the step. In this case, "a user visits the signin page" is implemented by

```
visit signin_path
```

If this looks familiar, it should: It's just Capybara, which is included by default in Cucumber step files. The next two lines should also look familiar; the scenario steps

```
When he submits invalid signin information
Then he should see an error message
```

in the feature file are handled by these steps:

```
When /^he submits invalid signin information$/ do
  click_button "Sign in"
end

Then /^he should see an error message$/ do
  page.should have_selector('div.alert.alert-error')
end
```

The first step also uses Capybara, while the second uses Capybara's **page** object with RSpec. Evidently, all the testing work we've done so far with RSpec and Capybara is also useful with Cucumber.

The rest of the steps proceed similarly. The final step definition file appears in Listing 8.33. Try adding one step at a time, running

```
$ bundle exec cucumber features/
```

each time until the tests pass.

Listing 8.33 The complete steps needed to get the signin features to pass.
`features/step_definitions/authentication_steps.rb`

```
Given /^a user visits the signin page$/ do
  visit signin_path
end

When /^he submits invalid signin information$/ do
  click_button "Sign in"
end

Then /^he should see an error message$/ do
  page.should have_selector('div.alert.alert-error')
end

Given /^the user has an account$/ do
  @user = User.create(name: "Example User", email: "user@example.com",
                      password: "foobar", password_confirmation: "foobar")
end

When /^the user submits valid signin information$/ do
  fill_in "Email",    with: @user.email
  fill_in "Password", with: @user.password
  click_button "Sign in"
end

Then /^he should see his profile page$/ do
  page.should have_selector('title', text: @user.name)
end

Then /^he should see a signout link$/ do
  page.should have_link('Sign out', href: signout_path)
end
```

With the code in Listing 8.33, the Cucumber tests should pass:

```
$ bundle exec cucumber features/
```

8.3.3   Counterpoint: RSpec Custom Matchers

Having written some simple Cucumber scenarios, it's worth comparing the result to the equivalent RSpec examples. First, take a look at the Cucumber feature in Listing 8.32 and the corresponding step definitions in Listing 8.33. Then take a look at the RSpec request specs (integration tests):

```ruby
describe "Authentication" do

  subject { page }

  describe "signin" do
    before { visit signin_path }

    describe "with invalid information" do
      before { click_button "Sign in" }

      it { should have_selector('title', text: 'Sign in') }
      it { should have_selector('div.alert.alert-error', text: 'Invalid') }
    end

    describe "with valid information" do
      let(:user) { FactoryGirl.create(:user) }
      before do
        fill_in "Email",    with: user.email
        fill_in "Password", with: user.password
        click_button "Sign in"
      end

      it { should have_selector('title', text: user.name) }
      it { should have_selector('a', 'Sign out', href: signout_path) }
    end
  end
end
```

You can see how a case could be made for either Cucumber or integration tests. Cucumber features are easily readable, but they are entirely separate from the code that implements them—a property that cuts both ways. I find that Cucumber is easy to read and awkward to write, while integration tests are (for a programmer) a little harder to read and *much* easier to write.

One nice effect of Cucumber's separation of concerns is that it operates at a higher level of abstraction. For example, we write

```
Then he should see an error message
```

to express the expectation of seeing an error message, and

```ruby
Then /^he should see an error message$/ do
  page.should have_selector('div.alert.alert-error', text: 'Invalid')
end
```

to implement the test. What's especially convenient about this is that only the second element (the step) is dependent on the implementation, so that if we change, for example, the CSS class used for error messages, the feature file would stay the same.

In this vein, it might make you unhappy to write

```
should have_selector('div.alert.alert-error', text: 'Invalid')
```

in a bunch of places, when what you really want is to indicate that the page should have an error message. This practice couples the test tightly to the implementation, and we would have to change it everywhere if the implementation changed. In the context of pure RSpec, there is a solution, which is to use a *custom matcher*, allowing us to write the following instead:

```
should have_error_message('Invalid')
```

We can define such a matcher in the same utilities file where we put the `full_title` test helper in Section 5.3.4. The code itself looks like this:

```
RSpec::Matchers.define :have_error_message do |message|
  match do |page|
    page.should have_selector('div.alert.alert-error', text: message)
  end
end
```

We can also define helper functions for common operations:

```
def valid_signin(user)
  fill_in "Email",    with: user.email
  fill_in "Password", with: user.password
  click_button "Sign in"
end
```

The resulting support code is shown in Listing 8.34 (which incorporates the results of Listing 5.37 and Listing 5.38 from Section 5.6). I find this approach to be more flexible than Cucumber step definitions, particularly when the matchers or should helpers naturally take an argument, such as `valid_signin(user)`. Step definitions can replicate this functionality with regex matchers, but I generally find this approach to be more (cu)cumbersome.

Listing 8.34 Adding a helper method and a custom RSpec matcher.
spec/support/utilities.rb

```
include ApplicationHelper

def valid_signin(user)
  fill_in "Email",    with: user.email
  fill_in "Password", with: user.password
  click_button "Sign in"
end

RSpec::Matchers.define :have_error_message do |message|
  match do |page|
    page.should have_selector('div.alert.alert-error', text: message)
  end
end
```

With the code in Listing 8.34, we can write

```
it { should have_error_message('Invalid') }
```

and

```
describe "with valid information" do
  let(:user) { FactoryGirl.create(:user) }
  before { valid_signin(user) }
  .
  .
  .
```

There are many other examples of coupling between our tests and the site's implementation. Sweeping through the current test suite and decoupling the tests from the implementation details by making custom matchers and methods is left as an exercise (Section 8.5).

8.4 Conclusion

We've covered a lot of ground in this chapter, transforming our promising but unformed application into a site capable of the full suite of registration and login behaviors. All that is needed to complete the authentication functionality is to restrict access to pages based on signin status and user identity. We'll accomplish this task en route to giving users the ability to edit their information and giving administrators the ability to remove users from the system, which are the main goals of Chapter 9.

Before moving on, merge your changes back into the master branch:

```
$ git add .
$ git commit -m "Finish sign in"
$ git checkout master
$ git merge sign-in-out
```

Then push up the remote GitHub repository and the Heroku production server:

```
$ git push
$ git push heroku
$ heroku run rake db:migrate
```

If you've created any users on the production server, I recommend following the steps in Section 8.2.4 to give each user a valid remember token. The only difference is using the Heroku console instead of the local one:

```
$ heroku run console
>> User.all.each { |user| user.save(validate: false) }
```

8.5 Exercises

1. Refactor the signin form to use **form_tag** in place of **form_for**. Make sure the test suite still passes. *Hint*: See the RailsCast on authentication in Rails 3.1, and note in particular the change in the structure of the **params** hash.

2. Following the example in Section 8.3.3, go through the user and authentication request specs (i.e., the files currently in the **spec/requests** directory) and define utility functions in **spec/support/utilities.rb** to decouple the test from the implementation. *Extra credit*: Organize the support code into separate files and modules, and get everything to work by including the modules properly in the spec helper file

CHAPTER 9
Updating, Showing, and Deleting Users

In this chapter, we will complete the REST actions for the Users resource (Table 7.1) by adding **edit**, **update**, **index**, and **destroy** actions. We'll start by giving users the ability to update their profiles, which will also provide a natural opportunity to enforce a security model (made possible by the authorization code in Chapter 8). Then we'll make a listing of all users (also requiring authorization), which will motivate the introduction of sample data and pagination. Finally, we'll add the ability to destroy users, wiping them clear from the database. Since we can't allow just any user to have such dangerous powers, we'll take care to create a privileged class of administrative users (admins) authorized to delete other users.

To get started, let's start work on an **updating-users** topic branch:

```
$ git checkout -b updating-users
```

9.1 Updating Users

The pattern for editing user information closely parallels that for creating new users (Chapter 7). Instead of a **new** action rendering a view for new users, we have an **edit** action rendering a view to edit users; instead of **create** responding to a POST request, we have an **update** action responding to a PUT request (Box 3.2). The biggest difference is that, while anyone can sign up, only the current user should be able to update his information. This means that we need to enforce access control so that only authorized users can edit and update; the authentication machinery from Chapter 8 will allow us to use a *before filter* to ensure that this is the case.

9.1.1 Edit Form

We start with the edit form, whose mockup appears in Figure 9.1.[1] As usual, we'll begin with some tests. First, note the link to change the Gravatar image; if you poke around the Gravatar site, you'll see that the page to add or edit images is located at http://gravatar.com/emails, so we test the **edit** page for a link with that URI.[2]

The tests for the edit user form are analogous to the test for the new user form in Listing 7.31 from the Chapter 7 exercises, which added a test for the error message on invalid submission. The result appears in Listing 9.1.

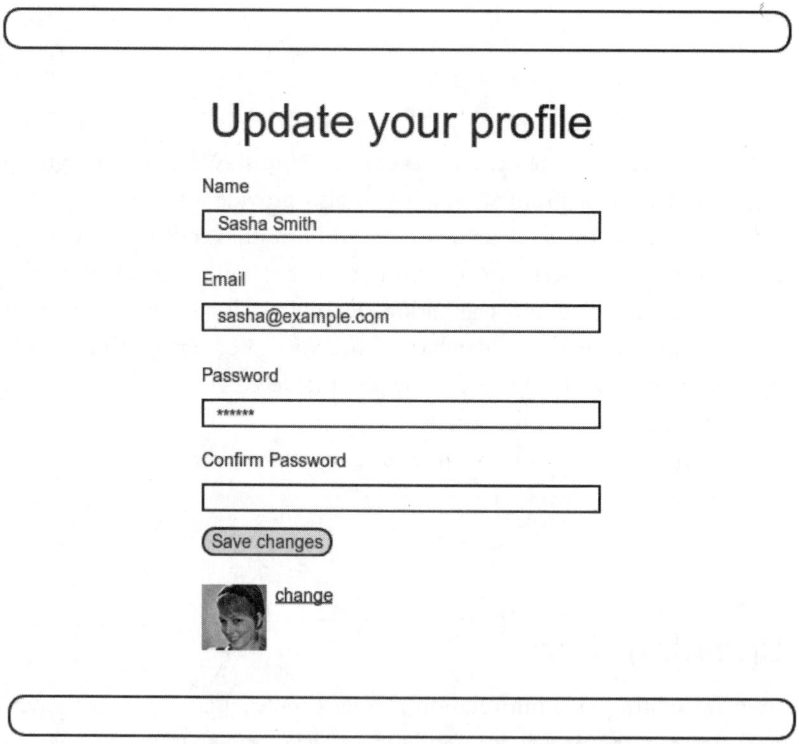

Figure 9.1 A mockup of the user edit page.

---

1. Image from www.flickr.com/photos/sashawolff/4598355045/.

2. The Gravatar site actually redirects this to http://en.gravatar.com/emails, which is for English language users, but I've omitted the en part to account for the use of other languages.

Listing 9.1 Tests for the user edit page.
spec/requests/user_pages_spec.rb

```ruby
require 'spec_helper'

describe "User pages" do
  .
  .
  .
  describe "edit" do
    let(:user) { FactoryGirl.create(:user) }
    before { visit edit_user_path(user) }

    describe "page" do
      it { should have_selector('h1',    text: "Update your profile") }
      it { should have_selector('title', text: "Edit user") }
      it { should have_link('change', href: 'http://gravatar.com/emails') }
    end

    describe "with invalid information" do
      before { click_button "Save changes" }

      it { should have_content('error') }
    end
  end
end
```

To write the application code, we need to fill in the **edit** action in the Users controller. Note from Table 7.1 that the proper URI for a user's edit page is /users/1/edit (assuming the user's id is 1). Recall that the id of the user is available in the **params[:id]** variable, which means that we can find the user with the code in Listing 9.2.

Listing 9.2 The user **edit** action.
app/controllers/users_controller.rb

```ruby
class UsersController < ApplicationController
  .
  .
  .
  def edit
    @user = User.find(params[:id])
  end
end
```

Getting the tests to pass requires making the actual edit view, shown in Listing 9.3. Note how closely this resembles the new user view from Listing 7.17; the large overlap suggests factoring the repeated code into a partial, which is left as an exercise (Section 9.6).

Listing 9.3 The user edit view.
`app/views/users/edit.html.erb`

```
<% provide(:title, "Edit user") %>
<h1>Update your profile</h1>

<div class="row">
  <div class="span6 offset3">
  <%= form_for(@user) do |f| %>
      <%= render 'shared/error_messages' %>

      <%= f.label :name %>
      <%= f.text_field :name %>

      <%= f.label :email %>
      <%= f.text_field :email %>

      <%= f.label :password %>
      <%= f.password_field :password %>

      <%= f.label :password_confirmation, "Confirm Password" %>
      <%= f.password_field :password_confirmation %>

      <%= f.submit "Save changes", class: "btn btn-large btn-primary" %>
    <% end %>

    <%= gravatar_for @user %>
    <a href="http://gravatar.com/emails">change</a>
  </div>
</div>
```

Here we have reused the shared **error_messages** partial introduced in Section 7.3.2.

With the **@user** instance variable from Listing 9.2, the edit page tests from Listing 9.1 should pass:

```
$ bundle exec rspec spec/requests/user_pages_spec.rb -e "edit page"
```

The corresponding page appears in Figure 9.2, which shows how Rails automatically pre-fills the Name and Email fields using the attributes of the **@user** variable.

Looking at the HTML source for Figure 9.2, we see a form tag as expected (Listing 9.4).

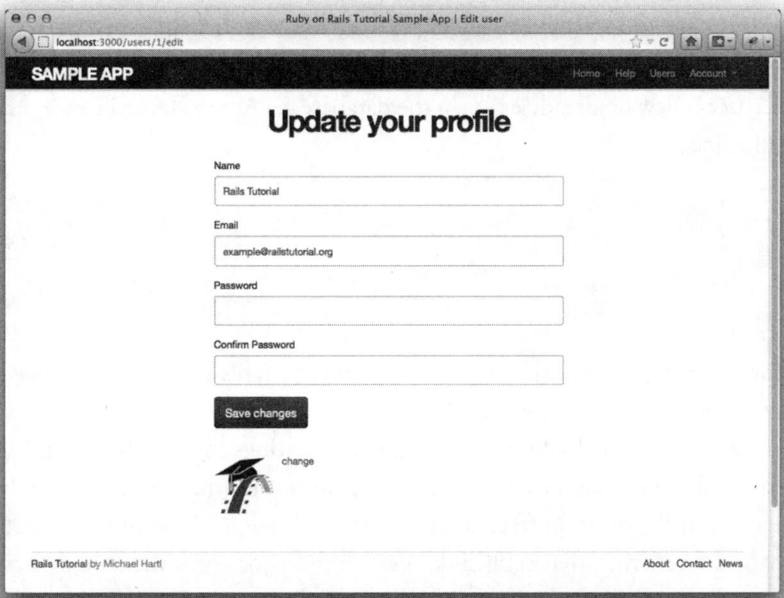

Figure 9.2 The initial user edit page with pre-filled name and email.

Listing 9.4 HTML for the edit form defined in Listing 9.3 and shown in Figure 9.2.

```
<form action="/users/1" class="edit_user" id="edit_user_1" method="post">
  <input name="_method" type="hidden" value="put" />
    .
    .
    .
</form>
```

Note here the hidden input field

```
<input name="_method" type="hidden" value="put" />
```

Since web browsers can't natively send PUT requests (as required by the REST conventions from Table 7.1), Rails fakes it with a POST request and a hidden **input** field.[3]

---

3. Don't worry about how this works; the details are of interest to developers of the Rails framework itself, and by design are not important for Rails application developers.

There's another subtlety to address here: The code **form_for(@user)** in Listing 9.3 is *exactly* the same as the code in Listing 7.17—so how does Rails know to use a POST request for new users and a PUT for editing users? The answer is that it is possible to tell whether a user is new or already exists in the database via Active Record's **new_record?** boolean method:

```
$ rails console
>> User.new.new_record?
=> true
>> User.first.new_record?
=> false
```

When constructing a form using **form_for(@user)**, Rails uses POST if **@user.new_record?** is **true** and PUT if it is **false**.

As a final touch, we'll add a URI to the user settings link to the site navigation. Since it depends on the signin status of the user, the test for the "Settings" link belongs with the other authentication tests, as shown in Listing 9.5. (It would be nice to have additional tests verifying that such links *don't* appear for users who aren't signed in; writing these tests is left as an exercise (Section 9.6).)

Listing 9.5 Adding a test for the "Settings" link.
spec/requests/authentication_pages_spec.rb

```
require 'spec_helper'

describe "Authentication" do
    .
    .
    .
    describe "with valid information" do
      let(:user) { FactoryGirl.create(:user) }
      before { sign_in user }

      it { should have_selector('title', text: user.name) }
      it { should have_link('Profile',  href: user_path(user)) }
      it { should have_link('Settings', href: edit_user_path(user)) }
      it { should have_link('Sign out', href: signout_path) }
      it { should_not have_link('Sign in', href: signin_path) }
      .
      .
      .
    end
  end
end
```

For convenience, the code in Listing 9.5 uses a helper to sign in a user inside the tests. The method is to visit the signin page and submit valid information, as shown in Listing 9.6.

Listing 9.6 A test helper to sign users in.
`spec/support/utilities.rb`

```
.
.
.
def sign_in(user)
  visit signin_path
  fill_in "Email",    with: user.email
  fill_in "Password", with: user.password
  click_button "Sign in"
  # Sign in when not using Capybara as well.
  cookies[:remember_token] = user.remember_token
end
```

As noted in the comment line, filling in the form doesn't work when not using Capybara, so to cover this case we also add the user's remember token to the cookies:

```
# Sign in when not using Capybara as well.
cookies[:remember_token] = user.remember_token
```

This is necessary when using one of the HTTP request methods directly (**get**, **post**, **put**, or **delete**), as we'll see in Listing 9.47. (Note that the test **cookies** object isn't a perfect simulation of the real cookies object; in particular, the **cookies.permanent** method seen in Listing 8.19 doesn't work inside tests.) As you might suspect, the **sign_in** method will prove useful in future tests, and in fact it can already be used to eliminate some duplication (Section 9.6).

The application code to add the URI for the "Settings" link is simple: We just use the named route **edit_user_path** from Table 7.1, together with the handy **current_user** helper method defined in Listing 8.22:

```
<%= link_to "Settings", edit_user_path(current_user) %>
```

The full application code appears in Listing 9.7.

Listing 9.7 Adding a "Settings" link.
`app/views/layouts/_header.html.erb`

```erb
<header class="navbar navbar-fixed-top">
  <div class="navbar-inner">
    <div class="container">
      <%= link_to "sample app", root_path, id: "logo" %>
      <nav>
        <ul class="nav pull-right">
          <li><%= link_to "Home", root_path %></li>
          <li><%= link_to "Help", help_path %></li>
          <% if signed_in? %>
            <li><%= link_to "Users", '#' %></li>
            <li id="fat-menu" class="dropdown">
              <a href="#" class="dropdown-toggle" data-toggle="dropdown">
                Account <b class="caret"></b>
              </a>
              <ul class="dropdown-menu">
                <li><%= link_to "Profile", current_user %></li>
                <li><%= link_to "Settings", edit_user_path(current_user) %></li>
                <li class="divider"></li>
                <li>
                  <%= link_to "Sign out", signout_path, method: "delete" %>
                </li>
              </ul>
            </li>
          <% else %>
            <li><%= link_to "Sign in", signin_path %></li>
          <% end %>
        </ul>
      </nav>
    </div>
  </div>
</header>
```

9.1.2 Unsuccessful Edits

In this section we'll handle unsuccessful edits and get the error messages test in Listing 9.1 to pass. The application code creates an **update** action that uses **update_attributes** (Section 6.1.5) to update the user based on the submitted **params** hash, as shown in Listing 9.8. With invalid information, the update attempt returns **false**, so the **else** branch re-renders the edit page. We've seen this pattern before; the structure closely parallels the first version of the **create** action (Listing 7.21).

Listing 9.8 The initial user **update** action.
`app/controllers/users_controller.rb`

```
class UsersController < ApplicationController
  .
  .
  .
  def edit
    @user = User.find(params[:id])
  end

  def update
    @user = User.find(params[:id])
    if @user.update_attributes(params[:user])
      # Handle a successful update.
    else
      render 'edit'
    end
  end
end
```

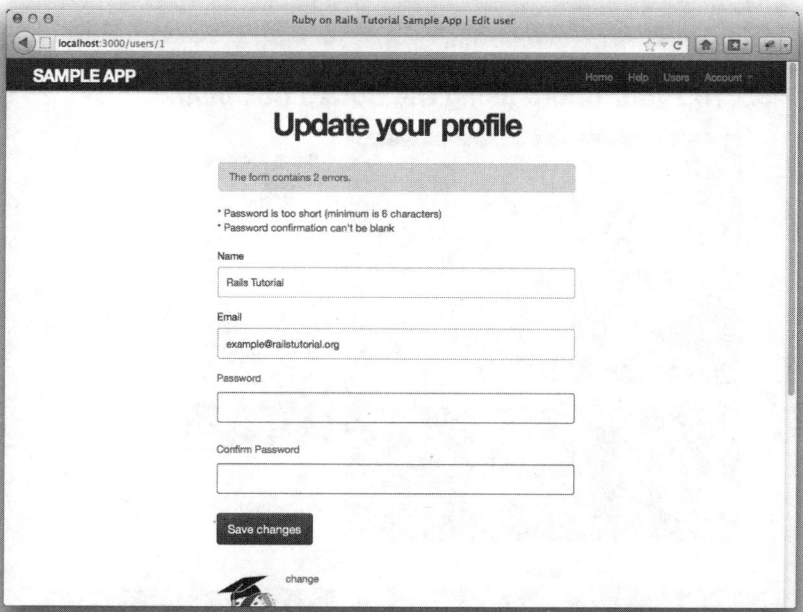

Figure 9.3 Error message from submitting the update form.

The resulting error message (Figure 9.3) is the one needed to get the error message test to pass, as you should verify by running the test suite:

```
$ bundle exec rspec spec/
```

9.1.3 Successful Edits

Now it's time to get the edit form to work. Editing the profile images is already functional since we've outsourced image upload to Gravatar; we can edit gravatars by clicking on the "change" link from Figure 9.2, as shown in Figure 9.4. Let's get the rest of the user edit functionality working as well.

The tests for the **update** action are similar to those for **create**. Listing 9.9 shows how to use Capybara to fill in the form fields with valid information and then test that the resulting behavior is correct. This is a lot of code; see if you can work through it by referring back to the tests in Chapter 7.

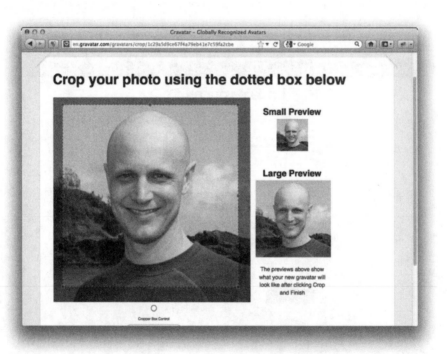

Figure 9.4   The Gravatar image-cropping interface, with a picture of some dude.

Listing 9.9 Tests for the user **update** action.
`spec/requests/user_pages_spec.rb`

```
require 'spec_helper'

describe "User pages" do
  .
  .
  .
  describe "edit" do
    let(:user) { FactoryGirl.create(:user) }
    before { visit edit_user_path(user) }
    .
    .
    .
    describe "with valid information" do
      let(:new_name)  { "New Name" }
      let(:new_email) { "new@example.com" }
      before do
        fill_in "Name",             with: new_name
        fill_in "Email",            with: new_email
        fill_in "Password",         with: user.password
        fill_in "Confirm Password", with: user.password
        click_button "Save changes"
      end

      it { should have_selector('title', text: new_name) }
      it { should have_selector('div.alert.alert-success') }
      it { should have_link('Sign out', href: signout_path) }
      specify { user.reload.name.should  == new_name }
      specify { user.reload.email.should == new_email }
    end
  end
end
```

The only real novelty in Listing 9.9 is the **reload** method, which appears in the test for changing the user's attributes:

```
specify { user.reload.name.should  == new_name }
specify { user.reload.email.should == new_email }
```

This reloads the **user** variable from the test database using **user.reload**, then verifies that the user's new name and email match the new values.

The **update** action needed to get the tests in Listing 9.9 to pass is similar to the final form of the **create** action (Listing 8.27), as seen in Listing 9.10. All this does is add

```
flash[:success] = "Profile updated"
sign_in @user
redirect_to @user
```

to the code in Listing 9.8. Note that we sign in the user as part of a successful profile update; this is because the remember token gets reset when the user is saved (Listing 8.18), which invalidates the user's session (Listing 8.22). This is a nice security feature, because it means that any hijacked sessions will automatically expire when the user information is changed.

Listing 9.10 The user **update** action.
app/controllers/users_controller.rb

```
class UsersController < ApplicationController
  .
  .
  .
  def update
    @user = User.find(params[:id])
    if @user.update_attributes(params[:user])
      flash[:success] = "Profile updated"
      sign_in @user
      redirect_to @user
    else
      render 'edit'
    end
  end
end
```

Note that, as currently constructed, every edit requires the user to reconfirm the password (as implied by the empty confirmation text box in Figure 9.2), which is a minor annoyance but makes updates much more secure.

With the code in this section, the user edit page should be working, as you can double-check by re-running the test suite, which should now be green:

```
$ bundle exec rspec spec/
```

9.2 Authorization

One nice effect of building the authentication machinery in Chapter 8 is that we are now in a position to implement authorization as well: *Authentication* allows us to identify users of our site, and *authorization* lets us control what they can do.

Although the edit and update actions from Section 9.1 are functionally complete, they suffer from a ridiculous security flaw: They allow anyone (even non-signed-in users) to access either action, and any signed-in user can update the information for any other user. In this section, we'll implement a security model that requires users to be signed in and prevents them from updating any information other than their own. Users who aren't signed in and who try to access protected pages will be forwarded to the signin page with a helpful message, as mocked up in Figure 9.5.

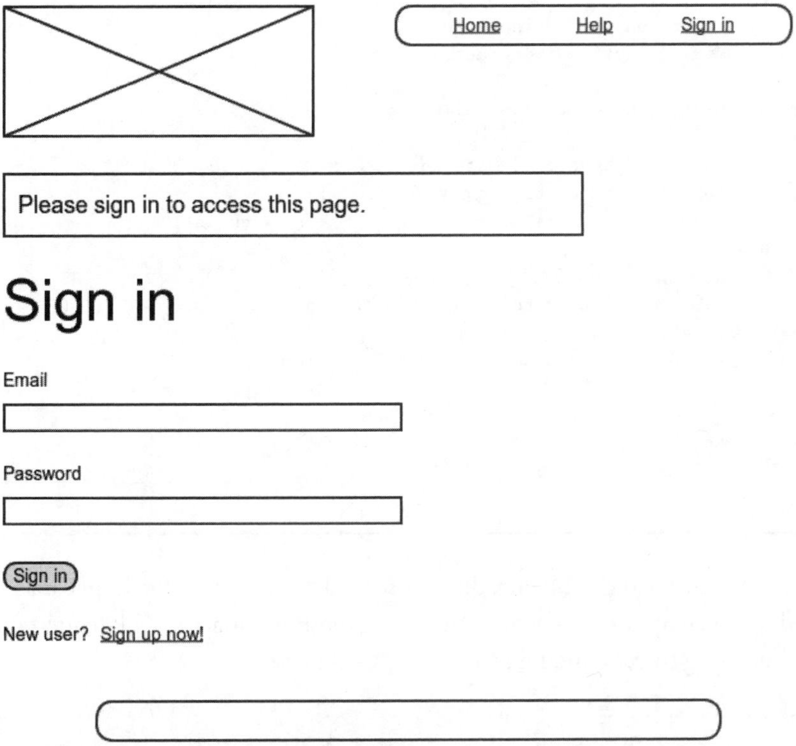

Figure 9.5   A mockup of the result of visiting a protected page.

9.2.1 Requiring Signed-in Users

Since the security restrictions for the **edit** and **update** actions are identical, we'll handle them in a single RSpec **describe** block. Starting with the sign-in requirement, our initial tests verify that non-signed-in users attempting to access either action are simply sent to the signin page, as seen in Listing 9.11.

Listing 9.11 Testing that the **edit** and **update** actions are protected.
spec/requests/authentication_pages_spec.rb

```
require 'spec_helper'

describe "Authentication" do
  .
  .
  .
  describe "authorization" do

    describe "for non-signed-in users" do
      let(:user) { FactoryGirl.create(:user) }

      describe "in the Users controller" do

        describe "visiting the edit page" do
          before { visit edit_user_path(user) }
          it { should have_selector('title', text: 'Sign in') }
        end

        describe "submitting to the update action" do
          before { put user_path(user) }
          specify { response.should redirect_to(signin_path) }
        end
      end
    end
  end
end
```

The code in Listing 9.11 introduces a second way, apart from Capybara's **visit** method, to access a controller action: By issuing the appropriate HTTP request directly, in this case using the **put** method to issue a PUT request:

```
describe "submitting to the update action" do
  before { put user_path(user) }
  specify { response.should redirect_to(signin_path) }
end
```

This issues a PUT request directly to **/users/1**, which gets routed to the **update** action of the Users controller (Table 7.1). This is necessary because there is no way for a browser to visit the **update** action directly—it can only get there indirectly by submitting the edit form—so Capybara can't do it either. But visiting the edit page only tests the authorization for the **edit** action, not for **update**. As a result, the only way to test the proper authorization for the **update** action itself is to issue a direct request. (As you might guess, in addition to **put** Rails tests support **get**, **post**, and **delete** as well.)

When using one of the methods to issue HTTP requests directly, we get access to the low-level **response** object. Unlike the Capybara **page** object, **response** lets us test for the server response itself, in this case verifying that the **update** action responds by redirecting to the signin page:

```
specify { response.should redirect_to(signin_path) }
```

The authorization application code uses a *before filter*, which arranges for a particular method to be called before the given actions. To require users to be signed in, we define a **signed_in_user** method and invoke it using **before_filter :signed_in_user**, as shown in Listing 9.12.

Listing 9.12 Adding a **signed_in_user** before filter.
app/controllers/users_controller.rb

```
class UsersController < ApplicationController
  before_filter :signed_in_user, only: [:edit, :update]
  .
  .
  .
  private

    def signed_in_user
      redirect_to signin_path, notice: "Please sign in." unless signed_in?
    end
end
```

By default, before filters apply to *every* action in a controller, so here we restrict the filter to act only on the **:edit** and **:update** actions by passing the appropriate **:only** options hash.

Note that Listing 9.12 uses a shortcut for setting **flash[:notice]** by passing an options hash to the **redirect_to** function. The code in Listing 9.12 is equivalent to the more verbose

```
flash[:notice] = "Please sign in."
redirect_to signin_path
```

(The same construction works for the **:error** key, but not for **:success**.)

Together with **:success** and **:error**, the **:notice** key completes our triumvirate of **flash** styles, all of which are supported natively by Bootstrap CSS. By signing out and attempting to access the user edit page /users/1/edit, we can see the resulting yellow "notice" box, as seen in Figure 9.6.

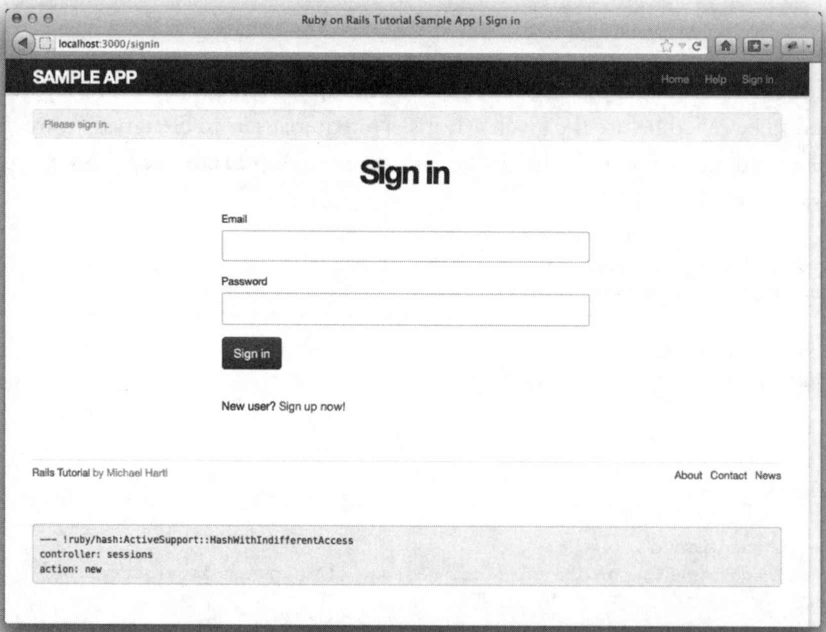

Figure 9.6   The signin form after trying to access a protected page.

Unfortunately, in the process of getting the authorization tests from Listing 9.11 to pass, we've broken the tests in Listing 9.1. Code like

```
describe "edit" do
  let(:user) { FactoryGirl.create(:user) }
  before { visit edit_user_path(user) }
  .
  .
  .
```

no longer works because visiting the edit user path requires a signed-in user. The solution is to sign in the user with the **sign_in** utility from Listing 9.6, as shown in Listing 9.13.

Listing 9.13 Adding a signin step to the edit and update tests.
spec/requests/user_pages_spec.rb

```
require 'spec_helper'

describe "User pages" do
  .
  .
  .
  describe "edit" do
    let(:user) { FactoryGirl.create(:user) }
    before do
      sign_in user
      visit edit_user_path(user)
    end
    .
    .
    .
  end
end
```

At this point our test suite should be green:

```
$ bundle exec rspec spec/
```

9.2.2 Requiring the Right User

Of course, requiring users to sign in isn't quite enough; users should only be allowed to edit their *own* information. We can test for this by first signing in as an incorrect user and then hitting the **edit** and **update** actions (Listing 9.14). Note that, since users should never even *try* to edit another user's profile, we redirect not to the signin page but to the root URL.

Listing 9.14 Testing that the **edit** and **update** actions require the right user.
spec/requests/authentication_pages_spec.rb

```
require 'spec_helper'

describe "Authentication" do
  .
  .
  .
  describe "authorization" do
    .
    .
    .
    describe "as wrong user" do
      let(:user) { FactoryGirl.create(:user) }
      let(:wrong_user) { FactoryGirl.create(:user, email: "wrong@example.com") }
      before { sign_in user }

      describe "visiting Users#edit page" do
        before { visit edit_user_path(wrong_user) }
        it { should_not have_selector('title', text: full_title('Edit user')) }
      end

      describe "submitting a PUT request to the Users#update action" do
        before { put user_path(wrong_user) }
        specify { response.should redirect_to(root_path) }
      end
    end
  end
end
```

Note here that a factory can take an option:

```
FactoryGirl.create(:user, email: "wrong@example.com")
```

This creates a user with a different email address from the default. The tests specify that this wrong user should not have access to the original user's **edit** or **update** actions.

The application code adds a second before filter to call the **correct_user** method, as shown in Listing 9.15.

Listing 9.15 A **correct_user** before filter to protect the edit/update pages.
app/controllers/users_controller.rb

```
class UsersController < ApplicationController
  before_filter :signed_in_user, only: [:edit, :update]
  before_filter :correct_user,   only: [:edit, :update]
  .
  .
  .
  def edit
  end

  def update
    if @user.update_attributes(params[:user])
      flash[:success] = "Profile updated"
      sign_in @user
      redirect_to @user
    else
      render 'edit'
    end
  end
  .
  .
  .
  private

    def signed_in_user
      redirect_to signin_path, notice: "Please sign in." unless signed_in?
    end

    def correct_user
      @user = User.find(params[:id])
      redirect_to(root_path) unless current_user?(@user)
    end
end
```

The **correct_user** filter uses the **current_user?** boolean method, which we define in the Sessions helper (Listing 9.16).

Listing 9.16 The `current_user?` method.
`app/helpers/sessions_helper.rb`

```ruby
module SessionsHelper
  .
  .
  .
  def current_user
    @current_user ||= User.find_by_remember_token(cookies[:remember_token])
  end

  def current_user?(user)
    user == current_user
  end
  .
  .
  .
end
```

Listing 9.15 also shows the updated **edit** and **update** actions. Before, in Listing 9.2, we had

```ruby
def edit
  @user = User.find(params[:id])
end
```

and similarly for **update**. Now that the **correct_user** before filter defines **@user**, we can omit it from both actions.

Before moving on, you should verify that the test suite passes:

```
$ bundle exec rspec spec/
```

9.2.3 Friendly Forwarding

Our site authorization is complete as written, but there is one minor blemish: When users try to access a protected page, they are currently redirected to their profile pages regardless of where they were trying to go. In other words, if a non-logged-in user tries to visit the edit page, after signing in the user will be redirected to /users/1 instead of /users/1/edit. It would be much friendlier to redirect them to their intended destination instead.

To test for such "friendly forwarding," we first visit the user edit page, which redirects to the signin page. We then enter valid signin information and click the "Sign in" button. The resulting page, which by default is the user's profile, should in this case be the "Edit user" page. The test for this sequence appears in Listing 9.17.

Listing 9.17 A test for friendly forwarding.
spec/requests/authentication_pages_spec.rb

```
require 'spec_helper'

describe "Authentication" do
  .
  .
  .
  describe "authorization" do

    describe "for non-signed-in users" do
      let(:user) { FactoryGirl.create(:user) }

      describe "when attempting to visit a protected page" do
        before do
          visit edit_user_path(user)
          fill_in "Email",    with: user.email
          fill_in "Password", with: user.password
          click_button "Sign in"
        end

        describe "after signing in" do

          it "should render the desired protected page" do
            page.should have_selector('title', text: 'Edit user')
          end
        end
      end
    end
  .
  .
  .
  end
end
```

Now for the implementation.[4] In order to forward users to their intended destination, we need to store the location of the requested page somewhere, and then redirect

---

4. The code in this section is adapted from the Clearance gem by thoughtbot.

to that location instead. We accomplish this with a pair of methods, **store_location**
and **redirect_back_or**, both defined in the Sessions helper (Listing 9.18).

Listing 9.18 Code to implement friendly forwarding.
app/helpers/sessions_helper.rb

```
module SessionsHelper
  .
  .
  .
  def redirect_back_or(default)
    redirect_to(session[:return_to] || default)
    session.delete(:return_to)
  end

  def store_location
    session[:return_to] = request.fullpath
  end
end
```

The storage mechanism is the **session** facility provided by Rails, which you can
think of as being like an instance of the **cookies** variable from Section 8.2.1 that
automatically expires upon browser close. (Indeed, as noted in Section 8.5, **session** is
implemented in just this way.) We also use the **request** object to get the **fullpath**,
i.e., the full path (URI) of the requested page. The **store_location** method puts the
requested URI in the **session** variable under the key **:return_to**.

To make use of **store_location**, we need to add it to the **signed_in_user**
before filter, as shown in Listing 9.19.

Listing 9.19 Adding **store_location** to the signed-in user before filter.
app/controllers/users_controller.rb

```
class UsersController < ApplicationController
  before_filter :signed_in_user, only: [:edit, :update]
  before_filter :correct_user,   only: [:edit, :update]
  .
  .
  .
  def edit
  end
  .
  .
  .
  private

    def signed_in_user
```

```
      unless signed_in?
        store_location
        redirect_to signin_path, notice: "Please sign in."
      end
  end

  def correct_user
    @user = User.find(params[:id])
    redirect_to(root_path) unless current_user?(@user)
  end
end
```

To implement the forwarding itself, we use the **redirect_back_or** method to redirect to the requested URI if it exists, or some default URI otherwise, which we add to the Sessions controller **create** action to redirect after successful signin (Listing 9.20). The **redirect_back_or** method uses the or operator **||** through

```
session[:return_to] || default
```

This evaluates to **session[:return_to]** unless it's **nil**, in which case it evaluates to the given default URI. Note that Listing 9.18 is careful to remove the forwarding URI; otherwise, subsequent signin attempts would forward to the protected page until the user closed his browser. (Testing for this is left as an exercise [Section 9.6.])

Listing 9.20 The Sessions **create** action with friendly forwarding.
app/controllers/sessions_controller.rb

```
class SessionsController < ApplicationController
  .
  .
  .
  def create
    user = User.find_by_email(params[:session][:email])
    if user && user.authenticate(params[:session][:password])
      sign_in user
      redirect_back_or user
    else
      flash.now[:error] = 'Invalid email/password combination'
      render 'new'
    end
  end
  .
  .
  .
end
```

With that, the friendly forwarding integration test in Listing 9.17 should pass, and the basic user authentication and page protection implementation is complete. As usual, it's a good idea to verify that the test suite is green before proceeding:

```
$ bundle exec rspec spec/
```

9.3 Showing All Users

In this section, we'll add the penultimate user action, the **index** action, which is designed to display *all* the users instead of just one. Along the way, we'll learn about populating the database with sample users and *paginating* the user output so that the index page can scale up to display a potentially large number of users. A mockup of the result—users, pagination links, and a "Users" navigation link—appears in Figure 9.7.[5] In Section 9.4, we'll add an administrative interface to the user index so that (presumably troublesome) users can be destroyed.

9.3.1 User Index

Although we'll keep individual user **show** pages visible to all site visitors, the user **index** will be restricted to signed-in users so that there's a limit to how much unregistered users can see by default. We'll start by testing that the **index** action is protected by visiting the **users_path** (Table 7.1) and verifying that we are redirected to the signin page. As with other authorization tests, we'll put this example in the authentication integration test, as shown in Listing 9.21.

Listing 9.21 Testing that the **index** action is protected.
spec/requests/authentication_pages_spec.rb

```
require 'spec_helper'

describe "Authentication" do
  .
  .
  .
  describe "authorization" do

    describe "for non-signed-in users" do
      .
```

---

5. Baby photo from www.flickr.com/photos/glasgows/338937124/.

```
      .
      .
      .
    describe "in the Users controller" do
      .
      .
      .
      describe "visiting the user index" do
        before { visit users_path }
        it { should have_selector('title', text: 'Sign in') }
      end
    end
      .
      .
      .
    end
  end
end
```

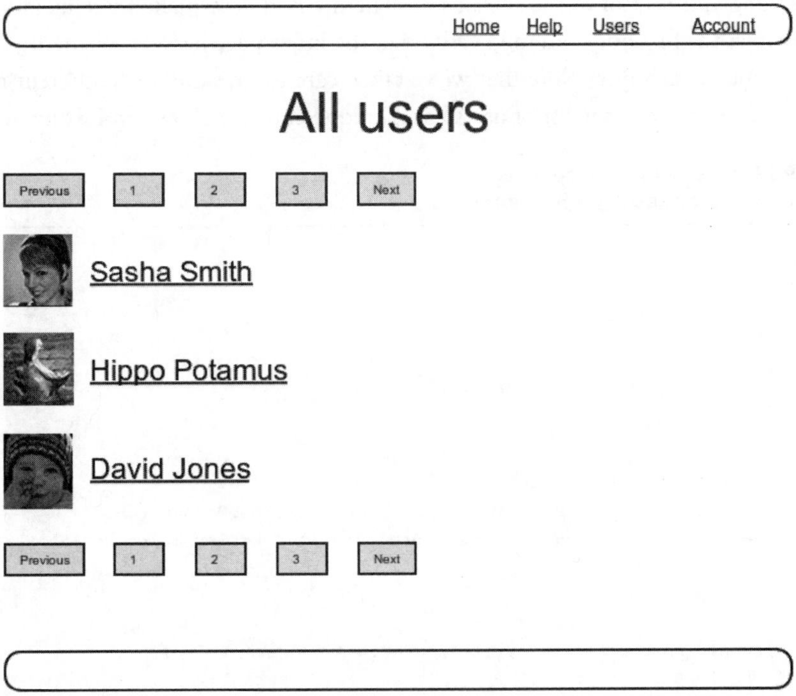

All users

Figure 9.7   A mockup of the user index, with pagination and a "Users" nav link.

The corresponding application code simply involves adding **index** to the list of actions protected by the **signed_in_user** before filter, as shown in Listing 9.22.

Listing 9.22 Requiring a signed-in user for the **index** action.
app/controllers/users_controller.rb

```
class UsersController < ApplicationController
  before_filter :signed_in_user, only: [:index, :edit, :update]
    .
    .
    .
  def index
  end
    .
    .
    .
end
```

The next set of tests makes sure that, for signed-in users, the index page has the right title/heading and lists all of the site's users. The method is to make three factory users (signing in as the first one) and then verify that the index page has a list element (**li**) tag for the name of each one. Note that we've taken care to give the users different names so that each element in the list of users has a unique entry, as shown in Listing 9.23.

Listing 9.23 Tests for the user index page.
spec/requests/user_pages_spec.rb

```
require 'spec_helper'

describe "User pages" do

  subject { page }

  describe "index" do
    before do
      sign_in FactoryGirl.create(:user)
      FactoryGirl.create(:user, name: "Bob", email: "bob@example.com")
      FactoryGirl.create(:user, name: "Ben", email: "ben@example.com")
      visit users_path
    end

    it { should have_selector('title', text: 'All users') }
    it { should have_selector('h1',    text: 'All users') }
```

```
    it "should list each user" do
      User.all.each do |user|
        page.should have_selector('li', text: user.name)
      end
    end
  end
  .
  .
  .
end
```

As you may recall from the corresponding action in the demo app (Listing 2.4), the application code uses **User.all** to pull all the users out of the database, assigning them to an **@users** instance variable for use in the view, as seen in Listing 9.24. (If displaying all the users at once seems like a bad idea, you're right, and we'll remove this blemish in Section 9.3.3.)

Listing 9.24 The user **index** action.
app/controllers/users_controller.rb

```
class UsersController < ApplicationController
  before_filter :signed_in_user, only: [:index, :edit, :update]
  .
  .
  .
  def index
    @users = User.all
  end
  .
  .
  .
end
```

To make the actual index page, we need to make a view that iterates through the users and wraps each one in an **li** tag. We do this with the **each** method, displaying each user's Gravatar and name, while wrapping the whole thing in an unordered list (**ul**) tag (Listing 9.25). The code in Listing 9.25 uses the result of Listing 7.29 from Section 7.6, which allows us to pass an option to the Gravatar helper specifying a size other than the default. If you didn't do that exercise, update your Users helper file with the contents of Listing 7.29 before proceeding.

Listing 9.25 The user index view.
app/views/users/index.html.erb

```erb
<% provide(:title, 'All users') %>
<h1>All users</h1>

<ul class="users">
  <% @users.each do |user| %>
    <li>
      <%= gravatar_for user, size: 52 %>
      <%= link_to user.name, user %>
    </li>
  <% end %>
</ul>
```

Let's also add a little CSS (or, rather, SCSS) for style (Listing 9.26).

Listing 9.26 CSS for the user index.
app/assets/stylesheets/custom.css.scss

```scss
.
.
.

/* users index */

.users {
  list-style: none;
  margin: 0;
  li {
    overflow: auto;
    padding: 10px 0;
    border-top: 1px solid $grayLighter;
    &:last-child {
      border-bottom: 1px solid $grayLighter;
    }
  }
}
```

Finally, we'll add the URI to the users link in the site's navigation header using **users_path**, thereby using the last of the unused named routes in Table 7.1. The test (Listing 9.27) and application code (Listing 9.28) are both straightforward.

Listing 9.27 A test for the "Users" link URI.
`spec/requests/authentication_pages_spec.rb`

```
require 'spec_helper'

describe "Authentication" do
    .
    .
    .
    describe "with valid information" do
      let(:user) { FactoryGirl.create(:user) }
      before { sign_in user }

      it { should have_selector('title', text: user.name) }

      it { should have_link('Users',    href: users_path) }
      it { should have_link('Profile',  href: user_path(user)) }
      it { should have_link('Settings', href: edit_user_path(user)) }
      it { should have_link('Sign out', href: signout_path) }

      it { should_not have_link('Sign in', href: signin_path) }
      .
      .
      .
    end
  end
end
```

Listing 9.28 Adding the URI to the users link.
`app/views/layouts/_header.html.erb`

```
<header class="navbar navbar-fixed-top">
  <div class="navbar-inner">
    <div class="container">
      <%= link_to "sample app", root_path, id: "logo" %>
      <nav>
        <ul class="nav pull-right">
          <li><%= link_to "Home", root_path %></li>
          <li><%= link_to "Help", help_path %></li>
          <% if signed_in? %>
            <li><%= link_to "Users", users_path %></li>
            <li id="fat-menu" class="dropdown">
              <a href="#" class="dropdown-toggle" data-toggle="dropdown">
                Account <b class="caret"></b>
```

```
      </a>
      <ul class="dropdown-menu">
        <li><%= link_to "Profile", current_user %></li>
        <li><%= link_to "Settings", edit_user_path(current_user) %></li>
        <li class="divider"></li>
        <li>
          <%= link_to "Sign out", signout_path, method: "delete" %>
        </li>
      </ul>
    </li>
  <% else %>
    <li><%= link_to "Sign in", signin_path %></li>
  <% end %>
      </ul>
    </nav>
  </div>
  </div>
</header>
```

With that, the user index is fully functional, with all tests passing:

```
$ bundle exec rspec spec/
```

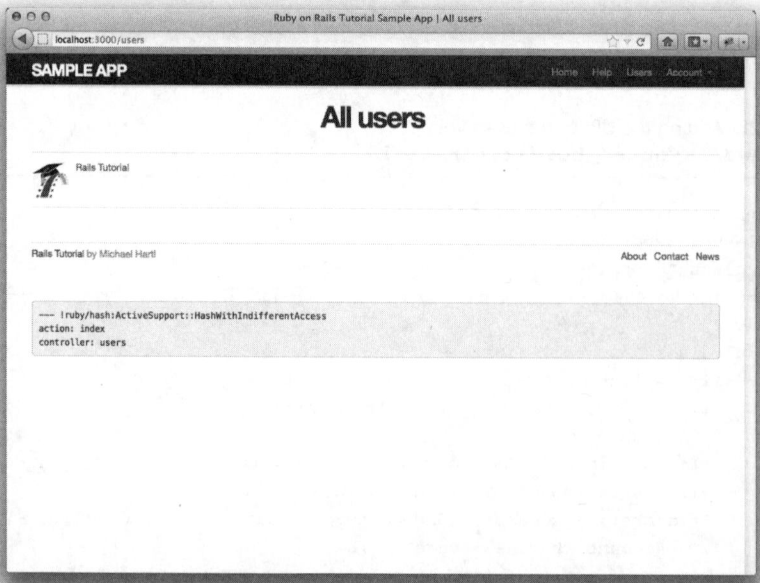

Figure 9.8   The user index page /users with only one user.

On the other hand, as seen in Figure 9.8, it is a bit . . . lonely. Let's remedy this sad situation.

9.3.2 Sample Users

In this section, we'll give our lonely sample user some company. Of course, to create enough users to make a decent user index, we *could* use our web browser to visit the signup page and make the new users one by one, but far a better solution is to use Ruby (and Rake) to make the users for us.

First, we'll add the *Faker* gem to the **Gemfile**, which will allow us to make sample users with semi-realistic names and email addresses (Listing 9.29).

Listing 9.29 Adding the Faker gem to the **Gemfile**.

```
source 'https://rubygems.org'

gem 'rails', '3.2.13'
gem 'bootstrap-sass', '2.0.0'
gem 'bcrypt-ruby', '3.0.1'
gem 'faker', '1.0.1'
 .
 .
 .
```

Then install as usual:

```
$ bundle install
```

Next, we'll add a Rake task to create sample users. Rake tasks live in the **lib/tasks** directory, and are defined using *namespaces* (in this case, **:db**), as seen in Listing 9.30. (This is a bit advanced, so don't worry too much about the details.)

Listing 9.30 A Rake task for populating the database with sample users.
lib/tasks/sample_data.rake

```
namespace :db do
  desc "Fill database with sample data"
  task populate: :environment do
    User.create!(name: "Example User",
                 email: "example@railstutorial.org",
                 password: "foobar",
                 password_confirmation: "foobar")
    99.times do |n|
      name  = Faker::Name.name
```

```
      email = "example-#{n+1}@railstutorial.org"
      password  = "password"
      User.create!(name: name,
                    email: email,
                    password: password,
                    password_confirmation: password)
    end
  end
end
```

This defines a task **db:populate** that creates an example user with name and email address replicating our previous one, and then makes 99 more. The line

```
task populate: :environment do
```

ensures that the Rake task has access to the local Rails environment, including the User model (and hence **User.create!**). Here **create!** is just like the **create** method, except it raises an exception (Section 6.1.4) for an invalid user rather than returning **false**. This noisier construction makes debugging easier by avoiding silent errors.

With the **:db** namespace as in Listing 9.30, we can invoke the Rake task as follows:

```
$ bundle exec rake db:reset
$ bundle exec rake db:populate
$ bundle exec rake db:test:prepare
```

After running the Rake task, our application has 100 sample users, as seen in Figure 9.9. (I've taken the liberty of associating the first few sample addresses with photos so that they're not all the default Gravatar image.)

9.3.3 Pagination

Our original user doesn't suffer from loneliness any more, but now we have the opposite problem: Our user has *too many* companions, and they all appear on the same page. Right now there are a hundred, which is already a reasonably large number, and on a real site it could be thousands. The solution is to *paginate* the users, so that (for example) only 30 show up on a page at any one time.

There are several pagination methods in Rails; we'll use one of the simplest and most robust, called will_paginate. To use it, we need to include both the will_paginate gem and bootstrap-will_paginate, which configures will_paginate to use Bootstrap's pagination styles. The updated **Gemfile** appears in Listing 9.31.

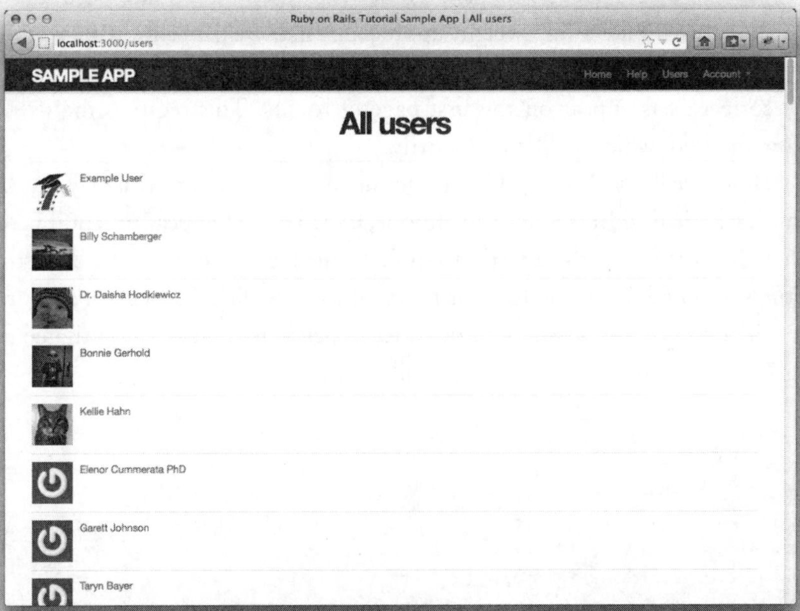

Figure 9.9 The user index page /users with 100 sample users.

Listing 9.31 Including `will_paginate` in the **Gemfile**.

```
source 'https://rubygems.org'

gem 'rails', '3.2.3'
gem 'bootstrap-sass', '2.0.0'
gem 'bcrypt-ruby', '3.0.1'
gem 'faker', '1.0.1'
gem 'will_paginate', '3.0.3'
gem 'bootstrap-will_paginate', '0.0.6'
.
.
.
```

Then run **bundle install**:

```
$ bundle install
```

You should also restart the web server to insure that the new gems are loaded properly.

Because the `will_paginate` gem is in wide use, there's no need to test it thoroughly, so we'll take a lightweight approach. First, we'll test for a **div** with CSS class "pagination", which is what gets output by `will_paginate`. Then we'll verify that the correct users appear on the first page of results. This requires the use of the **paginate** method, which we'll cover shortly.

As before, we'll use Factory Girl to simulate users, but immediately we have a problem: User email addresses must be unique, which would appear to require creating more than 30 users by hand—a terribly cumbersome job. In addition, when testing for user listings it would be convenient for them all to have different names. Fortunately, Factory Girl anticipates this issue, and provides *sequences* to solve it. Our original factory (Listing 7.8) hard-coded the name and email address:

```
FactoryGirl.define do
  factory :user do
    name     "Michael Hartl"
    email    "michael@example.com"
    password "foobar"
    password_confirmation "foobar"
  end
end
```

Instead, we can arrange for a sequence of names and email addresses using the **sequence** method:

```
factory :user do
  sequence(:name)  { |n| "Person #{n}" }
  sequence(:email) { |n| "person_#{n}@example.com"}
  .
  .
  .
```

Here **sequence** takes a symbol corresponding to the desired attribute (such as **:name**) and a block with one variable, which we have called **n**. Upon successive invocations of the **FactoryGirl** method,

```
FactoryGirl.create(:user)
```

The block variable **n** is automatically incremented, so that the first user has name "Person 1" and email address "person_1@example.com", the second user has name "Person 2" and email address "person_2@example.com", and so on. The full code appears in Listing 9.32.

Listing 9.32 Defining a Factory Girl sequence.
`spec/factories.rb`

```ruby
FactoryGirl.define do
  factory :user do
    sequence(:name)  { |n| "Person #{n}" }
    sequence(:email) { |n| "person_#{n}@example.com"}
    password "foobar"
    password_confirmation "foobar"
  end
end
```

Applying the idea of factory sequences, we can make 30 users in our test, which (as we will see) will be sufficient to invoke pagination:

```ruby
before(:all) { 30.times { FactoryGirl.create(:user) } }
after(:all)  { User.delete_all }
```

Note here the use of **before(:all)**, which ensures that the sample users are created *once*, before all the tests in the block. This is an optimization for speed, as creating 30 users can be slow on some systems. We use the complementary method **after(:all)** to delete the users once we're done.

The tests for the appearance of the pagination **div** and the right users appears in Listing 9.33. Note the replacement of the **User.all** array from Listing 9.23 with **User.paginate(page: 1)**, which (as we'll see momentarily) is how to pull out the first page of users from the database. Note also that Listing 9.33 uses **before(:each)** to emphasize the contrast with **before(:all)**.

Listing 9.33 Tests for pagination.
`spec/requests/user_pages_spec.rb`

```ruby
require 'spec_helper'

describe "User pages" do

  subject { page }

  describe "index" do

    let(:user) { FactoryGirl.create(:user) }

    before(:each) do
      sign_in user
      visit users_path
    end
```

```ruby
  it { should have_selector('title', text: 'All users') }
  it { should have_selector('h1',    text: 'All users') }

  describe "pagination" do

    it { should have_selector('div.pagination') }

    it "should list each user" do
      User.paginate(page: 1).each do |user|
        page.should have_selector('li', text: user.name)
      end
    end
  end
end

  .
  .
  .
end
```

To get pagination working, we need to add some code to the index view telling Rails to paginate the users, and we need to replace **User.all** in the **index** action with an object that knows about pagination. We'll start by adding the special **will_paginate** method in the view (Listing 9.34); we'll see in a moment why the code appears both above and below the user list.

Listing 9.34 The user index with pagination.
app/views/users/index.html.erb

```erb
<% provide(:title, 'All users') %>
<h1>All users</h1>

<%= will_paginate %>

<ul class="users">
  <% @users.each do |user| %>
    <li>
      <%= gravatar_for user, size: 52 %>
      <%= link_to user.name, user %>
    </li>
  <% end %>
</ul>

<%= will_paginate %>
```

The `will_paginate` method is a little magical; inside a **users** view, it automatically looks for an **@users** object, then displays pagination links to access other pages. The view in Listing 9.34 doesn't work yet, though, because currently **@users** contains the results of **User.all** (Listing 9.24), which is of class **Array**, whereas **will_paginate** expects an object of class **ActiveRecord::Relation**. Happily, this is just the kind of object returned by the **paginate** method added by the `will_paginate` gem to all Active Record objects:

```
$ rails console
>> User.all.class
=> Array
>> User.paginate(page: 1).class
=> ActiveRecord::Relation
```

Note that **paginate** takes a hash argument with key **:page** and value equal to the page requested. **User.paginate** pulls the users out of the database one chunk at a time (30 by default), based on the **:page** parameter. So, for example, page 1 is users 1–30, page 2 is users 31–60, etc. If the page is **nil**, **paginate** simply returns the first page.

Using the **paginate** method, we can paginate the users in the sample application by using **paginate** in place of **all** in the **index** action (Listing 9.35). Here the **:page** parameter comes from **params[:page]**, which is generated automatically by **will_paginate**.

Listing 9.35 Paginating the users in the **index** action.
app/controllers/users_controller.rb

```
class UsersController < ApplicationController
  before_filter :signed_in_user, only: [:index, :edit, :update]
  .
  .
  .
  def index
    @users = User.paginate(page: params[:page])
  end
  .
  .
  .
end
```

The user index page should now be working, appearing as in Figure 9.10. (On some systems, you may have to restart the Rails server at this point.) Because we included

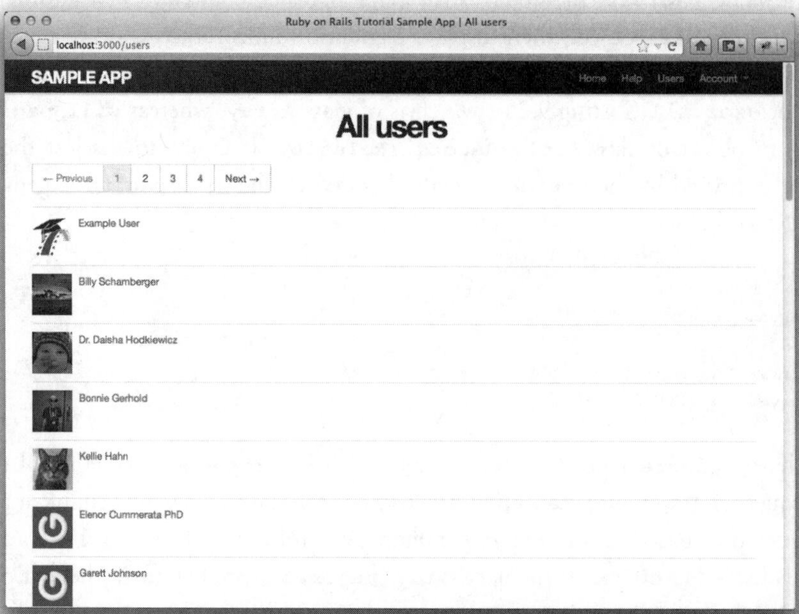

Figure 9.10 The user index page /users with pagination.

`will_paginate` both above and below the user list, the pagination links appear in both places.

If you now click on either the 2 link or Next link, you'll get the second page of results, as shown in Figure 9.11.

You should also verify that the tests are passing:

```
$ bundle exec rspec spec/
```

9.3.4 Partial Refactoring

The paginated user index is now complete, but there's one improvement I can't resist including: Rails has some incredibly slick tools for making compact views, and in this section we'll refactor the index page to use them. Because our code is well-tested, we can refactor with confidence, assured that we are unlikely to break our site's functionality.

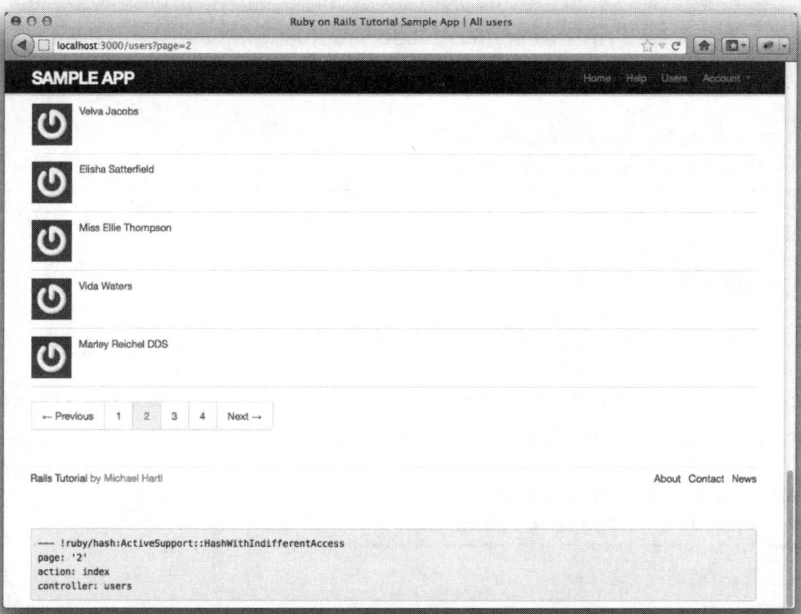

Figure 9.11 Page 2 of the user index (/users?page=2).

The first step in our refactoring is to replace the user **li** from Listing 9.34 with a **render** call (Listing 9.36).

Listing 9.36 The first refactoring attempt at the index view.
app/views/users/index.html.erb

```
<% provide(:title, 'All users') %>
<h1>All users</h1>

<%= will_paginate %>

<ul class="users">
  <% @users.each do |user| %>
    <%= render user %>
  <% end %>
</ul>

<%= will_paginate %>
```

Here we call **render** not on a string with the name of a partial, but rather on a **user** variable of class **User**;[6] in this context, Rails automatically looks for a partial called **_user.html.erb**, which we must create (Listing 9.37).

Listing 9.37 A partial to render a single user.
app/views/users/_user.html.erb

```
<li>
  <%= gravatar_for user, size: 52 %>
  <%= link_to user.name, user %>
</li>
```

This is a definite improvement, but we can do even better: We can call **render** *directly* on the **@users** variable (Listing 9.38).

Listing 9.38 The fully refactored user index.
app/views/users/index.html.erb

```
<% provide(:title, 'All users') %>
<h1>All users</h1>

<%= will_paginate %>

<ul class="users">
  <%= render @users %>
</ul>

<%= will_paginate %>
```

Here Rails infers that **@users** is a list of **User** objects; moreover, when called with a collection of users, Rails automatically iterates through them and renders each one with the **_user.html.erb** partial. The result is the impressively compact code in Listing 9.38. As with any refactoring, you should verify that the test suite is still green after changing the application code:

```
$ bundle exec rspec spec/
```

---

6. The name **user** is immaterial—we could have written **@users.each do |foobar|** and then used **render foobar**. The key is the *class* of the object—in this case, **User**.

9.4 Deleting Users

Now that the user index is complete, there's only one canonical REST action left: **destroy**. In this section, we'll add links to delete users, as mocked up in Figure 9.12, and define the **destroy** action necessary to accomplish the deletion. But first, we'll create the class of administrative users authorized to do so.

9.4.1 Administrative Users

We will identify privileged administrative users with a boolean **admin** attribute in the User model, which, as we'll see, will automatically lead to an **admin?** boolean method to test for admin status. We can write tests for this attribute as in Listing 9.39.

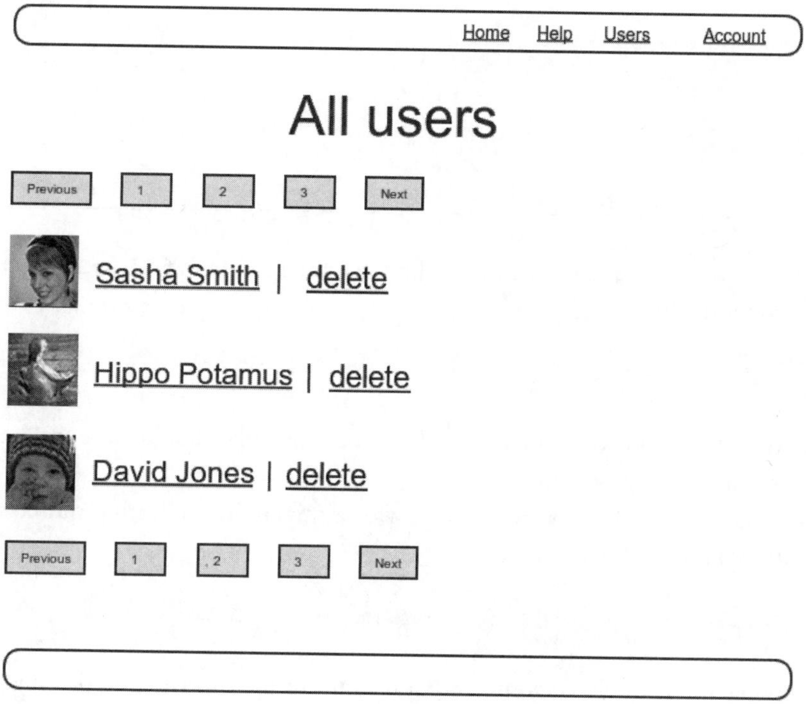

Figure 9.12 A mockup of the user index with delete links.

Listing 9.39 Tests for an **admin** attribute.
spec/models/user_spec.rb

```
require 'spec_helper'

describe User do
  .
  .
  .
  it { should respond_to(:admin) }
  it { should respond_to(:authenticate) }

  it { should be_valid }
  it { should_not be_admin }

  describe "with admin attribute set to 'true'" do
    before { @user.toggle!(:admin) }

    it { should be_admin }
  end
  .
  .
  .
end
```

Here we've used the **toggle!** method to flip the **admin** attribute from **false** to **true**. Also note that the line

```
it { should be_admin }
```

implies (via the RSpec boolean convention) that the user should have an **admin?** boolean method.

As usual, we add the **admin** attribute with a migration, indicating the **boolean** type on the command line:

```
$ rails generate migration add_admin_to_users admin:boolean
```

The migration simply adds the **admin** column to the **users** table (Listing 9.40), yielding the data model in Figure 9.13.

users	
id	integer
name	string
email	string
encrypted_password	string
salt	string
remember_token	string
admin	boolean
created_at	datetime
updated_at	datetime

Figure 9.13   The User model with an added **admin** boolean attribute.

Listing 9.40   The migration to add a boolean **admin** attribute to users.
db/migrate/[timestamp]_add_admin_to_users.rb

```ruby
class AddAdminToUsers < ActiveRecord::Migration
  def change
    add_column :users, :admin, :boolean, default: false
  end
end
```

Note that we've added the argument **default: false** to **add_column** in Listing 9.40, which means that users will *not* be administrators by default. (Without the **default: false** argument, **admin** will be **nil** by default, which is still **false**, so this step is not strictly necessary. It is more explicit, though, and communicates our intentions more clearly both to Rails and to readers of our code.)

Finally, we migrate the development database and prepare the test database:

```
$ bundle exec rake db:migrate
$ bundle exec rake db:test:prepare
```

As expected, Rails figures out the boolean nature of the **admin** attribute and automatically adds the question-mark method **admin?**:

```
$ rails console --sandbox
>> user = User.first
>> user.admin?
=> false
```

```
>> user.toggle!(:admin)
=> true
>> user.admin?
=> true
```

As a result, the admin tests should pass:

```
$ bundle exec rspec spec/models/user_spec.rb
```

As a final step, let's update our sample data populator to make the first user an admin by default (Listing 9.41).

Listing 9.41 The sample data populator code with an admin user.
lib/tasks/sample_data.rake

```ruby
namespace :db do
  desc "Fill database with sample data"
  task populate: :environment do
    admin = User.create!(name: "Example User",
                         email: "example@railstutorial.org",
                         password: "foobar",
                         password_confirmation: "foobar")
    admin.toggle!(:admin)
    .
    .
    .
  end
end
```

Then reset the database and re-populate the sample data:

```
$ bundle exec rake db:reset
$ bundle exec rake db:populate
$ bundle exec rake db:test:prepare
```

Revisiting `attr_accessible`

You might have noticed that Listing 9.41 makes the user an admin with `toggle!(:admin)`, but why not just add `admin: true` to the initialization hash? The answer is, it won't work, and this is by design: Only `attr_accessible` attributes can be assigned through mass assignment, and the `admin` attribute isn't accessible. Listing 9.42 reproduces the most recent list of `attr_accessible` attributes—note that `:admin` is *not* on the list.

Listing 9.42 The `attr_accessible` attributes for the User model *without* an `:admin` attribute.
`app/models/user.rb`

```
class User < ActiveRecord::Base
  attr_accessible :name, :email, :password, :password_confirmation
  .
  .
  .
end
```

Explicitly defining accessible attributes is crucial for good site security. If we omitted the `attr_accessible` list in the User model (or foolishly added `:admin` to the list), a malicious user could send a PUT request as follows:[7]

```
put /users/17?admin=1
```

This request would make user 17 an admin, which would be a potentially serious security breach, to say the least. Because of this danger, it is a good practice to define `attr_accessible` for every model. In fact, it's a good idea to write a test for any attribute that *isn't* accessible; writing such a test for the `admin` attribute is left as an exercise (Section 9.6).

9.4.2 The `destroy` Action

The final step needed to complete the Users resource is to add delete links and a `destroy` action. We'll start by adding a delete link for each user on the user index page, restricting access to administrative users.

To write tests for the delete functionality, it's helpful to be able to have a factory to create admins. We can accomplish this by adding an `:admin` block to our factories, as shown in Listing 9.43.

Listing 9.43 Adding a factory for administrative users.
`spec/factories.rb`

```
FactoryGirl.define do
  factory :user do
    sequence(:name)  { |n| "Person #{n}" }
    sequence(:email) { |n| "person_#{n}@example.com"}
    password "foobar"
    password_confirmation "foobar"
```

---

7. Command-line tools such as `curl` can issue PUT requests of this form.

```
    factory :admin do
      admin true
    end
  end
end
```

With the code in Listing 9.43, we can now use `FactoryGirl.create(:admin)` to create an administrative user in our tests.

Our security model requires that ordinary users not see delete links:

```
it { should_not have_link('delete') }
```

But administrative users should see such links, and by clicking on a delete link we expect an admin to delete the user, i.e., to change the `User` count by `-1`:

```
it { should have_link('delete', href: user_path(User.first)) }
it "should be able to delete another user" do
  expect { click_link('delete') }.to change(User, :count).by(-1)
end
it { should_not have_link('delete', href: user_path(admin)) }
```

Note that we have added a test to verify that the admin does not see a link to delete himself. The full set of delete link tests appears in Listing 9.44.

Listing 9.44 Tests for delete links.
spec/requests/user_pages_spec.rb

```
require 'spec_helper'

describe "User pages" do

  subject { page }

  describe "index" do

    let(:user) { FactoryGirl.create(:user) }

    before do
      sign_in user
      visit users_path
    end

    it { should have_selector('title', text: 'All users') }
    it { should have_selector('h1',    text: 'All users') }
```

```
    describe "pagination" do
      .
      .
      .
    end

    describe "delete links" do

      it { should_not have_link('delete') }

      describe "as an admin user" do
        let(:admin) { FactoryGirl.create(:admin) }
        before do
          sign_in admin
          visit users_path
        end

        it { should have_link('delete', href: user_path(User.first)) }
        it "should be able to delete another user" do
          expect { click_link('delete') }.to change(User, :count).by(-1)
        end
        it { should_not have_link('delete', href: user_path(admin)) }
      end
    end
  end
end
```

The application code links to **"delete"** if the current user is an admin (Listing 9.45). Note the **method: :delete** argument, which arranges for the link to issue the necessary DELETE request. We've also wrapped each link inside an **if** statement so that only admins can see them. The result for our admin user appears in Figure 9.14.

Listing 9.45 User delete links (viewable only by admins).
app/views/users/_user.html.erb

```
<li>
  <%= gravatar_for user, size: 52 %>
  <%= link_to user.name, user %>
  <% if current_user.admin? && !current_user?(user) %>
    | <%= link_to "delete", user, method: :delete, confirm: "You sure?" %>
  <% end %>
</li>
```

Web browsers can't send DELETE requests natively, so Rails fakes them with JavaScript. This means that the delete links won't work if the user has JavaScript

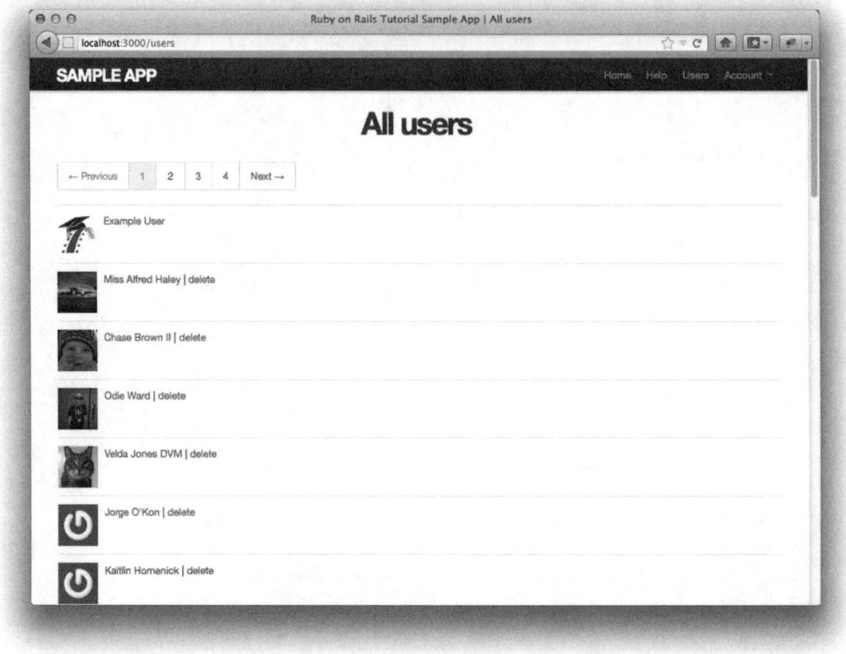

Figure 9.14   The user index /users with delete links.

disabled. If you must support non-JavaScript-enabled browsers you can fake a DELETE request using a form and a POST request, which works even without JavaScript; see the RailsCast on "Destroy Without JavaScript" for details.

To get the delete links to work, we need to add a **destroy** action (Table 7.1), which finds the corresponding user and destroys it with the Active Record **destroy** method, finally redirecting to the user index, as seen in Listing 9.46. Note that we also add **:destroy** to the **signed_in_user** before filter.

Listing 9.46 Adding a working **destroy** action.
app/controllers/users_controller.rb

```
class UsersController < ApplicationController
  before_filter :signed_in_user, only: [:index, :edit, :update, :destroy]
  before_filter :correct_user,   only: [:edit, :update]
  .
  .
  .
  def destroy
    User.find(params[:id]).destroy
```

```
    flash[:success] = "User destroyed."
    redirect_to users_path
  end
  .
  .
  .
end
```

Note that the **destroy** action uses method chaining to combine the **find** and **destroy** into one line:

```
User.find(params[:id]).destroy
```

As constructed, only admins can destroy users through the web, because only admins can see the delete links. Unfortunately, there's still a terrible security hole: Any sufficiently sophisticated attacker could simply issue DELETE requests directly from the command line to delete any user on the site. To secure the site properly, we also need access control on the **destroy** action, so our tests should check not only that admins *can* delete users, but also that other users *can't*. The results appear in Listing 9.47. Note that, in analogy with the **put** method from Listing 9.11, we use **delete** to issue a DELETE request directly to the specified URI (in this case, the user path, as required by Table 7.1).

Listing 9.47 A test for protecting the **destroy** action.
spec/requests/authentication_pages_spec.rb

```
require 'spec_helper'

describe "Authentication" do
  .
  .
  .
  describe "authorization" do
    .
    .
    .
    describe "as non-admin user" do
      let(:user) { FactoryGirl.create(:user) }
      let(:non_admin) { FactoryGirl.create(:user) }

      before { sign_in non_admin }

      describe "submitting a DELETE request to the Users#destroy action" do
        before { delete user_path(user) }
```

```
        specify { response.should redirect_to(root_path) }
      end
    end
  end
end
```

In principle, there's still a minor security hole, which is that an admin could delete himself by issuing a DELETE request directly. One might argue that such an admin is only getting what he deserves, but it would be nice to prevent such an occurrence, and doing so is left as an exercise (Section 9.6).

As you might suspect by now, the application code uses a before filter, this time to restrict access to the **destroy** action to admins. The resulting **admin_user** before filter appears in Listing 9.48.

Listing 9.48 A before filter restricting the **destroy** action to admins.
app/controllers/users_controller.rb

```
class UsersController < ApplicationController
  before_filter :signed_in_user, only: [:index, :edit, :update, :destroy]
  before_filter :correct_user,   only: [:edit, :update]
  before_filter :admin_user,     only: :destroy
  .
  .
  .
  private
    .
    .
    .
    def admin_user
      redirect_to(root_path) unless current_user.admin?
    end
end
```

At this point, all the tests should be passing, and the Users resource—with its controller, model, and views—is functionally complete.

```
$ bundle exec rspec spec/
```

9.5 Conclusion

We've come a long way since introducing the Users controller way back in Section 5.4. Those users couldn't even sign up; now users can sign up, sign in, sign out, view their profiles, edit their settings, and see an index of all users—and some can even destroy other users.

The rest of this book builds on the foundation of the Users resource (and associated authorization system) to make a site with Twitter-like microposts (Chapter 10) and a status feed of posts from followed users (Chapter 11). These chapters will introduce some of the most powerful features of Rails, including data modeling with **has_many** and **has_many through**.

Before moving on, be sure to merge all the changes into the master branch:

```
$ git add .
$ git commit -m "Finish user edit, update, index, and destroy actions"
$ git checkout master
$ git merge updating-users
```

You can also deploy the application and even populate the production database with sample users (using the **pg:reset** task to reset the production database):

```
$ git push heroku
$ heroku pg:reset SHARED_DATABASE --confirm <name-heroku-gave-to-your-app>
$ heroku run rake db:migrate
$ heroku run rake db:populate
```

(If you forgot the name of the Heroku app, just run **heroku pg:reset SHARED_ DATABASE** by itself and Heroku will remind you.)

It's also worth noting that this chapter saw the last of the necessary gem installations. For reference, the final **Gemfile** is shown in Listing 9.49.

Listing 9.49 The final **Gemfile** for the sample application.

```
source 'https://rubygems.org'

gem 'rails', '3.2.13'
gem 'bootstrap-sass', '2.0.0'
gem 'bcrypt-ruby', '3.0.1'
gem 'faker', '1.0.1'
gem 'will_paginate', '3.0.3'
gem 'bootstrap-will_paginate', '0.0.6'

group :development do
  gem 'sqlite3', '1.3.5'
  gem 'annotate', '~> 2.4.1.beta'
end
```

```
# Gems used only for assets and not required
# in production environments by default.
group :assets do
  gem 'sass-rails',   '3.2.4'
  gem 'coffee-rails', '3.2.2'
  gem 'uglifier', '1.2.3'
end

gem 'jquery-rails', '2.0.0'

group :test, :development do
  gem 'rspec-rails', '2.10.0'
  gem 'guard-rspec', '0.5.5'
  gem 'guard-spork', '0.3.2'
  gem 'spork', '0.9.0'
end

group :test do
  gem 'capybara', '1.1.2'
  gem 'factory_girl_rails', '1.4.0'
  gem 'cucumber-rails', '1.2.1', require: false
  gem 'database_cleaner', '0.7.0'
end

group :production do
  gem 'pg', '0.12.2'
end
```

9.6 Exercises

1. Following the model in Listing 10.8, add a test to verify that the User **admin** attribute isn't accessible. Be sure to get first to Red, and then to Green. (*Hint*: Your first step should be to *add* **admin** to the accessible list.)

2. Arrange for the Gravatar "change" link in Listing 9.3 to open in a new window (or tab). *Hint:* Search the web; you should find one particularly robust method involving something called **_blank**.

3. The current authentication tests check that navigation links such as "Profile" and "Settings" appear when a user is signed in. Add tests to make sure that these links *don't* appear when a user isn't signed in.

4. Use the **sign_in** test helper from Listing 9.6 in as many places as you can find.

5. Remove the duplicated form code by refactoring the **new.html.erb** and **edit.html.erb** views to use the partial in Listing 9.50. Note that you will have to pass the form variable **f** explicitly as a local variable, as shown in Listing 9.51. You will

also have to update the tests, as the forms aren't currently *exactly* the same; identify the slight difference and update the tests accordingly.

6. Signed-in users have no reason to access the **new** and **create** actions in the Users controller. Arrange for such users to be redirected to the root URL if they do try to hit those pages.

7. Learn about the **request** object by inserting some of the methods listed in the Rails API[8] into the site layout. (Refer to Listing 7.1 if you get stuck.)

8. Write a test to make sure that the friendly forwarding only forwards to the given URI the first time. On subsequent signin attempts, the forwarding URI should revert to the default (i.e., the profile page). See Listing 9.52 for a hint (and, by a hint, I mean the solution).

9. Modify the **destroy** action to prevent admin users from destroying themselves. (Write a test first.)

Listing 9.50 A partial for the new and edit form fields.
`app/views/users/_fields.html.erb`

```
<%= render 'shared/error_messages' %>

<%= f.label :name %>
<%= f.text_field :name %>

<%= f.label :email %>
<%= f.text_field :email %>

<%= f.label :password %>
<%= f.password_field :password %>

<%= f.label :password_confirmation, "Confirm Password" %>
<%= f.password_field :password_confirmation %>
```

Listing 9.51 The new user view with partial.
`app/views/users/new.html.erb`

```
<% provide(:title, 'Sign up') %>
<h1>Sign up</h1>

<div class="row">
  <div class="span6 offset3">
```

---

8. http://api.rubyonrails.org/v3.2.0/classes/ActionDispatch/Request.html.

```erb
  <%= form_for(@user) do |f| %>
    <%= render 'fields', f: f %>
    <%= f.submit "Create my account", class: "btn btn-large btn-primary" %>
  <% end %>
  </div>
</div>
```

Listing 9.52 A test for forwarding to the default page after friendly forwarding.
spec/requests/authentication_pages_spec.rb

```ruby
require 'spec_helper'

describe "Authentication" do
  .
  .
  .
  describe "authorization" do

    describe "for non-signed-in users" do
      .
      .
      .
      describe "when attempting to visit a protected page" do
        before do
          visit edit_user_path(user)
          fill_in "Email",    with: user.email
          fill_in "Password", with: user.password
          click_button "Sign in"
        end

        describe "after signing in" do

          it "should render the desired protected page" do
            page.should have_selector('title', text: 'Edit user')
          end

          describe "when signing in again" do
            before do
              visit signin_path
              fill_in "Email",    with: user.email
              fill_in "Password", with: user.password
              click_button "Sign in"
            end
```

```
            it "should render the default (profile) page" do
              page.should have_selector('title', text: user.name)
            end
          end
        end
      end
    end
    .
    .
    .

  end
end
```

CHAPTER 10
User Microposts

Chapter 9 saw the completion of the REST actions for the Users resource, so the time has finally come to add a second full resource: user *microposts*.[1] These are short messages associated with a particular user, first seen in larval form in Chapter 2. In this chapter, we will make a full-strength version of the sketch from Section 2.3 by constructing the Micropost data model, associating it with the User model using the **has_many** and **belongs_to** methods, and then making the forms and partials needed to manipulate and display the results. In Chapter 11, we'll complete our tiny Twitter clone by adding the notion of *following* users in order to receive a *feed* of their microposts.

If you're using Git for version control, I suggest making a topic branch as usual:

```
$ git checkout -b user-microposts
```

10.1 A Micropost Model

We begin the Microposts resource by creating a Micropost model, which captures the essential characteristics of microposts. What follows builds on the work from Section 2.3; as with the model in that section, our new Micropost model will include data validations and an association with the User model. Unlike that model, the present Micropost model will be fully tested and will also have a default *ordering* and automatic *destruction* if its parent user is destroyed.

---

1. Technically, we treated sessions as a resource in Chapter 8, but sessions are not saved to the database the way users and microposts are.

10.1.1 The Basic Model

The Micropost model needs only two attributes: a **content** attribute to hold the micropost's content,[2] and a **user_id** to associate a micropost with a particular user. As with the case of the User model (Listing 6.1), we generate it using **generate model**:

```
$ rails generate model Micropost content:string user_id:integer
```

This produces a migration to create a **microposts** table in the database (Listing 10.1); compare it to the analogous migration for the **users** table from Listing 6.2.

Listing 10.1 The Micropost migration. (Note the index on **user_id** and **created_at**.)
db/migrate/[timestamp]_create_microposts.rb

```
class CreateMicroposts < ActiveRecord::Migration
  def change
    create_table :microposts do |t|
      t.string :content
      t.integer :user_id

      t.timestamps
    end
    add_index :microposts, [:user_id, :created_at]
  end
end
```

Note that, since we expect to retrieve all the microposts associated with a given user id in reverse order of creation, Listing 10.1 adds an index (Box 6.2) on the **user_id** and **created_at** columns:

```
add_index :microposts, [:user_id, :created_at]
```

By including both the **user_id** and **created_at** columns as an array, we arrange for Rails to create a *multiple key index*, which means that Active Record uses *both* keys at the same time. Note also the **t.timestamps** line, which (as mentioned in Section 6.1.1) adds the magic **created_at** and **updated_at** columns. We'll put the **created_at** column to work in Section 10.1.4 and Section 10.2.1.

---

2. The **content** attribute will be a **string**, but, as noted briefly in Section 2.1.2, for longer text fields you should use the **text** data type.

We'll start with some minimal tests for the Micropost model based on the analogous tests for the User model (Listing 6.8). In particular, we verify that a micropost object responds to the **content** and **user_id** attributes, as shown in Listing 10.2.

Listing 10.2 The initial Micropost spec.
spec/models/micropost_spec.rb

```
require 'spec_helper'

describe Micropost do

  let(:user) { FactoryGirl.create(:user) }
  before do
    # This code is wrong!
    @micropost = Micropost.new(content: "Lorem ipsum", user_id: user.id)
  end

  subject { @micropost }

  it { should respond_to(:content) }
  it { should respond_to(:user_id) }
end
```

We can get these tests to pass by running the microposts migration and preparing the test database:

```
$ bundle exec rake db:migrate
$ bundle exec rake db:test:prepare
```

The result is a Micropost model with the structure shown in Figure 10.1.

You should verify that the tests pass:

```
$ bundle exec rspec spec/models/micropost_spec.rb
```

Even though the tests are passing, you might have noticed this code:

microposts	
id	integer
content	string
user_id	integer
created_at	datetime
updated_at	datetime

Figure 10.1 The Micropost data model.

```
let(:user) { FactoryGirl.create(:user) }
before do
  # This code is wrong!
  @micropost = Micropost.new(content: "Lorem ipsum", user_id: user.id)
end
```

The comment indicates that the code in the **before** block is wrong. See if you can guess why. We'll see the answer in the next section.

10.1.2 Accessible Attributes and the First Validation

To see why the code in the **before** block is wrong, we first start with validation tests for the Micropost model (Listing 10.3). (Compare with the User model tests in Listing 6.11.)

Listing 10.3 Tests for the validity of a new micropost.
spec/models/micropost_spec.rb

```
require 'spec_helper'

describe Micropost do

  let(:user) { FactoryGirl.create(:user) }
  before do
    # This code is wrong!
    @micropost = Micropost.new(content: "Lorem ipsum", user_id: user.id)
  end

  subject { @micropost }

  it { should respond_to(:content) }
  it { should respond_to(:user_id) }

  it { should be_valid }

  describe "when user_id is not present" do
    before { @micropost.user_id = nil }
    it { should_not be_valid }
  end
end
```

This code requires that the micropost be valid and tests for the presence of the **user_id** attribute. We can get these tests to pass with the simple presence validation shown in Listing 10.4.

Listing 10.4 A validation for the micropost's `user_id`.
`app/models/micropost.rb`

```
class Micropost < ActiveRecord::Base
  attr_accessible :content, :user_id
  validates :user_id, presence: true
end
```

Now we're prepared to see why

```
@micropost = Micropost.new(content: "Lorem ipsum", user_id: user.id)
```

is wrong. The problem is that by default (as of Rails 3.2.3) *all* of the attributes for our Micropost model are accessible. As discussed in Section 6.1.2 and Section 9.4.1, this means that anyone could change any aspect of a micropost object simply by using a command-line client to issue malicious requests. For example, a malicious user could change the `user_id` attributes on microposts, thereby associating microposts with the wrong users. This means that we should remove `:user_id` from the `attr_accessible` list, and once we do, the code above will fail. We'll fix this issue in Section 10.1.3.

10.1.3 User/Micropost Associations

When constructing data models for web applications, it is essential to be able to make *associations* between individual models. In the present case, each micropost is associated with one user, and each user is associated with (potentially) many microposts—a relationship seen briefly in Section 2.3.3 and shown schematically in Figure 10.2 and Figure 10.3. As part of implementing these associations, we'll write tests for the Micropost model that, unlike Listing 10.2, are compatible with the use of `attr_accessible` in Listing 10.7.

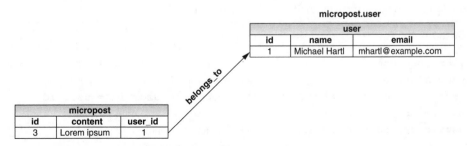

Figure 10.2   The `belongs_to` relationship between a micropost and its user.

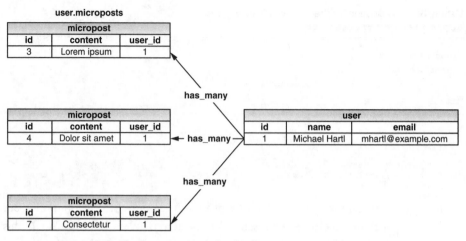

Figure 10.3   The **has_many** relationship between a user and its microposts.

Using the **belongs_to/has_many** association defined in this section, Rails constructs the methods shown in Table 10.1.

Note from Table 10.1 that instead of

```
Micropost.create
Micropost.create!
Micropost.new
```

we have

```
user.microposts.create
user.microposts.create!
user.microposts.build
```

Table 10.1   A summary of user/micropost association methods.

Method	Purpose
micropost.user	Return the User object associated with the micropost.
user.microposts	Return an array of the user's microposts.
user.microposts.create(arg)	Create a micropost (**user_id = user.id**).
user.microposts.create!(arg)	Create a micropost (exception on failure).
user.microposts.build(arg)	Return a new Micropost object (**user_id = user.id**).

This pattern is the canonical way to make a micropost: *through* its association with a user. When a new micropost is made in this way, its **user_id** is *automatically* set to the right value, which fixes the issue noted in Section 10.1.2. In particular, we can replace the code

```
let(:user) { FactoryGirl.create(:user) }
before do
  # This code is wrong!
  @micropost = Micropost.new(content: "Lorem ipsum", user_id: user.id)
end
```

from Listing 10.3 with

```
let(:user) { FactoryGirl.create(:user) }
before { @micropost = user.microposts.build(content: "Lorem ipsum") }
```

Once we define the proper associations, the resulting **@micropost** variable will automatically have **user_id** equal to its associated user.

Building the micropost through the User association doesn't fix the security problem of having an accessible **user_id**, and because this is such an important security concern we'll add a failing test to catch it, as shown in Listing 10.5.

Listing 10.5 A test to ensure that the **user_id** isn't accessible.
spec/models/micropost_spec.rb

```
require 'spec_helper'

describe Micropost do

  let(:user) { FactoryGirl.create(:user) }
  before { @micropost = user.microposts.build(content: "Lorem ipsum") }

  subject { @micropost }
  .
  .
  .
  describe "accessible attributes" do
    it "should not allow access to user_id" do
      expect do
        Micropost.new(user_id: user.id)
      end.should raise_error(ActiveModel::MassAssignmentSecurity::Error)
    end
  end
end
```

This test verifies that calling **Micropost.new** with a nonempty **user_id** raises a mass assignment security error exception. This behavior is on by default as of Rails 3.2.3, but previous versions had it off, so you should make sure that your application is configured properly, as shown in Listing 10.6.

Listing 10.6 Ensuring that Rails throws errors on invalid mass assignment.
config/application.rb

```
.
.
.
module SampleApp
  class Application < Rails::Application
    .
    .
    .
    config.active_record.whitelist_attributes = true
    .
    .
    .
  end
end
```

In the case of the Micropost model, there is only *one* attribute that needs to be editable through the web, namely, the **content** attribute, so we need to remove **:user_id** from the accessible list, as shown in Listing 10.7.

Listing 10.7 Making the **content** attribute (and *only* the **content** attribute) accessible.
app/models/micropost.rb

```
class Micropost < ActiveRecord::Base
  attr_accessible :content

  validates :user_id, presence: true
end
```

As seen in Table 10.1, another result of the user/micropost association is **microp-ost.user**, which simply returns the micropost's user. We can test this with the **it** and **its** methods as follows:

```
it { should respond_to(:user) }
its(:user) { should == user }
```

The resulting Micropost model tests are shown in Listing 10.8.

Listing 10.8 Tests for the micropost's user association.
`spec/models/micropost_spec.rb`

```
require 'spec_helper'

describe Micropost do

  let(:user) { FactoryGirl.create(:user) }
  before { @micropost = user.microposts.build(content: "Lorem ipsum") }

  subject { @micropost }

  it { should respond_to(:content) }
  it { should respond_to(:user_id) }
  it { should respond_to(:user) }
  its(:user) { should == user }

  it { should be_valid }

  describe "accessible attributes" do
    it "should not allow access to user_id" do
      expect do
        Micropost.new(user_id: user.id)
      end.should raise_error(ActiveModel::MassAssignmentSecurity::Error)
    end
  end

  describe "when user_id is not present" do
    before { @micropost.user_id = nil }
    it { should_not be_valid }
  end
end
```

On the User model side of the association, we'll defer the more detailed tests to Section 10.1.4; for now, we'll simply test for the presence of a **microposts** attribute (Listing 10.9).

Listing 10.9 A test for the user's **microposts** attribute.
`spec/models/user_spec.rb`

```
require 'spec_helper'

describe User do

  before do
    @user = User.new(name: "Example User", email: "user@example.com",
                     password: "foobar", password_confirmation: "foobar")
  end
```

```
subject { @user }
.
.
.
it { should respond_to(:authenticate) }
it { should respond_to(:microposts) }
.
.
.
end
```

After all that work, the code to implement the association is almost comically short: We can get the tests in both Listing 10.8 and Listing 10.9 to pass by adding just two lines: **belongs_to :user** (Listing 10.10) and **has_many :microposts** (Listing 10.11).

Listing 10.10 A micropost **belongs_to** a user.
app/models/micropost.rb

```
class Micropost < ActiveRecord::Base
  attr_accessible :content
  belongs_to :user

  validates :user_id, presence: true
end
```

Listing 10.11 A user has_many microposts.
app/models/user.rb

```
class User < ActiveRecord::Base
  attr_accessible :name, :email, :password, :password_confirmation
  has_secure_password
  has_many :microposts
  .
  .
  .
end
```

At this point, you should compare the entries in Table 10.1 with the code in Listing 10.8 and Listing 10.9 to satisfy yourself that you understand the basic nature of the associations. You should also check that the tests pass:

```
$ bundle exec rspec spec/models
```

10.1.4   Micropost Refinements

The test in Listing 10.9 of the **has_many** association doesn't test for much—it merely verifies the *existence* of a **microposts** attribute. In this section, we'll add *ordering* and *dependency* to microposts, while also testing that the **user.microposts** method actually returns an array of microposts.

We will need to construct some microposts in the User model test, which means that we should make a micropost factory at this point. To do this, we need a way to make an association in Factory Girl. Happily, this is easy, as seen in Listing 10.12.

Listing 10.12 The complete factory file, including a new factory for microposts.
spec/factories.rb

```
FactoryGirl.define do
  factory :user do
    sequence(:name)  { |n| "Person #{n}" }
    sequence(:email) { |n| "person_#{n}@example.com"}
    password "foobar"
    password_confirmation "foobar"

    factory :admin do
      admin true
    end
  end

  factory :micropost do
    content "Lorem ipsum"
    user
  end
end
```

Here we tell Factory Girl about the micropost's associated user just by including a user in the definition of the factory:

```
factory :micropost do
  content "Lorem ipsum"
  user
end
```

As we'll see in the next section, this allows us to define factory microposts as follows:

```
FactoryGirl.create(:micropost, user: @user, created_at: 1.day.ago)
```

Default Scope

By default, using **user.microposts** to pull a user's microposts from the database makes no guarantees about the order of the posts, but (following the convention of blogs and Twitter) we want the microposts to come out in reverse order of when they were created, i.e., most recent first. To test this ordering, we first create a couple of microposts as follows:

```
FactoryGirl.create(:micropost, user: @user, created_at: 1.day.ago)
FactoryGirl.create(:micropost, user: @user, created_at: 1.hour.ago)
```

Here we indicate (using the time helpers discussed in Box 8.1) that the second post was created more recently, i.e., **1.hour.ago**, while the first post was created **1.day.ago**. Note how convenient the use of Factory Girl is: Not only can we assign the user using mass assignment (since factories bypass **attr_accessible**), we can also set **created_ at** manually, which Active Record won't allow us to do. (Recall that **created_at** and **updated_at** are "magic" columns, automatically set to the proper creation and update timestamps, so any explicit initialization values are overwritten by the magic.)

Most database adapters (including the one for SQLite) return the microposts in order of their ids, so we can arrange for an initial test that almost certainly fails using the code in Listing 10.13. This uses the **let!** (read "let bang") method in place of **let**; the reason is that **let** variables are *lazy*, meaning that they only spring into existence when referenced. The problem is that we want the microposts to exist immediately, so that the timestamps are in the right order and so that **@user.microposts** isn't empty. We accomplish this with **let!**, which forces the corresponding variable to come into existence.

Listing 10.13 Testing the order of a user's microposts.
spec/models/user_spec.rb

```
require 'spec_helper'

describe User do
  .
  .
  .
  describe "micropost associations" do

    before { @user.save }
    let!(:older_micropost) do
      FactoryGirl.create(:micropost, user: @user, created_at: 1.day.ago)
    end
```

```
  let!(:newer_micropost) do
    FactoryGirl.create(:micropost, user: @user, created_at: 1.hour.ago)
  end

  it "should have the right microposts in the right order" do
    @user.microposts.should == [newer_micropost, older_micropost]
  end
  end
end
```

The key line here is

```
@user.microposts.should == [newer_micropost, older_micropost]
```

indicating that the posts should be ordered newest first. This should fail because by default the posts will be ordered by id, i.e., **[older_micropost, newer_micropost]**. This test also verifies the basic correctness of the **has_many** association itself, by checking (as indicated in Table 10.1) that **user.microposts** is an array of microposts.

To get the ordering test to pass, we use a Rails facility called **default_scope** with an **:order** parameter, as shown in Listing 10.14. (This is our first example of the notion of *scope*. We will learn about scope in a more general context in Chapter 11.)

Listing 10.14 Ordering the microposts with **default_scope**.
app/models/micropost.rb

```
class Micropost < ActiveRecord::Base
  .
  .
  .
  default_scope order: 'microposts.created_at DESC'
end
```

The order here is **'microposts.created_at DESC'**, where **DESC** is SQL for "descending," i.e., in descending order from newest to oldest.

Dependent: Destroy

Apart from proper ordering, there is a second refinement we'd like to add to microposts. Recall from Section 9.4 that site administrators have the power to *destroy* users. It stands to reason that, if a user is destroyed, the user's microposts should be destroyed as well. We can test for this by first destroying a micropost's user and then verifying that the associated microposts are no longer in the database (Listing 10.15).

Listing 10.15 Testing that microposts are destroyed when users are.
spec/models/user_spec.rb

```
require 'spec_helper'

describe User do
  .
  .
  .
  describe "micropost associations" do

    before { @user.save }
    let!(:older_micropost) do
      FactoryGirl.create(:micropost, user: @user, created_at: 1.day.ago)
    end
    let!(:newer_micropost) do
      FactoryGirl.create(:micropost, user: @user, created_at: 1.hour.ago)
    end
    .
    .
    .
    it "should destroy associated microposts" do
      microposts = @user.microposts
      @user.destroy
      microposts.each do |micropost|
        Micropost.find_by_id(micropost.id).should be_nil
      end
    end
  end
  .
  .
  .
end
```

Here we have used **Micropost.find_by_id**, which returns **nil** if the record is not found, whereas **Micropost.find** raises an exception on failure, which is a bit harder to test for. (In case you're curious,

```
lambda do
  Micropost.find(micropost.id)
end.should raise_error(ActiveRecord::RecordNotFound)
```

does the trick in this case.)

The application code to get Listing 10.15 to pass is less than one line; in fact, it's just an option to the **has_many** association method, as shown in Listing 10.16.

Listing 10.16 Ensuring that a user's microposts are destroyed along with the user.
`app/models/user.rb`

```
class User < ActiveRecord::Base
  attr_accessible :name, :email, :password, :password_confirmation
  has_secure_password
  has_many :microposts, dependent: :destroy
  .
  .
  .
end
```

Here the option **dependent: :destroy** in

```
has_many :microposts, dependent: :destroy
```

arranges for the dependent microposts (i.e., the ones belonging to the given user) to be destroyed when the user itself is destroyed. This prevents userless microposts from being stranded in the database when admins choose to remove users from the system.

With that, the final form of the user/micropost association is in place, and all the tests should be passing:

```
$ bundle exec rspec spec/
```

10.1.5   Content Validations

Before leaving the Micropost model, we'll add validations for the micropost **content** (following the example from Section 2.3.2). Like the **user_id**, the **content** attribute must be present, and it is further constrained to be no longer than 140 characters, making it an honest *micro*post. The tests generally follow the examples from the User model validation tests in Section 6.2, as shown in Listing 10.17.

Listing 10.17 Tests for the Micropost model validations.
`spec/models/micropost_spec.rb`

```
require 'spec_helper'

describe Micropost do

  let(:user) { FactoryGirl.create(:user) }
  before { @micropost = user.microposts.build(content: "Lorem ipsum") }
  .
  .
  .
```

```
    describe "when user_id is not present" do
      before { @micropost.user_id = nil }
      it { should_not be_valid }
    end

    describe "with blank content" do
      before { @micropost.content = " " }
      it { should_not be_valid }
    end

    describe "with content that is too long" do
      before { @micropost.content = "a" * 141 }
      it { should_not be_valid }
    end
  end
```

As in Section 6.2, the code in Listing 10.17 uses string multiplication to test the micropost length validation:

```
$ rails console
>> "a" * 10
=> "aaaaaaaaaa"
>> "a" * 141
=> "aaaaaaaaaaaaaaaaaaaaaaaaaaaaaaaaaaaaaaaaaaaaaaaaaaaaaaaaaaaaaaaaaaaaaaaa
aaaaaaaaaaaaaaaaaaaaaaaaaaaaaaaaaaaaaaaaaaaaaaaaaaaaaaaaaaaaaaaaaaaaaaaa"
```

The application code is a one-liner:

```
validates :content, presence: true, length: { maximum: 140 }
```

The resulting Micropost model is shown in Listing 10.18.

Listing 10.18 The Micropost model validations.
app/models/micropost.rb

```
class Micropost < ActiveRecord::Base
  attr_accessible :content

  belongs_to :user

  validates :content, presence: true, length: { maximum: 140 }
  validates :user_id, presence: true

  default_scope order: 'microposts.created_at DESC'
end
```

10.2 Showing Microposts

Although we don't yet have a way to create microposts through the web—that comes in Section 10.3.2—that won't stop us from displaying them (and testing that display). Following Twitter's lead, we'll plan to display a user's microposts not on a separate microposts **index** page, but rather directly on the user **show** page itself, as mocked up in Figure 10.4. We'll start with fairly simple ERb templates for adding a micropost display to the user profile, and then we'll add microposts to the sample data populator from Section 9.3.2 so that we have something to display.

As with the discussion of the signin machinery in Section 8.2.1, Section 10.2.1 will often push several elements onto the stack at a time, and then pop them off one by one. If you start getting bogged down, be patient; there's some nice payoff in Section 10.2.2.

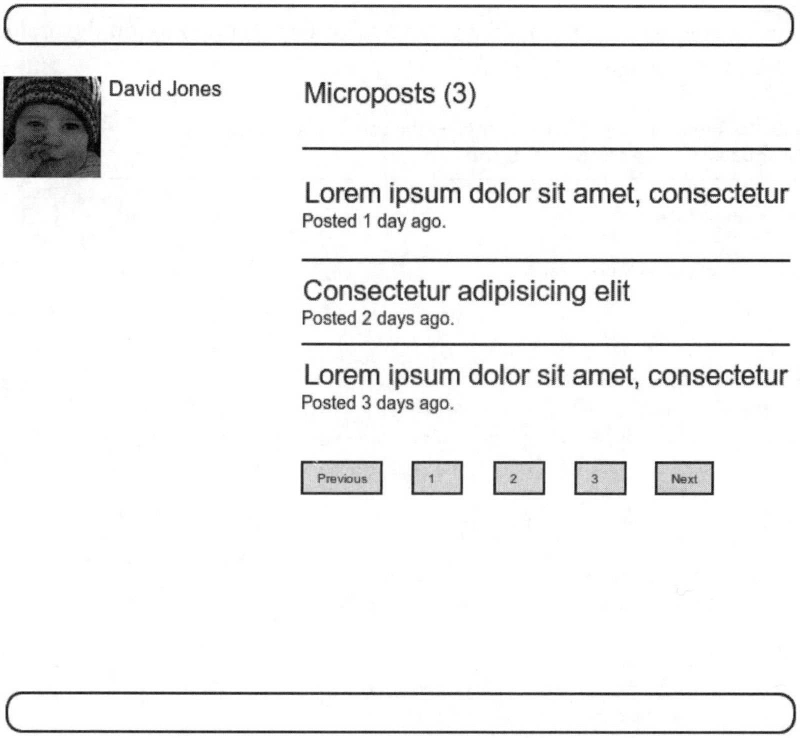

Figure 10.4   A mockup of a profile page with microposts.

10.2.1 Augmenting the User Show Page

We begin with tests for displaying the user's microposts, which we'll create in the request spec for Users. Our strategy is to create a couple of factory microposts associated with the user, and then verify that the show page contains each post's content. We'll also verify that, as in Figure 10.4, the total number of microposts also gets displayed.

We can create the posts with the **let** method, but as in Listing 10.13 we want the association to exist immediately so that the posts appear on the user show page. To accomplish this, we use the **let!** variant:

```
let(:user) { FactoryGirl.create(:user) }
let!(:m1) { FactoryGirl.create(:micropost, user: user, content: "Foo") }
let!(:m2) { FactoryGirl.create(:micropost, user: user, content: "Bar") }

before { visit user_path(user) }
```

With the microposts so defined, we can test for their appearance on the profile page using the code in Listing 10.19.

Listing 10.19 A test for showing microposts on the user **show** page.
spec/requests/user_pages_spec.rb

```
require 'spec_helper'

describe "User pages" do
  .
  .
  .
  describe "profile page" do
    let(:user) { FactoryGirl.create(:user) }
    let!(:m1) { FactoryGirl.create(:micropost, user: user, content: "Foo") }
    let!(:m2) { FactoryGirl.create(:micropost, user: user, content: "Bar") }

    before { visit user_path(user) }

    it { should have_selector('h1',    text: user.name) }
    it { should have_selector('title', text: user.name) }

    describe "microposts" do
      it { should have_content(m1.content) }
      it { should have_content(m2.content) }
      it { should have_content(user.microposts.count) }
    end
```

```
  end
    .
    .
    .
end
```

Note here that we can use the **count** method *through* the association:

```
user.microposts.count
```

The association **count** method is smart and performs the count directly in the database. In particular, it does *not* pull all the microposts out of the database and then call **length** on the resulting array, as this could become inefficient as the number of microposts grew. Instead, it asks the database to count the microposts with the given **user_id**. In the unlikely event that finding the count is still a bottleneck in your application, you can make it even faster with a *counter cache*.

Although the tests in Listing 10.19 won't pass until Listing 10.21, we'll get started on the application code by inserting a list of microposts into the user profile page, as shown in Listing 10.20.

Listing 10.20 Adding microposts to the user **show** page.
app/views/users/show.html.erb

```erb
<% provide(:title, @user.name) %>
<div class="row">
  .
  .
  .
  <aside>
    .
    .
    .
  </aside>
  <div class="span8">
    <% if @user.microposts.any? %>
      <h3>Microposts (<%= @user.microposts.count %>)</h3>
      <ol class="microposts">
        <%= render @microposts %>
      </ol>
      <%= will_paginate @microposts %>
    <% end %>
  </div>
</div>
```

We will deal with the microposts list momentarily, but there are several other things to note first. In Listing 10.20, the use of `if @user.microposts.any?` (a construction we saw before in Listing 7.23) makes sure that an empty list won't be displayed when the user has no microposts.

Also note from Listing 10.20 that we've preemptively added pagination for microposts through

```
<%= will_paginate @microposts %>
```

If you compare this with the analogous line on the user index page, Listing 9.34, you'll see that before we had just

```
<%= will_paginate %>
```

This worked because, in the context of the Users controller, `will_paginate` *assumes* the existence of an instance variable called `@users` (which, as we saw in Section 9.3.3, should be of class `ActiveRecord::Relation`). In the present case, since we are still in the Users controller but want to paginate *microposts* instead, we pass an explicit `@microposts` variable to `will_paginate`. Of course, this means that we will have to define such a variable in the user `show` action (Listing 10.22).

Finally, note that we have taken this opportunity to add a count of the current number of microposts:

```
<h3>Microposts (<%= @user.microposts.count %>)</h3>
```

As noted, `@user.microposts.count` is the analogue of the `User.count` method, except that it counts the microposts belonging to a given user through the user/micropost association.

We come finally to the micropost list itself:

```
<ol class="microposts">
  <%= render @microposts %>
</ol>
```

This code, which uses the *ordered list* tag `ol`, is responsible for generating the list of microposts, but you can see that it just defers the heavy lifting to a micropost partial. We saw in Section 9.3.4 that the code

```
<%= render @users %>
```

automatically renders each of the users in the **@users** variable using the **_user .html.erb** partial. Similarly, the code

```
<%= render @microposts %>
```

does exactly the same thing for microposts. This means that we must define a **_micropost.html.erb** partial (along with a **micropost** views directory), as shown in Listing 10.21.

Listing 10.21 A partial for showing a single micropost.
app/views/microposts/_micropost.html.erb

```
<li>
  <span class="content"><%= micropost.content %></span>
  <span class="timestamp">
    Posted <%= time_ago_in_words(micropost.created_at) %> ago.
  </span>
</li>
```

This uses the awesome **time_ago_in_words** helper method, whose effect we will see in Section 10.2.2.

Thus far, despite defining all the relevant ERb templates, the test in Listing 10.19 should have been failing for want of an **@microposts** variable. We can get it to pass with Listing 10.22.

Listing 10.22 Adding an **@microposts** instance variable to the user **show** action.
app/controllers/users_controller.rb

```
class UsersController < ApplicationController
  .
  .
  .
  def show
    @user = User.find(params[:id])
    @microposts = @user.microposts.paginate(page: params[:page])
  end
end
```

Notice here how clever **paginate** is—it even works through the microposts association, reaching into the microposts table and pulling out the desired page of microposts.

At this point, we can get a look at our new user profile page in Figure 10.5. It's rather . . . disappointing. Of course, this is because there are not currently any microposts. It's time to change that.

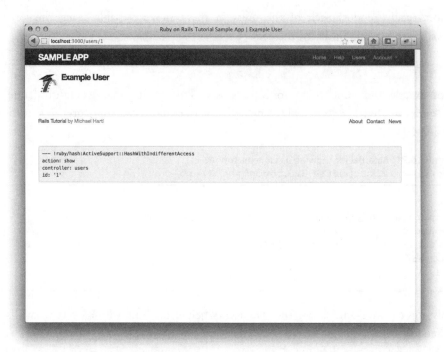

Figure 10.5   The user profile page with code for microposts—but no microposts.

10.2.2   Sample Microposts

With all the work making templates for user microposts in Section 10.2.1, the ending was rather anticlimactic. We can rectify this sad situation by adding microposts to the sample populator from Section 9.3.2. Adding sample microposts for *all* the users actually takes a rather long time, so first we'll select just the first six users[3] using the `:limit` option to the `User.all` method:[4]

```
users = User.all(limit: 6)
```

We then make 50 microposts for each user (plenty to overflow the pagination limit of 30), generating sample content for each micropost using the Faker gem's handy `Lorem.sentence` method. (**`Faker::Lorem.sentence`** returns *lorem ipsum* text; as

---

3. (i.e., the five users with custom Gravatars, and one with the default Gravatar)

4. Tail your `log/development.log` file if you're curious about the SQL this method generates.

noted in Chapter 6, *lorem ipsum* has a fascinating back story.) The result is the new sample data populator shown in Listing 10.23.

Listing 10.23 Adding microposts to the sample data.
lib/tasks/sample_data.rake

```
namespace :db do
  desc "Fill database with sample data"
  task populate: :environment do
    .
    .
    .
    users = User.all(limit: 6)
    50.times do
      content = Faker::Lorem.sentence(5)
      users.each { |user| user.microposts.create!(content: content) }
    end
  end
end
```

Of course, to generate the new sample data we have to run the **db:populate** Rake task:

```
$ bundle exec rake db:reset
$ bundle exec rake db:populate
$ bundle exec rake db:test:prepare
```

With that, we are in a position to enjoy the fruits of our Section 10.2.1 labors by displaying information for each micropost.[5] The preliminary results appear in Figure 10.6.

The page shown in Figure 10.6 has no micropost-specific styling, so let's add some (Listing 10.24) and take a look the resulting pages.[6] Figure 10.7, which displays the user profile page for the first (signed-in) user, while Figure 10.8 shows the profile for a second user. Finally, Figure 10.9 shows the *second* page of microposts for the first user, along with the pagination links at the bottom of the display. In all three cases, observe that each micropost display indicates the time since it was created (e.g., "Posted 1 minute ago."); this is the work of the **time_ago_in_words** method from Listing 10.21. If you wait a couple minutes and reload the pages, you'll see how the text gets automatically updated based on the new time.

---

5. By design, the Faker gem's *lorem ipsum* text is randomized, so the contents of your sample microposts will differ.

6. For convenience, Listing 10.24 actually has *all* the CSS needed for this chapter.

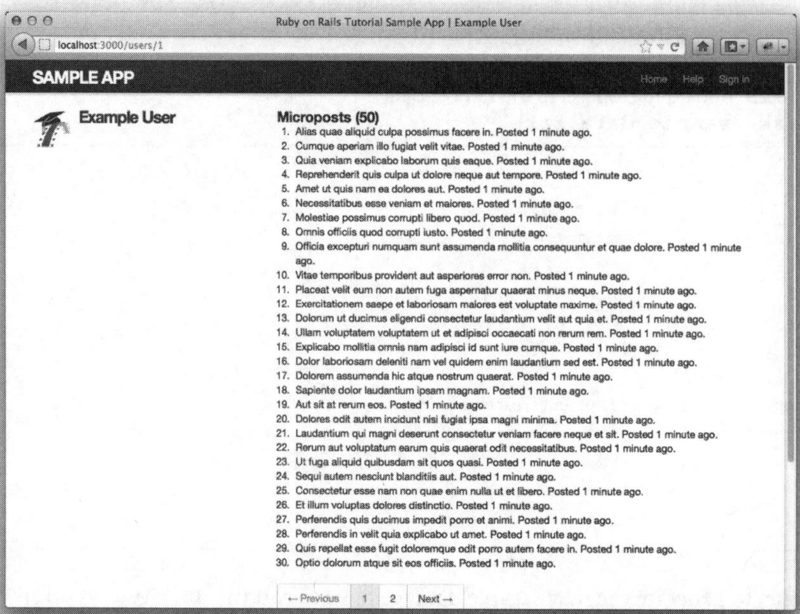

Figure 10.6   The user profile (/users/1) with unstyled microposts.

Listing 10.24   The CSS for microposts (including all the CSS for this chapter).
`app/assets/stylesheets/custom.css.scss`

```
.
.
.
/* microposts */

.microposts {
  list-style: none;
  margin: 10px 0 0 0;

  li {
    padding: 10px 0;
    border-top: 1px solid #e8e8e8;
  }
}
```

```scss
.content {
  display: block;
}
.timestamp {
  color: $grayLight;
}
.gravatar {
  float: left;
  margin-right: 10px;
}
aside {
  textarea {
    height: 100px;
    margin-bottom: 5px;
  }
}
```

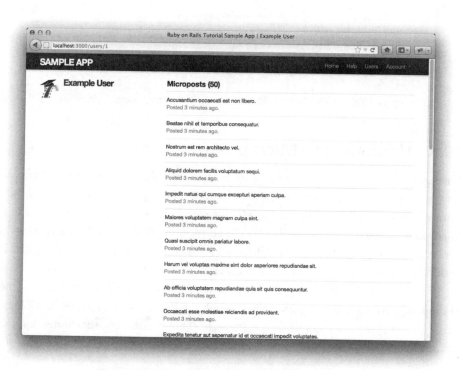

Figure 10.7   The user profile (/users/1) with microposts.

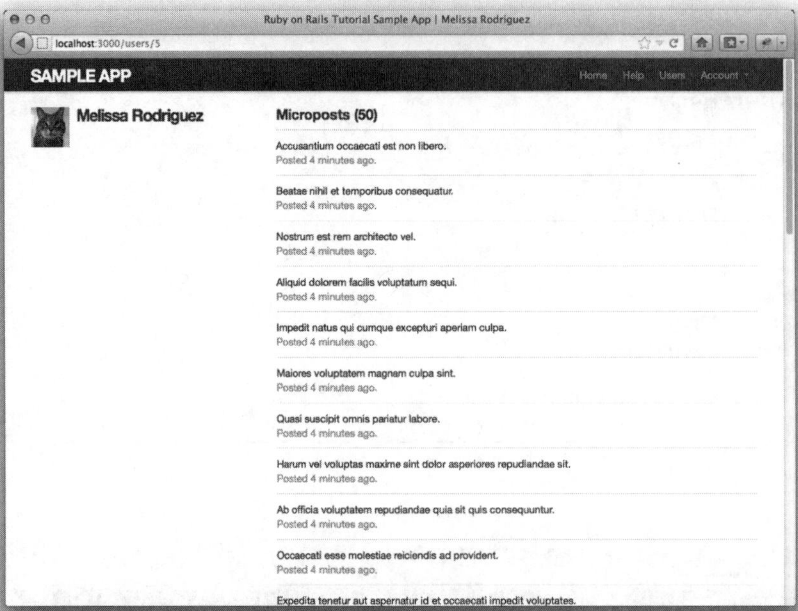

Figure 10.8   The profile of a different user, also with microposts (/users/3).

10.3   Manipulating Microposts

Having finished both the data modeling and display templates for microposts, we now turn our attention to the interface for creating them through the web. The result will be our third example of using an HTML form to create a resource—in this case, a Microposts resource.[7] In this section, we'll also see the first hint of a *status feed*—a notion brought to full fruition in Chapter 11. Finally, as with users, we'll make it possible to destroy microposts through the web.

There is one break with past convention worth noting: The interface to the Microposts resource will run principally through the Users and StaticPages controllers, rather than relying on a controller of its own. This means that the routes for the Microposts resource are unusually simple, as seen in Listing 10.25. The code in

---

7. The other two resources are Users in Section 7.2 and Sessions in Section 8.1.

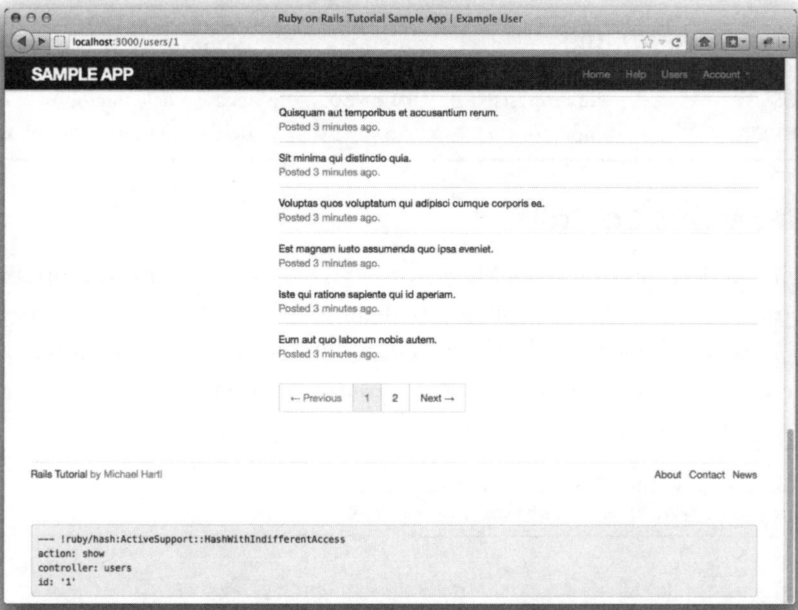

Figure 10.9   Micropost pagination links (/users/1?page=2).

Listing 10.25 leads in turn to the RESTful routes shown in Table 10.2, which is a small subset of the full set of routes seen in Table 2.3. Of course, this simplicity is a sign of being *more* advanced, not less—we've come a long way since our reliance on scaffolding in Chapter 2, and we no longer need most of its complexity.

Listing 10.25   Routes for the Microposts resource.
`config/routes.rb`

```
SampleApp::Application.routes.draw do
  resources :users
  resources :sessions,   only: [:new, :create, :destroy]
  resources :microposts, only: [:create, :destroy]
  .
  .
  .
end
```

Table 10.2 RESTful routes provided by the Microposts resource in Listing 10.25.

HTTP request	URI	Action	Purpose
POST	/microposts	**create**	create a new micropost
DELETE	/microposts/1	**destroy**	delete micropost with id **1**

10.3.1 Access Control

We begin our development of the Microposts resource with some access control in the Microposts controller. The idea is simple: Both the **create** and **destroy** actions should require users to be signed in. The RSpec code to test for this appears in Listing 10.26. (We'll test for and add a third protection—ensuring that only a micropost's user can destroy it—in Section 10.3.4.)

Listing 10.26 Access control tests for microposts.
`spec/requests/authentication_pages_spec.rb`

```
require 'spec_helper'

describe "Authentication" do
  .
  .
  .
  describe "authorization" do

    describe "for non-signed-in users" do
      let(:user) { FactoryGirl.create(:user) }
      .
      .
      .
      describe "in the Microposts controller" do

        describe "submitting to the create action" do
          before { post microposts_path }
          specify { response.should redirect_to(signin_path) }
        end

        describe "submitting to the destroy action" do
          before do
            micropost = FactoryGirl.create(:micropost)
            delete micropost_path(micropost)
          end
          specify { response.should redirect_to(signin_path) }
```

```
          end
        end
          .
          .
          .

      end
    end
  end
end
```

Rather than using the (yet-to-be-built) web interface for microposts, the code in Listing 10.26 operates at the level of the individual micropost actions, a strategy we first saw in Listing 9.14. In this case, a non-signed-in user is redirected upon submitting a POST request to /microposts (**post microposts_path**, which hits the **create** action) or submitting a DELETE request to /microposts/1 (**delete micropost_path(micropost)**, which hits the **destroy** action).

Writing the application code needed to get the tests in Listing 10.26 to pass requires a little refactoring first. Recall from Section 9.2.1 that we enforced the signin requirement using a before filter that called the **signed_in_user** method (Listing 9.12). At the time, we only needed that method in the Users controller, but now we find that we need it in the Microposts controller as well, so we'll move it into the Sessions helper, as shown in Listing 10.27.[8]

Listing 10.27 Moving the **signed_in_user** method into the Sessions helper.
app/helpers/sessions_helper.rb

```ruby
module SessionsHelper
  .
  .
  .
  def current_user?(user)
    user == current_user
  end

  def signed_in_user
    unless signed_in?
      store_location
      redirect_to signin_path, notice: "Please sign in."
```

---

8. We noted in Section 8.2.1 that helper methods are available only in *views* by default, but we arranged for the Sessions helper methods to be available in the controllers as well by adding **include SessionsHelper** to the Application controller (Listing 8.14).

```
      end
  end
  .
  .
  .
end
```

To avoid code repetition, you should also remove **signed_in_user** from the Users controller at this time.

With the code in Listing 10.27, the **signed_in_user** method is now available in the Microposts controller, which means that we can restrict access to the **create** and **destroy** actions with the before filter shown in Listing 10.28. (Since we didn't generate it at the command line, you will have to create the Microposts controller file by hand.)

Listing 10.28 Adding authentication to the Microposts controller actions.
`app/controllers/microposts_controller.rb`

```ruby
class MicropostsController < ApplicationController
  before_filter :signed_in_user

  def create
  end

  def destroy
  end
end
```

Note that we haven't restricted the actions the before filter applies to since it applies to them both by default. If we were to add, say, an **index** action accessible even to non-signed-in users, we would need to specify the protected actions explicitly:

```ruby
class MicropostsController < ApplicationController
  before_filter :signed_in_user, only: [:create, :destroy]

  def index
  end

  def create
  end

  def destroy
  end
end
```

At this point, the tests should pass:

```
$ bundle exec rspec spec/requests/authentication_pages_spec.rb
```

10.3.2 Creating Microposts

In Chapter 7, we implemented user signup by making an HTML form that issued an HTTP POST request to the **create** action in the Users controller. The implementation of micropost creation is similar; the main difference is that, rather than using a separate page at /microposts/new, we will (following Twitter's convention) put the form on the Home page itself (i.e., the root path /), as mocked up in Figure 10.10.

When we last left the Home page, it appeared as in Figure 5.6—that is, it had a "Sign up now!" button in the middle. Since a micropost creation form only makes

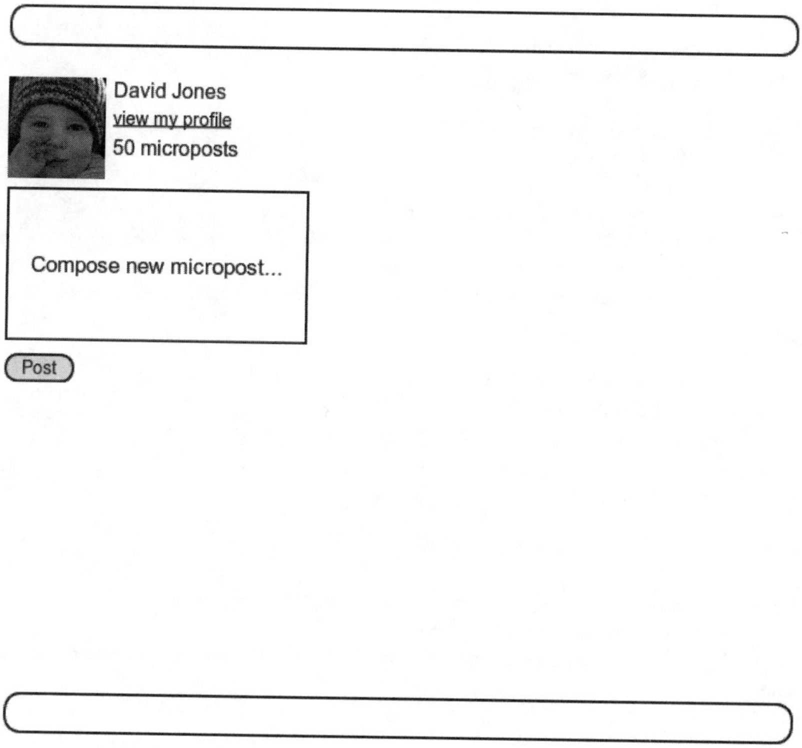

Figure 10.10   A mockup of the Home page with a form for creating microposts.

sense in the context of a particular signed-in user, one goal of this section will be to serve different versions of the Home page depending on a visitor's signin status. We'll implement this in Listing 10.31 below, but we can still write the tests now. As with the Users resource, we'll use an integration test:

```
$ rails generate integration_test micropost_pages
```

The micropost creation tests then parallel those for user creation from Listing 7.16; the result appears in Listing 10.29.

Listing 10.29 Tests for creating microposts.
spec/requests/micropost_pages_spec.rb

```ruby
require 'spec_helper'

describe "Micropost pages" do

  subject { page }

  let(:user) { FactoryGirl.create(:user) }
  before { sign_in user }

  describe "micropost creation" do
    before { visit root_path }

    describe "with invalid information" do

      it "should not create a micropost" do
        expect { click_button "Post" }.should_not change(Micropost, :count)
      end

      describe "error messages" do
        before { click_button "Post" }
        it { should have_content('error') }
      end
    end

    describe "with valid information" do

      before { fill_in 'micropost_content', with: "Lorem ipsum" }
      it "should create a micropost" do
        expect { click_button "Post" }.should change(Micropost, :count).by(1)
      end
    end
  end
end
```

We'll start with the **create** action for microposts, which is similar to its user analogue (Listing 7.25); the principal difference lies in using the user/micropost association to **build** the new micropost, as seen in Listing 10.30.

Listing 10.30 The Microposts controller **create** action.
app/controllers/microposts_controller.rb

```
class MicropostsController < ApplicationController
  before_filter :signed_in_user

  def create
    @micropost = current_user.microposts.build(params[:micropost])
    if @micropost.save
      flash[:success] = "Micropost created!"
      redirect_to root_path
    else
      render 'static_pages/home'
    end
  end

  def destroy
  end
end
```

To build a form for creating microposts, we use the code in Listing 10.31, which serves up different HTML based on whether the site visitor is signed in or not.

Listing 10.31 Adding microposts creation to the Home page (/).
app/views/static_pages/home.html.erb

```
<% if signed_in? %>
  <div class="row">
    <aside class="span4">
      <section>
        <%= render 'shared/user_info' %>
      </section>
      <section>
        <%= render 'shared/micropost_form' %>
      </section>
    </aside>
  </div>
<% else %>
  <div class="center hero-unit">
    <h1>Welcome to the Sample App</h1>
```

```
  <h2>
    This is the home page for the
    <a href="http://railstutorial.org/">Ruby on Rails Tutorial</a>
    sample application.
  </h2>

  <%= link_to "Sign up now!", signup_path,
                           class: "btn btn-large btn-primary" %>
</div>

  <%= link_to image_tag("rails.png", alt: "Rails"), 'http://rubyonrails.org/' %>
<% end %>
```

Having so much code in each branch of the **if-else** conditional is a bit messy, and cleaning it up using partials is left as an exercise (Section 10.5). Filling in the necessary partials from Listing 10.31 isn't an exercise, though; we fill in the new Home page sidebar in Listing 10.32 and the micropost form partial in Listing 10.33.

Listing 10.32 The partial for the user info sidebar.
app/views/shared/_user_info.html.erb

```
<a href="<%= user_path(current_user) %>">
  <%= gravatar_for current_user, size: 52 %>
</a>
<h1>
  <%= current_user.name %>
</h1>
<span>
  <%= link_to "view my profile", current_user %>
</span>
<span>
  <%= pluralize(current_user.microposts.count, "micropost") %>
</span>
```

As in Listing 9.25, the code in Listing 10.32 uses the version of the **gravatar_for** helper defined in Listing 7.29.

Note that, as in the profile sidebar (Listing 10.20), the user info in Listing 10.32 displays the total number of microposts for the user. There's a slight difference in the display, though; in the profile sidebar, "Microposts" is a label, and showing "Microposts (1)" makes sense. In the present case, though, saying "1 microposts" is ungrammatical, so we arrange to display "1 micropost" (but "2 microposts") using **pluralize**.

We next define the form for creating microposts (Listing 10.33), which is similar to the signup form in Listing 7.17.

Listing 10.33 The form partial for creating microposts.
`app/views/shared/_micropost_form.html.erb`

```erb
<%= form_for(@micropost) do |f| %>
  <%= render 'shared/error_messages', object: f.object %>
  <div class="field">
    <%= f.text_area :content, placeholder: "Compose new micropost..." %>
  </div>
  <%= f.submit "Post", class: "btn btn-large btn-primary" %>
<% end %>
```

We need to make two changes before the form in Listing 10.33 will work. First, we need to define **@micropost**, which (as before) we do through the association:

```
@micropost = current_user.microposts.build
```

The result appears in Listing 10.34.

Listing 10.34 Adding a micropost instance variable to the **home** action.
`app/controllers/static_pages_controller.rb`

```ruby
class StaticPagesController < ApplicationController

  def home
    @micropost = current_user.microposts.build if signed_in?
  end
  .
  .
  .
end
```

The code in Listing 10.34 has the advantage that it will break the test suite if we forget to require the user to sign in.

The second change needed to get Listing 10.33 to work is to redefine the error messages partial so that

```erb
<%= render 'shared/error_messages', object: f.object %>
```

works. You may recall from Listing 7.22 that the error messages partial references the **@user** variable explicitly, but in the present case we have an **@micropost** variable instead. We should define an error messages partial that works regardless of the kind of object passed to it. Happily, the form variable **f** can access the associated object through **f.object**, so that in

```
form_for(@user) do |f|
```

f.object is **@user**, and in

```
form_for(@micropost) do |f|
```

f.object is **@micropost**.

To pass the object to the partial, we use a hash with value equal to the object and key equal to the desired name of the variable in the partial, which is what this code accomplishes:

```
<%= render 'shared/error_messages', object: f.object %>
```

In other words, **object: f.object** creates a variable called **object** in the **error_messages** partial. We can use this object to construct a customized error message, as shown in Listing 10.35.

Listing 10.35 Updating the error-messages partial from Listing 7.23 to work with other objects. **app/views/shared/_error_messages.html.erb**

```
<% if object.errors.any? %>
  <div id="error_explanation">
    <div class="alert alert-error">
      The form contains <%= pluralize(object.errors.count, "error") %>.
    </div>
    <ul>
    <% object.errors.full_messages.each do |msg| %>
      <li>* <%= msg %></li>
    <% end %>
    </ul>
  </div>
<% end %>
```

As this point, the tests in Listing 10.29 should be passing:

```
$ bundle exec rspec spec/requests/micropost_pages_spec.rb
```

Unfortunately, the User request spec is now broken because the signup and edit forms use the old version of the error messages partial. To fix them, we'll update them with the more general version, as shown in Listing 10.36 and Listing 10.37. (*Note*: Your code will differ if you implemented Listing 9.50 and Listing 9.51 from the exercises in Section 9.6. *Mutatis mutandis*.)

Listing 10.36 Updating the rendering of user signup errors.
`app/views/users/new.html.erb`

```
<% provide(:title, 'Sign up') %>
<h1>Sign up</h1>

<%= form_for(@user) do |f| %>
  <%= render 'shared/error_messages', object: f.object %>
  .
  .
  .
<% end %>
```

Listing 10.37 Updating the errors for editing users.
`app/views/users/edit.html.erb`

```
<% provide(:title, "Edit user") %>
<h1>Update your profile</h1>

<%= form_for(@user) do |f| %>
  <%= render 'shared/error_messages', object: f.object %>
  .
  .
  .
<% end %>

<%= gravatar_for(@user) %>
<a href="http://gravatar.com/emails">change</a>
```

At this point, all the tests should be passing:

```
$ bundle exec rspec spec/
```

Additionally, all the HTML in this section should render properly, showing the form as in Figure 10.11, and a form with a submission error as in Figure 10.12. You are invited

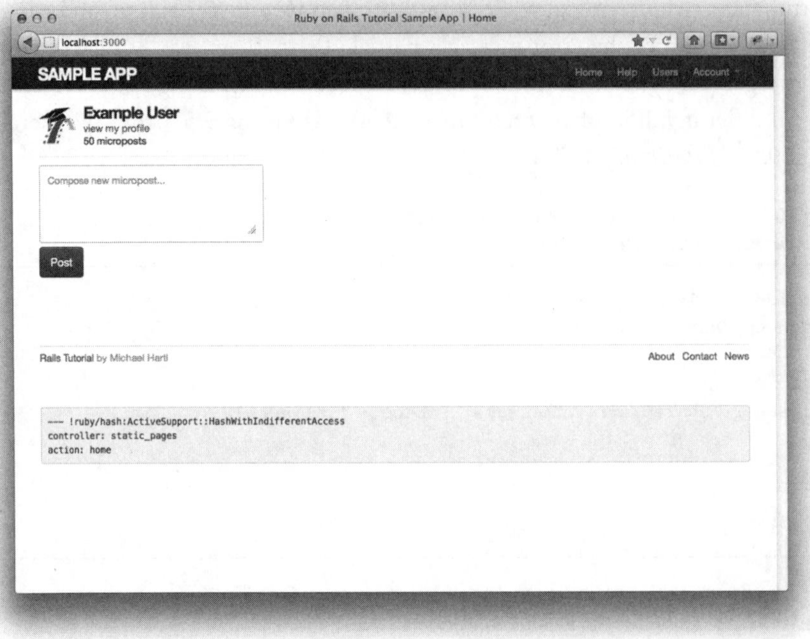

Figure 10.11   The Home page (/) with a new micropost form.

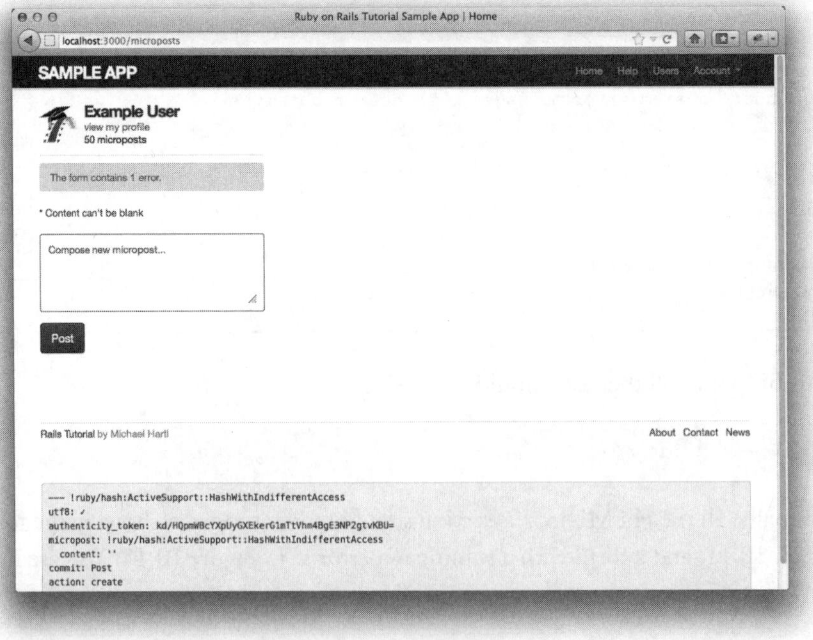

Figure 10.12   The Home page with form errors.

at this point to create a new post for yourself and verify that everything is working—but you should probably wait until after Section 10.3.3.

10.3.3   A Proto-feed

The comment at the end of Section 10.3.2 alluded to a problem: The current Home page doesn't display any microposts. If you like, you can verify that the form shown in Figure 10.11 is working by submitting a valid entry and then navigating to the profile page to see the post, but that's rather cumbersome. It would be far better to have a *feed* of microposts that includes the user's own posts, as mocked up in Figure 10.13. (In Chapter 11, we'll generalize this feed to include the microposts of users being *followed* by the current user.)

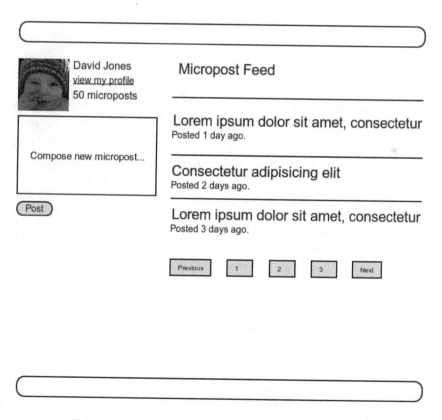

Figure 10.13   A mockup of the Home page with a proto-feed.

Since each user should have a feed, we are led naturally to a **feed** method in the User model. Eventually, we will test that the feed returns the microposts of the users being followed, but for now we'll just test that the **feed** method *includes* the current user's microposts but *excludes* the posts of a different user. We can express these requirements in code with Listing 10.38.

Listing 10.38 Tests for the (proto-)status feed.
spec/models/user_spec.rb

```ruby
require 'spec_helper'

describe User do
  .
  .
  .
  it { should respond_to(:microposts) }
  it { should respond_to(:feed) }
  .
  .
  .
  describe "micropost associations" do

    before { @user.save }
    let!(:older_micropost) do
      FactoryGirl.create(:micropost, user: @user, created_at: 1.day.ago)
    end
    let!(:newer_micropost) do
      FactoryGirl.create(:micropost, user: @user, created_at: 1.hour.ago)
    end
    .
    .
    .
    describe "status" do
      let(:unfollowed_post) do
        FactoryGirl.create(:micropost, user: FactoryGirl.create(:user))
      end

      its(:feed) { should include(newer_micropost) }
      its(:feed) { should include(older_micropost) }
      its(:feed) { should_not include(unfollowed_post) }
    end
  end
end
```

These tests introduce (via the RSpec boolean convention) the array **include?** method, which simply checks if an array includes the given element:[9]

```
$ rails console
>> a = [1, "foo", :bar]
>> a.include?("foo")
=> true
>> a.include?(:bar)
=> true
>> a.include?("baz")
=> false
```

This example shows just how flexible the RSpec boolean convention is; even though **include** is already a Ruby keyword (used to include a module, as seen in, e.g., Listing 8.14), in this context RSpec correctly guesses that we want to test array inclusion.

We can arrange for an appropriate micropost **feed** method by selecting all the microposts with **user_id** equal to the current user's id, which we accomplish using the **where** method on the **Micropost** model, as shown in Listing 10.39.[10]

Listing 10.39 A preliminary implementation for the micropost status feed.
app/models/user.rb

```
class User < ActiveRecord::Base
  .
  .
  def feed
    # This is preliminary. See "Following users" for the full implementation.
    Micropost.where("user_id = ?", id)
  end
  .
  .
end
```

---

9. Learning about methods such as **include?** is one reason why, as noted in Section 1.1.1, I recommend reading a pure Ruby book after finishing this one.

10. See the Rails Guide on the Active Record Query Interface for more on **where** and the like.

The question mark in

```
Micropost.where("user_id = ?", id)
```

ensures that **id** is properly *escaped* before being included in the underlying SQL query, thereby avoiding a serious security hole called *SQL injection*. The **id** attribute here is just an integer, so there is no danger in this case, but *always* escaping variables injected into SQL statements is a good habit to cultivate.

Alert readers might note at this point that the code in Listing 10.39 is essentially equivalent to writing

```
def feed
  microposts
end
```

We've used the code in Listing 10.39 instead because it generalizes much more naturally to the full status feed needed in Chapter 11.

To test the display of the status feed, we first create a couple of microposts and then verify that a list element (**li**) appears on the page for each one (Listing 10.40).

Listing 10.40 A test for rendering the feed on the Home page.
spec/requests/static_pages_spec.rb

```
require 'spec_helper'

describe "Static pages" do

  subject { page }

  describe "Home page" do
    .
    .
    .
    describe "for signed-in users" do
      let(:user) { FactoryGirl.create(:user) }
      before do
        FactoryGirl.create(:micropost, user: user, content: "Lorem ipsum")
        FactoryGirl.create(:micropost, user: user, content: "Dolor sit amet")
        sign_in user
        visit root_path
      end
```

```
      it "should render the user's feed" do
        user.feed.each do |item|
          page.should have_selector("li##{item.id}", text: item.content)
        end
      end
    end
  end
  .
  .
  .
end
```

Listing 10.40 assumes that each feed item has a unique CSS id, so that

```
page.should have_selector("li##{item.id}", text: item.content)
```

will generate a match for each item. (Note that the first **#** in **li##{item.id}** is Capybara syntax for a CSS id, whereas the second **#** is the beginning of a Ruby string interpolation **#{}**.)

To use the feed in the sample application, we add an **@feed_items** instance variable for the current user's (paginated) feed, as in Listing 10.41, and then add a feed partial (Listing 10.42) to the Home page (Listing 10.44). (Adding tests for pagination is left as an exercise; see Section 10.5.)

Listing 10.41 Adding a feed instance variable to the **home** action.
app/controllers/static_pages_controller.rb

```
class StaticPagesController < ApplicationController

  def home
    if signed_in?
      @micropost  = current_user.microposts.build
      @feed_items = current_user.feed.paginate(page: params[:page])
    end
  end
  .
  .
  .
end
```

Listing 10.42 The status feed partial.
`app/views/shared/_feed.html.erb`

```erb
<% if @feed_items.any? %>
  <ol class="microposts">
    <%= render partial: 'shared/feed_item', collection: @feed_items %>
  </ol>
  <%= will_paginate @feed_items %>
<% end %>
```

The status feed partial defers the feed item rendering to a feed item partial using the code

```erb
<%= render partial: 'shared/feed_item', collection: @feed_items %>
```

Here we pass a `:collection` parameter with the feed items, which causes **render** to use the given partial (`'feed_item'` in this case) to render each item in the collection. (We have omitted the `:partial` parameter in previous renderings, writing, e.g., **render** `'shared/micropost'`, but with a `:collection` parameter that syntax doesn't work.) The feed item partial itself appears in Listing 10.43.

Listing 10.43 A partial for a single feed item.
`app/views/shared/_feed_item.html.erb`

```erb
<li id="<%= feed_item.id %>">
  <%= link_to gravatar_for(feed_item.user), feed_item.user %>
  <span class="user">
    <%= link_to feed_item.user.name, feed_item.user %>
  </span>
  <span class="content"><%= feed_item.content %></span>
  <span class="timestamp">
    Posted <%= time_ago_in_words(feed_item.created_at) %> ago.
  </span>
</li>
```

Listing 10.43 also adds a CSS id for each feed item using

```erb
<li id="<%= feed_item.id %>">
```

as required by the test in Listing 10.40.

We can then add the feed to the Home page by rendering the feed partial as usual (Listing 10.44). The result is a display of the feed on the Home page, as required (Figure 10.14).

Listing 10.44 Adding a status feed to the Home page.
`app/views/static_pages/home.html.erb`

```erb
<% if signed_in? %>
  <div class="row">
    .
    .
    .
    <div class="span8">
      <h3>Micropost Feed</h3>
      <%= render 'shared/feed' %>
    </div>
  </div>
<% else %>
  .
  .
  .
<% end %>
```

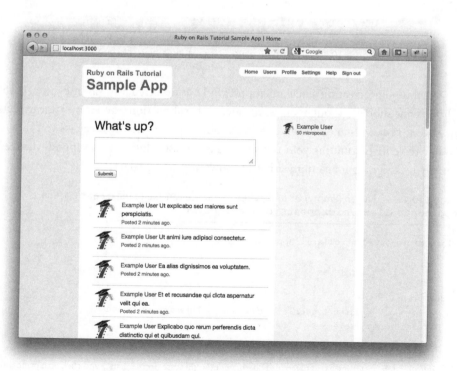

Figure 10.14   The Home page (/) with a proto-feed.

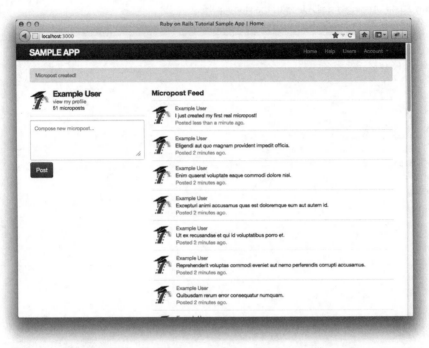

Figure 10.15   The Home page after creating a new micropost.

At this point, creating a new micropost works as expected, as seen in Figure 10.15. There is one subtlety, though: on *failed* micropost submission, the Home page expects an **@feed_items** instance variable, so failed submissions currently break (as you should be able to verify by running your test suite). The easiest solution is to suppress the feed entirely by assigning it an empty array, as shown in Listing 10.45.[11]

Listing 10.45 Adding an (empty) **@feed_items** instance variable to the **create** action.
app/controllers/microposts_controller.rb

```
class MicropostsController < ApplicationController
  .
  .
  .
  def create
    @micropost = current_user.microposts.build(params[:micropost])
    if @micropost.save
```

---

11. Unfortunately, returning a paginated feed doesn't work in this case. Implement it and click on a pagination link to see why.

```
      flash[:success] = "Micropost created!"
      redirect_to root_path
    else
      @feed_items = []
      render 'static_pages/home'
    end
  end
  .
  .
  .
end
```

At this point, the proto-feed should be working, and the test suite should pass:

```
$ bundle exec rspec spec/
```

10.3.4 Destroying Microposts

The last piece of functionality to add to the Microposts resource is the ability to destroy posts. As with user deletion (Section 9.4.2), we accomplish this with "delete" links, as mocked up in Figure 10.16. Unlike that case, which restricted user destruction to admin users, the delete links will work only for microposts created by the current user.

Our first step is to add a delete link to the micropost partial as in Listing 10.43, and while we're at it we'll add a similar link to the feed item partial from Listing 10.43. The results appear in Listing 10.46 and Listing 10.47. (The two cases are almost identical, and eliminating this duplication is left as an exercise (Section 10.5).)

Listing 10.46 Adding a delete link to the micropost partial.
app/views/microposts/_micropost.html.erb

```
<li>
  <span class="content"><%= micropost.content %></span>
  <span class="timestamp">
    Posted <%= time_ago_in_words(micropost.created_at) %> ago.
  </span>
  <% if current_user?(micropost.user) %>
    <%= link_to "delete", micropost, method: :delete,
                                     confirm: "You sure?",
                                     title:  micropost.content %>
  <% end %>
</li>
```

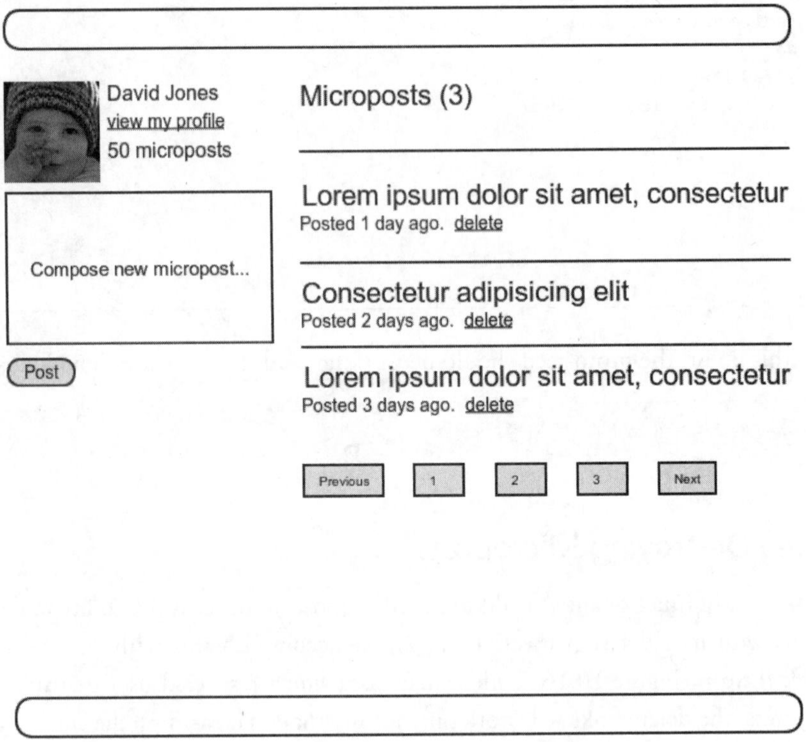

Figure 10.16 A mockup of the proto-feed with micropost delete links.

Listing 10.47 The feed item partial with added delete link.
app/views/shared/_feed_item.html.erb

```
<li id="<%= feed_item.id %>">
  <%= link_to gravatar_for(feed_item.user), feed_item.user %>
    <span class="user">
      <%= link_to feed_item.user.name, feed_item.user %>
    </span>
    <span class="content"><%= feed_item.content %></span>
    <span class="timestamp">
      Posted <%= time_ago_in_words(feed_item.created_at) %> ago.
    </span>
  <% if current_user?(feed_item.user) %>
    <%= link_to "delete", feed_item, method:  :delete,
                                     confirm: "You sure?",
                                     title:   feed_item.content %>
  <% end %>
</li>
```

The test for destroying microposts uses Capybara to click the "delete" link and expects the Micropost count to decrease by 1 (Listing 10.48).

Listing 10.48 Tests for the Microposts controller **destroy** action.
`spec/requests/micropost_pages_spec.rb`

```
require 'spec_helper'

describe "Micropost pages" do
  .
  .
  .
  describe "micropost destruction" do
    before { FactoryGirl.create(:micropost, user: user) }

    describe "as correct user" do
      before { visit root_path }

      it "should delete a micropost" do
        expect { click_link "delete" }.should change(Micropost, :count).by(-1)
      end
    end
  end
end
```

The application code is also analogous to the user case in Listing 9.48; the main difference is that, rather than using an **admin_user** before filter, in the case of microposts we have a **correct_user** before filter to check that the current user actually has a micropost with the given id. The code appears in Listing 10.49, and the result of destroying the second-most-recent post appears in Figure 10.17.

Listing 10.49 The Microposts controller **destroy** action.
`app/controllers/microposts_controller.rb`

```
class MicropostsController < ApplicationController
  before_filter :signed_in_user, only: [:create, :destroy]
  before_filter :correct_user,   only: :destroy
  .
  .
  .
  def destroy
    @micropost.destroy
    redirect_back_or root_path
  end
```

```
  private

    def correct_user
      @micropost = current_user.microposts.find_by_id(params[:id])
      redirect_to root_path if @micropost.nil?
    end
end
```

In the **correct_user** before filter, note that we find microposts *through* the association:

```
current_user.microposts.find_by_id(params[:id])
```

This automatically ensures that we find only microposts belonging to the current user. In this case, we use **find_by_id** instead of **find** because the latter raises an exception when the micropost doesn't exist instead of returning **nil**. By the way, if you're comfortable with exceptions in Ruby, you could also write the **correct_user** filter like this:

```
def correct_user
  @micropost = current_user.microposts.find(params[:id])
rescue
  redirect_to root_path
end
```

It might occur to you that we could implement the **correct_user** filter using the **Micropost** model directly, like this:

```
@micropost = Micropost.find_by_id(params[:id])
redirect_to root_path unless current_user?(@micropost.user)
```

This would be equivalent to the code in Listing 10.49, but, as explained by Wolfram Arnold in the blog post Access Control 101 in Rails and the Citibank Hack, for security purposes it is a good practice always to run lookups through the association.

With the code in this section, our Micropost model and interface are complete, and the test suite should pass:

```
$ bundle exec rspec spec/
```

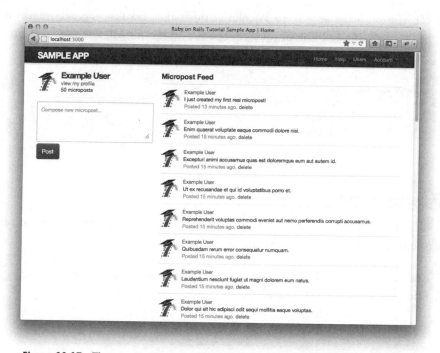

Figure 10.17 The user Home page after deleting the second-most-recent micropost.

10.4 Conclusion

With the addition of the Microposts resource, we are nearly finished with our sample application. All that remains is to add a social layer by letting users follow each other. We'll learn how to model such user relationships and see the implications for the status feed in Chapter 11.

Before proceeding, be sure to commit and merge your changes if you're using Git for version control:

```
$ git add .
$ git commit -m "Add user microposts"
$ git checkout master
$ git merge user-microposts
$ git push
```

You can also push the app up to Heroku at this point. Because the data model has changed through the addition of the **microposts** table, you will also need to migrate the production database:

```
$ git push heroku
$ heroku pg:reset SHARED_DATABASE --confirm <name-heroku-gave-to-your-app>
$ heroku run rake db:migrate
$ heroku run rake db:populate
```

10.5 Exercises

We've covered enough material now that there is a combinatorial explosion of possible extensions to the application. Below are just a few of the many possibilities.

1. Add tests for the sidebar micropost counts (including proper pluralization).
2. Add tests for micropost pagination.

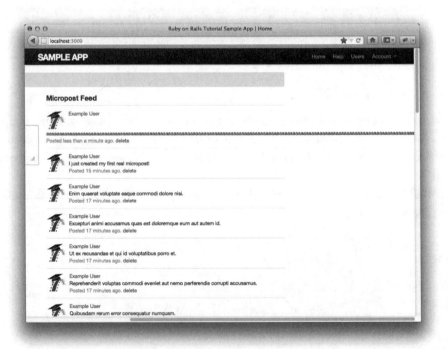

Figure 10.18 The (broken) site layout with a particularly long word.

3. Refactor the Home page to use separate partials for the two branches of the `if-else` statement.

4. Write a test to make sure delete links do not appear for microposts not created by the current user.

5. Using partials, eliminate the duplication in the delete links from Listing 10.46 and Listing 10.47.

6. Very long words currently break our layout, as shown in Figure 10.18. Fix this problem using the **wrap** helper defined in Listing 10.50. Note the use of the **raw** method to prevent Rails from escaping the resulting HTML, together with the **sanitize** method needed to prevent cross-site scripting. This code also uses the strange-looking but useful *ternary operator* (Box 10.1).

7. **(challenging)** Add a JavaScript display to the Home page to count down from 140 characters.

Listing 10.50 A helper to wrap long words.
`app/helpers/microposts_helper.rb`

```
module MicropostsHelper

  def wrap(content)
    sanitize(raw(content.split.map{ |s| wrap_long_string(s) }.join(' ')))
  end

  private

    def wrap_long_string(text, max_width = 30)
      zero_width_space = "&#8203;"
      regex = /.{1,#{max_width}}/
      (text.length < max_width) ? text :
                                  text.scan(regex).join(zero_width_space)
    end
end
```

Box 10.1 Ten Types of People

There are ten kinds of people in the world: Those who like the ternary operator, those who don't, and those who don't know about it. (If you happen to be in the third category, soon you won't be any longer.)

When you do a lot of programming, you quickly learn that one of the most common bits of control flow goes something like this:

```
if boolean?
  do_one_thing
else
  do_something_else end
```

Ruby, like many other languages (including C/C++, Perl, PHP, and Java), allows you to replace this with a much more compact expression using the *ternary operator* (so called because it consists of three parts):

```
boolean? ? do_one_thing : do_something_else
```

You can also use the ternary operator to replace assignment:

```
if boolean?
  var = foo
else
  var = bar
end
```

becomes

```
var = boolean? ? foo : bar
```

Another common use is in a function's return value:

```
def foo
  do_stuff
  boolean? ? "bar" : "baz" end
```

Since Ruby implicitly returns the value of the last expression in a function, here the foo method returns "bar" or "baz" depending on the value of boolean?. It is this final construction that appears in Listing 10.50.

CHAPTER 11
Following Users

In this chapter, we will complete the core sample application by adding a social layer that allows users to follow (and unfollow) other users, resulting in each user's Home page displaying a status feed of the followed users' microposts. We will also make views to display both a user's followers and the users each user is following. We will learn how to model relationships between users in Section 11.1, then make the web interface in Section 11.2 (including an introduction to Ajax). Finally, we'll end by developing a fully functional status feed in Section 11.3.

This final chapter contains some of the most challenging material in the tutorial, including some Ruby/SQL trickery to make the status feed. Through these examples, you will see how Rails can handle even rather intricate data models, which should serve you well as you go on to develop your own applications with their own specific requirements. To help with the transition from tutorial to independent development, Section 11.4 contains suggested extensions to the core sample application, along with pointers to more advanced resources.

As usual, Git users should create a new topic branch:

```
$ git checkout -b following-users
```

Because the material in this chapter is particularly challenging, before writing any code, we'll pause for a moment and take a tour of the interface. As in previous chapters, at this early stage we'll represent pages using mockups.[1] The full page flow runs as follows: A user (John Calvin) starts at his profile page (Figure 11.1) and navigates to

---

[1]. The photographs in the mockup tour are from www.flickr.com/photos/john_lustig/2518452221 and www.flickr.com/photos/30775272@N05/2884963755.

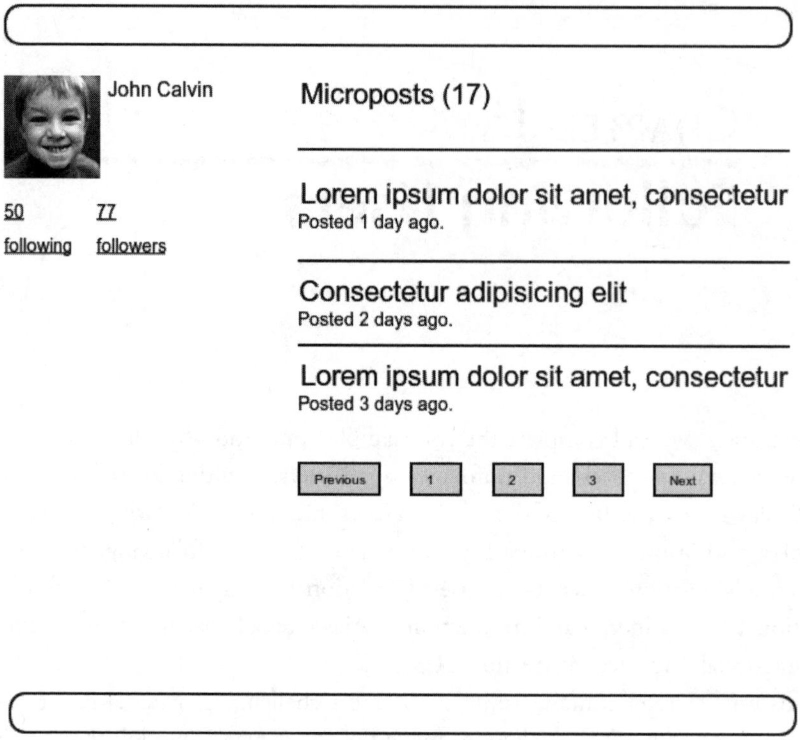

Figure 11.1 The current user's profile.

the Users page (Figure 11.2) to select a user to follow. Calvin navigates to the profile of a second user, Thomas Hobbes (Figure 11.3), clicking on the "Follow" button to follow that user. This changes the "Follow" button to "Unfollow" and increments Hobbes's "followers" count by one (Figure 11.4). Navigating to his Home page, Calvin now sees an incremented "following" count and finds Hobbes's microposts in his status feed (Figure 11.5). The rest of this chapter is dedicated to making this page flow actually work.

11.1 The Relationship Model

Our first step in implementing following users is to construct a data model, which is not as straightforward as it seems. Naïvely, it seems that a **has_many** relationship should do: A user **has_many** followed users and **has_many** followers. As we will see, there is a problem with this approach, and we'll learn how to fix it using **has_many through**.

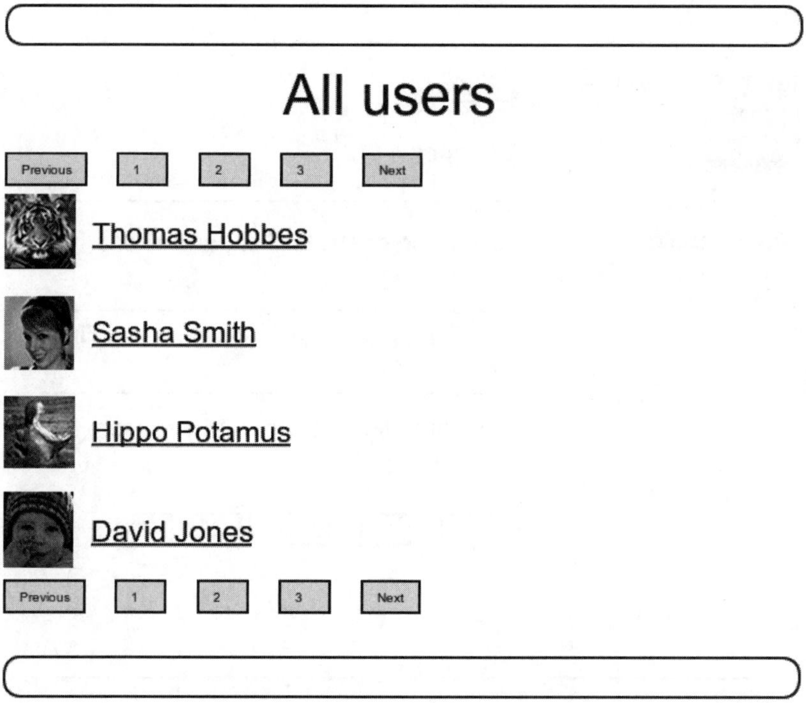

Figure 11.2 Finding a user to follow.

It's likely that many of the ideas in this section won't seem obvious at first, and it may take a while for the rather complicated data model to sink in. If you find yourself getting confused, try pushing forward to the end, then read the section a second time through to see if things are clearer.

11.1.1 A Problem with the Data Model (and a Solution)

As a first step toward constructing a data model for following users, let's examine a typical case. For instance, consider a user who follows a second user: We could say that, e.g., Calvin is following Hobbes, and Hobbes is followed by Calvin, so that Calvin is the *follower* and Hobbes is *followed*. Using Rails' default pluralization convention, the set of all users following a given user is that user's *followers*, and `user.followers` is an array of those users. Unfortunately, the reverse doesn't work: By default, the set of all followed users would be called the *followeds*, which is ungrammatical and clumsy.

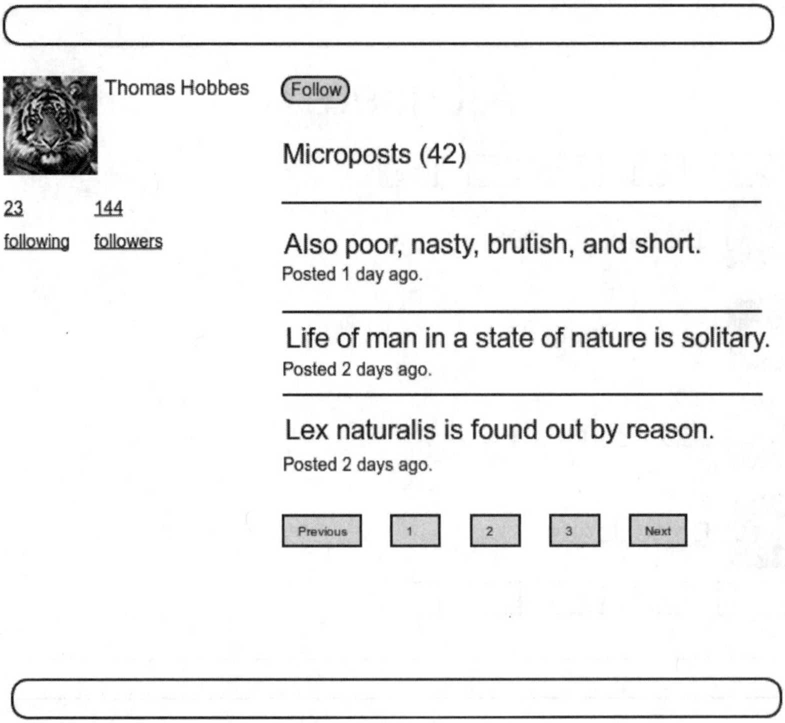

Figure 11.3 The profile of a user to follow, with a follow button.

We could call them *following*, but that's ambiguous: In normal English, a "following" is the set of people following *you*, i.e., your followers—exactly the opposite of the intended meaning. Although we will use "following" as a label, as in "50 following, 75 followers," we'll use "followed users" for the users themselves, with a corresponding `user.followed_users` array.[2]

This discussion suggests modeling the followed users as in Figure 11.6, with a `followed_users` table and a `has_many` association. Since `user.followed_users` should be an array of users, each row of the `followed_users` table would need to be a user, as identified by the `followed_id`, together with the `follower_id` to establish

---

2. The first edition of this book used the `user.following` terminology, which even I found confusing at times. Thanks to reader Cosmo Lee for convincing me to change the terminology and for offering suggestions on how to make it clearer. (I didn't follow his exact advice, though, so if it's still confusing he bears none of the blame.)

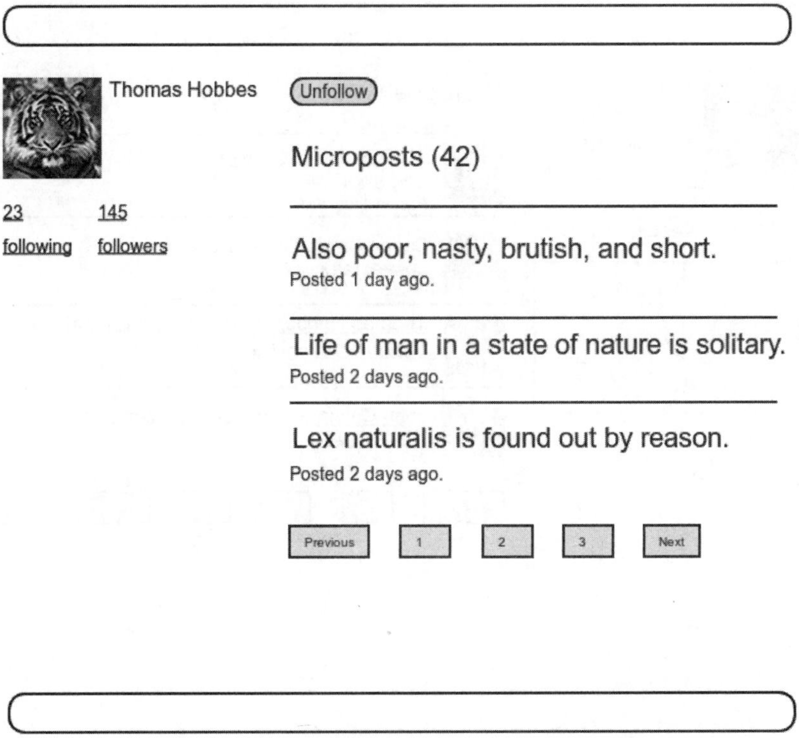

Figure 11.4   A profile with an unfollow button and incremented followers count.

the association.[3] In addition, since each row is a user, we would need to include the user's other attributes, including the name, password, etc.

The problem with the data model in Figure 11.6 is that it is terribly redundant: Each row contains not only each followed user's id, but all their other information as well—all of which are *already* in the **users** table. Even worse, to model user *followers* we would need a separate, similarly redundant **followers** table. Finally, this data model is a maintainability nightmare: Each time a user changed (say) his name, we would need to update not just the user's record in the **users** table but also *every row containing that user* in both the **followed_users** and **followers** tables.

The problem here is that we are missing an underlying abstraction. One way to find the proper abstraction is to consider how we might implement the act of *following*

---

3. For simplicity, Figure 11.6 suppresses the **followed_users** table's **id** column.

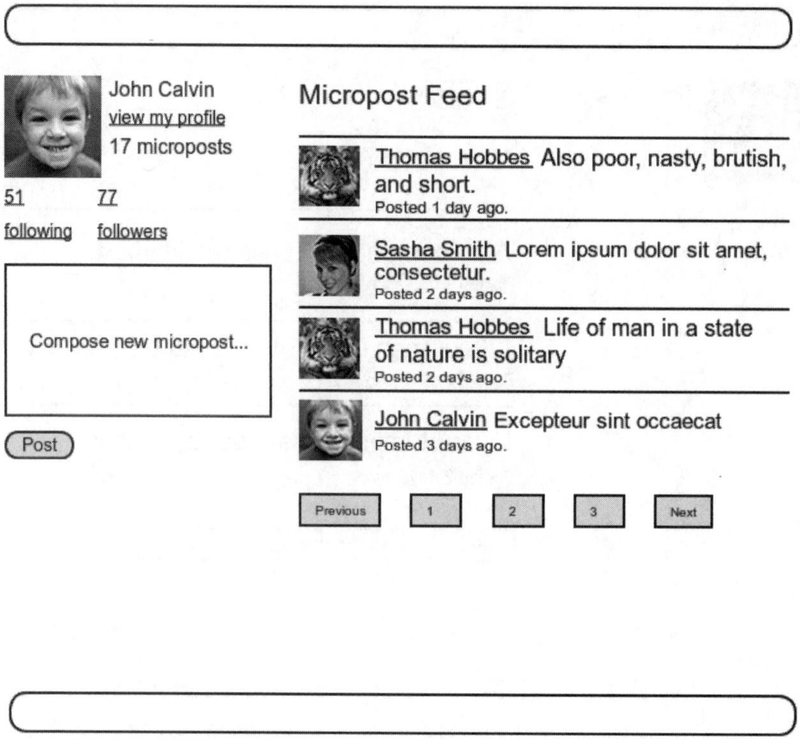

Figure 11.5 The Home page with status feed and incremented following count.

in a web application. Recall from Section 7.1.2 that the REST architecture involves *resources* that are created and destroyed. This leads us to ask two questions: When a user follows another user, what is being created? When a user *un*follows another user, what is being destroyed?

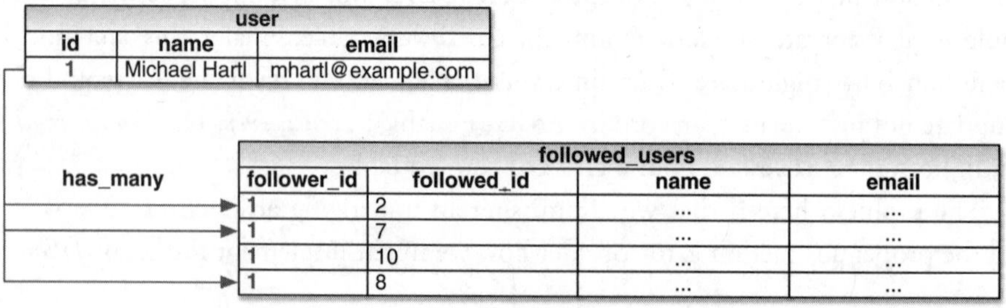

user		
id	name	email
1	Michael Hartl	mhartl@example.com

	followed_users			
	follower_id	followed_id	name	email
has_many	1	2	...	...
	1	7	...	...
	1	10	...	...
	1	8	...	...

Figure 11.6 A naïve implementation of user following.

Upon reflection, we see that in these cases the application should either create or destroy a *relationship* between two users. A user then **has_many :relationships**, and has many **followed_users** (or **followers**) *through* these relationships. Indeed, Figure 11.6 already contains most of the implementation: Since each followed user is uniquely identified by **followed_id**, we could convert **followed_users** to a **relationships** table, omit the user details and use **followed_id** to retrieve the followed user from the **users** table. Moreover, by considering *reverse* relationships, we could use the **follower_id** column to extract an array of user's followers.

To make a **followed_users** array of users, it would be possible to pull out an array of **followed_id** attributes and then find the user for each one. As you might expect, though, Rails has a way to make this procedure more convenient, and the relevant technique is known as **has_many through**. As we will see in Section 11.1.4, Rails allows us to say that a user is following many users *through* the relationships table, using the succinct code

```
has_many :followed_users, through: :relationships, source: "followed_id"
```

This code automatically populates **user.followed_users** with an array of followed users. A diagram of the data model appears in Figure 11.7.

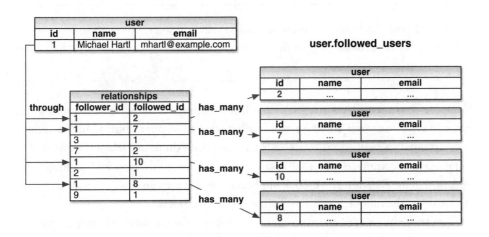

```
User has_many :followed_users, through: :relationships,
                                   source: "followed_id"
```

Figure 11.7   A model of followed users through user relationships.

To get started with the implementation, we first generate a Relationship model as follows:

```
$ rails generate model Relationship follower_id:integer followed_id:integer
```

Since we will be finding relationships by **follower_id** and by **followed_id**, we should add an index on each column for efficiency, as shown in Listing 11.1.

Listing 11.1 Adding indices for the **relationships** table.
db/migrate/[timestamp]_create_relationships.rb

```ruby
class CreateRelationships < ActiveRecord::Migration
  def change
    create_table :relationships do |t|
      t.integer :follower_id
      t.integer :followed_id

      t.timestamps
    end

    add_index :relationships, :follower_id
    add_index :relationships, :followed_id
    add_index :relationships, [:follower_id, :followed_id], unique: true
  end
end
```

Listing 11.1 also includes a *composite* index that enforces uniqueness of pairs of (**follower_id**, **followed_id**), so that a user can't follow another user more than once:

```
add_index :relationships, [:follower_id, :followed_id], unique: true
```

(Compare to the email uniqueness index from Listing 6.22.) As we'll see starting in Section 11.1.4, our user interface won't allow this to happen, but adding a unique index arranges to raise an error if a user tries to create duplicate relationships anyway (using, e.g., a command-line tool such as curl). We could also add a uniqueness validation to the Relationship model, but because it is *always* an error to create duplicate relationships, the unique index is sufficient for our purposes.

To create the **relationships** table, we migrate the database and prepare the test database as usual:

```
$ bundle exec rake db:migrate
$ bundle exec rake db:test:prepare
```

The result is the Relationship data model shown in Figure 11.8.

relationships	
id	integer
follower_id	integer
followed_id	integer
created_at	datetime
updated_at	datetime

Figure 11.8 The Relationship data model.

11.1.2 User/Relationship Associations

Before implementing followed users and followers, we first need to establish the association between users and relationships. A user **has_many** relationships, and—since relationships involve *two* users—a relationship **belongs_to** both a follower and a followed user.

As with microposts in Section 10.1.3, we will create new relationships using the user association, with code such as

```
user.relationships.build(followed_id: ...)
```

We start with some tests, shown in Listing 11.2, which make a **relationship** variable, checks that it is valid, and ensures that the **follower_id** isn't accessible. (If the test for accessible attributes doesn't fail, be sure that your **application.rb** has been updated in accordance with Listing 10.6.)

Listing 11.2 Testing Relationship creation and attributes.
spec/models/relationship_spec.rb

```ruby
require 'spec_helper'

describe Relationship do

  let(:follower) { FactoryGirl.create(:user) }
  let(:followed) { FactoryGirl.create(:user) }
  let(:relationship) { follower.relationships.build(followed_id: followed.id) }

  subject { relationship }

  it { should be_valid }

  describe "accessible attributes" do
    it "should not allow access to follower_id" do
      expect do
```

```
        Relationship.new(follower_id: follower.id)
      end.should raise_error(ActiveModel::MassAssignmentSecurity::Error)
    end
  end
end
```

Note that, unlike the tests for the User and Micropost models, which use **@user** and **@micropost**, respectively, Listing 11.2 uses **let** in preference to an instance variable. The differences rarely matter,[4] but I consider **let** to be cleaner than using an instance variable. We originally used instance variables both because instance variables are important to introduce early and because **let** is a little more advanced.

We should also test the User model for a **relationships** attribute, as shown in Listing 11.3.

Listing 11.3 Testing for the **user.relationships** attribute.
spec/models/user_spec.rb

```
require 'spec_helper'

describe User do
  .
  .
  .
  it { should respond_to(:feed) }
  it { should respond_to(:relationships) }
  .
  .
  .
end
```

At this point, you might expect application code as in Section 10.1.3, and it's similar, but there is one critical difference: In the case of the Micropost model, we could say

```
class Micropost < ActiveRecord::Base
  belongs_to :user
  .
  .
  .
end
```

---

4. See the discussion on when to use let at Stack Overflow for more information.

and

```
class User < ActiveRecord::Base
  has_many :microposts
  .
  .
  .
end
```

because the **microposts** table has a **user_id** attribute to identify the user (Section 10.1.1). An id used in this manner to connect two database tables is known as a *foreign key*, and when the foreign key for a User model object is **user_id**, Rails infers the association automatically: By default, Rails expects a foreign key of the form **<class>_id**, where **<class>** is the lowercase version of the class name.[5] In the present case, although we are still dealing with users, they are now identified with the foreign key **follower_id**, so we have to tell that to Rails, as shown in Listing 11.4.[6]

Listing 11.4 Implementing the user/relationships **has_many** association.
app/models/user.rb

```
class User < ActiveRecord::Base
  .
  .
  has_many :microposts, dependent: :destroy
  has_many :relationships, foreign_key: "follower_id", dependent: :destroy
  .
  .
end
```

Since destroying a user should also destroy that user's relationships, we've gone ahead and added **dependent: :destroy** to the association; writing a test for this is left as an exercise (Section 11.5).

As with the Micropost model, the Relationship model has a **belongs_to** relationship with users; in this case, a relationship object belongs to both a **follower** and a **followed** user, which we test for in Listing 11.5.

---

5. Technically, Rails uses the **underscore** method to convert the class name to an id. For example, **"FooBar".underscore** is **"foo_bar"**, so the foreign key for a **FooBar** object would be **foo_bar_id**. (Incidentally, the inverse of **underscore** is **camelize**, which converts **"camel_case"** to **"CamelCase"**.)

6. If you've noticed that **followed_id** also identifies a user and are concerned about the asymmetric treatment of followed and follower, you're ahead of the game. We'll deal with this issue in Section 11.1.5.

Listing 11.5 Testing the user/relationships **belongs_to** association.
spec/models/relationship_spec.rb

```
describe Relationship do
  .
  .
  .
  describe "follower methods" do
    it { should respond_to(:follower) }
    it { should respond_to(:followed) }
    its(:follower) { should == follower }
    its(:followed) { should == followed }
  end
end
```

To write the application code, we define the **belongs_to** relationship as usual. Rails infers the names of the foreign keys from the corresponding symbols (i.e., **follower_id** from **:follower**, and **followed_id** from **:followed**), but since there is neither a Followed nor a Follower model we need to supply the class name **User**. The result is shown in Listing 11.6. Note that, unlike the default generate Relationship model, in this case only the **followed_id** is accessible.

Listing 11.6 Adding the **belongs_to** associations to the Relationship model.
app/models/relationship.rb

```
class Relationship < ActiveRecord::Base
  attr_accessible :followed_id

  belongs_to :follower, class_name: "User"
  belongs_to :followed, class_name: "User"
end
```

The **followed** association isn't actually needed until Section 11.1.5, but the parallel follower/followed structure is clearer if we implement them both at the same time.

At this point, the tests in Listing 11.2 and Listing 11.3 should pass.

```
$ bundle exec rspec spec/
```

11.1.3 Validations

Before moving on, we'll add a couple of Relationship model validations for completeness. The tests (Listing 11.7) and application code (Listing 11.8) are straightforward.

Listing 11.7 Testing the Relationship model validations.
spec/models/relationship_spec.rb

```ruby
describe Relationship do
  .
  .
  .
  describe "when followed id is not present" do
    before { relationship.followed_id = nil }
    it { should_not be_valid }
  end

  describe "when follower id is not present" do
    before { relationship.follower_id = nil }
    it { should_not be_valid }
  end
end
```

Listing 11.8 Adding the Relationship model validations.
app/models/relationship.rb

```ruby
class Relationship < ActiveRecord::Base
  attr_accessible :followed_id

  belongs_to :follower, class_name: "User"
  belongs_to :followed, class_name: "User"

  validates :follower_id, presence: true
  validates :followed_id, presence: true
end
```

11.1.4 Followed users

We come now to the heart of the Relationship associations: **followed_users** and **followers**. We start with **followed_users**, as shown Listing 11.9.

Listing 11.9 A test for the `user.followed_users` attribute.
`spec/models/user_spec.rb`

```
require 'spec_helper'

describe User do
  .
  .
  .
  it { should respond_to(:relationships) }
  it { should respond_to(:followed_users) }
  .
  .
  .
end
```

The implementation uses **has_many through** for the first time: A user has many following *through* relationships, as illustrated in Figure 11.7. By default, in a **has_many through** association Rails looks for a foreign key corresponding to the singular version of the association; in other words, code like

```
has_many :followeds, through: :relationships
```

would assemble an array using the **followed_id** in the **relationships** table. But, as noted in Section 11.1.1, **user.followeds** is rather awkward; far more natural is to use "followed users" as a plural of "followed," and write instead **user.followed_users** for the array of followed users. Naturally, Rails allows us to override the default, in this case using the **:source** parameter (Listing 11.10), which explicitly tells Rails that the source of the **followed_users** array is the set of **followed** ids.

Listing 11.10 Adding the User model **followed_users** association.
`app/models/user.rb`

```
class User < ActiveRecord::Base
  .
  .
  .
  has_many :microposts, dependent: :destroy
  has_many :relationships, foreign_key: "follower_id", dependent: :destroy
  has_many :followed_users, through: :relationships, source: :followed
  .
  .
  .
end
```

To create a following relationship, we'll introduce a **follow!** utility method so that we can write **user.follow!(other_user)**. (This **follow!** method should always work, so, as with **create!** and **save!**, we indicate with an exclamation point that an exception will be raised on failure.) We'll also add an associated **following?** boolean method to test if one user is following another.[7] The tests in Listing 11.11 show how we expect these methods to be used in practice.

Listing 11.11 Tests for some "following" utility methods.
spec/models/user_spec.rb

```
require 'spec_helper'

describe User do
  .
  .
  .
  it { should respond_to(:followed_users) }
  it { should respond_to(:following?) }
  it { should respond_to(:follow!) }
  .
  .
  .
  describe "following" do
    let(:other_user) { FactoryGirl.create(:user) }
    before do
      @user.save
      @user.follow!(other_user)
    end

    it { should be_following(other_user) }
    its(:followed_users) { should include(other_user) }
  end
end
```

In the application code, the **following?** method takes in a user, called **other_user**, and checks to see if a followed user with that id exists in the database; the **follow!** method calls **create!** through the **relationships** association to create the following relationship. The results appear in Listing 11.12.

---

7. Once you have a lot of experience modeling a particular domain, you can often guess such utility methods in advance, and even when you can't, you'll often find yourself writing them to make the tests cleaner. In this case, though, it's OK if you wouldn't have guessed them. Software development is usually an iterative process—you write code until it starts getting ugly, and then you refactor it—but for brevity the tutorial presentation is streamlined a bit.

Listing 11.12 The **following?** and **follow!** utility methods.
app/models/user.rb

```ruby
class User < ActiveRecord::Base
  .
  .
  .
  def feed
    .
    .
    .
  end

  def following?(other_user)
    relationships.find_by_followed_id(other_user.id)
  end

  def follow!(other_user)
    relationships.create!(followed_id: other_user.id)
  end
  .
  .
  .
end
```

Note that in Listing 11.12 we have omitted the user itself, writing just

```ruby
relationships.create!(...)
```

instead of the equivalent code

```ruby
self.relationships.create!(...)
```

Whether to include the explicit **self** is largely a matter of taste.

Of course, users should be able to unfollow other users as well as follow them, which leads to the somewhat predictable **unfollow!** method, as shown in Listing 11.13.[8]

---

8. The **unfollow!** method *doesn't* raise an exception on failure—in fact, I don't even know how Rails indicates a failed destroy—but we use an exclamation point to maintain the symmetry with **follow!**.

Listing 11.13 A test for unfollowing a user.
`spec/models/user_spec.rb`

```ruby
require 'spec_helper'

describe User do
  .
  .
  .
  it { should respond_to(:follow!) }
  it { should respond_to(:unfollow!) }
  .
  .
  .
  describe "following" do
    .
    .
    .
    describe "and unfollowing" do
      before { @user.unfollow!(other_user) }

      it { should_not be_following(other_user) }
      its(:followed_users) { should_not include(other_user) }
    end
  end
end
```

The code for **`unfollow!`** is straightforward: Just find the relationship by followed id and destroy it (Listing 11.14).

Listing 11.14 Unfollowing a user by destroying a user relationship.
`app/models/user.rb`

```ruby
class User < ActiveRecord::Base
  .
  .
  .
  def following?(other_user)
    relationships.find_by_followed_id(other_user.id)
  end

  def follow!(other_user)
    relationships.create!(followed_id: other_user.id)
  end
```

```
def unfollow!(other_user)
  relationships.find_by_followed_id(other_user.id).destroy
end
  .
  .
  .

end
```

11.1.5 Followers

The final piece of the relationships puzzle is to add a **user.followers** method to go with **user.followed_users**. You may have noticed from Figure 11.7 that all the information needed to extract an array of followers is already present in the **relationships** table. Indeed, the technique is exactly the same as for user following, with the roles of **follower_id** and **followed_id** reversed. This suggests that, if we could somehow arrange for a **reverse_relationships** table with those two columns reversed (Figure 11.9), we could implement **user.followers** with little effort.

We begin with the tests, having faith that the magic of Rails will come to the rescue (Listing 11.15).

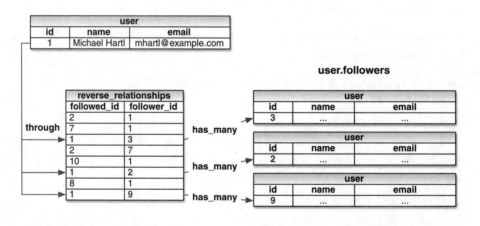

```
User has_many :followers, through: :reverse_relationships,
                          source:  "follower_id"
```

Figure 11.9 A model for user followers using a reverse Relationship model.

Listing 11.15 Testing for reverse relationships.
`spec/models/user_spec.rb`

```
require 'spec_helper'

describe User do
  .
  .
  .
  it { should respond_to(:relationships) }
  it { should respond_to(:followed_users) }
  it { should respond_to(:reverse_relationships) }
  it { should respond_to(:followers) }
  .
  .
  .

  describe "following" do
    .
    .
    .
    it { should be_following(other_user) }
    its(:followed_users) { should include(other_user) }

    describe "followed user" do
      subject { other_user }
      its(:followers) { should include(@user) }
    end
    .
    .
    .

  end
end
```

Notice how we switch subjects using the **subject** method, replacing **@user** with **other_user**, allowing us to test the follower relationship in a natural way:

```
subject { other_user }
its(:followers) { should include(@user) }
```

As you probably suspect, we will not be making a whole database table just to hold reverse relationships. Instead, we will exploit the underlying symmetry between followers and followed users to simulate a **reverse_relationships** table by passing

followed_id as the primary key. In other words, where the **relationships** association uses the **follower_id** foreign key,

```
has_many :relationships, foreign_key: "follower_id"
```

the **reverse_relationships** association uses **followed_id**:

```
has_many :reverse_relationships, foreign_key: "followed_id"
```

The **followers** association then gets built through the reverse relationships, as shown in Listing 11.16.

Listing 11.16 Implementing **user.followers** using reverse relationships.
app/models/user.rb

```
class User < ActiveRecord::Base
  .
  .
  .
  has_many :reverse_relationships, foreign_key: "followed_id",
                                   class_name: "Relationship",
                                   dependent:  :destroy
  has_many :followers, through: :reverse_relationships, source: :follower
  .
  .
  .
end
```

(As with Listing 11.4, the test for **dependent :destroy** is left as an exercise [Section 11.5].) Note that we actually have to include the *class* name for this association, i.e.,

```
has_many :reverse_relationships, foreign_key: "followed_id",
                                 class_name: "Relationship"
```

because otherwise Rails would look for a **ReverseRelationship** class, which doesn't exist.

It's also worth noting that we could actually omit the **:source** key in this case, using simply

```
has_many :followers, through: :reverse_relationships
```

since, in the case of a **:followers** attribute, Rails will singularize "followers" and automatically look for the foreign key **follower_id** in this case. I've kept the **:source** key to emphasize the parallel structure with the **has_many :followed_users** association, but you are free to leave it off.

With the code in Listing 11.16, the following/follower associations are complete, and all the tests should pass:

```
$ bundle exec rspec spec/
```

This section has placed rather heavy demands on your data modeling skills, and it's fine if it takes a while to soak in. In fact, one of the best ways to understand the associations is to use them in the web interface, as seen in the next section.

11.2   A Web Interface for Following Users

In the introduction to this chapter, we saw a preview of the page flow for user following. In this section, we will implement the basic interface and following/unfollowing functionality shown in those mockups. We will also make separate pages to show the user following and followers arrays. In Section 11.3, we'll complete our sample application by adding the user's status feed.

11.2.1   Sample Following Data

As in previous chapters, we will find it convenient to use the sample data Rake task to fill the database with sample relationships. This will allow us to design the look and feel of the web pages first, deferring the back-end functionality until later in this section.

When we last left the sample data populator in Listing 10.23, it was getting rather cluttered, so we begin by defining separate methods to make users and microposts, and then add sample relationship data using a new **make_relationships** method. The results are shown in Listing 11.17.

Listing 11.17 Adding following/follower relationships to the sample data.
lib/tasks/sample_data.rake

```
namespace :db do
  desc "Fill database with sample data"
  task populate: :environment do
    make_users
    make_microposts
    make_relationships
  end
end
```

```ruby
def make_users
  admin = User.create!(name:     "Example User",
                       email:    "example@railstutorial.org",
                       password: "foobar",
                       password_confirmation: "foobar")
  admin.toggle!(:admin)
  99.times do |n|
    name  = Faker::Name.name
    email = "example-#{n+1}@railstutorial.org"
    password = "password"
    User.create!(name:     name,
                 email:    email,
                 password: password,
                 password_confirmation: password)
  end
end

def make_microposts
  users = User.all(limit: 6)
  50.times do
    content = Faker::Lorem.sentence(5)
    users.each { |user| user.microposts.create!(content: content) }
  end
end

def make_relationships
  users = User.all
  user  = users.first
  followed_users = users[2..50]
  followers      = users[3..40]
  followed_users.each { |followed| user.follow!(followed) }
  followers.each      { |follower| follower.follow!(user) }
end
```

Here the sample relationships are created using the code

```ruby
def make_relationships
  users = User.all
  user  = users.first
  followed_users = users[2..50]
  followers      = users[3..40]
  followed_users.each { |followed| user.follow!(followed) }
  followers.each      { |follower| follower.follow!(user) }
end
```

We somewhat arbitrarily arrange for the first user to follow users 3 through 51, then have users 4 through 41 follow that user back. The resulting relationships will be sufficient for developing the application interface.

To execute the code in Listing 11.17, populate the database as usual:

```
$ bundle exec rake db:reset
$ bundle exec rake db:populate
$ bundle exec rake db:test:prepare
```

11.2.2   Stats and a Follow Form

Now that our sample users have both followed user and followers arrays, we need to update the profile page and Home page to reflect this. We'll start by making a partial to display the following and follower statistics on the profile and home pages. We'll next add a follow/unfollow form, then make dedicated pages for showing user followed users and followers.

As noted in Section 11.1.1, the word "following" is ambiguous as an attribute (where **user.following** could reasonably mean either the followed users or the user's followers), it makes sense as a label, as in "50 following." Indeed, this is the label used by Twitter itself, a usage adopted in the mockups starting in Figure 11.1 and shown in close-up in Figure 11.10.

The stats in Figure 11.10 consist of the number of users the current user is following and the number of followers, each of which should be a link to its respective dedicated display page. In Chapter 5, we stubbed out such links with the dummy text **'#'**, but that was before we had much experience with routes. This time, although we'll defer the actual pages to Section 11.2.3, we'll make the routes now, as seen in Listing 11.18. This code uses the **:member** method inside a **resources** *block*, which we haven't seen before, but see if you can guess what it does. (*Note*: The code in Listing 11.18 should *replace* the **resources :users**.)

Figure 11.10   A mockup of the stats partial.

506

Chapter 11: Following Users

Listing 11.18 Adding **followed_users** and **followers** actions to the Users controller. **config/routes.rb**

```
SampleApp::Application.routes.draw do
  resources :users do
    member do
      get :following, :followers
    end
  end
  .
  .
  .
end
```

You might suspect that the URIs will look like /users/1/following and /users/1/followers, and that is exactly what the code in Listing 11.18 does. Since both pages will be showing data, we use **get** to arrange for the URIs to respond to GET requests (as required by the REST convention for such pages), and the **member** method means that the routes respond to URIs containing the user id. The other possibility, **collection**, works without the id, so that

```
resources :users do
  collection do
    get :tigers
  end
end
```

would respond to the URI /users/tigers (presumably to display all the tigers in our application). For more details on such routing options, see the Rails Guides article entitled "Rails Routing from the Outside In." A table of the routes generated by Listing 11.18 appears in Table 11.1; note the named routes for the followed user and followers pages, which we'll put to use shortly. The unfortunate hybrid usage in the "following" route is forced by our choice to use the unambiguous "followed users" terminology along with the "following" usage from Twitter. Since the former would lead to routes of the form **followed_users_user_path**, which sounds strange, we've opted for the latter in the context of Table 11.1, yielding **following_user_path**.

Table 11.1 RESTful routes provided by the custom rules in resource in Listing 11.18.

HTTP request	URI	Action	Named route
GET	/users/1/following	**following**	**following_user_path(1)**
GET	/users/1/followers	**followers**	**followers_user_path(1)**

With the routes defined, we are now in a position to make tests for the stats partial. (We could have written the tests first, but the named routes would have been hard to motivate without the updated routes file.) The stats partial will appear on both the profile page and the Home page; Listing 11.19 opts to test it on the latter.

Listing 11.19 Testing the following/follower statistics on the Home page.
spec/requests/static_pages_spec.rb

```ruby
require 'spec_helper'

describe "StaticPages" do
  .
  .
  .
  describe "Home page" do
    .
    .
    .
    describe "for signed-in users" do
      let(:user) { FactoryGirl.create(:user) }
      before do
        FactoryGirl.create(:micropost, user: user, content: "Lorem")
        FactoryGirl.create(:micropost, user: user, content: "Ipsum")
        sign_in user
        visit root_path
      end

      it "should render the user's feed" do
        user.feed.each do |item|
          page.should have_selector("li##{item.id}", text: item.content)
        end
      end

      describe "follower/following counts" do
        let(:other_user) { FactoryGirl.create(:user) }
        before do
          other_user.follow!(user)
          visit root_path
        end

        it { should have_link("0 following", href: following_user_path(user)) }
        it { should have_link("1 follower",  href: followers_user_path(user)) }
      end
    end
  end
  .
  .
  .
end
```

The core of this test is the expectation that the following and follower counts appear on the page, together with the right URIs:

```
it { should have_link("0 following", href: following_user_path(user)) }
it { should have_link("1 follower",  href: followers_user_path(user)) }
```

Here we have used the named routes shown in Table 11.1 to verify that the links have the right addresses.

The application code for the stats partial is just a couple of links inside a div, as shown in Listing 11.20.

Listing 11.20 A partial for displaying follower stats.
app/views/shared/_stats.html.erb

```
<% @user ||= current_user %>
<div class="stats">
  <a href="<%= following_user_path(@user) %>">
    <strong id="following" class="stat">
      <%= @user.followed_users.count %>
    </strong>
    following
  </a>
  <a href="<%= followers_user_path(@user) %>">
    <strong id="followers" class="stat">
      <%= @user.followers.count %>
    </strong>
    followers
  </a>
</div>
```

Since we will be including the stats on both the user show pages and the Home page, the first line of Listing 11.20 picks the right one using

```
<% @user ||= current_user %>
```

As discussed in Box 8.2, this does nothing when **@user** is not **nil** (as on a profile page), but when it is (as on the Home page) it sets **@user** to the current user.

Note also that the following/follower counts are calculated through the associations using

```
@user.followed_users.count
```

and

```
@user.followers.count
```

Compare these to the microposts count from Listing 10.20, where we wrote

```
@user.microposts.count
```

to count the microposts.

One final detail worth noting is the presence of CSS ids on some elements, as in

```
<strong id="following" class="stat">
. . .
</strong>
```

This is for the benefit of the Ajax implementation in Section 11.2.5, which accesses elements on the page using their unique ids.

With the partial in hand, including the stats on the Home page is easy, as shown in Listing 11.21. (This also gets the test in Listing 11.19 to pass.)

Listing 11.21 Adding follower stats to the Home page.
app/views/static_pages/home.html.erb

```
<% if signed_in? %>
    .
    .
    .
    <section>
      <%= render 'shared/user_info' %>
    </section>
    <section>
      <%= render 'shared/stats' %>
    </section>
    <section>
      <%= render 'shared/micropost_form' %>
    </section>
    .
    .
    .
<% else %>
    .
    .
    .
<% end %>
```

To style the stats, we'll add some SCSS, as shown in Listing 11.22 (which contains all the stylesheet code needed in this chapter). The result appears in Figure 11.11.

Listing 11.22 SCSS for the Home page sidebar.
app/assets/stylesheets/custom.css.scss

```scss
.
.
.
/* sidebar */
.
.
.
.stats {
  overflow: auto;
  a {
    float: left;
    padding: 0 10px;
    border-left: 1px solid $grayLighter;
    color: gray;
    &:first-child {
      padding-left: 0;
      border: 0;
    }
    &:hover {
      text-decoration: none;
      color: $blue;
    }
  }
  strong {
    display: block;
  }
}

.user_avatars {
  overflow: auto;
  margin-top: 10px;
  .gravatar {
    margin: 1px 1px;
  }
}
.
.
.
```

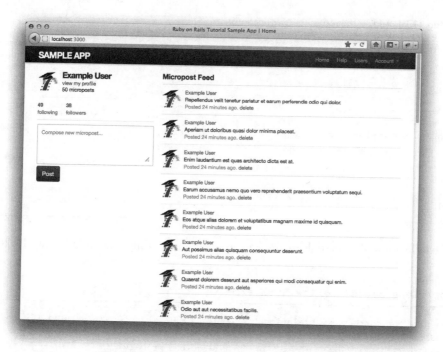

Figure 11.11   The Home page (/) with follow stats.

We'll render the stats partial on the profile page in a moment, but first let's make a partial for the follow/unfollow button, as shown in Listing 11.23.

Listing 11.23 A partial for a follow/unfollow form.
app/views/users/_follow_form.html.erb

```erb
<% unless current_user?(@user) %>
  <div id="follow_form">
  <% if current_user.following?(@user) %>
    <%= render 'unfollow' %>
  <% else %>
    <%= render 'follow' %>
  <% end %>
  </div>
<% end %>
```

This does nothing but defer the real work to **follow** and **unfollow** partials, which need a new routes file with rules for the Relationships resource, which follows the Microposts resource example (Listing 10.25), as seen in Listing 11.24.

Listing 11.24 Adding the routes for user relationships.
`config/routes.rb`

```
SampleApp::Application.routes.draw do
  .
  .
  .
  resources :sessions,      only: [:new, :create, :destroy]
  resources :microposts,    only: [:create, :destroy]
  resources :relationships, only: [:create, :destroy]
  .
  .
  .
end
```

The follow/unfollow partials themselves are shown in Listing 11.25 and Listing 11.26.

Listing 11.25 A form for following a user.
`app/views/users/_follow.html.erb`

```
<%= form_for(current_user.relationships.build(followed_id: @user.id)) do |f| %>
  <div><%= f.hidden_field :followed_id %></div>
  <%= f.submit "Follow", class: "btn btn-large btn-primary" %>
<% end %>
```

Listing 11.26 A form for unfollowing a user.
`app/views/users/_unfollow.html.erb`

```
<%= form_for(current_user.relationships.find_by_followed_id(@user),
             html: { method: :delete }) do |f| %>
  <%= f.submit "Unfollow", class: "btn btn-large" %>
<% end %>
```

These two forms both use **form_for** to manipulate a Relationship model object; the main difference between the two is that Listing 11.25 builds a *new* relationship, whereas Listing 11.26 finds the existing relationship. Naturally, the former sends a POST request to the Relationships controller to **create** a relationship, while the latter sends a DELETE request to **destroy** a relationship. (We'll write these actions in Section 11.2.4.) Finally, you'll note that the follow/unfollow form doesn't have any content other than the button, but it still needs to send the **followed_id**, which we accomplish with the **hidden_field** method, which produces HTML of the form

```
<input id="followed_relationship_followed_id"
name="followed_relationship[followed_id]"
type="hidden" value="3" />
```

The "hidden" **input** tag puts the relevant information on the page without displaying it in the browser.

We can now include the follow form and the following statistics on the user profile page simply by rendering the partials, as shown in Listing 11.27. Profiles with follow and unfollow buttons, respectively, appear in Figure 11.12 and Figure 11.13.

Listing 11.27 Adding the follow form and follower stats to the user profile page.
app/views/users/show.html.erb

```
<% provide(:title, @user.name) %>
<div class="row">
  <aside class="span4">
    <section>
      <h1>
        <%= gravatar_for @user %>
        <%= @user.name %>
      </h1>
    </section>
    <section>
      <%= render 'shared/stats' %>
    </section>
  </aside>
  <div class="span8">
    <%= render 'follow_form' if signed_in? %>
    .
    .
    .
  </div>
</div>
```

We'll get these buttons working soon enough—in fact, we'll do it two ways, the standard way (Section 11.2.4) and using Ajax (Section 11.2.5)—but first we'll finish the HTML interface by making the following and followers pages.

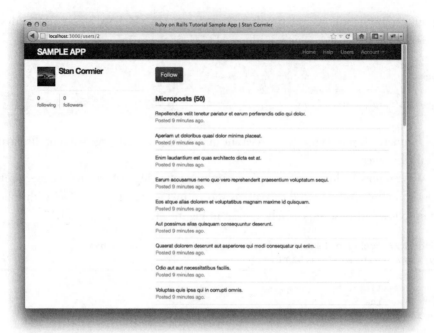

Figure 11.12 A user profile with a follow button (/users/2).

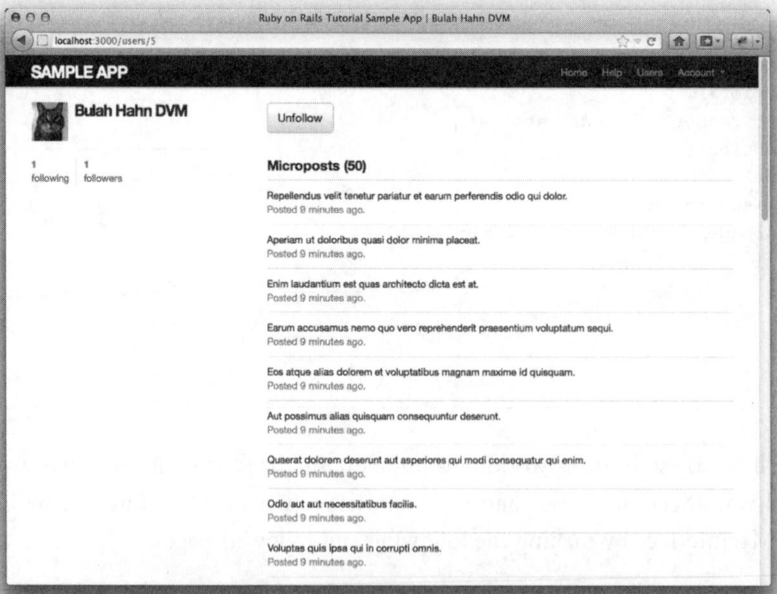

Figure 11.13 A user profile with an unfollow button (/users/6).

11.2.3 Following and Followers Pages

Pages to display followed users and followers will resemble a hybrid of the user profile page and the user index page (Section 9.3.1), with a sidebar of user information (including the following stats) and a list of users. In addition, we'll include a raster of user profile image links in the sidebar. Mockups matching these requirements appear in Figure 11.14 (following) and Figure 11.15 (followers).

Our first step is to get the following and followers links to work. We'll follow Twitter's lead and have both pages to require user signin, as tested in Listing 11.28. For signed-in users, the pages should have links for following and followers, respectively, as tested in Listing 11.29.

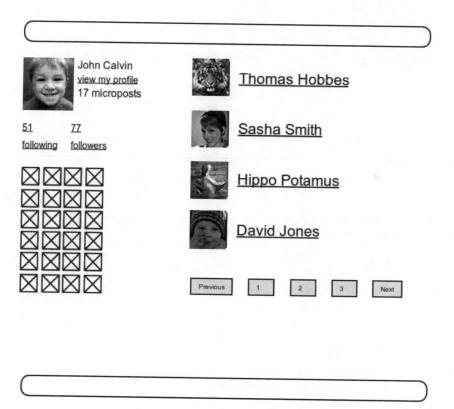

Figure 11.14 A mockup of the user following page.

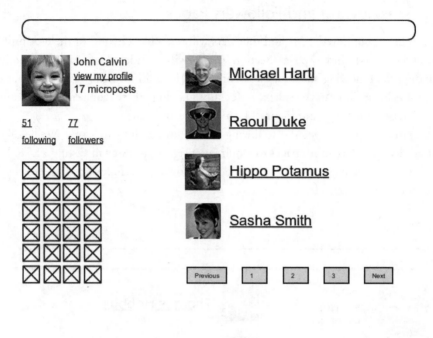

Figure 11.15   A mockup of the user followers page.

Listing 11.28 Tests for the authorization of the following and followers pages.
spec/requests/authentication_pages_spec.rb

```
require 'spec_helper'

describe "Authentication" do
  .
  .
  .
  describe "authorization" do

    describe "for non-signed-in users" do
      let(:user) { FactoryGirl.create(:user) }

      describe "in the Users controller" do
        .
        .
        .
```

```
            describe "visiting the following page" do
              before { visit following_user_path(user) }
              it { should have_selector('title', text: 'Sign in') }
            end

            describe "visiting the followers page" do
              before { visit followers_user_path(user) }
              it { should have_selector('title', text: 'Sign in') }
            end
          end
          .
          .
          .
      end
      .
      .
      .
  end
  .
  .
  .
end
```

Listing 11.29 Test for the **followed_users** and **followers** pages.
spec/requests/user_pages_spec.rb

```
require 'spec_helper'

describe "User pages" do
  .
  .
  .
  describe "following/followers" do
    let(:user) { FactoryGirl.create(:user) }
    let(:other_user) { FactoryGirl.create(:user) }
    before { user.follow!(other_user) }

    describe "followed users" do
      before do
        sign_in user
        visit following_user_path(user)
      end

      it { should have_selector('title', text: full_title('Following')) }
      it { should have_selector('h3', text: 'Following') }
      it { should have_link(other_user.name, href: user_path(other_user)) }
    end
```

```
describe "followers" do
  before do
    sign_in other_user
    visit followers_user_path(other_user)
  end

  it { should have_selector('title', text: full_title('Followers')) }
  it { should have_selector('h3', text: 'Followers') }
  it { should have_link(user.name, href: user_path(user)) }
  end
 end
end
```

The only tricky part of the implementation is realizing that we need to add two new actions to the Users controller; based on the routes defined in Listing 11.18, we need to call them **following** and **followers**. Each action needs to set a title, find the user, retrieve either **@user.followed_users** or **@user.followers** (in paginated form), and then render the page. The result appears in Listing 11.30.

Listing 11.30 The **following** and **followers** actions.
app/controllers/users_controller.rb

```
class UsersController < ApplicationController
  before_filter :signed_in_user,
                only: [:index, :edit, :update, :destroy, :following, :followers]
  .
  .
  .
  def following
    @title = "Following"
    @user = User.find(params[:id])
    @users = @user.followed_users.paginate(page: params[:page])
    render 'show_follow'
  end

  def followers
    @title = "Followers"
    @user = User.find(params[:id])
    @users = @user.followers.paginate(page: params[:page])
    render 'show_follow'
  end
  .
  .
  .
end
```

Note here that both actions make an *explicit* call to **render**, in this case rendering a view called **show_follow**, which we must create. The reason for the common view is that the ERb is nearly identical for the two cases, and Listing 11.31 covers them both.

Listing 11.31 The **show_follow** view used to render following and followers.
app/views/users/show_follow.html.erb

```erb
<% provide(:title, @title) %>
<div class="row">
  <aside class="span4">
    <section>
      <%= gravatar_for @user %>
      <h1><%= @user.name %></h1>
      <span><%= link_to "view my profile", @user %></span>
      <span><b>Microposts:</b> <%= @user.microposts.count %></span>
    </section>
    <section>
      <%= render 'shared/stats' %>
      <% if @users.any? %>
        <div class="user_avatars">
          <% @users.each do |user| %>
            <%= link_to gravatar_for(user, size: 30), user %>
          <% end %>
        </div>
      <% end %>
    </section>
  </aside>
  <div class="span8">
    <h3><%= @title %></h3>
    <% if @users.any? %>
    <ul class="users">
      <%= render @users %>
    </ul>
    <%= will_paginate %>
    <% end %>
  </div>
</div>
```

With that, the tests should now be passing, and the pages should render as shown in Figure 11.16 (following) and Figure 11.17 (followers).

11.2.4 A Working Follow Button the Standard Way

Now that our views are in order, it's time to get the follow/unfollow buttons working. The tests for these buttons combine many of the testing techniques covered throughout

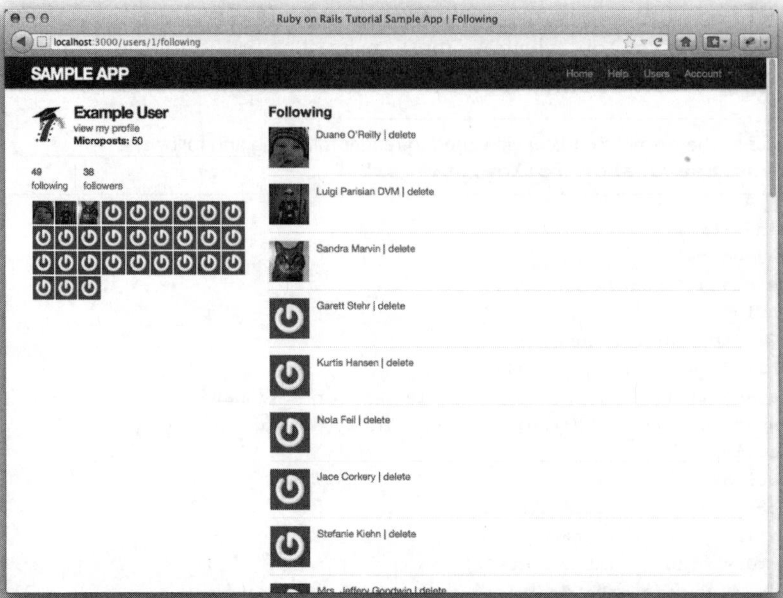

Figure 11.16   Showing the users being followed by the current user.

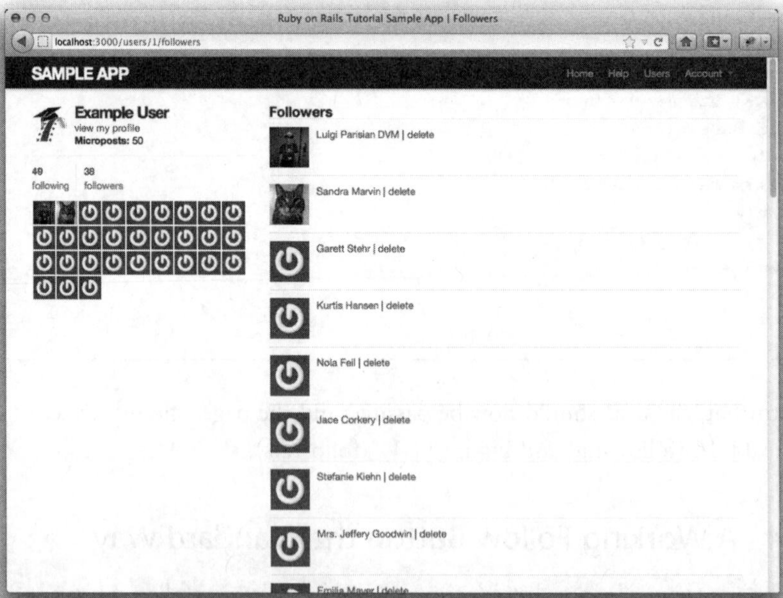

Figure 11.17   Showing the current user's followers.

this tutorial and make for a good exercise in reading code. Study Listing 11.32 until you are convinced that you understand what it's testing and why. (There's one minor security omission as well; see if you can spot it. We'll cover it momentarily.)

Listing 11.32 Tests for the Follow/Unfollow button.
spec/requests/user_pages_spec.rb

```ruby
require 'spec_helper'

describe "User pages" do
  .
  .
  .
  describe "profile page" do
    let(:user) { FactoryGirl.create(:user) }
    .
    .
    .
    describe "follow/unfollow buttons" do
      let(:other_user) { FactoryGirl.create(:user) }
      before { sign_in user }

      describe "following a user" do
        before { visit user_path(other_user) }

        it "should increment the followed user count" do
          expect do
            click_button "Follow"
          end.to change(user.followed_users, :count).by(1)
        end

        it "should increment the other user's followers count" do
          expect do
            click_button "Follow"
          end.to change(other_user.followers, :count).by(1)
        end

        describe "toggling the button" do
          before { click_button "Follow" }
          it { should have_selector('input', value: 'Unfollow') }
        end
      end

      describe "unfollowing a user" do
        before do
          user.follow!(other_user)
          visit user_path(other_user)
        end
```

```
      it "should decrement the followed user count" do
        expect do
          click_button "Unfollow"
        end.to change(user.followed_users, :count).by(-1)
      end

      it "should decrement the other user's followers count" do
        expect do
          click_button "Unfollow"
        end.to change(other_user.followers, :count).by(-1)
      end

      describe "toggling the button" do
        before { click_button "Unfollow" }
        it { should have_selector('input', value: 'Follow') }
      end
     end
    end
   end
  end
  .
  .
  .
end
```

Listing 11.32 tests the following buttons by clicking on them and specifying the proper behavior. Writing the implementation involves digging a little deeper: Following and unfollowing involve *creating* and *destroying* relationships, which means defining **create** and **destroy** actions in a Relationships controller (which we must create). Although the following buttons only appear for signed-in users, giving us a superficial layer of security, the tests in Listing 11.32 miss a lower-level issue, namely, the **create** and **destroy** actions themselves should only be accessible to signed-in users. (This is the security hole alluded to above.) Listing 11.33 expresses this requirement using the **post** and **delete** methods to hit those actions directly.

Listing 11.33 Tests for the Relationships controller authorization.
spec/requests/authentication_pages_spec.rb

```
require 'spec_helper'

describe "Authentication" do
  .
  .
  .
  describe "authorization" do
```

```
    describe "for non-signed-in users" do
      let(:user) { FactoryGirl.create(:user) }
        .
        .
        .
      describe "in the Relationships controller" do
        describe "submitting to the create action" do
          before { post relationships_path }
          specify { response.should redirect_to(signin_path) }
        end

        describe "submitting to the destroy action" do
          before { delete relationship_path(1) }
          specify { response.should redirect_to(signin_path) }
        end
      end
        .
        .
        .
    end
  end
end
```

Note that, in order to avoid the overhead of creating a virtually useless Relationship object, the **delete** test hard-codes the id **1** in the named route:

```
before { delete relationship_path(1) }
```

This works because the user should be redirected before the application ever tries to retrieve the relationship with this id.

The controller code needed to get these tests to pass is remarkably concise: We just retrieve the user followed or to be followed, then follow or unfollow the user using the relevant utility method. The full implementation appears in Listing 11.34.

Listing 11.34 The Relationships controller.
app/controllers/relationships_controller.rb

```
class RelationshipsController < ApplicationController
  before_filter :signed_in_user

  def create
    @user = User.find(params[:relationship][:followed_id])
    current_user.follow!(@user)
    redirect_to @user
  end
```

```
def destroy
  @user = Relationship.find(params[:id]).followed
  current_user.unfollow!(@user)
  redirect_to @user
end
end
```

We can see from Listing 11.34 why the security issue mentioned above is minor: If an unsigned-in user were to hit either action directly (e.g., using a command-line tool), **current_user** would be **nil**, and in both cases the action's second line would raise an exception, resulting in an error but no harm to the application or its data. It's best not to rely on that, though, so we've taken the extra step and added an extra layer of security.

With that, the core follow/unfollow functionality is complete, and any user can follow (or unfollow) any other user, which you should verify both by clicking around in the sample application and by running the test suite:

```
$ bundle exec rspec spec/
```

11.2.5 A Working Follow Button with Ajax

Although our user following implementation is complete as it stands, we have one bit of polish left to add before starting work on the status feed. You may have noticed in Section 11.2.4 that both the **create** and **destroy** actions in the Relationships controller simply redirect *back* to the original profile. In other words, a user starts on a profile page, follows the user, and is immediately redirected back to the original page. It is reasonable to ask why the user needs to leave that page at all.

This is exactly the problem solved by *Ajax*, which allows web pages to send requests asynchronously to the server without leaving the page.[9] Because the practice of adding Ajax to web forms is quite common, Rails makes Ajax easy to implement. Indeed, updating the follow/unfollow form partials is trivial: Just change

```
form_for
```

to

```
form_for ..., remote: true
```

---

9. Because it is nominally an acronym for *asynchronous JavaScript and XML*, Ajax is sometimes misspelled "AJAX," even though the original Ajax article spells it as "Ajax" throughout.

and Rails automagically uses Ajax.[10] The updated partials appear in Listing 11.35 and Listing 11.36.

Listing 11.35 A form for following a user using Ajax.
app/views/users/_follow.html.erb

```
<%= form_for(current_user.relationships.build(followed_id: @user.id),
              remote: true) do |f| %>
  <div><%= f.hidden_field :followed_id %></div>
  <%= f.submit "Follow", class: "btn btn-large btn-primary" %>
<% end %>
```

Listing 11.36 A form for unfollowing a user using Ajax.
app/views/users/_unfollow.html.erb

```
<%= form_for(current_user.relationships.find_by_followed_id(@user),
              html: { method: :delete },
              remote: true) do |f| %>
  <%= f.submit "Unfollow", class: "btn btn-large" %>
<% end %>
```

The actual HTML generated by this ERb isn't particularly relevant, but you might be curious, so here's a peek:

```
<form action="/relationships/117" class="edit_relationship" data-remote="true"
    id="edit_relationship_117" method="post">
    .
    .
    .
</form>
```

This sets the variable **data-remote="true"** inside the form tag, which tells Rails to allow the form to be handled by JavaScript. By using a simple HTML property instead of inserting the full JavaScript code (as in previous versions of Rails), Rails 3 follows the philosophy of *unobtrusive JavaScript*.

Having updated the form, we now need to arrange for the Relationships controller to respond to Ajax requests. Testing Ajax is quite tricky, and doing it thoroughly is a large subject in its own right, but we can get started with the code in Listing 11.37. This uses the **xhr** method (for "XmlHttpRequest") to issue an Ajax request; compare to the **get**, **post**, **put**, and **delete** methods used in previous tests. We then verify that

---

10. This only works if JavaScript is enabled in the browser, but it degrades gracefully, working exactly as in Section 11.2.4 if JavaScript is disabled.

the **create** and **destroy** actions do the correct things when hit with an Ajax request. (To write more thorough test suites for Ajax-heavy applications, take a look at Selenium and Watir.)

Listing 11.37 Tests for the Relationships controller responses to Ajax requests.
spec/controllers/relationships_controller_spec.rb

```ruby
require 'spec_helper'

describe RelationshipsController do

  let(:user) { FactoryGirl.create(:user) }
  let(:other_user) { FactoryGirl.create(:user) }

  before { sign_in user }

  describe "creating a relationship with Ajax" do

    it "should increment the Relationship count" do
      expect do
        xhr :post, :create, relationship: { followed_id: other_user.id }
      end.should change(Relationship, :count).by(1)
    end

    it "should respond with success" do
      xhr :post, :create, relationship: { followed_id: other_user.id }
      response.should be_success
    end
  end

  describe "destroying a relationship with Ajax" do

    before { user.follow!(other_user) }
    let(:relationship) { user.relationships.find_by_followed_id(other_user) }

    it "should decrement the Relationship count" do
      expect do
        xhr :delete, :destroy, id: relationship.id
      end.should change(Relationship, :count).by(-1)
    end

    it "should respond with success" do
      xhr :delete, :destroy, id: relationship.id
      response.should be_success
    end
  end
end
```

The code in Listing 11.37 is our first example of a *controller* test, which I used to use extensively (as in the previous edition of this book) but now mainly eschew in favor of integration tests. In this case, though, the **xhr** method is (somewhat inexplicably) not available in integration tests. Although our use of **xhr** is new, at this point in the tutorial you should be able to infer from context what the code does:

```
xhr :post, :create, relationship: { followed_id: other_user.id }
```

We see that **xhr** takes as arguments a symbol for the relevant HTTP method, a symbol for the action, and a hash representing the contents of **params** in the controller itself. As in previous examples, we use **expect** to wrap the operation in a block and test for an increment or decrement in the relevant count.

As implied by the tests, the application code uses the same **create** and **destroy** actions to respond to the Ajax requests that it uses to respond to ordinary POST and DELETE HTTP requests. All we need to do is respond to a normal HTTP request with a redirect (as in Section 11.2.4) and respond to an Ajax request with JavaScript. The controller code appears as in Listing 11.38. (See Section 11.5 for an exercise showing an even more compact way to accomplish the same thing.)

Listing 11.38 Responding to Ajax requests in the Relationships controller.
app/controllers/relationships_controller.rb

```ruby
class RelationshipsController < ApplicationController
  before_filter :signed_in_user

  def create
    @user = User.find(params[:relationship][:followed_id])
    current_user.follow!(@user)
    respond_to do |format|
      format.html { redirect_to @user }
      format.js
    end
  end

  def destroy
    @user = Relationship.find(params[:id]).followed
    current_user.unfollow!(@user)
    respond_to do |format|
      format.html { redirect_to @user }
      format.js
    end
  end
end
```

This code uses **respond_to** to take the appropriate action depending on the kind of request. (There is no relationship between this **respond_to** and the **respond_to** used in the RSpec examples.) The syntax is potentially confusing, and it's important to understand that in

```
respond_to do |format|
  format.html { redirect_to @user }
  format.js
end
```

only *one* of the lines gets executed (based on the nature of the request).

In the case of an Ajax request, Rails automatically calls a *JavaScript Embedded Ruby* (**.js.erb**) file with the same name as the action, i.e., **create.js.erb** or **destroy.js.erb**. As you might guess, the files allow us to mix JavaScript and Embedded Ruby to perform actions on the current page. It is these files that we need to create and edit in order to update the user profile page upon being followed or unfollowed.

Inside a JS-ERb file, Rails automatically provides the jQuery JavaScript helpers to manipulate the page using the Document Object Model (DOM). The jQuery library provides a large number of methods for manipulating the DOM, but here we will need only two. First, we will need to know about the dollar-sign syntax to access a DOM element based in its unique CSS id. For example, to manipulate the **follow_form** element, we will use the syntax

```
$("#follow_form")
```

(Recall from Listing 11.23 that this is a **div** that wraps the form, not the form itself.) This syntax, inspired by CSS, uses the **#** symbol to indicate a CSS id. As you might guess, jQuery, like CSS, uses a dot **.** to manipulate CSS classes.

The second method we'll need is **html**, which updates the HTML inside the relevant element with the contents of its argument. For example, to replace the entire follow form with the string **"foobar"**, we would write

```
$("#follow_form").html("foobar")
```

Unlike plain JavaScript files, JS-ERb files also allow the use of Embedded Ruby, which we apply in the **create.js.erb** file to update the follow form with the **unfollow** partial (which is what should show after a successful following) and update the follower count. The result is shown in Listing 11.39. This uses the `escape_javascript` function, which is needed to escape out the result when inserting HTML in a JavaScript file.

Listing 11.39 The JavaScript Embedded Ruby to create a following relationship.
`app/views/relationships/create.js.erb`

```
$("#follow_form").html("<%= escape_javascript(render('users/unfollow')) %>")
$("#followers").html('<%= @user.followers.count %>')
```

The `destroy.js.erb` file is analogous (Listing 11.40).

Listing 11.40 The Ruby JavaScript (RJS) to destroy a following relationship.
`app/views/relationships/destroy.js.erb`

```
$("#follow_form").html("<%= escape_javascript(render('users/follow')) %>")
$("#followers").html('<%= @user.followers.count %>')
```

With that, you should navigate to a user profile page and verify that you can follow and unfollow without a page refresh, and the test suite should also pass:

```
$ bundle exec rspec spec/
```

Using Ajax in Rails is a large and fast-moving subject, so we've only been able to scratch the surface here, but (as with the rest of the material in this tutorial) our treatment should give you a good foundation for more advanced resources.

11.3 The Status Feed

We come now to the pinnacle of our sample application: the status feed. Appropriately, this section contains some of the most advanced material in the entire tutorial. The full status feed builds on the proto-feed from Section 10.3.3 by assembling an array of the microposts from the users being followed by the current user, along with the current user's own microposts. To accomplish this feat, we will need some fairly advanced Rails, Ruby, and even SQL programming techniques.

Because of the heavy lifting ahead, it's especially important to review where we're going. A recap of the final user status feed, shown in Figure 11.5, appears again in Figure 11.18.

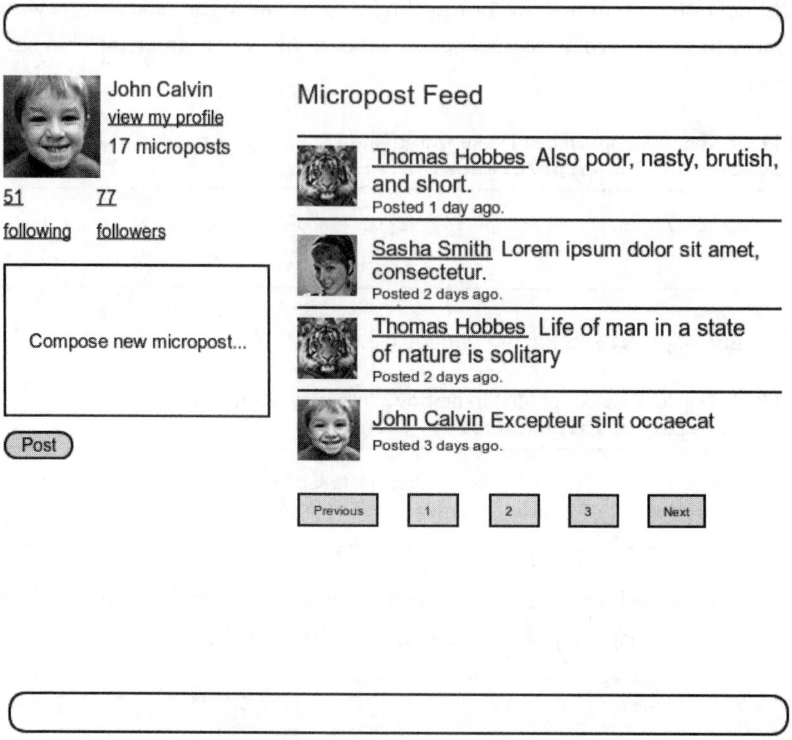

John Calvin
view my profile
17 microposts

51   77
following   followers

Compose new micropost...

Post

Micropost Feed

Thomas Hobbes Also poor, nasty, brutish, and short.
Posted 1 day ago.

Sasha Smith Lorem ipsum dolor sit amet, consectetur.
Posted 2 days ago.

Thomas Hobbes Life of man in a state of nature is solitary
Posted 2 days ago.

John Calvin Excepteur sint occaecat
Posted 3 days ago.

Previous   1   2   3   Next

Figure 11.18   A mockup of a user's Home page with a status feed.

11.3.1 Motivation and Strategy

The basic idea behind the feed is simple. Figure 11.19 shows a sample **microposts** database table and the resulting feed. The purpose of a feed is to pull out the microposts whose user ids correspond to the users being followed by the current user (and the current user itself), as indicated by the arrows in the diagram.

Since we need a way to find all the microposts from users followed by a given user, we'll plan on implementing a method called **from_users_followed_by**, which we will use as follows:

```
Micropost.from_users_followed_by(user)
```

Although we don't yet know how to implement it, we can already write tests for for its functionality. The key is to check all three requirements for the feed: microposts for followed users and the user itself should be included in the feed, but a post from an

microposts		
id	**content**	**user_id**
1	...	1
2	...	2
3	...	4
4	...	7
5	...	1
6	...	18
7	...	8
8	...	9
9	...	10
10	...	2

user.feed

1	...	1
2	...	2
4	...	7
5	...	1
7	...	8
9	...	10
10	...	2

Figure 11.19   The feed for a user (id 1) following users 2, 7, 8, and 10.

unfollowed user should not be included. Two of these requirements already appear in our tests: Listing 10.38 verifies that a user's own microposts appear in the feed, while the micropost from an unfollowed user doesn't appear. Now that we know how to follow users, we can add a third type of test, this time checking that the microposts of a followed user appear in the feed, as shown in Listing 11.41.

Listing 11.41 The final tests for the status feed.
spec/models/user_spec.rb

```ruby
require 'spec_helper'

describe User do
  .
  .
  .
  describe "micropost associations" do
    before { @user.save }
    let!(:older_micropost) do
      FactoryGirl.create(:micropost, user: @user, created_at: 1.day.ago)
    end
    let!(:newer_micropost) do
      FactoryGirl.create(:micropost, user: @user, created_at: 1.hour.ago)
    end
    .
    .
    .
    describe "status" do
      let(:unfollowed_post) do
        FactoryGirl.create(:micropost, user: FactoryGirl.create(:user))
      end
      let(:followed_user) { FactoryGirl.create(:user) }
```

```
      before do
        @user.follow!(followed_user)
        3.times { followed_user.microposts.create!(content: "Lorem ipsum") }
      end

      its(:feed) { should include(newer_micropost) }
      its(:feed) { should include(older_micropost) }
      its(:feed) { should_not include(unfollowed_post) }
      its(:feed) do
        followed_user.microposts.each do |micropost|
          should include(micropost)
        end
      end
    end
  end
end
```

Implementing the feed simply defers the hard work to `Micropost.from_users_followed_by`, as shown in Listing 11.42.

Listing 11.42 Adding the completed feed to the User model.
`app/models/user.rb`

```
class User < ActiveRecord::Base
  .
  .
  .
  def feed
    Micropost.from_users_followed_by(self)
  end
  .
  .
  .
end
```

11.3.2 A First Feed Implementation

Now it's time to implement `Micropost.from_users_followed_by`, which for simplicity we'll just refer to as "the feed." Since the final result is rather intricate, we'll build up to the final feed implementation by introducing one piece at a time.

The first step is to think of the kind of query we'll need. What we want to do is select from the **microposts** table all the microposts with ids corresponding to the users being followed by a given user (or the user itself). We might write this schematically as follows:

```
SELECT * FROM microposts
WHERE user_id IN (<list of ids>) OR user_id = <user id>
```

In writing this code, we've guessed that SQL supports an **IN** keyword that allows us to test for set inclusion. (Happily, it does.)

Recall from the proto-feed in Section 10.3.3 that Active Record uses the **where** method to accomplish the kind of select shown above, as illustrated in Listing 10.39. There, our select was very simple; we just picked out all the microposts with user id corresponding to the current user:

```
Micropost.where("user_id = ?", id)
```

Here, we expect it to be more complicated, something like

```
where("user_id in (?) OR user_id = ?", following_ids, user)
```

(Here we've used the Rails convention of **user** instead of **user.id** in the condition; Rails automatically uses the **id**. We've also omitted the leading **Micropost.** since we expect this method to live in the Micropost model itself.)

We see from these conditions that we'll need an array of ids corresponding to the users being followed. One way to do this is to use Ruby's **map** method, available on any "enumerable" object, i.e., any object (such as an Array or a Hash) that consists of a collection of elements.[11] We saw an example of this method in Section 4.3.2; it works like this:

```
$ rails console
>> [1, 2, 3, 4].map { |i| i.to_s }
=> ["1", "2", "3", "4"]
```

---

11. The main requirement is that enumerable objects must implement an **each** method to iterate through the collection.

Situations like the one illustrated above, where the same method (e.g., **to_s**) gets called on each element, are common enough that there's a shorthand notation using an *ampersand* **&** and a symbol corresponding to the method:[12]

```
>> [1, 2, 3, 4].map(&:to_s)
=> ["1", "2", "3", "4"]
```

Using the **join** method (Section 4.3.1), we can create a string composed of the ids by joining them on comma-space :

```
>> [1, 2, 3, 4].map(&:to_s).join(', ')
=> "1, 2, 3, 4"
```

We can use the above method to construct the necessary array of followed user ids by calling **id** on each element in **user.followed_users**. For example, for the first user in the database this array appears as follows:

```
>> User.first.followed_users.map(&:id)
=> [4, 5, 6, 7, 8, 9, 10, 11, 12, 13, 14, 15, 16, 17, 18, 19, 20, 21, 22, 23,
24, 25, 26, 27, 28, 29, 30, 31, 32, 33, 34, 35, 36, 37, 38, 39, 40, 41, 42,
43, 44, 45, 46, 47, 48, 49, 50, 51]
```

In fact, because this sort of construction is so useful, Active Record provides it by default:

```
>> User.first.followed_user_ids
=> [4, 5, 6, 7, 8, 9, 10, 11, 12, 13, 14, 15, 16, 17, 18, 19, 20, 21, 22, 23,
24, 25, 26, 27, 28, 29, 30, 31, 32, 33, 34, 35, 36, 37, 38, 39, 40, 41, 42,
43, 44, 45, 46, 47, 48, 49, 50, 51]
```

Here the **followed_user_ids** method is synthesized by Active Record based on the **has_many :followed_users** association (Listing 11.10); the result is that we need only append **_ids** to the association name to get the ids corresponding to the **user.followed_users** collection. A string of followed user ids then appears as follows:

```
>> User.first.followed_user_ids.join(', ')
=> "4, 5, 6, 7, 8, 9, 10, 11, 12, 13, 14, 15, 16, 17, 18, 19, 20, 21, 22, 23,
24, 25, 26, 27, 28, 29, 30, 31, 32, 33, 34, 35, 36, 37, 38, 39, 40, 41, 42,
43, 44, 45, 46, 47, 48, 49, 50, 51"
```

---

12. This notation actually started as an extension Rails made to the core Ruby language; it was so useful that it has now been incorporated into Ruby itself. How cool is that?

When inserting into an SQL string, though, you don't need to do this; the **?** interpolation takes care of it for you (and in fact eliminates some database-dependent incompatibilities). This means we can use

```
user.followed_user_ids
```

by itself.

At this point, you might guess that code like

```
Micropost.from_users_followed_by(user)
```

will involve a class method in the **Micropost** class (a construction mentioned briefly in Section 4.4.1). A proposed implementation along these lines appears in Listing 11.43.

Listing 11.43 A first cut at the **from_users_followed_by** method.
app/models/micropost.rb

```
class Micropost < ActiveRecord::Base
  .
  .
  .
  def self.from_users_followed_by(user)
    followed_user_ids = user.followed_user_ids
    where("user_id IN (?) OR user_id = ?", followed_user_ids, user)
  end
end
```

Although the discussion leading up to Listing 11.43 was couched in hypothetical terms, it actually works! You can verify this yourself by running the test suite, which should pass:

```
$ bundle exec rspec spec/
```

In some applications, this initial implementation might be good enough for most practical purposes. But it's not the final implementation; see if you can make a guess about why not before moving on to the next section. (*Hint*: What if a user is following 5,000 other users?)

11.3.3   Subselects

As hinted at in the last section, the feed implementation in Section 11.3.2 doesn't scale well when the number of microposts in the feed is large, as would likely happen if a user were following, say, 5000 other users. In this section, we'll reimplement the status feed in a way that scales better with the number of followed users.

The problem with the code in Section 11.3.2 is that

```
followed_user_ids = user.followed_user_ids
```

pulls *all* the followed users' ids into memory and creates an array the full length of the followed users array. Since the condition in Listing 11.43 actually just checks inclusion in a set, there must be a more efficient way to do this, and indeed SQL is optimized for just such set operations. The solution involves pushing the finding of followed user ids into the database using a *subselect*.

We'll start by refactoring the feed with the slightly modified code in Listing 11.44

Listing 11.44 Improving **`from_users_followed_by`**.
`app/models/micropost.rb`

```
class Micropost < ActiveRecord::Base
  .
  .
  .
  # Returns microposts from the users being followed by the given user.
  def self.from_users_followed_by(user)
    followed_user_ids = user.followed_user_ids
    where("user_id IN (:followed_user_ids) OR user_id = :user_id",
          followed_user_ids: followed_user_ids, user_id: user)
  end
end
```

As preparation for the next step, we have replaced

```
where("user_id IN (?) OR user_id = ?", followed_user_ids, user)
```

with the equivalent

```
where("user_id IN (:followed_user_ids) OR user_id = :user_id",
      followed_user_ids: followed_user_ids, user_id: user)
```

The question mark syntax is fine, but when we want the *same* variable inserted in more than one place the second syntax is more convenient.

The above discussion mentions that we will be adding a *second* occurrence of `user_id` in the SQL query. In particular, we can replace the Ruby code

```
followed_user_ids = user.followed_user_ids
```

with the SQL snippet

```
followed_user_ids = "SELECT followed_id FROM relationships
                     WHERE follower_id = :user_id"
```

This code contains a SQL *subselect*, and internally the entire select for user 1 would look something like this:

```
SELECT * FROM microposts
WHERE user_id IN (SELECT followed_id FROM relationships
                  WHERE follower_id = 1)
    OR user_id = 1
```

This subselect arranges for all the set logic to be pushed into the database, which is more efficient.[13]

With this foundation, we are ready for an efficient feed implementation, as seen in Listing 11.45. Note that, because it is now raw SQL, `followed_user_ids` is *interpolated*, not escaped. (It actually works either way, but logically it makes more sense to interpolate in this context.)

Listing 11.45 The final implementation of `from_users_followed_by`.
`app/models/micropost.rb`

```
class Micropost < ActiveRecord::Base
  attr_accessible :content
  belongs_to :user

  validates :user_id, presence: true
  validates :content, presence: true, length: { maximum: 140 }

  default_scope order: 'microposts.created_at DESC'
```

---

13. For a more advanced way to create the necessary subselect, see the blog post "Hacking a subselect in ActiveRecord."

```
  def self.from_users_followed_by(user)
    followed_user_ids = "SELECT followed_id FROM relationships
                         WHERE follower_id = :user_id"
    where("user_id IN (#{followed_user_ids}) OR user_id = :user_id",
          user_id: user.id)
  end
end
```

This code has a formidable combination of Rails, Ruby, and SQL, but it does the job, and does it well. (Of course, even the subselect won't scale forever. For bigger sites, you would probably need to generate the feed asynchronously using a background job. Such scaling subtleties are beyond the scope of this tutorial, but the Scaling Rails screencasts are a good place to start.)

11.3.4 The New Status Feed

With the code in Listing 11.45, our status feed is complete. As a reminder, the code for the Home page appears in Listing 11.46; this code creates a paginated feed of the relevant microposts for use in the view, as seen in Figure 11.20.[14] Note that the **paginate** method actually reaches all the way into the Micropost model method in Listing 11.45, arranging to pull out only 30 microposts at a time from the database. (You can verify this by examining the SQL statements in the development server log file.)

Listing 11.46 The **home** action with a paginated feed.
app/controllers/static_pages_controller.rb

```
class StaticPagesController < ApplicationController

  def home
    if signed_in?
      @micropost  = current_user.microposts.build
      @feed_items = current_user.feed.paginate(page: params[:page])
    end
  end
  .
  .
  .
end
```

14. In order to make a prettier feed for Figure 11.20, I've added a few extra microposts by hand using the Rails console.

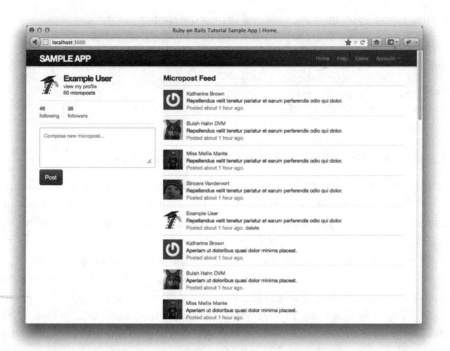

Figure 11.20   The Home page with a working status feed.

11.4 Conclusion

With the addition of the status feed, we've finished the core sample application for the *Rails Tutorial*. This application includes examples of all the major features of Rails, including models, views, controllers, templates, partials, filters, validations, callbacks, **has_many/belongs_to** and **has_many through** associations, security, testing, and deployment. Despite this impressive list, there is still much to learn about Rails. As a first step in this process, this section contains some suggested extensions to the core application, as well as suggestions for further learning.

Before moving on to tackle any of the application extensions, it's a good idea to merge in your changes:

```
$ git add .
$ git commit -m "Add user following"
$ git checkout master
$ git merge following-users
```

As usual, you can also push the code and deploy the application if you want:

```
$ git push
$ git push heroku
$ heroku pg:reset SHARED_DATABASE --confirm <name-heroku-gave-to-your-app>
$ heroku run rake db:migrate
$ heroku run rake db:populate
```

11.4.1 Extensions to the Sample Application

The proposed extensions in this section are mostly inspired either by general features common to web applications, such as password reminders and email confirmation, or features specific to our type of sample application, such as search, replies, and messaging. Implementing one or more of these application extensions will help you make the transition from following a tutorial to writing original applications of your own.

Don't be surprised if it's tough going at first; the blank slate of a new feature can be quite intimidating. To help get you started, I can give two pieces of general advice. First, before adding any feature to a Rails application, take a look at the RailsCasts archive to see if Ryan Bates has already covered the subject.[15] If he has, watching the relevant RailsCast first will often save you a ton of time. Second, always do extensive Google searches on your proposed feature to find relevant blog posts and tutorials. Web application development is hard, and it helps to learn from the experience (and mistakes) of others.

Many of the following features are quite challenging, and I have given some hints about the tools you might need to implement them. Even with hints, they are *much* more difficult than the book's end-of-chapter exercises, so don't be discouraged if you can't solve them without considerable effort. Due to time constraints, I am not available for one-on-one assistance, but if there is sufficient interest I might release standalone article/screencast bundles on some of these extensions in the future; go to the main Rails Tutorial website at http://railstutorial.org and subscribe to the news feed to get the latest updates.

---

15. Note that RailsCasts usually omit the tests, which is probably necessary to keep the episodes nice and short, but you could get the wrong idea about the importance of testing. Once you've watched the relevant RailsCast to get a basic idea of how to proceed, I suggest writing the new feature using test-driven development. (In this context, I recommend taking a look at the RailsCast on "How I test." You'll see that Ryan Bates himself often uses TDD for real-life development, and in fact his testing style is similar to style used in this tutorial.)

Replies

Twitter allows users to make "@replies", which are microposts whose first characters are the user's login preceded by the @ sign. These posts only appear in the feed of the user in question or users following that user. Implement a simplified version of this, restricting @replies to appear only in the feeds of the recipient and the sender. This might involve adding an **in_reply_to** column in the **microposts** table and an extra **including_replies** scope to the Micropost model.

Since our application lacks unique user logins, you will also have to decide on a way to represent users. One option is to use a combination of the id and the name, such as **@1-michael-hartl**. Another is to *add* a unique username to the signup process and then use it in @replies.

Messaging

Twitter supports direct (private) messaging by prefixing a micropost with the letter "d." Implement this feature for the sample application. The solution will probably involve a Message model and a regular expression match on new microposts.

Follower Notifications

Implement a feature to send each user an email notification when they gain a new follower. Then make the notification optional, so that users can opt out if desired. Among other things, adding this feature requires learning how to send mail with Rails. To get started, I suggest viewing the RailsCast on Action Mailer in Rails 3.

Password Reminders

Currently, if our application's users forget their passwords, they have no way to retrieve them. Because of the one-way secure password hashing in Chapter 6, our application can't email the user's password, but it can send a link to a reset form. Follow the steps in the RailsCast on Remember Me & Reset Password to fix this omission.

Signup Confirmation

Apart from an email regular expression, the sample application currently has no way to verify the validity of a user's email address. Add an email address verification step to confirm a user's signup. The new feature should create users in an inactive state, email the user an activation URI, then change the user to an active state when the URI gets hit. You might want to read up on state machines in Rails to help you with the inactive/active transition.

RSS Feed

For each user, implement an RSS feed for their microposts. Then implement an RSS feed for each status feed, optionally restricting access to that feed using an authentication scheme. The RailsCast on generating RSS feeds will help get you started.

REST API

Many websites expose an Application Programmer Interface (API) so that third-party applications can get, post, put, and delete the application's resources. Implement such a REST API for the sample application. The solution will involve adding `respond_to` blocks (Section 11.2.5) to many of the application's controller actions; these should respond to requests for XML. Be careful about security; the API should only be accessible to authorized users.

Search

Currently, there is no way for users to find each other, apart from paging through the user index or viewing the feeds of other users. Implement a search feature to remedy this. Then add another search feature for microposts. The RailsCast on simple search forms will help get you started. If you deploy using a shared host or a dedicated server, I suggest using Thinking Sphinx (following the RailsCast on Thinking Sphinx). If you deploy on Heroku, you should follow the Heroku full text search instructions.

11.4.2   Guide to Further Resources

There are a wealth of Rails resources in stores and on the web—indeed, the supply is so rich that it can be overwhelming. The good news is that, having gotten this far, you're ready for almost anything else out there. Here are some suggestions for further learning:

- The *Rails Tutorial* screencasts: I have prepared a full-length screencast course based on this book. In addition to covering all the material in the book, the screencasts are filled with tips, tricks, and the kind of see-how-it's-done demos that are hard to capture in print. They are available for purchase through the *Rails Tutorial* website. (*Note*: The screencasts for the second edition are currently in preparation. They will be a paid upgrade, but current customers will receive a substantial discount.)

- RailsCasts: It's hard to overemphasize what a great resource the RailsCasts are. I suggest starting by visiting the RailsCasts episode archive and clicking on subjects that catch your eye.

- Scaling Rails: One topic we've hardly covered in the *Rails Tutorial* book is performance, optimization, and scaling. Luckily, most sites will never run into serious scaling issues, and using anything beyond plain Rails is probably premature optimization. If you do run into performance issues, the Scaling Rails series from Gregg Pollack of Envy Labs is a good place to start. I also recommend investigating the site monitoring applications Scout and New Relic.[16] And, as you might suspect by now, there are RailsCasts on many scaling subjects, including profiling, caching, and background jobs.

- Ruby and Rails books: As mentioned in Chapter 1, I recommend *Beginning Ruby* by Peter Cooper, *The Well-Grounded Rubyist* by David A. Black, and *The Ruby Way* by Hal Fulton for further Ruby learning, and *The Rails 3 Way* by Obie Fernandez and *Rails 3 in Action* (wait for the second edition) by Ryan Bigg and Yehuda Katz for more about Rails.

- PeepCode and Code School: The screencasts at PeepCode and interactive courses at Code School are consistently high-quality, and I warmly recommend them.

11.5 Exercises

1. Add tests for destroying relationships associated with a given user (i.e., as implemented by `dependent :destroy` in Listing 11.4 and Listing 11.16). *Hint*: Follow the example in Listing 10.15.
2. The `respond_to` method seen in Listing 11.38 can actually be hoisted out of the actions into the Relationships controller itself, and the `respond_to` blocks can be replaced with a Rails method called `respond_with`. Prove that the resulting code, shown in Listing 11.47, is correct by verifying that the test suite still passes. (For details on this method, do a Google search on "rails respond_with".)
3. Refactor Listing 11.31 by adding partials for the code common to the following/followers pages, the Home page, and the user show page.
4. Following the model in Listing 11.19, write tests for the stats on the profile page.

---

16. In addition to being a clever phrase—*new relic* being a contradiction in terms—New Relic is also an anagram for the name of the company's founder, Lew Cirne.

Listing 11.47 A compact refactoring of Listing 11.38.

```
class RelationshipsController < ApplicationController
  before_filter :signed_in_user

  respond_to :html, :js

  def create
    @user = User.find(params[:relationship][:followed_id])
    current_user.follow!(@user)
    respond_with @user
  end

  def destroy
    @user = Relationship.find(params[:id]).followed
    current_user.unfollow!(@user)
    respond_with @user
  end
end
```

Index

Note: Page numbers in *italics* indicate figures, those with *t* indicate tables, and those with n indicate footnotes.

Symbols

" (double quote character), 135
(hash symbol), 21
/ (forward slash), 8
|| = construction, 354–355
! (not) operator, 139
&& (and) operator, 139
+ (plus) operator, 135
|| (or) operator, 139

A

About page
   about route, adding (Listing 3.14), 100–101
   about view, adding, 101–102
   adding, 99–103
   adding code to test contents of (Listing 3.13), 99
   code for (Listing 3.16), 102
   footer partial with links for (Listing 5.25), 206
   with HTML structure (Listing 3.21), 108
   with HTML structure removed (Listing 3.28), 113
   new, *102*
   refactoring, 103
   StaticPages controller with added about action (Listing 3.15), 101

tests for static pages (Listing 5.27), 210
view for, with Embedded Ruby title (Listing 3.24), 110–111
writing a failing test for, 99–100
abstraction layers, 226n4
access control, 456–459
access control in manipulating Microposts, 456–459
accessible attributes and first validation, 432–433
accessible attributes in model file, 230
actions, 85–86
Active Record, 222
   callback, 253
   count method, 295
   creating user objects, 230–233
   finding user objects, 233–235
   updating user objects, 235–236
   See also Validations
adding files, in Git, 30–31
administrative users, 413–417
   attr_accessible, 416–417
   attr_accessible attributes for User model without :admin attribute (Listing 9.42), 417
   deleting, 413–417
   migration to add boolean admin attribute to users (Listing 9.40), 415

administrative users (*continued*)
  sample data populator code with admin user
      (Listing 9.41), 416
  tests for admin attribute (Listing 9.39), 414
  user delete links (viewable by admins)
      (Listing 9.45), 419
  User model with admin boolean attribute, *415*
administrative users, deleting, 413–417
Ajax
  follow button with, 524–529
  form for following a user using (Listing 11.35),
      525
  form for unfollowing a user using
      (Listing 11.36), 525
  JavaScript Embedded Ruby to create following
      relationship (Listing 11.39), 529
  problem solved by, 524
  Ruby JavaScript to destroy following
      relationship (Listing 11.40), 529
Ajax requests, responding to, 525–529
  JS-ERb, 528–529
  in Relationships controller (Listing 11.38), 527
  tests for Relationships controller
      (Listing 11.37), 526
ampersand (&), 534
anchor tag, 97
annotate, 229–230
annotated User model (Listing 6.5), 229–230
ApplicationController class with inheritance
      (Listing 2.16), 72
Application Programmer Interface (API), 542
application root, 9, 28–29, 125, 161
Architectural Styles and the Design of Network-based
      Software Architectures (Fielding), 60n4
arrays, in Ruby data structures, 142–145
asset directory in asset pipeline, 187–188
asset pipeline, Sass and, 187–190
  asset directory, 187–188
  efficiency in production, 189–190
  manifest files, 188–189
  preprocessor engines, 189
assignment, 352
  See also Mass assignment
associations
  Micropost resource, 68–70
  user/micropost, 433–438
  user/relationship, 491–494

associative arrays, 148
asynchronous JavaScript and XML. *See* Ajax
attr_accessible
  administrative users, 416–417
  attributes for User model without :admin
      attribute (Listing 9.42), 417
  making name and email attributes accessible
      (Listing 6.6), 230
  to prevent mass assignment, 230, 416–417
attribute accessors, 162
authenticate method
  has_secure_password, 264, 338
  moving the authenticate method into the
      Sessions helper (Listing 10.27), 457–458
  test for (Listing 6.29), 262–263
authentication, 260–263
  adding authentication to Microposts controller
      actions (Listing 10.28), 458
  vs. authorization, 385
  sessions and, 325–326
  signin failure, 325–343
  signin success, 343–363
  See also Authenticate method
authenticity token, 301
authorization, 385–396
  vs. authentication, 385
  of following and followers pages, tests for
      (Listing 11.28), 516–517
  friendly forwarding, 392–396
  for relationships controller, tests for
      (Listing 11.33), 522–523
  requiring right user, 390–392
  requiring signed-in users, 386–389
automated testing, 77
Automattic, 286
avatar, 286n7

B

Bates, Ryan, 6, 7, 540
BCrypt cost factor in test environment, redefining
      (Listing 7.11), 286
before filters, 373
  adding a signed_in_user before filter
      (Listing 9.12), 387
  applied to every action in controller, 387
  correct_user before filter in microposts,
      477–478

correct_user before filter to protect edit/update pages (Listing 9.15), 391
current_user boolean method, 391–392
in requiring right user, 390–392
restricting destroy action to admins (Listing 9.48), 422
Beginning Ruby (Cooper), 4, 5, 129, 543
Black, David A., 6, 543
blocks, in Ruby data structures, 146–148
Booleans, 133, 138–139, 142
Bootstrap
  adding bootstrap-sass gem to (Listing 5.3), 175
  adding to application.js (Listing 8.25), 358
  and custom CSS in layout structure, 175–186
  framework, 176, 317
browsers, 11–12
built-in Ruby classes, modifying, 158–159
bundle exec, eliminating, 118–119
  binstubs, 119
  RVM Bundler integration, 118–119
Bundler, 19–23
business logic, 25

C

callback, 253, 346–348
Capybara, 79
  in Cucumber step files, 367
  integration tests, 93
  signin tests, 330
  signup tests, 294
  syntax for CSS id, 471
  in test-driven development, 94–95
  test for destroying microposts, 477
  tests for user update action (Listing 9.9), 383
cascading style sheets (CSS), 152–153, 190–197
  asset directory, 187–188
  Bootstrap framework, 176, 317
  Capybara syntax for CSS id, 471
  custom CSS, 175–186
  efficiency in production, 189–190
  HTML source produced by CSS includes (Listing 4.7), 153
  layout links, 197–211
  manifest files, 188–189
  for microposts (Listing 10.24), 452–453
  mixins, 274–275
  nesting, 190–192

partials, 181–186
preprocessor engines, 189
in Ruby data structures, 152–153
Sass, 187–197
site navigation, 169–175
structure, adding, 167–186
for styling error messages (Listing 7.24), 311
for user index (Listing 9.26), 400
user signup, 211–215
variables, 193–197
Celadon Cedar Stack, 40
chaining, 139, 421
checkout command, 28, 32
Chrome, 11–12, 103, 170
classes, 153–163
  built-in, modifying, 158–159
  code for example user (Listing 4.9), 161
  constructor, 153–154
  container class, 172
  controller, 159–161
  defining Word class in console (Listing 4.8), 156
  inheritance, 155–157
  user, 161–163
class methods, 154–155
class name converted to id, 493n5
Code School, 6, 543
command lines, 10, *11*
comments, 134–135
commit command, in Git, 31
config directory, 9, 88, *89*
constructor classes, 153–154
Contact page
  action for (Listing 5.18), 199
  adding, 197–199
  adding route for (Listing 5.17), 199
  footer partial with links for (Listing 5.25), 206
  for sample app, 114–117
  tests for (Listing 5.16), 198
  tests for static pages (Listing 5.27), 210
  view for (Listing 5.19), 199
container class, 172
content validations, Micropost model, 443–444
controller classes, 159–161
cookies, 349–351
  expiring 20 years in the future, 350
  remember token added to, 379

cookies (*continued*)
    remember token removed from, 363
    used as a hash, 349–351
Cooper, Peter, 4, 5, 543
correct_user before filter
    in microposts, 477–478
    to protect edit/update pages (Listing 9.15), 391
counting columns, 105n12
count method, 295
create action
    adding (empty) @feed_items instance variable
        to (Listing 10.45), 474–475
    completed, 313
    completed Sessions controller create action (not
        yet working) (Listing 8.13), 343
    handling signup failure (but not success)
        (Listing 7.21), 305
    for microposts, 461
    Microposts controller create action
        (Listing 10.30), 461
    preliminary version of sessions create action
        (Listing 8.9), 337
    for Sessions controller, 326, 336–338, 343,
        395
    Sessions create action with friendly forwarding
        (Listing 9.20), 395
    in signup failure, 304–305
    strategy for using, 304
    tests for post-save behavior in (Listing 7.32),
        323
    user create action with save and redirect
        (Listing 7.25), 314
    for Users controller, 425, 459
creating microposts, 459–467
    adding micropost instance variable to home
        action (Listing 10.34), 463
    adding microposts creation to Home page
        (Listing 10.31), 461
    form partial for creating microposts
        (Listing 10.33), 463
    Microposts controller create action
        (Listing 10.30), 461
    partial for user info sidebar (Listing 10.32), 462
    tests for (Listing 10.29), 460
    updating error-messages partial from
        Listing 7.23 to work with other objects
        (Listing 10.35), 464
    updating errors for editing users
        (Listing 10.37), 465
    updating rendering of user signup errors
        (Listing 10.36), 465
cross-site request forgery (CSRF), 301
cross-site scripting attack, 481
CSS. *See* Cascading style sheets (CSS)
CSS: The Missing Manual (McFarland), 5
Cucumber, 363–371
    adding cucumber-rails gem to Gemfile
        (Listing 8.31), 364
    adding helper method and custom RSpec
        matcher (Listing 8.34), 371
    features and steps, 365–368
    features to test user signin (Listing 8.32), 366
    installation and setup, 364–365
    RSpec examples, equivalent, 368–371
    signin tests using, 363–371
    steps needed to get signin features to pass
        (Listing 8.33), 368
current user, 351–355
    defining assignment to (Listing 8.20), 352
    definition for (Listing 8.21), 353
    finding, using remember_token (Listing 8.22),
        353
    non-nil, 356
    in signin success, 351–355
current_user? boolean method, 391–392

D

database indices, 254
database migration. *See* Migration
data model
    defined, 47
    micropost, 48–49
    user, 47–48
debug
    adding code for debug box, including Sass
        mixin (Listing 7.2), 274
    information, adding to site layout (Listing 7.1),
        273–274
    information, restricting to development
        environment, 276
    information in sign up, 271–276
    output, *275*
    in Rails environments, 276
default Rails directory structure, 19*t*

default Rails page, *24*
  with the app environment, *25*
default scope in Micropost model refinements, 440–441
demo app, 45–75
  conclusion, 74–75
  Microposts resource, 63–74
  planning the application, 45–49
  Users resource, 49–63
demo app, deploying, 73–74
dependent refinements in Micropost model, 441–443
deploying Rails, 39–42
destroy action
  adding factory for administrative users (Listing 9.43), 417–418
  adding working destroy action (Listing 9.46), 420–421
  in deleting users, 417–422
  before filter restricting destroy action to admins (Listing 9.48), 422
  test for protecting destroy action (Listing 9.47), 421–422
  tests for delete links (Listing 9.44), 418–419
  user index /users with delete links, *420*
destroying microposts
  ensuring that user's microposts are destroyed along with user (Listing 10.16), 443
  feed item partial with added delete link (Listing 10.47), 476
  Microposts controller destroy action (Listing 10.49), 477–478
  mockup of proto-feed with micropost delete links, *476*
  testing that microposts are destroyed when users are (Listing 10.15), 442
  tests for Microposts controller destroy action (Listing 10.48), 477
  user home page after deleting second-most-recent micropost, *479*
development environment, 9–27
  browsers, 11–12
  command lines, 10, *11*
  IDEs, 10
  terminals, 11
  text editors, 10, *11*
  time learning tools, 12

development log, 231–232, 450n4
directories
  standard directory and file structure, *18*
  summary of default Rails directory structure, 19*t*
div tags, 171
doctype, 84
Document Object Model (DOM), 528
domain logic, 25
domain-specific language (DSL), 3, 94, 283
drb option, 125
duplication, eliminating, 103, 111–113
dynamic pages. *See* Slightly dynamic pages

E

each method, 146, 151, 245, 399, 533n11
edit form, in updating users, 374–380
edits in updating users, successful, 382–384
edits in updating users, unsuccessful, 380–382
Emacs, 29
Embedded Ruby
  instance variables and, 162
  JavaScript, to create following relationship (Listing 11.39), 529
  slightly dynamic pages, 108–111
Embedded Ruby title
  view for About page with (Listing 3.24), 110–111
  view for Help page with (Listing 3.23), 110
  view for Home page with (Listing 3.22), 109
empty? method, 138, 139, 310
encrypted passwords, 255–257
Engine Yard, 13, 16
Engine Yard Cloud, 39
environment loading, adding to Spork.prefork block (Listing 3.36), 124
equality comparison operator, 144
ERb. *See* Embedded Ruby
error messages, signup, 308–312
  code to display error messages on signup form (Listing 7.22), 309
  CSS for styling error messages (Listing 7.24), 311
  failed signup with error messages, *312*
  partial for displaying form submission error messages (Listing 7.23), 309
exceptions, 234n8

F

factories
  complete factory file, including new factory for
      microposts (Listing 10.12), 439
  to simulate User model objects (Listing 7.8),
      284
  test for user show page (Listing 7.9),
      285
  testing user show page with, 282–286
Factory Girl, 283–286
  adding to Gemfile (Listing 7.7), 284
  in micropost refinements, 439–440
  sequence, defining (Listing 9.32),
      407
  sequence, solving problems in, 406
  slow nature of running, 285–286
Faker gem, 403
  adding to Gemfile (Listing 9.29), 403
  lorem ipsum text, 450–451, 451n5
feed, 429
  proto-, 467–475
  RSS, 542
  status, 529–539
Fernandez, Obie, 6, 142n5, 543
Fielding, Roy, 60
Files
  standard directory and file structure, 18
  summary of default Rails directory structure,
      19t
Firebug, 12, 301
Firefox, 11–12, 89, 170
first feed implementation, 532–535
flash, 315–317
  adding contents of flash variable to site layout
      (Listing 7.26), 315–316
  adding flash message to user signup
      (Listing 7.27), 317
  ERb in site layout using content tag
      (Listing 7.33), 324
  vs. flash.now, 316n11
  message for failed signin, 339–343, 340
flash.now, 316n11, 342
follow and unfollow buttons, 519–529
  with Ajax, 524–529
  current user's followers, 520
  profile of user to follow, with follow button,
      486

profile with unfollow button and incremented
    followers count, 487
Relationships controller (Listing 11.34),
    523–524
tests for (Listing 11.32), 521–522
tests for relationships controller authorization
    (Listing 11.33), 522–523
user profile with follow button, 514
users being followed by current user, 520
working follow button, 519–524
followed users in relationship model, 495–500
follower notifications, 541
followers, 500–503
  implementing user.followers using reverse
      relationships (Listing 11.16), 502
  model for user followers using reverse
      Relationship model, 500
  testing for reverse relationships (Listing 11.15),
      501
followers relationship model, 500–503
follow form, 505–514
  adding followed_users and followers actions
      to Users controller (Listing 11.18),
      506
  adding follow form and follower stats to user
      profile page (Listing 11.27), 513
  for following a user using (Listing 11.35), 525
  form for following user (Listing 11.25), 512
  form for unfollowing user (Listing 11.26), 512
  partial for follow/unfollow form
      (Listing 11.23), 511
  RESTful routes provided by custom rules in
      resource, 506t
  routes added for user relationships
      (Listing 11.24), 512
  for unfollowing a user using (Listing 11.36),
      525
following
  adding following/follower relationships to
      sample data (Listing 11.17), 503–504
  following? and follow! utility methods
      (Listing 11.12), 498
  problem with the data model (and a solution),
      485–490
  relationship model, 484–503
  sample following data, 503–505
  user/relationship associations, 491–494

users, 503–544
utility methods, tests for (Listing 11.11), 497
following and followers pages, 515–519
following and followers actions (Listing 11.30), 518
mockups of, *515–516*
show_follow view used to render following and followers (Listing 11.31), 519
test for followed_users and followers pages (Listing 11.29), 517–518
tests for authorization of (Listing 11.28), 516–517
following data, sample, 503–505
following? method, 497–500
follow! method, 497–500
forgery, 112
format, validating, 245–248
form_for, 297–300
form tag, 303, 334, 372
forward slash (/), 8
Fowler, Martin, 222n1
friendly forwarding, 392–396
adding store_location to signed-in user before filter (Listing 9.19), 394–395
code to implement (Listing 9.18), 394
Sessions create action with (Listing 9.20), 395
test for friendly forwarding (Listing 9.17), 393
full-table scan, 254
Fulton, Hal, 6, 543
functions, 91

G

gem configuration file
creating (Listing 1.1), 16
suppressing ri and rdoc documentation in (Listing 1.2), 16
Gemfile
adding annotate gem to (Listing 6.4), 229
adding bcrypt-ruby to (Listing 6.24), 255
adding bootstrap-sass gem to (Listing 5.3), 175
adding cucumber-rails gem to (Listing 8.31), 364
adding Factory Girl to (Listing 7.7), 284
adding Faker gem to (Listing 9.29), 403
default, in the first_app directory (Listing 1.4), 20

default Gemfile in the first app directory (Listing 1.4), 20
for demo app (Listing 2.1), 46
with explicit version of each Ruby gem (Listing 1.5), 21–22
including will paginate in (Listing 9.31), 405
needed to use PostgreSQL instead of SQLite (Listing 3.31), 117
for sample app (Listing 3.1), 78
for sample app (Listing 3.35), 123
for sample app, final (Listing 9.49), 423–424
for sample app including Guard (Listing 3.33), 120
gems, 14
gemsets, 14–15
generated code, scaffolding and, 3
generate script, 49, 86, 94
GET, 89–90
Git, 27–39
adding files in, 30–31
benefit of using, 31–32
branches, 35–36
commit command, 31
committing, 36–37
editing, 36
first-time repository setup, 28–30
first-time setup, 27–28
installing, 13
merging, 37–38
pushing, 38–39
README file, 34–35, *35*
README file, README.md (Listing 1.8), 36
README file formatted with Markdown, *39*
status command, 30
GitHub, 32–34
creating first app repository at, *33*
creating sample app repository at, *81*
initial README file for project at, *35*
repository page, *34*
.gitignore
augmented .gitignore file (Listing 1.7), 29–30
default .gitignore created by rails command (Listing 1.6), 29
Goia, Mircea, 14

Gravatar, 286–291
    adding sidebar to user show view (Listing 7.14),
        290
    defining gravatar_for helper method
        (Listing 7.13), 288
    editing, 382–384
    SCSS for styling user show page, including
        sidebar (Listing 7.15), 290–291
    in sign up, 286–291
    user profile page /users/1 with default Gravatar,
        289
    user show page /users/1 with sidebar and CSS,
        291
    user show page with custom Gravatar, 289
    user show view with name and (Listing 7.12),
        287
Guard
    automated tests with, 120–122
    Gemfile for sample app including
        (Listing 3.33), 120
    Spork with Guard, 126–127
gVim, 28

H

Hansson, David Heinemeier, 2, 4
hashes, 337
    nested (Listing 4.6), 151
    in Ruby data structures, 148–152
hash symbol, 21
has_secure_password
    authenticate method, 264, 338
    User, 263–265
have_selector method, 104
Head First HTML, 5
Help page
    code added to test (Listing 3.11), 98
    generated view for (Listing 3.8), 92
    with HTML structure (Listing 3.20), 107
    with HTML structure removed (Listing 3.27),
        113
    tests for static pages (Listing 5.27), 210
    view for, with Embedded Ruby title
        (Listing 3.23), 110
Heroku
    commands, 41–42
    creating a new application at (Listing 1.9), 40
    deployment, 40–41
    setup, 39–40

hierarchies, inheritance, 70–73, *73*
Home page
    adding follower stats to (Listing 11.21), 509
    adding microposts creation to (Listing 10.31),
        461–462
    with follow stats, *511*
    generated view for (Listing 3.7), 92
    with HTML structure (Listing 3.19), 107
    with HTML structure removed (Listing 3.26),
        113
    with link to signup page (Listing 5.2), 173
    mockup with form for creating microposts,
        459
    mockup with proto-feed, *467*
    SCSS for Home page sidebar (Listing 11.22),
        510
    with status feed, mockup of, *530*
    with status feed and incremented following
        count, *488*
    testing following/follower statistics on
        (Listing 11.19), 507
    view for, with Embedded Ruby title
        (Listing 3.22), 109
    view for, with HTML structure (Listing 3.19),
        107
    with working status feed, *539*
href, 97
HTML
    About page with HTML structure removed
        (Listing 3.28), 113
    About page with structure (Listing 3.21), 108
    code for signin form (Listing 8.7), 334
    for edit form defined in Listing 9.3 and shown
        in Figure 9.2. (Listing 9.4), 377
    for form in Figure 7.12 (Listing 7.20), 301
    initial user edit page with pre-filled name and
        email, *377*
    produced by CSS includes (Listing 4.7), 153
    for signin form produced by Listing 8.7, 335
    signup form, 301–303, *335*
    for signup form/signup for new users, *300*
    typical, with friendly greeting (Listing 3.3), 84
    user edit action (Listing 9.2), 375
    for user edit form (Listing 9.2), 377
HTTP, 89–90
HTTP verbs, 89, 90
hypertext reference (href), 97
hypertext transfer protocol. *See* HTTP

I

IDEs, 10
implicit return, 141
index, user. *See* User index
index action, simplified for demo app
    (Listing 2.4), 61
index.html file, 82–84, *83*
index page
    with 100 sample users, *405*
    correspondence between pages and URIs for
        Users resource, *52t*
    initial, for Users resource, *52*
    micropost, *68*
    with one user, *402*
    with second user, *55*
    tests for (Listing 9.23), 398–399
    users with pagination, *410*
inheritance
    ApplicationController class with (Listing 2.16),
        72
    class, 155–157
    classes, 155–157
    hierarchies, 70–73, *73*
    Micropost class with (Listing 2.13), 71
    MicropostsController class with (Listing 2.15),
        72
    User class with (Listing 2.12), 71
    UsersController class with (Listing 2.14), 72
inheritance class, 155–157
inheritance hierarchies, 70–73, *73*
initialization hash, 231
inspect method, 151
installing Rails, 16–17
instance variables, 61, 162
    adding (empty) @feed items to create action
        (Listing10.45), 474–475
    adding to home action (Listing 10.41), 471
    adding to the home action (Listing 10.34),
        463
    adding to user show action (Listing 10.22),
        449
integrated development environments (IDEs), 10
integration tests, 93
    See also Tests
interpolation, 136–137
    string, 115, 133, 142, 162, 209
IRC client, 14n10
iTerm, 11

J

JavaScript
    adding Bootstrap to application.js
        (Listing 8.25), 358
    to create following relationship (Listing 11.39),
        529
    to destroy following relationship
        (Listing 11.40), 529
    unobtrusive, 525
JavaScript Embedded Ruby (JS-ERb), 528–529
    to create a following relationship
        (Listing 11.39), 529
join method, 145, 534
JS-ERb. *See* JavaScript Embedded Ruby
    (JS-ERb)

K

Katz, Yehuda, 364, 543

L

layout, filling in, 167–219
    adding structure, 167–186
    asset pipeline, Sass and, 187–190
    conclusion, 215–216
    exercises, 217–219
    layout links, 197–211
    stylesheets and, improving with Sass, 190–197
    user signup, 211–215
layout files
    duplication eliminated with, 103, 111–113
    sample application site layout (Listing 3.25),
        112
    sample application site layout (Listing 4.1), 130
    sample application site layout (Listing 4.3),
        132
    site layout with added structure (Listing 5.1),
        169
layout links, 197–211
    changing for signed-in users (Listing 8.24),
        357–358
    named routes, 205–207
    Rails routes, 202–205
    route tests, 200–202
    RSpec, 207–211
    test for links on layout (Listing 5.36), 218
layout links, changing, 355–359
    adding Bootstrap JavaScript library to
        application.js (Listing 8.25), 358

layout links, changing (*continued*)
   the signed in? helper method (Listing 8.23),
     356
   for signed-in users (Listing 8.24), 357–358
   signin success and, 355–359
length validations, 243–244
   adding for name attribute (Listing 6.15), 244
   constraining micropost characters (Listing 2.9),
     67
   test name for (Listing 6.14), 244
Linux, 13–14
Linux Mint, 14
Linux Ubuntu, 14
lists, unordered, 172
literal constructor, 153–154
literal strings, 135
Loeffler, David, 10
log, development, 231–232
log files, ignoring, 29

M

Macintosh OS X, 11
MacVim, 28
magic columns, 226, 232
manifest files in asset pipeline, 188–189
map method, 147–148, 533
mapping for site links, 198*t*
mass assignment
   attr_accessible used to prevent, 230, 416
   invalid, ensuring Rails throws errors on
     (Listing 10.6), 436
memoization, 354n7
Merb, merger with Rails, 4
message passing in Ruby, objects and, 138–141
messaging, 541
method chaining, 139, 421
method definitions, 141
micropost associations, 433–438
Micropost class with inheritance (Listing 2.13), 71
micropost data model, 48–49
micropost migration (Listing 10.1), 430
Micropost model, 429–444, *431*
   accessible attributes and first validation,
     432–433
   basic model, 430–432
   content validations, 443–444
   initial Micropost spec (Listing 10.2), 431

micropost migration (Listing 10.1), 430
   refinements, 439–443
   tests for (Listing 10.17), 443–444
   tests for validity of new micropost
     (Listing 10.3), 432
   user has many microposts (Listing 10.11), 438
   user/micropost associations, 433–438
   validation for user (Listing 10.4), 433
   validations (Listing 10.18), 444
microposts
   adding to sample data (Listing 10.23), 451
   CSS for (Listing 10.24), 452–453
   destroying along with user (Listing 10.16), 443
   form partial for creating (Listing 10.33), 463
   ordering with default scope (Listing 10.14), 441
   partial for showing single micropost
     (Listing 10.21), 449
   sample microposts, 450–454
   summary of user/micropost association
     methods, 434*t*
   testing that microposts are destroyed when
     users are (Listing 10.15), 442
   testing the order of a user's microposts
     (Listing 10.13), 440–441
Microposts, manipulating, 454–479
   access control, 456–459
   creating microposts, 459–467
   destroying microposts, 475–479
   micropost pagination links, *455*
   proto-feed, 467–475
Microposts, showing, 445–454
   profile page with microposts, mockup of, *445*
   sample microposts, 450–454
   user show page, augmenting, 446–450
Microposts controller
   create action (Listing 10.30), 461
   destroy action (Listing 10.49), 477–478
   in schematic form (Listing 2.8), 65–66
   tests for destroy action (Listing 10.48), 477
MicropostsController class with inheritance
     (Listing 2.15), 72
Microposts resource, 63–75
   access control, 456–459
   associations, 68–70
   demo app, deploying, 73–74
   error messages for failed micropost creation, *69*
   inheritance hierarchies, 70–73, *73*

length validations, 243–244
micropost belonging to user (Listing 2.11), 69
between microposts and users, *70*
microtour, 63–66
Rails routes with new rule (Listing 2.7), 65
RESTful routes provided by, 65*t*
routes for (Listing 10.25), 455
user has many microposts (Listing 2.10), 68
validations, 66–68
microtour, 63–66
migration
    to add boolean admin attribute to users
        (Listing 9.40), 415
    micropost (Listing 10.1), 430
    password, 256–257
    Rake used in, 50
    user model, 223–228
    for User model (to create users table)
        (Listing 6.2), 225
mockups, 167–168
model annotation in model file, 228–230
model file, 228–230
    accessible attributes, 230
    model annotation, 228–230
modeling demo microposts, 48–49
modeling demo users, 47–48
modeling users, 221–269
    conclusion, 267
    exercises, 268–269
    passwords, 254–267
    user model, 222–236
    user validations, 236–254
model-view-controller (MVC), 25–27
    in action, 56–62
    in Rails, diagram of, *57*
    schematic representation of, *26*
motivation
    in Ruby, 129–133
    in status feed, 529–532
MVC. *See* Model-view-controller (MVC)

N

name attribute
    adding length validation for (Listing 6.15), 244
    failing test for validation of (Listing 6.11), 241
    validating presence of (Listing 6.9), 240
named routes

footer partial with links (Listing 5.25), 206
header partial with links (Listing 5.24),
        205–206
namespaces, 403
nested hashes (Listing 4.6), 151
nesting, 190–192
newline, 105n11
new status feed, 538–539
nil, 136
non-nil current user, 356

O

objects and message passing, in Ruby, 138–141
OS X. *See* Macintosh OS X

P

PagesController. *See* StaticPages controller
pagination, for showing all users, 404–410
    paginating users in index action (Listing 9.35),
        409
    tests for pagination (Listing 9.33), 407–408
pagination links, micropost, *455*
palindrome? method, 155–156, 158
Paperclip gem, 287n8
partial refactoring, for showing all users, 410–412
partials, 181–186
    adding CSS for site footer (Listing 5.13),
        185–186
    for displaying form submission error messages
        (Listing 7.23), 309
    for HTML shim (Listing 5.9), 183
    for the site footer (Listing 5.11), 184
    for the site header (Listing 5.10), 184
    site layout with footer partial (Listing 5.12),
        185
    site layout with partials for stylesheets and
        header (Listing 5.8), 182–183
    updating error-messages (Listing 10.35), 464
passwords, 254–267
    adding bcrypt-ruby to Gemfile (Listing 6.24),
        255
    and confirmation, 257–260
    creating a user, 265–267
    encrypted, 255–257
    ensuring that User object has password_digest
        column (Listing 6.25), 256

passwords (*continued*)

   migration, 256–257

   migration to add password_digest column to
      users table (Listing 6.26), 256

   reminders, 540, 541

   secure, adding, 254–260

   test for password and password confirmation
      (Listing 6.28), 259–260

   testing for password and password_confirmation
      attributes (Listing 6.27), 257

   user authentication, 260–263

   user has secure password, 263–265

   User model with added password_digest
      attribute, *255*

   See also Authenticate method

Patterns of Enterprise Application Architecture
   (Fowler), 222n1

PeepCode, 6, 543

pending spec, 237

persistence, 223

Phusion Passenger, 39

Pik project, 13

pluralize text helper, 310

PostgreSQLn, 46–47, 115, 117, 223, 253n15

pound sign. *See* Hash symbol

preprocessor engines in asset pipeline, 189

presence, validating, 239–243

Preston-Werner, Tom, 286

private keyword, 348

production in asset pipeline, efficiency in,
   189–190

profile images, 286, 382

profile links, 332

protected page

   mockup of, *385*

   signin form after trying to access, *388*

proto-feed, 467–475

   adding feed instance variable to home action
      (Listing 10.41), 471

   adding (empty) @feed items instance
      variable to create action (Listing10.45),
      474–475

   adding status feed to Home page
      (Listing 10.44), 473

   Home page after creating micropost, *474*

   Home page with, *473*

   mockup of Home page with, *467*

preliminary implementation for micropost
      status feed (Listing 10.39), 469

single feed item partial (Listing 10.43), 472

status feed partial (Listing 10.42), 472

test for rendering feed on Home page
      (Listing 10.40), 470–471

tests for (Listing 10.38), 468

public/index.html file, *83*

puts method, 136

R

Rails

   approach to learning, 4–6

   deploying, 39–42

   development environment setup, 9–27

   environments, 276–277

   intermediate-to-advanced resources, 6–7

   introduction, 3–9

   Merb merger and, 4

   Ruby and, importance of, 129–165 (*See also*
      Ruby)

   running to generate new application
      (Listing 1.3), 17–18

   scaling, 7

   version control with Git, 27–39

Rails, installing

   Git, installing, 13

   Rails, installing (Windows), 13, 16–17

   Ruby, installing, 13–15

   RubyGems, installing, 15–16

The Rails 3 Way (Fernandez), 6, 82n5, 142n5, 543

RailsCasts, 6, 7, 540, 543

Rails command, 17–19

   default .gitignore created by (Listing 1.6), 29

   to generate new application (Listing 1.3),
      17–18

Rails console, 134

Rails Guides, 6, 189, 202, 228, 506, 543

Rails Machine, 39

Rails root, 8–9

Rails routes, 202–205

   adding mapping for the (Listing 5.23), 204

   adding Users resource to (Listing 7.3), 279

   commented-out hint for defining
      (Listing 5.22), 204

   with new rule for Microposts resource
      (Listing 2.7), 65

with rule for Users resource (Listing 2.2), 58
for static pages (Listing 5.21), 202
Rails server, 23–25
The Rails 3 Way (Fernandez), 6, 142n5, 543
Rails Tutorial help page, 9n6
Rake, 50, 51
task for populating database with sample users
(Listing 9.30), 403–404
ranges, 145–146
README file
Git, 34–35, *35*
improved, formatted with Markdown (Listing),
39
improved, for sample app (Listing 3.2), 80
initial, for project at GitHub, *35*
new README file, README.md
(Listing 1.8), 36
updating, 80
Red, Green, Refactor, 94
Green, 100–102
Red, 99–100
Refactor, 103
refactoring
in adding static pages, 103
compact, of Listing 11.38 (Listing 11.47),
544
first attempt at index view (Listing 9.36), 411
partial, 410–412
refactored following and followers actions
(Listing 11.30), 518
refinements in Micropost model, 439–443
default scope, 440–441
dependent: destroy, 441–443
regular expression (regex), 246
relationship model, 484–503, *491*
adding belongs to associations to (Listing 11.6),
494
adding indices for relationships table
(Listing 11.1), 490
adding User model followed_users association
(Listing 11.10), 496
followed users, 495–500
of followed users through user relationships,
489
followers, 500–503
following? and follow! utility methods
(Listing 11.12), 498

implementing user.followers using reverse
relationships (Listing 11.16), 502
implementing user/relationships has_many
association (Listing 11.4), 493
problem with, 485–491
for reverse relationships, 500–503
test for unfollowing a user (Listing 11.12), 499
test for user.followed_users attribute
(Listing 11.9), 496
testing for reverse relationships (Listing 11.15),
501
testing for user.relationships attribute
(Listing 11.3), 492
testing Relationship creation and attributes
(Listing 11.2), 491–492
testing Relationship model validations
(Listing 11.7), 495
testing user/relationships belongs_to association
(Listing 11.5), 494
tests for "following" utility methods
(Listing 11.11), 497
unfollowing user by destroying user
relationship (Listing 11.14), 499–500
for user followers using reverse relationship
model, *500*
user/relationship associations, 491–494
validations, 495
relationships attribute, 492
Relationships controller
Ajax requests in, responding to (Listing 11.38),
527
follow and unfollow buttons (Listing 11.34),
523–524
responses to Ajax requests, tests for
(Listing 11.37), 526
reload method, 383
remember token, 344
added to cookies, 379
before_save callback to create (Listing 8.18),
348–349
cookie in local browser, *360*
current user found by using (Listing 8.22), 353
first test for (Listing 8.15), 345
migration to add to users table (Listing 8.16),
346
removed from cookies, 363
test for valid (nonblank) (Listing 8.17), 347

remember token (*continued*)
  User model with added remember_token
      attribute, *345*
render, 183
replies, 541
repository setup, 28–30
request specs. *See* Tests
resources
  advanced Rails, 4, 6
  guide to further, 542–543
REST API, 542
REST architecture, 45, 59, 65, 86, 90
RESTful routes
  provided by Microposts resource, 65*t*
  provided by Users resource, 65*t*
reverse relationships, 500–503
  followers using reverse relationship model, *500*
  implementing user.followers using reverse
      relationships (Listing 11.16), 502
  testing for reverse relationships (Listing 11.15),
      501
root, 8–9
routes in layout links
  named, 205–207
  Rails, 202–205
  tests, 200–202
RSpec
  adding helper method and custom RSpec
      matcher (Listing 8.34), 371
  Cucumber equivalent, 368–371
  custom matchers, 368–371
  layout links, 207–211
  request specs, 93, 368
RSS feed, 542
Rubular, 247, *248*
Ruby, 129–165
  comments, 134–135
  conclusion, 164
  exercises, 164–165
  gems, 14
  gemsets, 14–15
  installing, 13–15
  method defintions, 141
  motivation, 129–133
  objects and message passing, 138–141
  strings, 135–138
  title helper, 142

Ruby classes. *See* Classes
Ruby data structures, 142–153
  arrays, 142–145
  blocks, 146–148
  cascading style sheets, 152–153
  hashes and symbols, 148–152
  ranges, 145–146
RubyGems, installing, 15–16
Ruby JavaScript (RJS)
  to create following relationship (Listing 11.39),
      529
  to destroy following relationship
      (Listing 11.40), 529
RubyMine, 10
Ruby on Rails. *See* Rails
Ruby Version Manager (RVM), 8, 13, 118
The Ruby Way (Fulton), 6, 129, 543

S

Safari, 11–12, 89, 170
sample application, extensions to, 540–542
  follower notifications, 541
  messaging, 541
  password reminders, 541
  replies, 541
  REST API, 542
  RSS feed, 542
  search, 542
  signup confirmation, 541
sample users, showing all, 403–404
sandbox, 231, 252, 265
Sass, 187–197
  asset pipeline and, 187–190
  improving stylesheets with, 190–197
save!, 497
scaffolding, 2–3
scaling Rails, 7
scope, 440–441
screencasts, 538, 542
SCSS
  converting to CSS, 192
  error messages styled with, 311
  for Home page sidebar (Listing 11.22), 510
  initial SCSS file converted to use nesting and
      variables (Listing 5.15), 195–197
  rewriting, 193–194
  Sass supported by, 190

for styling user show page, including sidebar
    (Listing 7.15), 290–291
search, 542
Secure Sockets Layer (SSL), 318
    deploying production with, in signup success,
        317–321
Seguin, Wayne E., 13, 14
self, 157, 348
session hijacking attack, 318, 351
sessions
    authentication and, 325–326
    defined, 325–326
    destroying a session (user signout)
        (Listing 8.29), 362
    preliminary version of sessions create action
        (Listing 8.9), 337
    sessions create action with friendly forwarding
        (Listing 9.20), 395
    signin failure and, 325–326
    sign out method in Sessions helper module
        (Listing 8.30), 363
Sessions controller
    adding resource to get standard RESTful
        actions for sessions (Listing 8.2), 328
    completed Sessions controller create action (not
        yet working) (Listing 8.13), 343
    create action for, 326, 336–338, 343, 395
    signin failure and, 326–329
    tests for new session action and view
        (Listing 8.1), 327
short-circuit evaluation, 355
showing microposts. See Microposts, showing
sidebar
    partial for the user info sidebar (Listing 10.32),
        462
    SCSS for Home page (Listing 11.22), 510
    in SCSS for styling user show page
        (Listing 7.15), 290–291
    in sign up, 288–291
signed in? helper method (Listing 8.23), 356
signed-in users
    authorization of, 386–389
    requiring, 386–389
sign in, 325–372
    conclusion, 371–372
    Cucumber, signin tests using, 363–371
    exercises, 372

signin failure, 325–343
    flash message, rendering with, 339–343
    reviewing from submission, 336–338
    sessions, 325–326
    Sessions controller, 326–329
    signin form, 333–336, 335
    signin tests, 330–333
signin form, 333–336, 335
    code for (Listing 8.7), 334
    HTML for signin form produced by Listing 8.7
        (Listing 8.8), 335
    initial failed signin, with create as in
        Listing 8.9., 336
    signin failure and, 333–336
signing out, 361–363
    destroying a session (user signout)
        (Listing 8.29), 362
    sign out method in Sessions helper module
        (Listing 8.30), 363
sign_in method, signin success and, 349–351
signin success, 343–363
    current user, 351–355
    layout links, changing, 355–359
    remembering user signin status, 343–349
    signing out, 361–363
    sign_in method, 349–351
    signin upon signup, 359–361
signin tests
    signin failure and, 330–333
    using Cucumber, 363–371
signin upon signup, 359–361
sign up, 271–324
    conclusion, 321
    exercises, 321–324
    failure in (See Signup failure)
    Rails environments in, 276–277
    showing users, 271–291
    success in (See Signup success)
signup confirmation, 541
signup failure, 303–312, 306
    a partial for displaying form submission
        error messages (Listing 7.23),
        309
    code to display error messages on signup form
        (Listing 7.23), 309
    create action that can handle (but not success)
        (Listing 7.21), 305

signup failure (*continued*)
  CSS for styling error messages (Listing 7.24),
      311
  debug information, *307*
  mockup of signup failure page, *304*
  signup error messages, 308–312, *312*
  working form, 303–308
signup form, 292–303
  adding @user variable to the new action
      (Listing 7.18), 299
  CSS for (Listing 7.19), 300
  filled-in form with text and password fields, *302*
  form_for, using, 297–300
  form to sign up new users (Listing 7.17), 298
  HTML, 301–303
  HTML for form in figure 7.12 (Listing 7.20),
      301
  for new users, *300*
  tests for signing up users (Listing 7.16),
      296–297
  tests for user signup, 293–297
  using form_for, 297–300
signup page
  initial (stub) (Listing 5.33), 214
  linking the button to (Listing 5.34), 215
  route for (Listing 5.32), 214
  signing in user upon signup (Listing 8.27), 361
  signin upon signup, 359–361
  testing that newly signed-up users are also
      signed in (Listing 8.26), 360–361
  Users controller, 212
signup success, 312–321
  deploying production with SSL, 317–321
  finished signup form, 313–315
  first signup, 317
  flash, 315–319
  mockup of, *314*
signup URI, in user signup, 213–215
site navigation in filling in layout, 169–175
  Home page with link to signup page
      (Listing 5.2), 173
  site layout with added structure (Listing 5.1),
      169
skeleton for a shuffle method attached to the
    String class (Listing 4.11), 165
skeleton for a string shuffle function
    (Listing 4.10), 164

slightly dynamic pages, 103–113
  duplication, eliminating with layouts, 103,
      111–113
  Embedded Ruby, 108–111
  instance variables and Embedded Ruby, 162
  passing title tests, 106–108
  testing a title change, 103–107
  testing title page, 103–106
spike, 93
split method, 143
Spork, 123–127
  adding environment loading to Spork.prefork
      block (Listing 3.36), 124
  configuring RSpec to automatically use
      (Listing 3.37), 125
  Gemfile for sample app (Listing 3.35), 123
  Guardfile updated for Spork (Listing 3.38),
      126
  Guard with Spork, 126–127
  speeding up tests with, 123–127
SQL injection, 470
SQLite Database Browser, 226, *227,* 266
Stack Overflow, 301, 492n4
staging area, 30
static pages, 77–128
  conclusion, 114
  exercises, 114–117
  test-driven development, 93–99
  testing, 93–103
  See also Slightly dynamic pages
static pages, adding, 99–103
  green, 100–102
  red, 99–100
  refactor, 103
static pages, advanced setup, 117–128
  bundle exec, eliminating, 118–119
  Guard, automated tests with, 120–122
  Spork, speeding up tests with, 123–127
  Sublime Text, tests inside, 127–128
static pages, making, 82–92
  with Rails, 85–92
  truly static pages, 82–85
  undoing things, 87–88
StaticPages controller
  with about action (Listing 3.15), 101
  generating (Listing 3.4), 86
  inheritance hierarchy for, *160*

made by Listing 3.4 (Listing 3.6), 91
routes for home and help actions in
    (Listing 3.5), 88
spec with base title (Listing 3.29), 115–116
spec with title tests (Listing 3.18), 105
stats, 505–514
    adding follower stats to Home page
        (Listing 11.21), 509
    adding follow form and follower stats to user
        profile page (Listing 11.27), 513
    Home page with follow stats, *511*
    mockup of stats partial, *505*
    a partial for displaying follower stats
        (Listing 11.20), 508
    SCSS for Home page sidebar (Listing 11.22),
        510
    testing following/follower statistics on the
        Home page (Listing 11.19), 507
stats form, 505–514
status command, in Git, 30
status feed, 529–539
    adding completed feed to User model
        (Listing 11.42), 532
    final implementation of from_users_followed_by
        (Listing 11.45), 537–538
    final tests for (Listing 11.41), 531–532
    first cut at from_users_followed_by
        (Listing 11.43), 535
    first feed implementation, 532–535
    home action with paginated feed
        (Listing 11.46), 538
    Home page with working status feed, *539*
    improving from_users_followed_by
        (Listing 11.44), 536
    mockup of a user's Home page with, *530*
    motivation and strategy, 529–532
    new, 538–539
    partial for a single feed item (Listing 10.43),
        472
    preliminary implementation for micropost
        (Listing 10.39), 469
    subselects, 535–538
    for user following users, *531*
strategy in status feed, 529–532
string interpolation, 115, 133, 142, 162,
    209
string literals, 135

strings
    double-quoted, 137–138
    printing, 136–137
    in Ruby, 135–138
    single-quoted, 137–138
structure in filling in layout, 167–186
    bootstrap and custom CSS, 175–186
    partials, 181–186
    site navigation, 169–175
stylesheets. *See* Cascading style sheets (CSS)
Sublime Text, tests inside, 127–128
Sublime Text 2, 10, 16, 127
subselects in status feed, 535–538
sudo, 8
superclass method, 155
symbols, 148–152
system setups, 27

T

TDD. *See* Test-driven development (TDD)
terminals, 11
ternary operator, 481, 482
test-driven development (TDD), 5
    Green, 100–102
    Red, 99–100
    Red, Green, Refactor, 94
    Refactor, 103
    Spork, 123–127
    in testing static pages, 93–99
testing tools, 93
tests
    for admin attribute (Listing 9.39), 414
    for authorization of following and followers
        pages (Listing 11.28), 516–517
    automated tests with Guard, 120–122
    for Contact page (Listing 5.16), 198
    for creating microposts (Listing 10.29), 460
    for delete links (Listing 9.44), 418–419
    for destroy action in Microposts controller
        (Listing 10.48), 477
    for email format validation (Listing 6.16),
        245–246
    for follow and unfollow buttons
        (Listing 11.32), 521–522
    for "following" utility methods (Listing 11.11),
        497
    for friendly forwarding (Listing 9.17), 393

tests (*continued*)
    for full_title helper (Listing 5.37), 219
    Guard, automated tests with, 120–122
    for index page (Listing 9.23), 398–399
    integration tests, 93
    for Micropost model (Listing 10.17), 443–444
    for Microposts controller destroy action
        (Listing 10.48), 477
    for micropost's user association (Listing 10.8),
        437
    for new session action and view (Listing 8.1),
        327
    for pagination (Listing 9.33), 407–408
    passing title, 106–108
    for post-save behavior in (Listing 7.32), 323
    for proto-feed (Listing 10.38), 468
    for Relationships controller (Listing 11.37),
        526
    for relationships controller authorization
        (Listing 11.33), 522–523
    for Relationships controller authorization
        (Listing 11.33), 522–523
    for responses to Ajax requests (Listing 11.37),
        526
    for reverse relationships (Listing 11.15),
        501
    for routes in layout links, 200–202
    for showing microposts on user show page
        (Listing 10.19), 446
    signin, using Cucumber, 363–371
    for signin failure, 330–333
    for signing up users (Listing 7.16), 296–297
    signin tests using Capybara, 294, 330
    signin tests using Cucumber, 363–371
    spec with title tests (Listing 3.18), 105
    speeding up with Spork, 123–127
    static pages (Listing 5.27), 210
    for static pages, 93–99
    for static pages (Listing 5.27), 210
    for status feed, final (Listing 11.41), 531–532
    Sublime Text, tests inside, 127–128
    for title change, 103–106
    title test (Listing 3.17), 104
    user, initial, 236–239
    for user index page (Listing 9.23), 398–399
    for user show page (Listing 7.9), 285
    for user signup, 293–297
    for user's microposts attribute (Listing 10.9),
        437–438
    for user update action (Listing 9.9), 383
    for user validations, initial, 236–239
    for utility methods, (Listing 11.11), 497
    for validity of new micropost (Listing 10.3),
        432
text editors, 10, *11*
TextMate, 10, 28, 105n12
time helpers, 350
timestamps, 225
title change
    passing title tests, 106–107
    testing, 103–106
title helper, 142
    tests for full_title helper (Listing 5.37), 219
title test (Listing 3.17), 104
toggle method, 414
tools, learning, 12
Torvalds, Linus, 27

U

underscore method, 493n5
unfollow and follow buttons. *See* Follow and
    unfollow buttons
unfollow form, using Ajax (Listing 11.36),
    525
unfollowing a user
    by destroying a user relationship
        (Listing 11.14), 499–500
    test for (Listing 11.13), 499
uniqueness, validating, 249–254
Unix-style command line, 7
unobtrusive JavaScript, 525
unordered list tag, 172
update action. *See* User update action
updating users, 373–384
    edit form, 374–380
    successful edits, 382–384
    unsuccessful edits, 380–382
URIs
    adding to users link (Listing 9.28), 401–402
    correspondence between pages and URIs for
        Users resource, 52*t*
    defined, 2n1
    signup, in user signup, 213–215
    test for "Users" link (Listing 9.27), 401

URLs
  correspondence between pages and Users
      resource, 52*t*
  defined, 2n1
user
  administrative, 413–417
  creating, 265–267
  current user? method (Listing 9.16), 392
  destroying, 499–500
  has secure password, 263–265
  new user view with partial (Listing 9.51), 425
  paginating, 404–410
  requiring signed-in users, 386–389
  requiring the right user, 390–392
  sample users, 403–404
  showing, 271–291
  signin status, remembering, 343–349
  stub view for showing user information
      (Listing 7.4), 280
  summary of user/micropost association
      methods/updating, 434*t*
  tests, initial, 236–239
user authentication. *See* Authentication
user authorization. *See* Authorization
user class, 161–163
User class with inheritance (Listing 2.12), 71
user data model, 47–48
user edit form
  adding test for Settings link (Listing 9.5), 378
  HTML for (Listing 9.2), 377
  mockup of, *374*
  partial for new and edit form fields
      (Listing 9.50), 425
  tests for user update action (Listing 9.9), 383
  updating error-messages partial from
      Listing 7.23 to work with other objects
      (Listing 10.35), 464
  updating trendering of user signup errors
      (Listing 10.36), 465
  user edit action (Listing 9.2), 375
  user edit view (Listing 9.3), 376
  user update action (Listing 9.10), 384
user.followers method, 500
user has_many microposts (Listing 10.11), 438
  micropost belongs to user (Listing 2.11), 69
  relationship between a user and its microposts,
      434

user index, 396–403
  adding URI to users link (Listing 9.28),
      401–402
  CSS for (Listing 9.26), 400
  first refactoring attempt at index view
      (Listing 9.36), 411
  including will paginate in Gemfile
      (Listing 9.31), 405
  mockup of, *397*
  paginating users in index action (Listing
      9.35), 409
  pagination, 404–410
  with pagination (Listing 9.34), 408
  partial refactoring, 410–412
  partial to render single user (Listing 9.37), 412
  refactored (Listing 9.38), 412
  requiring signed-in user for index action
      (Listing 9.22), 398
  for showing all users, 396–403
  test for "Users" link URI (Listing 9.27), 401
  testing that index action is protected
      (Listing 9.21), 396–397
  tests for pagination (Listing 9.33), 407–408
  user index action (Listing 9.24), 399
  user index view (Listing 9.25), 400
  view (Listing 9.25), 400
user index page
  page 2 of, *411*
  tests for (Listing 9.23), 398–399
  users with 100 sample users, *405*
  users with only one user, *402*
  users with pagination, *410*
user info sidebar, partial for (Listing 10.32),
    462
user/micropost associations, 433–438
User microposts, 429–482
  conclusion, 479–480
  exercises, 480–482
  manipulating, 454–479
  model, 429–444, *431*
  resources, 63–74
  showing, 445–454
User model, 222–236
  accessible attributes, 230
  with added password_digest attribute, *255*
  adding annotate gem to Gemfile (Listing 6.4),
      229

User model (*continued*)
  annotated User model (Listing 6.5), 229–230
  brand new (Listing 6.3), 228
  for demo application (Listing 2.5), 61
  generating (Listing 6.1), 224
  making name and email attributes accessible
    (Listing 6.6), 230
  migration for (to create a users table)
    (Listing 6.2), 225
  migrations, 223–228
  model file, 228–230
  user objects, 230–236
user objects
  creating, 230–233
  finding, 233–235
  updating, 235–236
user profile page, mockup of, *445*
user/relationship associations, 491–494
  implementing has_many association
    (Listing 11.4), 493
  See also Relationship model
users, deleting, 413–422
  administrative users, 413–417
  destroy action, 417–422
users, following, 483–544
  conclusion, 539–543
  current user's profile, *484*
  exercises, 543–544
  finding a user to follow, *485*
  Home page with status feed and incremented
    following count, *488*
  implementation of user following, *488*
  model of followed users through user
    relationships, *489*
  profile of user to follow, with follow button,
    486
  profile with unfollow button and incremented
    followers count, *487*
  resources, guide to further, 542–543
  sample application, extensions to, 540–542
  status feed, 529–539
  test for unfollowing (Listing 11.13), 499
  web interface for, 503–529
  See also Relationship model
users, showing all, 396–412
  pagination, 404–410
  partial refactoring, 410–412

  sample users, 403–404
  user index, 396–403
users, showing in sign up, 271–291
  debug information, 272–276
  Gravatar, 286–291
  Rails environments, 276–277
  sidebar, 288–291
  user show page, testing, 282–286
  Users resource, 278–281
users, updating, 373–385
  edit form, 374–380
  successful edits, 382–384
  unsuccessful edits, 380–382
Users controller, 212
  adding followed_users and followers
    actions to Users controller (Listing 11.18),
    506
  class with inheritance (Listing 2.14), 72
  create action for, 425, 459
  initial, with new action (Listing 5.29), 212
  in schematic form (Listing 2.3), 58
  with show action (Listing 7.5), 281
  testing the user show page with factories,
    282–286
  in user signup, 212
user show page, *53,* 282–286
  adding sidebar to user show view (Listing 7.14),
    290
  adding title and heading for user profile page
    (Listing 7.10), 285
  defining gravatar_for helper method
    (Listing 7.13), 288
  factories to simulate User model objects
    (Listing 7.8), 284
  Factory Girl added to Gemfile (Listing 7.7),
    284
  in Microposts, augmenting, 446–450
  recap of initial User pages spec (Listing 7.6),
    282–283
  redefining BCrypt cost factor in test
    environment (Listing 7.11), 286
  SCSS for styling, including sidebar
    (Listing 7.15), 290–291
  tests for (Listing 7.9), 285
  user profile page /users/1 with default
    Gravatar, *289*
  at /users/1 after adding Users resource, *282*

Users controller with show action
(Listing 7.5), 281
user show page /users/1 with sidebar and CSS,
291
user show page with custom Gravatar, *289*
user show view with name and (Listing 7.12),
287
user signup, 211–215
adding flash message to (Listing 7.27), 317
errors, updating rendering of (Listing 10.36),
465
signup URI, 213–215
tests for, 293–297
users controller, 212
Users resource, 49–63
adding to the routes file (Listing 7.3), 279
correspondence between pages and URLs, 52*t*
MVC in action, 56–62
Rails routes with rule for (Listing 2.2), 58
RESTful routes provided by, 65*t*
in sign up, 278–281
weaknesses of, 62–63
Users resource tour, 51–56
user update action (Listing 9.10), 384
initial (Listing 9.8), 381
tests for (Listing 9.9), 383
user validations, 236–254
format, 245–248
length, 243–244
presence, 239–243
uniqueness, 249–254
user tests, initial, 236–239

V

validations
commenting out a validation to ensure a failing
test (Listing 6.10), 241
email format with regular expression
(Listing 6.17), 246
format, 245–248
initial user pages spec (Listing 7.6), 282
length, 243–244
length, adding for name attribute
(Listing 6.15), 244
Microposts resource, 66–68
migration for enforcing email uniqueness
(Listing 6.22), 252

of name attribute, failing test for (Listing 6.11),
241
for password attribute (Listing 6.27), 257
practically blank default User spec (Listing 6.7),
237
of presence, 239–243
of presence of name and email attributes
(Listing 6.13), 243
of presence of name attribute (Listing 6.9), 240
Relationship data model, 495
Relationship model, adding (Listing 11.8), 495
in relationship model, 495
test for name length (Listing 6.14), 244
test for presence of email attribute
(Listing 6.12), 243
test for rejection of duplicate email addresses
(Listing 6.18), 249
test for rejection of duplicate email addresses,
insensitive to case (Listing 6.20), 250
testing Relationship model validations
(Listing 11.7), 495
tests for email format validation (Listing 6.16),
245–246
of uniqueness, 249–254
of uniqueness of email addresses
(Listing 6.19), 250
of uniqueness of email addresses, ignoring
case (Listing 6.21), 251
user, 236–254
validations, Micropost model, 432–444
accessible attributes and first, 432–433
content validations, 443–444
first validation, accessible attributes and,
432–433
tests for validity of new micropost
(Listing 10.3), 432
for user (Listing 10.4), 433
variables in improving stylesheets, 193–197
version control. *See* Git
Vim, 10, 12, 29, 82
virtual attributes, 257

W

web interface for following users, 503–529
adding following/follower relationships to
sample data (Listing 11.17), 503–504
follow button with Ajax, working, 524–529

web interface for following users (*continued*)
  follow form, 505–514
  following and followers pages, 515–519
  follow/unfollow buttons, working, 519–524
  sample following data, 503–505
  stats, 505–514
Webrat, 79n1
The Well-Grounded Rubyist (Black), 6, 129, 543
will paginate method, 408
Windows, 11

wireframes, 167
wrapping long words, helper for (Listing 10.50),
  481

Y

YAML, 276n3

Z

zero-offset, 143